The
Method and Task
of
THEOLOGY

PART I

The Method and Task
of
THEOLOGY

Sex, politics and theology—these are the only things worth talking about. This old saying is an exaggeration, perhaps, but it is an attempt to express a deep truth. Sex forces the question, "Who am I?" Politics asks, "How can we learn to live together?" Theology, which means literally "a word about God," asks questions like these: "What is your only comfort in life and in death?" "What is the chief end of human life?" "What are we by nature?" "In whom do you believe?"[1] But this means (to risk carrying the exaggeration even further) that of the three topics mentioned, theology is the most important and most interesting because it *includes* the questions raised by sex and politics! No theology is interested only in God. *The study of theology is by definition the quest for the ultimate truth about God, about ourselves and about the world we live in.* What else is there to talk about?

When it is put that way, you should not be awed to hear that you are about to begin a study of theology. Theology is not just an impractical, otherworldly subject for a few dreamy scholars who retire to ivory towers to devote themselves to such irrelevant, hairsplitting questions as, How many angels can dance on the head of a pin? It is the discipline which wrestles with the basic issues and decisions all of us face every day, whoever we are, whatever we do. Whether you know it or not, you are already a practicing theologian even before you begin this formal study of theology. Our purpose in this book is simply to articulate and seek some answers to questions you have been consciously or unconsciously struggling with all your life.

Before we can get to the content of the truth about God, man and the world, we have to ask how we should go about discovering this truth. That is the problem we shall tackle in the first two chapters. In the first chapter we shall discuss "How To Be a Theologian" as we study the method and task of theology. In the second we shall ask, "Who Says So?" This will involve a consideration of significant creeds and confessions of the Christian church and their authority over us as church members.

1

Who Is a Theologian?

This first chapter is actually the last. It is written after all the rest of this book has been finished. Its purpose is to tell you what to expect and to give you some guidelines to help you know how to go about your study. We shall begin not by talking about the content of the book as such, but by talking about *us*—you and me, the readers and the writer. Theology, of course, does have to do with ideas, truths and doctrines ("doctrine" means simply "teaching"). But these ideas, truths and doctrines themselves point to a living Person who confronts us as persons. So we go straight to the heart of theology when we get personal from the very beginning. As we become clear about who we theologians are, we will also understand our task as theologians and the purpose of this book.

As you read this chapter, make a list of the various things you need to keep in mind in order to go about your study as a good theologian.

Who Are You?

Most of you who will study this book are church members, and you will be working through it with other members of the church. But you will never understand Christian theology if you think of yourself and the others only as such.

1. **Your personal and social background.** You are not only a Christian; you are either a *male* or *female*, whose life,

in fact if not in theory, is as much determined by your sexual as by your religious needs and desires, thoughts and instincts.

The Christian community is not the only community you belong to; you are the member of a *family* community—husband or wife, father or mother, son or daughter, brother or sister. And much more of your life is spent (or should be) concentrating on the success or failure, happiness or misery of your family relationships (or lack of them) than on church activities.

You are the member of one *race* or another, one *economic class* or another—and more than likely even the particular congregation you belong to has been brought together far more obviously on the basis of common racial and class ties than on the basis of common theological convictions.

You are deeply involved not only in the Christian way of life but also in the American way of life, which is something quite different. Not all Christians are Americans, and not all Americans are Christians. But your understanding of the Christian faith is inevitably influenced by your American culture as well as by your reading of the Bible and study of church doctrine.

You are the citizens of a particular nation as well as "citizens of heaven," and your liberal or conservative politics affects your theology as much as your liberal or conservative theology affects your politics.

In short, part of your life is colored by what goes on in the church, but much of it is also colored by what goes on in the home, bank, supermarket, courthouse and movie and television studios. Even when you leave the "world" to go to church, you take your worldly life with you. Insofar as *you* are in the church, the world is there too. Even when you put aside the newspaper and other secular literature to read the Bible and this book about theology, you bring to your religious studies all your secular problems, desires and opinions—whether you want to or not.

This means that if Christian theology is to be more than an intellectual game, if it is to deal with you personally, it has to bring the word about God to bear not just on your church life but on your life in the world. At every point in this book, therefore, you will find that I have tried to relate Christian theology not just to purely religious questions and problems, but also to family and social and political and economic questions and problems. This is an essential part of Christian theology not only because it tries to deal with people where they really live, but because the God we have to talk about is a God who is at work to judge and help in every area of our lives.

It follows, then, that as you study the doctrines discussed in this book, your task is to ask at every point what they have to say about your social as well as your individual life, your everyday work and play as well as your private and public worship, your life here and now as well as your life in the "world to come." Only when you do that will you fulfill the task of a good theologian— one who thinks and speaks about both the true God and real men in the real world.

I have tried to help you fulfill this task throughout the book, but you will find specific and concrete help especially in the section called "For Further Reflection and Study" at the end of each chapter. You might find it helpful to glance first at this section every time you begin a new chapter.

2. Your religious background. You begin your study of theology not only with the whole personal and social background which makes you the particular kind of person you are. You begin also with some sort of religious background. Some of you who read this book are already deeply committed Christians. Some of you have serious doubts about the truth and meaning of the Christian faith. Some of you probably belong to the church because it's the thing to do, without either deep commitment or serious thought one way or the other. Some of you already know a lot about the Bible and the doctrines of your church. Others of you know practically nothing. For some of you, "The Bible says . . ." or "Our church teaches . . ." carries great weight. Others of you are not impressed with such statements and won't buy anything until you are *shown* its truth and relevance.

I have been troubled throughout the book about this wide divergence among you. How can I speak relevantly to all of you at once? If you are studying this book in a class with other people.

you will soon be confronted with the same problem: How can you discuss theology meaningfully with people whose religious background and faith are different? There is no easy solution to the problem. But as I have written, there are two rules I have tried to make for myself in order to include all of you in the conversation. I suggest that you keep them in mind as you study the book, and especially as you discuss it with other people. They are general rules for being a good theologian, for "doing theology."

a. Be honest! Be honest with yourself and with other people —and above all with God. Don't apologize for, or try to hide, what you believe, whether it is right or wrong in the eyes of others. And don't apologize for, or try to hide, what you cannot believe or have a hard time believing. Growth in understanding and growth in faith are possible only where there is neither self-deception nor an attempt to fool God and other people. An honest doubter is closer to the truth than a superficial or dishonest believer. And, to quote the words of the great Christian theologian, P. T. Forsyth, "A live heresy is better than a dead orthodoxy."

b. Recognize your own limitations. Theology deals with a God whose thoughts are not our thoughts and whose ways are not our ways (Isaiah 55:8). The theologian who is sure that he has all the answers to all questions and that his task is simply to convince others that this is so is a bad theologian. He only proves that he knows nothing at all of the majesty and mystery of the God who cannot be captured and mastered by any human system of thought. Sometimes it is more believing to say "I just don't know" than to be too smugly sure. Sometimes it is better to leave some questions open until we have more light. It is often the case that sincere, serious Christians disagree even on very important questions, so that it simply cannot be said that this or that is *the* Christian position. In other words, we will be good theologians when we are *modest* theologians, acknowledging our own limitations, recognizing that we may be wrong at this or that point, knowing that we need to be open to let ourselves be helped by as well as to help, to be changed by as well as to change, those who think differently from us.

I have tried to follow these rules myself. I have tried to be honest about what I think myself, yet to invite you to examine and criticize the positions I have taken. Instead of trying to give one right solution to every problem, I have often described several possible solutions, suggesting the arguments for and against each and leaving it up to you to decide. Sometimes I have only raised questions, suggesting some factors which have to be taken into consideration in searching for answers, without giving *any* answers as such.

You will be fortunate if different members of your study group choose *different* alternatives and *different* answers, and if you are willing to give them the same freedom to be honest about their faith and doubts that you want for yourself. You will learn far more from genuine open debate than from total agreement.

All this means that when you have finished your study, you will not have a nicely wrapped-up system of theology with every question answered and every problem solved. You will not have "arrived" in your understanding of the Christian faith; you will only be a little further along the way—and better theologians just because you have learned that our faith can only be in the God who is beyond all that any of us can ask or think, and not in our simple or complicated, liberal or conservative, orthodox or heretical theology.

Who Is the Author?

Your task as theologians is clarified not only by reflection about who you are, but also by some things you ought to remember about the theologian who wrote the book you are studying. One of the things you ought to keep in mind about me is that I am an ordained minister and professional theologian. This carries with it some advantages and disadvantages.

1. **Professional limitations.** On the one hand, it means that I am at least supposed to have more competence than most of you in understanding and explaining the teachings of the Bible and the church. But on the other hand, it means that most of my time and work are spent in an ecclesiastical and academic environment. If, as we have said, theology has to do with the

truth of God in relation to every aspect of life *in the world,* then many of you know more about that side of the theological task than I. I have done my best not to write from an ivory tower, but I have been very much aware of the limitations of my profession. You should keep this in mind also. And you can help counterbalance my limitations by carefully examining what I have written in the light of your own experience and by listening seriously to those who have competence in other fields. What are the reactions of an insurance salesman, a housewife, a medical doctor, someone involved in public affairs, a businessman, a scientist, to what you read in this book? You will study the book as good theologians just when you do not study it as if it had nothing to do with what people in such "worldly" vocations know, but when you constantly invite criticism and additional information from them. Good theology is a *two-way* conversation between preachers and laymen, church and world, professional theologians and experts in other areas. So take advantage of whatever help is available to you from *both* sides.

2. The problem of language. Part of my job is to interpret the language of the Bible and the technical terminology of the church. I have tried to do that in this book. You will find such words as justification, sanctification, sin, grace, salvation and eschatology throughout the book. I have used such religious language deliberately. Just as you have to learn the vocabulary of psychology or physics or sociology if you are going to study those sciences, so you have to understand the vocabulary of the Bible and the church if you are to understand the science of theology.

On the other hand, you must watch us professional theologians very carefully! Sometimes *we* know what we are talking about when we use the language of our profession, but do not explain it so that other people can understand it. And sometimes we unconsciously use technical jargon to avoid difficult problems, or to hide from ourselves and others the fact that we ourselves do not know what we are talking about. I have done my best to avoid both faults. But I may not have been successful always. So read this book very critically. Keep asking all the way through: "Does it make sense? What is the meaning of this biblical or technical word? Has the author explained it adequately? Is it my fault or his that I do not understand?" And be just as hard on other members of your study group. Don't let anyone get by with meaningless or ambiguous jargon. Keep asking for definitions and explanations—even of the most basic words such as God or Christ or Spirit or sin. Theology which is only intellectual or pious or undefined biblical jargon is always *bad* theology. It is not enough simply to say "The Bible says . . ." or "The church teaches . . ." or "Theologians say . . ." The job is not done until the *meaning* of such statements is clear.

3. The problem of theological bias. No matter how seriously a theologian tries to put aside his wishes and opinions and feelings in order to understand the truth about God and God's ways with men, his own personal prejudices will always color his understanding of the truth. That is true of this book also. Even when I have left questions open and have presented several alternative solutions, you probably will see what my own personal preferences are. Even when I have quoted Scripture or the teachings of the church or the writings of other theologians, what comes out is inevitably *my* interpretation of them. I have tried to be fair in describing the position of those with whom I differ, and to recognize the limitations and difficulties of my own position or inclinations. I have tried not to twist what others have written to suit my own taste and fancy. But still my biases will show through—more clearly to you than to me.

Now this means once again that you must study this book with a critical eye. Your task is not to learn just what I think, but what the truth is. But how can you distinguish between the truth itself and my biased interpretation of it? You must be careful here, because the temptation is simply to judge what the book says by *your* personal biases. If you do that, you still will not discover the truth, but only the confirmation of your own likes and dislikes. You will finish exactly where you began, having learned nothing.

What are the criteria, then, by which you can get past both my *and* your own prejudices? There are some. They are the criteria by which both what I have written and your study of it should be guided, and which define the task of Christian theology as such.

What Is the Task of Theology?

What we have to do and the way we should go about it comes into focus as soon as we say that what we are concerned with is not just theology in general but *Christian* theology. Our task is to try to understand a particular view of God, man and the world, the content and nature of which is no more a matter of personal opinion than is the content and nature of Marxist communism or Freudian psychology. As with the teachings of Marx or Freud, so with the religion identified with the name of Christ: We may like or dislike what we are told. We may believe it or not, accept it or not. We may and should criticize any particular interpretation of it. But when we are asked to say what Marxism or Freudianism or Christianity is, we are neither asked nor allowed simply to express our own likes, dislikes, wishes, opinions or prejudices about politics, psychology or religion. We have to try to understand a way of thinking and living that is identifiable quite apart from our own personal preferences and ideas.

In the case of Christian theology, there are three objective factors which have to be taken into consideration. They are the criteria which have guided me as I have tried to say what the Christian faith is. And they are the criteria which can help you to evaluate both what I have written and your own reactions. My purpose in writing and your task in studying this book is to understand the truth about God, man and the world as it is made known, believed and experienced in (1) Jesus Christ, (2) the Bible, (3) the church.

1. Jesus Christ. The name Christ is by definition a part of what Christian faith is. If you want to know what God is like, Christian theology says: Look at Christ. If you want to know what real humanity is, and how you can live a genuinely human life—look at Christ. If you want to know what God is doing in the world and in your individual lives—look at Christ. For Christian theology the person and work of Christ is the key to *all* truth about God, ourselves and the world we live in.

To say this does not mean that all questions are automatically answered, all problems automatically solved by repeating the magic words, "Jesus Christ." Christ is himself the question and problem of Christian theology, the mystery we have to try to understand. But to say that he stands at the center of all Christian theology does mean that at every point we must let all our own ideas, feelings and experiences be examined, measured, judged and interpreted by the problem, question and mystery of who he is and what he does.

Again, the claim that for Christian theologians everything turns around the truth to be discovered in Christ does not mean the arrogant claim that only we Christians know anything about God, man and the world, and that we have nothing to learn from anyone else. We learn from Christ himself that the whole world is God's world, and that there is no place where he cannot be about his creative, reconciling, renewing work—even among men who do not know him or believe in him. That means that in this book we shall also listen to and be open to learn from the natural sciences, psychology, political science, secular novels and plays, and even other religions. Consistent with our Christian standpoint, we shall do so in the light of the truth about God, man and the world given in Christ. But as we listen to these "outsiders" it will be vital not to confuse Christian truth with our own biased interpretation of it.

This, then, is the first objective reference point for our theological work: Recognizing that it is the problem as well as the answer of Christian theology, being wide open for the insights of other points of view, everything we do must be done with reference to the truth which is *in Christ Jesus* about God, about ourselves, and about the world.

2. The Bible. It is in this book that we come to know the Person who stands at the center of the Christian faith. The whole of the Old Testament looks forward to him and is fulfilled in him. The whole of the New Testament is an expression of the faith that in him is hid the secret of the past, present and future not only of Christian individuals but of the whole world. Christian theology is different from theology in general in that of all books this particular book is the source and norm of its attempt to understand the truth about God, man and the world. The fact of the Bible means that we are not left alone to talk about a God who is only the projection of our own desires and fears, a humanity which is only the result of our wishful thinking about ourselves, or a world which is only the reflection of our own pessimistic or optimistic view of life. If we want to know what Christians believe, we cannot look only to our own minds and hearts and personal experiences; we have to go to the Bible.

You will find, therefore, that Bible study is an essential part of the theological work ahead of you. Take the trouble to look up the passages mentioned and to do the Bible study suggested. Use the various Bible dictionaries and word study books at your disposal. That will give you a constant way of checking my biases and presuppositions as well as your own, and of exposing both of our subjective interpretations of Christian truth to the source and norm of that truth.

But Bible study in itself is no automatic guarantee of good theology. There is always the danger that we will find *in* the Bible only what we take with us *to* it, use it to confirm what we already think, hear only what we want to hear. Because they already hated Jews before they read the Bible, some German Christians once found in the Bible justification for slaughtering millions of Jews. Because they wanted to keep their human property, some American Christians once argued from the Bible that it is right to buy and sell human beings as if they were animals. Have you noticed that mean people usually find a mean God in the Bible, and that superficial people usually find a superficial God? Comfortable, powerful men usually find that the Bible supports political conservatism; poor, exploited people usually find that it supports social and political reform.

What is to keep us from simply using the Bible to give authority to our own religious, social, political and economic prejudices? What is to prevent us from using the study of this ancient book as a pious excuse for refusing to face the radical claims of the living God on every area of our lives, here and now?

First of all there are some questions we can keep asking. As you see the way I have used the Bible, and as you study together, keep asking me and each other: (a) Is that *all* the Bible says, or have you only picked out some passages which support your own ideas? (b) Have you forgotten or ignored some other passages which throw a different light, or more light, on the question at hand? (c) Have you quoted a passage out of context, so that it does not really mean what you say it means? (d) What does this or that text about God and those people who lived thousands of years ago have to say to us modern men in a technological world?

Another way we can avoid using the Bible only to confirm our personal prejudices is to listen to how other Christians, in different times and places and situations, have understood it. This brings us to the third objective guideline for Christian theologians.

3. The church. As soon as we say *Christian* theology we also say *church* theology. To be a follower of Christ has meant from the very beginning to join the community of disciples he draws together around himself. Christ himself promised to make himself known especially where people were gathered together in his name. The Bible was not written for and about isolated individuals; it was written for and about a *community* of people—Israel in the Old Testament, the church in the New Testament. You cannot be a Christian by yourself; you can only be a Christian together with other Christians who serve God in the world. It follows, then, that you cannot be a Christian *theologian* by reflecting on the meaning of Christ and studying the Bible only by yourself, to suit yourself. You can only be a Christian theologian as you do your work in conversation with other Christians in the Christian community, as together with them you seek to learn what God is doing and what he has for you to do also in the world outside the church.

There are several ways in which the theology of this book is church theology. (a) It will be genuine church theology when you really *listen* to the other members of your study group (instead of just waiting for them to stop talking so you can talk), when you are open to *learn* from them (instead of just defending to the death what you already think you know). (b) Secondly, this book is church theology in that it constantly depends on the work of the great theologians of the church, both past and present. Whether I have interpreted them correctly is always open to question. But the fact that they are there is at least a check on my and your ignorance, narrowness and personal prejudices. (c) Finally, this is church theology in that it constantly depends on the creeds and confessions which are the official statements of what the church believes. This is still another way in which our private opinions will be subject to examination and correction.

What Is the Reformed Tradition?

At this point we must confess quite frankly that it is especially the creeds and confessions of the *Reformed-Presbyterian* churches which will guide us. Does this mean that we have been trying to overcome personal theological biases only in order to substitute a narrow *denominational* bias? Several things need to be said from the very beginning about the particular place we shall stand to do our church theology.

1. One church. Every Christian theologian works from some one concrete part of the one "holy catholic church." He may be a Roman Catholic, Lutheran, Methodist, Anglican-Episcopalian, Baptist or some other "brand" of Christian, but none of us can belong to *the* church without belonging to *a* church. If we do our work from a particular perspective, this does not mean a claim that we are the real Christians while those others are false Christians, or that we have a monopoly on the truth. We can and we shall learn also from the thinkers and creeds and confessions of other parts of the church. Even when our tradition differs from theirs, we will not question the fact that they are truly and sincerely Christian too. But genuine and helpful conversation within the whole church is possible only where the individual partners in the conversation do not try to hide who they are and where they come from. In this book, we shall enter the conversation honestly and openly identifying our perspective as Presbyterian-Reformed—the tradition springing especially from John Calvin and guided by the creeds and confessions of the Calvinistic branch of the church.

2. The Apostles' Creed. At the heart of the Reformed tradition stands the one confession of faith which nearly all Christian churches, everywhere, have in common—the Apostles' Creed. The articles of this creed form the main outline of this book. This means that while you may expect some typically Reformed emphases in this book (for instance, the free sovereignty of God, man's total dependence on God, the claim of God on every area of man's life in the world), nevertheless you are not beginning a narrow denominational study. In following the Apostles' Creed, I have tried to write not just Reformed theology, but ecumenical (worldwide) *Christian* theology—from a Reformed point of view.

3. The reformed family. The word "Reformed" itself excludes narrowness and onesidedness. There is no such thing as *the* Reformed position; there is only a generally recognizable Reformed "perspective"—or "orientation," or perhaps best of all, "family."

All Reformed Christians recognize especially Calvin as their father. But Calvin can be understood in different ways, and, as is the case in any family, his children feel different degrees of dependence upon him. So, for instance, the American Reformed theologians, Charles Hodge (died 1878) and Benjamin Warfield (died 1921), stuck closer to home than have Emil Brunner and Karl Barth, two well-known contemporary theologians of the Swiss Reformed Church. But there is no doubt that Brunner and Barth are legitimate children and still belong to the family.

Moreover, there is no one authoritative statement of faith to which all Reformed churches subscribe. There are many different statements. They all bear a common family resemblance, but they differ from each other in emphasis, in the spirit in which they are written, and sometimes in theological content. We shall have to consider all of them, recognizing all as genuinely Reformed, honestly acknowledging their differences, refusing to let any one statement become the standard by which the others are judged. There is plenty of room in the Reformed family, in other words, for individual differences and freedom of movement.

Finally, we ought to point out that, strictly speaking, "Reformed" is a theological, not a denominational title. It is a mistake to limit it to any one denomination and organization. In 1964 there were ninety-six member churches in the World Alliance of Reformed Churches, representing sixty-six countries, with an estimated fifty million members. Perhaps it is important to emphasize that there are also Reformed churches and faithful Reformed Christians in communistic eastern Europe and Asia. "Reformed" is a doctrinal-theological description which cuts across all linguistic, national, racial, class, political and cultural distinctions.

In other words, when we say that we will be doing Christian theology from a Reformed perspective, we do not mean that we will be talking about just "me and my denomination, and those within it who think and live exactly like me." The Reformed perspective does not aim at setting up but at breaking down barriers between Christians.

This brings us to a last point, which summarizes everything we have been trying to say about the task of theology in this whole chapter.

4. Always reforming. This is an old slogan of the Reformed tradition. To say that this book is Christian theology from a Reformed point of view does not mean that our task is to try to master an already fixed system of theology which Reformed Christians believe has once and for all captured the truth about God, man and the world. According to the Reformed faith *no* system of theology can ever do that. *The* truth is the truth about God, man and the world in Jesus Christ as we know him in the Bible. *All* theology, whether that of an individual or of the whole church, is at best an inadequate, fallible, human attempt to understand that truth. According to the Reformed churches, therefore, there always has been and always will be the right and responsibility to question any individual's, any denomination's, any creedal document's grasp of the truth—not for the sake of our freedom to think anything we please, but for the sake of the freedom of biblical truth from every human attempt to capture and tame it.

To work at Christian theology from the Reformed perspective, then, does not mean that we are asked simply to hold the fort and defend what Calvin and his followers thought three or four hundred years ago. Being loyal to them means that we do *not* simply repeat what they said, but that we take seriously what they themselves taught us about the superiority of the Word of God over every word of men—including theirs! It means to ask the question they themselves taught us to ask: "What is the living God we know in Christ and in the Bible doing and saying in *our* time, *here* and *now*, where *we* have to think and live as Christians?" And that means that we will be faithful to our Reformed tradition when we *continue* the reformation begun in the sixteenth and seventeenth centuries and are willing when necessary to say things differently in the twentieth century.

Reformed means *always* reforming. That is the task—and the freedom—to which you are invited as you study in this book *Christian* theology from a *Reformed* point of view.

But what is the relation between the authority of Christ, the authority of the Bible, the authority of the church, and the authority of our individual attempts to measure the teachings of the church by the truth given in Christ and in the Bible? That is the problem we have to wrestle with in the next chapter.

FOR FURTHER REFLECTION AND STUDY

1. In light of what you have read in this chapter, evaluate the following statements:

   a. Religion is just a matter of personal opinion. It doesn't really matter what you believe so long as you are sincere.

   b. All religions are basically the same.

   c. Christ is the answer.

d. The church ought to stick to spiritual concerns and not meddle in social, political and economic problems.

e. "My reading is very limited and yet very extended; it begins with Moses and ends with John. The Bible and the Bible alone I read and study . . . . For it does not matter to me to learn how Ursin or Luther or Anselm or Augustine or Irenaeus [i.e., great theologians in the history of the church] thought about the matter and formulated and determined it—they and their decisions are too new. I want that which is old, original and solely authentic: Holy Scripture itself" (G. Menken, nineteenth-century theologian).[2]

2. What should your attitude be toward someone whose theological beliefs are different from yours?

3. What should be the attitude of Christian theology toward such secular disciplines as science and psychology? Toward other religions?

4. What is the difference between "Reformed" and "Presbyterian"?

5. Is "Always Reforming" a dangerous slogan?

6. Read Mark 9:14–24. Would the words of the father be a good motto for you as you study Christian theology?

2

Who Says So?

THE PROBLEM OF
AUTHORITY

Who has the right and ability to decide what is genuinely Christian?

The biblical writers? But whose *interpretation* of the Bible? The church? *Which* church?

Every individual Christian for himself? But how can we tell the difference between what is *Christian* and what is only *personal opinion?*

This is the problem we are going to tackle in this chapter— the problem of authority. It confronts many of us most directly and concretely with the question of our attitude toward the various creeds and confessions which attempt to describe the Christian faith and life. So we shall deal with the problem of authority in terms of the problem of the authority of creeds and confessions. Our perspective will be that of the Presbyterian-Reformed tradition. However, those who stand in this tradition need to remember that not all churches have sought to solve the problem of authority by preparing a creed or confession. The Moravians, for example, have preferred to express their theology in their hymns and in their ritual of worship rather than in creeds that are to be accepted as binding on the church. Nor are the various Baptist bodies creedal churches. They are content to say that their creed is the Bible, but at the heart of the life of these churches there is a solid body of convictions which are common to practically all Baptist churches. But most of the churches which stand in the

Presbyterian and Reformed tradition have felt it necessary at times to express their faith in creedal statements.

As we consider these creeds, this will be our procedure: We shall ask first what a creed or confession of faith is. Then we shall ask what authority creeds and confessions have for the church as a whole. Finally we shall ask what freedom and what responsibility individual Christians have in relation to them. In the appendix at the end of this chapter you will find a brief historical introduction to some of the particular creeds and confessions which are most important in the history of the church.

The Origin, Nature and Purpose of Creeds and Confessions

We want a living People's Church which is the expression of all the religious powers of our nation. . . . We demand a change in the legal constitution and open battle against Marxism, hostile to religion and to the nation, and against its socialist-Christian fellow travelers of all degrees. . . . We see in race, national character and nation orders of life given and entrusted to us by God, to maintain which is a law of God for us. Therefore racial mixing is to be opposed. . . . We know something of Christian duty and love toward the helpless, but we demand also the protection of the nation from the incapable and inferior. . . . We want an Evangelical Church which roots in the national character, and we repudiate the spirit of a Christian cosmopolitanism (The Platform of German Christians).[1]

These sentences, written in 1932, were a part of the platform of a group called the "German Christians," who wanted to make the church into the religious arm of Hitler's Nazi regime. In 1934, another group of Christians in Germany (from the Reformed, Lutheran and United Churches) made a declaration or "confession of faith." It said in part:

Jesus Christ, as he is testified to us in the Holy Scripture, is the one Word of God, whom we are to hear, whom we are to trust and obey in life and in death.

We repudiate the false teaching that the church can and must recognize yet other happenings and powers, images and truths as divine revelation alongside this one Word of God, as a source of her preaching.

. . . Jesus Christ . . . is also God's mighty claim on our whole life; in him we encounter a joyous liberation from the godless claims of this world to free and thankful service to his creatures.

We repudiate the false teaching that there are areas of our life in which we belong not to Jesus Christ but to another lord, areas in which we do not need justification and sanctifi· cation through him.

The Christian Church . . . has to witness in the midst of the world of sin as the church of forgiven sinners that she is his alone, that she lives and wishes to live only by his comfort and his counsel in expectation of his appearance.

We repudiate the false teaching that the church can turn over the form of her message and ordinances at will or according to some dominant ideological and political convictions (The Barmen Declaration, 1934).[2]

The Nazis got the point! Those who stood by this creed were considered traitors, and many of them gave their lives because they refused to compromise their faith in Jesus Christ to make it compatible with the Nazi ideology.

This Barmen Declaration is a modern example of what "creed" or "confession of faith" has always meant in the history of the Christian faith. It suggests several things about the origin, nature and purpose of creeds and confessions in general.

1. **The great creeds and confessions are rooted in a concrete *historical situation*.** They are not the work of otherworldly theologians who sit down to think up a creed, but the work of theologians faced with crucial issues of the church's life and witness in the world. To know and confess the God of the Bible is to know and confess him as the living, acting God who confronts us in the events of history—"secular" as well as "religious" history. The earliest Christian confession and the basic

Christian affirmation repeated in different ways, in different times and places, in *all* the creeds of the church is the simple New Testament confession "Jesus is Lord" (Romans 10:9; Philippians 2:11).

That sounds admirably pious and comfortably harmless—until its meaning is spelled out in the concrete situation of the church at various periods in its history. Then it has always become "subversive," "fanatical," "ridiculous," "explosive"—*alive! Jesus Christ* is Lord: not Caesar, not the pope, not Hitler, not Jim Crow! *Jesus Christ* rules our thinking and living: not the ancient Jewish, not the classical Greek, not the medieval European, not the modern American way of life. *Jesus Christ* is to be served and obeyed: above nation, above generally accepted ethical and religious values, above reason, above family, above economic prosperity—above *everything* else. We shall understand the creeds and confessions of the church only when we see that they have to do with life and death decisions of individual Christians and the Christian community, not just with some abstract intellectual theories.

2. **The great creeds and confessions are also a** *form of worship.* "I believe in God the Father Almighty, maker of heaven and earth" does not mean only, "I believe that God exists." It means, "I put my ultimate trust and confidence in this God— and no other." If I confess that Jesus Christ is Lord, I thankfully and prayerfully commit myself to his care and to his authority. "In confession the believer takes his stand, commits his life, declares what he believes to be true, affirms his ultimate loyalty, and defies every false claim upon his life."[3]

3. **The great creeds and confessions are intended to be a guide to the proper interpretation of Scripture for Christian** *preaching* **and** *witness.* They assume that the Bible is the norm for living and proclaiming Christian truth, and they seek to preserve its authority by ruling out false interpretations which in fact "put the word and work of the Lord in the service of some self-determined wishes, purposes or plans" (Barmen Declaration, par. 6).

4. The great creeds and confessions of the church are usually _polemical._ They attempt to defend and clarify Christian truth against attacks and perversions both from without and from within the church. Heresy from _within_ has often been more difficult to recognize and fight than heresy from without, and therefore it is more dangerous. The most dangerous heretics the creeds have had to fight are not the openly godless, immoral people who attack the church and the Christian faith from the outside. They are the people within the church (like the "German Christians") who are enthusiastically in favor of the Bible, religion, morality and the church—but use them to lend authority and respectability to ideologies and methods they consciously or unconsciously want to enthrone _in place of_ God in Christ.

On the other hand heretics, both within and without, have performed a real service to the church. They have forced the church to formulate and clarify its beliefs. Sometimes, by overemphasizing some aspect of Christian truth neglected by the church they have forced the church to correct its own onesidedness.

5. The great creeds and confessions are creeds and confessions of the _church._ Even when they have been composed by an individual or several individuals, and even when they say "I believe," they are intended to articulate the faith of the _whole community_ of Christians. They do not aim to confess the faith of a few extraordinarily orthodox or pious individuals, or the faith of a group within or among the churches who consider themselves spiritually and intellectually superior. They aim to be the voice of the "_one_ holy _catholic_" church. And even when they have to exclude, the great creeds and confessions do so for the sake of "one _holy_ catholic" church. We misunderstand and misuse the creeds when we use them intentionally to divide and set Christian against Christian, rather than as an attempt to express the unity of the Christian community.

6. The great creeds and confessions have been intended for the _instruction_ of Christians as manuals of educa-

tion. The earliest creeds grew out of the need for some standard of instruction and affirmation for new converts to the Christian faith before they were baptized. Creedal and confessional statements throughout the history of the church have often been in the form of catechisms to be used in the instruction of children, new Christians and mature Christians who need to learn to articulate their faith.

The Authority of Reformed Creeds and Confessions

What is the nature and extent of the authority of the church's confessional writings? Do we *have* to accept them? What makes them true? Not just the content of the doctrines of the Reformed churches, but the way Reformed. Christians answer this question is indicative of what it means to be a "Reformed" Christian. A clue to the Reformed confessional statements lies in the fact that there are *many* Reformed confessions, produced over a very *wide geographical area,* extending over a *long period of time.* That means, negatively, that no one doctrinal formulation, no one place, no one particular time in the history of the Reformed churches is decisive for what it means to be a Reformed Christian. But what does this plurality mean positively?

1. The authority of the creeds is only a limited authority. Only God himself has absolute, unquestionable authority. In creeds it is the human, fallible, sinful church—not God—speaking. All creeds are therefore subject to the correction of the higher authority of the Word of God himself—and therefore to the authority of *Scripture.* Because Reformed Christians believe this, it is characteristic of their creeds and confessions that they limit themselves and relativize their own authority! That is, they openly acknowledge that they could be wrong and in need of correction. Here is a well-known example. Many more could be quoted.[4]

The Supreme Judge, by whom all controversies of religion are to be determined, and all decrees of councils, opinions of ancient writers, doctrines of men, and private spirits, are to be examined, and in whose sentence we are to rest, can be no other but the Holy Spirit speaking in the Scripture . . . . All synods or councils since the apostles' times, whether general or particular, may err, and many have erred; therefore they are not to be made the rule of faith or practice, but to be used as a help in both. (Westminster Confession I, 10; XXXI, 3. Note that by implication the Westminster fathers subject also their *own* thoughts to the "Supreme Judge," and acknowledge that they too may have erred!)

2. **Any given confessional statement is authoritative only for the time being.** The Word of God is the same yesterday, today and forever. But the church *perceives* this word always in a broken, incomplete way. The truth does not change, but our *understanding* of the truth may need to change. Reformed Christians have therefore treated their creeds as open to discussion and improvement, and liable even to be superseded. Thus the Synod of Bern declared in 1528:

But where something is brought before us by our pastors or by others, which brings us closer to Christ, and in accordance with God's Word is more conducive to mutual friendship and Christian love than the interpretation now presented, we will gladly accept it and will not limit the course of the Holy Spirit, which does not go backwards towards the flesh but always forward towards the image of Jesus Christ our Lord.

3. **The authority of Reformed confessions lies in the truth to which they point,** not in the way they attempt to bear witness to that truth. In different times and situations, new and different confessions may need to be written, not because the truth changes, but because the *language* we use needs to change if we are to communicate the Reformed faith relevantly to new problems and needs and dangers. The Swiss reformers Bullinger and Judae are said to have signed the First Helvetic Confession of 1536 (the first confession to which all the Swiss cities agreed during the Reformation) with this statement:

We wish in no way to prescribe for all churches through these articles a single rule of faith. For we acknowledge no other rule of faith than Holy Scripture. We agree with whoever agrees with this, although he uses different expressions from our Confession. For we should have regard for the fact itself and for the truth, not for the words. We grant to everyone the freedom to use his own expressions which are suitable for his church and will make use of this freedom ourselves, at the same time defending the true sense of this Confession against distortions.

The multiplicity of Reformed creeds in different times and places is witness to the fact that the Reformed churches have in fact made use of this freedom.

4. **The authority of Reformed confessions relates to right *living* as well as to right *thinking*, to *life* as well as to *faith*.** Not only in the present, but ever since the Reformation itself, they have dealt not only with questions of doctrine and the inner life of the church, but with such "worldly" problems as sex, marriage and divorce; the Christian use of property; and politics. Ethics as well as theology is central to the Reformed faith. The creeds themselves are not intended to be norms for Christian living. Only Scripture can be that. But just because Scripture itself points to the claim of God both on our individual and on our social-political lives, Reformed creeds inevitably deal also with this area of Christian existence.

5. **The authority of Reformed creeds and confessions is limited by, and derived ultimately from, the authority of God himself through Scripture.** But that authority is expressed through the *church.* The Reformed creeds are the result of open discussion and subsequent voting, carried on with wide-open doors. Even when they are composed by an individual or by several individuals, it is the Christian *community* which decides. It is significant that the Reformed church is not named for the particular reformer who is its father. No man, not even John Cal-

vin (and certainly not lesser men), is allowed even to appear to assume the place that belongs to Christ alone, or stand between Christ and his church. The *democratic form* of the Reformed churches and the democratic way in which their creeds are made point to the absolute *autocracy* of Christ. We refuse to bestow unquestioned authority on any one man or group of men (including Calvin and our Dutch or Scottish fathers), and we insist that questions of faith and life must be decided by democratic procedures. But we do not do this so that the church may express the opinions and desires of the people. We do it so that it may be free to seek and attempt to express the will of God in Christ, for he alone is our Supreme Judge.

The Freedom and Responsibility of Individual Christians

When I begin to think about Christian doctrine for myself as a member of a Reformed Church, to what extent am I *bound* and to what extent am I *free in* relation to the creeds and confessions of the Reformed churches? How far am I committed to agree with them? What is the task of the individual Reformed Christian who reflects on Christian truth within the community of Reformed Christians? There are three possible answers to this question—the first two easy and wrong, the last very difficult but correct!

1. **Two easy answers.** One could argue that the task of theology is simply to *restate and interpret the given teachings of the church.* They are not to be criticized or questioned. The possibility of error and inadequacy is not to be considered. Perhaps they can be understood in a deeper and more complete way than they have been understood in the past. Perhaps new additions could even be made. But the task of the individual Christian thinker is essentially one of holding on to and defending what the church has said in the past. He is totally bound to it, not free at all to challenge or contradict it.

This is the conservative Roman Catholic understanding of the theologian's task (an understanding criticized by many contemporary Catholic theologians). While some Reformed thinkers have considered it to be their task also, such a conception contradicts the Reformed creeds and confessions themselves. This position may admit that Christ as he is given to us in Scripture is Lord *in* and *through* the church, but it does not see that he is Lord also *over* the church. Ultimately it deifies the church, because it attributes to its teachings an infallible authority that belongs to God alone.

Or one could go to the opposite extreme and say that the theologian's task is not to deify but to *ignore the church's creeds and confessions and to insist on total freedom from the church.* What the church has said in the past is of no importance; what *I* say *now* is of exclusive importance. Perhaps Protestantism has tended more than Catholicism toward too much individualism.

This understanding of the theologian's task can be conceived in a very conservative or a very liberal way. (As is often the case, extreme conservativism and extreme liberalism have a great deal in common here!) On the one hand, with the extreme conservative, I could appeal to the Reformation principle that every individual has immediate access to Scripture, and argue that I do not need and should not allow the interference of the church. The good theologian is the theologian alone with his Bible. Good theology is *my* interpretation of the Bible, not the church's interpretation. On the other hand, with the extreme liberal, I could argue that theology is not the result of the individual alone with the *external* authority of the Bible, but the individual alone with the *internal* authority of his reason, his personal religious experience, his conscience, or his innermost understanding of himself and the world in which he lives. Neither the church nor the Bible can have a higher authority than what I know to be true in one way or another deep within myself.

But neither the conservative nor the liberal individualist can be a Reformed theologian. If Roman Catholic theology of the past tended to deify the self-authority of the *church*, this kind of theology ultimately deifies the self-authority of the *individual*. In both cases, an exaggerated Roman Catholic "collectivism" and an exaggerated Protestant "individualism," the word of *man* is given final authority which according to the Reformed creeds belongs to the Word of God alone.

2. A more difficult answer. Reformed theologians are therefore neither totally bound to the church and its confessions and creeds, nor totally free from the church and its teachings. They are *relatively* bound and *relatively* free. In saying what this means, we at the same time summarize everything we have been saying about how we are to understand and use the creeds and confessions of our churches.

a. *The individual Reformed Christian is relatively bound to the confessional teachings of the church—*
(1) Because the creeds and confessions are attempts to understand and interpret Scripture. They help to preserve respect for the authority of Scripture by being a constant check on every theologian's tendency to let his own opinions and feelings instead of Scripture determine his thinking.
(2) Because God in Christ promised to be present and make himself known in the *church*. To ignore the creeds of the church is to cut oneself off from the community to which is promised the truth the theologian seeks to understand and interpret.
(3) Because the Holy Spirit who enlightens my mind, here, today, is the same Spirit who has been at work among other Christians in other places and times. To ignore the creeds and confessions of the church would mean that I am not really interested in what the Holy Spirit of God is saying and doing, and to run the risk of confusing some other spirit or spirits with the *Holy* Spirit.
(4) Because to be a Reformed Christian means to belong by free decision to the community of Reformed Christians who confess their faith through their creeds. To ignore the creeds is to contradict my own decision to participate in this community.

b. *The individual Reformed Christian is relatively free in relation to the confessional teaching of the church—*
(1) Because the creeds and confessions of the church are the words of fallible, sinful men—men who are "of themselves

liars," as the Belgic Confession strongly puts it. The church's understanding of Christian truth is therefore always subject to possible improvement and correction.

(2) Because the final truth of the Christian faith is the truth mediated to us by Scripture, not the truth of the church. Our first loyalty must be to God and his Word, not to the words of men.

(3) Because we can *serve* the church only when we are free to remind it of one who stands above it. Christians who want *only* and *always* to defend the church's past and present decisions contribute to the idolatrous substitute of the church's word for the Word of God, and thus help corrupt instead of serve the church.

(4) Because the Holy Spirit who has been at work guiding the church's thought and life in other times and places is *still* at work. He did not retire when Calvin died, or when the seventeenth century passed. He did not settle down to make his headquarters only in Switzerland or Holland or Scotland. We must be open to hear what he is saying and doing *here, now,* as well as what he did and said there, then.

(5) Because the Reformed confessions and creeds acknowledge their own authority to be relative, and invite continually renewed examination and, if necessary, correction in the light of Scripture. To deny the freedom to perform this task is to deny the creeds themselves.

Another way of describing what it means to be relatively free and relatively bound in relation to the creeds and confessions of the church is to say that Reformed theologians (that means all members of a Reformed church) stand at the same time under the First and Fifth Commandments: "You shall have no other gods before me," but at the same time "Honor your father and your mother." We should honor our theological "fathers" who were responsible for the creeds and confessions of our church. That means to respect them and to consider very carefully and seriously what we are doing when we disobey or contradict them. But we cannot make gods of them. There is still a higher authority to whom we are responsible, and we would do our "parents" no honor if we treated them like gods. We honor them just when we learn from them to be free *from* them—not free to think and live however we please, but free for the God whom they themselves have taught us to love and obey above all. On the other hand, we serve and obey our heavenly Father when we hear his commandment to give our human fathers no less but also no more honor than is due them.

It is not an easy task to which we are called. When we criticize and disagree with the church's teaching at this or that point, how can we be sure that we really are doing it in obedience to the Word of God and not just as an expression of our own personal biases? When we hold tenaciously to what the church teaches, how can we be sure that we really are doing it because we respect the truth of God, and not just because we are afraid or unwilling to subject our understanding of the truth to revision and correction? It is never easy to keep freedom and responsibility in proper balance. And it is especially difficult when we are trying to learn what it means to be properly free and properly bound in relation to the authority of the church.

But it is an exciting task to which we are called. How dull it would be if Christian truth were a neat package of information handed to us by the church to be memorized, mastered and dutifully recited when called upon. How exciting it is to know that we never "arrive" in our understanding of the depths of the truth of God—to be a part of a church whose motto is "*always* reforming." Growing up is painful sometimes. It is easier not to grow. But not to grow is to stagnate and die. The confessional teachings of the Reformed churches are not an invitation for us to *stop* growing, asking, seeking, moving, changing. They are not our final destination but signposts along the road which lead to mature manhood, to "the measure of the stature of the fulness of Christ" (Ephesians 4:13). Difficult as it is, we will use them correctly when we struggle to learn what it means to respect them as trustworthy signposts (being bound to them), but *only* as signposts which point beyond themselves (being free in relation to them). This will be our attitude toward the creeds and confessions of the church throughout our study of Christian doctrine according to the Reformed churches.

1. Scholars believe that the very earliest confessions of faith
    (used even before the New Testament was written down) are
    preserved in the following passages: Philippians 2:6–11; 1
    Corinthians 15:3–8; Romans 10:9; Ephesians 4:6. Make a list
    of the affirmations these brief confessions make about God and
    about Jesus. Which of these affirmations are included in the
    Apostles' Creed? Which affirmations in the Apostles' Creed are
    not mentioned in these passages? Do you think the added ele-
    ments in the Apostles' Creed are essential additions for a full
    summary of the Christian faith?

2. In view of the fact that the great creeds and confessions of the
    past were formulated to bring the truth of the Christian faith
    to bear on the needs and problems of a concrete historical
    situation, do you think that your denomination should try to
    formulate a new confession for our time?

3. What heresies (perversions of the Christian faith and life)
    in the modern world and in the modern church would need to
    be dealt with in a contemporary confession of faith?

4. Should a good Reformed Christian ever question the authori-
    tative confessional statements of his church?

5. How can we reconcile the basic Christian affirmation, "Jesus
    is Lord" (or King), with the democratic structure of our
    church?

6. Read pages 43–49, an historical introduction to creeds and
    confessions, to discover which of them are authoritative for
    your own denomination. How familiar are you with your own
    denomination's creed (or creeds)?

7. To what extent is your own creed determined by an official
    creedal statement? By your liturgy and especially by your
    hymns? By your pastor's views? By the prevailing local senti-
    ment in your community? What are the advantages of being
    controlled by a written creed? What are the advantages of
    other approaches such as those mentioned?

Introduction to the Creeds and Confessions

Our purpose in this appendix is simply to identify in outline form some of the great creeds and confessions in the history of the church. For convenience we shall divide them into four main groups: (1) the "ecumenical" creeds, (2) the confessions of the Reformed churches, (3) the confessions of other churches, and (4) confessional statements of the contemporary ecumenical movement. Because we shall be using especially the Reformed confessions in this book, we shall concentrate on them. You will find a detailed study of all these writings in Sara Little's *The Language of the Christian Community* (Richmond: The CLC Press, 1965), and in John H. Leith's *Creeds of the Churches* (New York: Doubleday and Co., 1963); both books are available in paperback. See also Philip Schaff, *Creeds of Christendom* (Grand Rapids: Baker Book House, 1966).

I. Ecumenical Creeds

The four creeds to be mentioned here are called "ecumenical" (worldwide) because they were the work of *all* the ancient church. They are the common root from which later confessions and creeds have grown. In our time also they are still formally or tacitly acknowledged by most Christian churches—Roman Catholic, Eastern Orthodox, and the various Protestant denominations. Since they contain the most basic articles of the Christian faith, they are an expression of a fundamental unity despite all the differences among the churches. Here Reformed Christians stand together with other Christians everywhere, in all times.

1. The Apostles' Creed. By legend attributed to the original apostles. Present form not found before the sixth or seventh century, but probably goes back to an ancient Roman baptismal creed of the second century. Used most widely in the Western churches.

2. Nicene Creed. As we recite it now, formulated at the Council of Nicea in 325 and completed at the Council of Constantinople in 381. Defined the relation between Father, Son, and Holy Spirit—the doctrine of the Trinity. Used most widely in the Eastern Orthodox Church.

3. Creed of Chalcedon. Formulation in 451 of the "two natures" of Christ—the relationship between his humanity and deity.

4. Athanasian Creed. Wrongly attributed by tradition to Athanasius, the great "Father of Orthodoxy" of the fourth century. Real author and origin unknown, but probably written between the fifth and seventh centuries. Doctrines of Trinity and Incarnation developed.

II. Presbyterian-Reformed Confessions

Whereas the ecumenical creeds, with the exception of the Apostles' Creed, concentrated on particular theological problems, most of the Reformation and post-Reformation confessions were attempts to summarize the whole of Christian teaching. From the Reformation to the present, more than sixty creeds have been written which could be considered as Reformed, although no exact number can be fixed since no one can say precisely what the qualifications are. We shall mention only a few of the most important, dividing them into three periods: (1) the period of the sixteenth century Reformation, (2) the period of seventeenth century "Orthodoxy" or "Scholasticism," (3) the modern period.

A. REFORMATION CONFESSIONS

1. SWITZERLAND:

   a. Catechism of Geneva, 1541. A summary of the Christian faith for children written by Calvin himself.

   b. The Second Helvetic Confession, 1566, by Heinrich Bullinger, a reformer from Zurich. One of the two most widely adopted of all continental Reformed confessions. A long, but moderate summary of central affirmations. Recently adopted into the *Book of Confessions* of the United Presbyterian Church.

2. GERMANY: *The Heidelberg Catechism,* 1563, by Zacharia Ursinus and Caspar Olevianus. (They were 28 and 26 years old when the catechism was composed.) A guide intended for instruction of youth, preachers and teachers, and for use in public worship. Most widely accepted of all Reformed confessions. In our country, one of the official standards of the United Presbyterian Church and the Reformed Church in America.

3. FRANCE: *The Gallican (or French) Confession,* 1559, prepared from a rough draft by Calvin.

4. HOLLAND: *The Belgic Confession,* 1561, by Guido de Bres. Similar in form and content to the French Confession. Together with the Westminster Confession perhaps the best summary of Calvinistic doctrine. An official standard of the Reformed Church in America.

5. SCOTLAND: *The Scots Confession,* 1560, by John Knox and a commission. Clear, fresh, sweet-spirited summary of Reformed faith as held in common by Protestants of England, Switzerland, France and Holland. Recently adopted as one of the standards of the United Presbyterian Church.

B. REFORMED CREEDS OF
THE SEVENTEENTH CENTURY

One has only to read the major Reformed confessions of the sixteenth and seventeenth centuries to notice the difference. The sixteenth century confessions and catechisms were usually written in the form of warm personal affirmation, with an obvious feeling of personal involvement. The seventeenth century confessions and catechisms were written in a more impersonal, rationalistic style. They were more concerned with right thinking about the truth than with personal involvement in it. In the seventeenth century the sense of joyous excitement of a new discovery of the gospel gave way to bitter arguments not only between Protestants and Catholics, but also between Reformed and Lutheran and even between Reformed and Reformed Christians. It now seemed necessary not simply to confess the new insights of the Reformation but to define them very precisely and defend them against other views. The seventeenth century is identified by the term "Protestant Orthodoxy" or "Protestant Scholasticism." A proper understanding of Reformed confessions includes the best of both: the joyful, modest, thankful, free personal character of the sixteenth century; and the careful, hard-thinking passion for correctness of the seventeenth century. Two writings from the latter period are most important for us:

1. *The Canons of the Synod of Dort,* 1619. Result of an international conference of Reformed thinkers in Holland. Dealt with problems related to predestination. Now recognized as a standard of doctrine in Holland and by the Reformed Church in America.

2. *Westminster Standards,* 1646. Came from the Westminster Assembly, meeting from 1643–1649, called to deal with issues of the Puritan conflict. The Westminster Confession of Faith, with the Larger and Shorter Catechisms, has become the most influential confessional standard in the English-speaking Reformed world and is accepted with various modifications by most American Presbyterian churches.

C. LATER REFORMED CONFESSIONS

The writing of Reformed confessions and creeds has continued after the great sixteenth and seventeenth century periods. For our purposes three are especially important:

1. *The Cumberland Presbyterian Confession,* 1829. A revision of the Westminster Confession, modifying the doctrine of predestination.

2. *The Barmen Declaration,* 1934. Especially important because it dealt with the modern heresies of nationalism and racism, as earlier creeds dealt with the heresies of their day. Written primarily by Karl Barth. Included by the United Presbyterian Church in its *Book of Confessions,* and by this action made one of the official standards of this church.

3. *The Confession of 1967.* First time in which American Reformed Christians have followed the classical Reformed tradition by which churches in different countries formulate the Reformed faith particularly for their time and situation. A confession of the United Presbyterian Church, restating

the Reformed faith in terms of the doctrine of reconciliation, and in a typically Reformed fashion relating reconciliation to concrete areas of alienation in modern American life.

III. The Confessional Writings of Other Churches

We shall divide the confessional writings of the non-Reformed Churches into two sections: (1) those of other "confessional" churches, (2) those of the "free churches."

A. CONFESSIONAL CHURCHES

1. THE LUTHERAN CHURCH. All the Lutheran confessions were written between 1529 and 1580, by Germans, in Germany, and are included in the Book of Concord of 1580. Besides the Apostles', Nicene and Athanasian Creeds, this book of confessions includes the following specifically Lutheran documents:

   a. *Augsburg Confession* (Melanchthon, 1530)

   b. *Apology of the Augsburg Confession* (Melanchthon, 1531)

   c. *Smalcald Articles* (Luther, 1537)

   d. *Treatise on the Power and Primacy of the Pope* (Melanchthon, 1537)

   e. *The Small Catechism* (Luther, 1529)

   f. *The Large Catechism* (Luther, 1529)

   g. *Formula of Concord* (by an assembly, 1577)

2. ANGLICAN AND EPISCOPAL CHURCHES

   a. *Book of Common Prayer.* First composed in 1549, and subsequently revised several times. Doctrine expressed in the form of public worship.

   b. *Thirty-Nine Articles,* 1563. A general doctrinal guide without the full authority given to creeds in Lutheran and Reformed Churches.

3. ROMAN CATHOLIC CHURCH. Recognizes the decisions of the ecumenical councils of the ancient church, and the doctrine formulated by other councils and by various promulgations of the popes. Some of the most distinctive statements of doctrine:

   a. *Council of Trent,* meeting with interruptions from 1545–1563. Catholic answer to the Protestant Reformation.

   b. *Dogma of the Immaculate Conception,* Pius IX, 1854.

c. *First Vatican Council,* 1870, called by Pius IX. Dealt with primacy of the pope and declared him infallible when he speaks officially regarding faith or morals.

d. *Dogma of the Assumption of the Virgin Mary,* Pius XII, 1950.

e. *Second Vatican Council.* First met in 1962 while John XXIII was still pope, and ended in 1964 under Pope Paul VI. Beginning of new conceptions in the Catholic Church concerning the nature of the church, revelation, liturgy, relation with non-Christian religions and with other churches, religious freedom, and the church's responsibility in the modern world. Marks a biblical and theological renewal which makes the eventual unity of all Christian churches seem less impossible than it once did.

4. *The Eastern Orthodox Church.* Acknowledges the decisions of the ecumenical councils of the ancient church. Most recent and authoritative summary of Orthodox doctrine is *The Confession of Dositheus,* 1672.

B. THE FREE CHURCHES

The so-called "free churches" are those which do not have officially binding confessional standards. Some of them have a congregationalist form of government, according to which there can be no denominational standards because each congregation is free to decide on its own creed or have no creed at all. Others may have a denomination-wide creed, but allow a great deal of freedom in relation to it. But even the former have produced statements of faith which help to identify where they stand. Some of the most important "confessional" writings of the nonconfessional churches are:

1. THE METHODISTS: *Twenty-Five Articles of Religion,* 1784. Revised by John Wesley from the Thirty-Nine Articles of the Church of England. A general guide, not strictly binding.

2. THE MORAVIANS: Doctrine embodied not in a theological statement but in *The Easter Litany of 1749.* An expression of the conviction that faith is best witnessed to not in formal logical affirmations but in life and worship.

3. THE BAPTISTS:
   a. The New Hampshire Confession, 1833. Prepared by a committee. Reflects a moderate Calvinism.
   b. Statement of Baptist Faith and Message, Southern Baptist Convention, 1925. Includes New Hampshire Confession, and adds the report of a committee on doctrinal issues of this period.

IV. The Contemporary Ecumenical Movement.

We have seen that the most ancient and most universal Christian creeds came from the "ecumenical" councils of the ancient church. All of the other confessional writings we have mentioned came not from *the* church, but from separate churches —a Christian church splintered into many parts. One of the most significant developments of the twentieth century is the reappearance of the word "ecumenical." At the heart of the ecumenical movement, there is a concern for the unity of the church, and an attempt on the part of the churches to speak with one united voice instead of many conflicting voices. We mention here only a few of the statements which have come from the modern ecumenical movement. Most of them deal with the question of the unity of the church and with the problem of the church's responsibility in the modern world. They are included in John H. Leith's *Creeds of the Churches.*

   1. The Call to Unity, Lausanne, 1927
   2. The Grace of Our Lord Jesus Christ, Edinburgh, 1937
   3. Affirmation of Union, Edinburgh, 1937
   4. Message of the First Assembly of the World Council of Churches, Amsterdam, 1948
   5. The Unity We Have and the Unity We Seek, Lund, 1952
   6. A Message from the Second Assembly of the World Council of Churches, Evanston, 1954
   7. The Church's Unity, World Council of Churches, New Delhi, 1961

We may hope that the continuing history of the great creeds and confessions of the church will not be the history of this or that denomination but of the one "holy Catholic Church."

GOD
and
MAN

PART II

GOD
and
MAN

"There are many gods" (1 Corinthians 8:5). "God" is whatever is more important than anything else, something for which a man will sacrifice everything else, something from which he expects everything worth having.[1] A man's god may be his own individual success or pleasure or happiness. It may be his family or his nation or even his church. It may be an ethical idea or a political cause. In our time it may even be "nothingness" or "meaninglessness." But whatever it is, a man's understanding of his god shapes his understanding of himself, and his understanding of himself shapes his understanding of his god. When I talk about what is most important to me, I give away what I think about myself. And when I talk about myself, I give away what my god really is (and it may turn out to be a different god from the god I claim I believe in!).

If, for instance, I understand myself basically as a kind of animal, my god will be something that fulfills what I consider my most essential animal needs: sex, hunger or self-preservation. And my god will in turn shape my life. I will use and sacrifice family, friends, the welfare of the society in which I live—everything—for sexual pleasure or economic security or sheer power. If some political cause is my god, I will understand myself as an exclusively political being, and my fellowmen not so much as fellow human beings as simply usable or not usable means in achieving my cause's victory. My self-understanding will lead me to make of my cause a god which demands and receives the sacrifice of anything or anyone who gets in the way. Understanding of my god and understanding of myself shape each other.

"There are many gods—yet for us there is one God" (1 Corinthians 8:5). What we have said in general about man and his gods is true also of Christians and their God. John Calvin begins his *Institutes of the Christian Religion* with the statement that ". . . true and sound wisdom, consists of two parts: the knowledge of God and of ourselves."[2] Without the knowledge of self, Calvin says, there can be no knowledge of God, and without the knowledge of God, there can be no knowledge of self.

This suggests that we could go about trying to understand the Christian faith in one of two ways. We could begin with the Christian understanding of man and try to grasp the Christian understanding of God from that point of view. Or we could speak first of the knowledge of God and in light of that try to reach the knowledge of man. Calvin himself, and following him, the Reformed confessional writings, chose the second alternative. That will also be our approach. A glance at the table of contents will show you that all the way along we shall speak first of God, then of man. But we must be careful that we do not make a separation here, as if we could ever talk *only* about God without at the same time talking about ourselves, or vice versa. From the very beginning and all the way along, we shall have to keep asking both questions at the same time: "What do our statements about God have to do with the way we understand ourselves, and what do our statements about ourselves imply about our understanding of God?"

"There are many gods, but for us there is one God." If Christians make such a claim, there is a series of questions we must answer before we do anything else. "How do we know this one God? Who is he? What is he like? What does he want with us?" These are the questions we shall try to answer in this first part of our study. As we answer them, some other questions will arise which will determine where we have to go from here.

3

How Can We Find God?

"Brother, have you found God?" a street-corner preacher once asked a man passing by. The man, who happened to be a Christian, answered, "I didn't know he was lost." For Christians, who believe that God has made himself known, the problem is not that *God* is lost, but that *men* are lost. But, while the man gave a good Christian answer, still we can understand what it means to ask "Have you found God?" We too can share the anguish of Job when he cried, "Oh, that I knew where I might find him!" Moreover, even when we do believe we know God, we have the responsibility to explain *how* we know. This is the first question usually taken up in Christian theology, and it is the first question we must wrestle with: How do we Christians—or anyone else—come to know God?

The broad stream of Christian thought, like the confessional writings of the Reformed Churches, gives two answers to this question.

First, God is known by the "light of nature and the works of creation" (Westminster Confession, I, 1). Or in other words, God is known "by the creation, preservation and government of the universe" (Belgic Confession, Art. II).

Secondly, God is known because "it pleased the Lord, at sundry times and in divers manners to reveal himself, and to declare that his will unto his church; and afterwards to commit the same wholly unto writing" (Westminster Confession, I, 1). Or more briefly: "Secondly, he makes himself known by his holy and divine Word" (Belgic Confession, Art. II).

Another way of identifying these two ways of knowing God is to speak of a general revelation and of a special revelation. Since we shall be using these technical terms and some concepts connected with them throughout this chapter, it is important that we get their meaning clearly in mind now.

General revelation refers to the self-disclosure of God which all men can perceive by contemplating evidences of his existence and nature in the world of nature, history and human life in general. The knowledge of God derived from this revelation is called the *natural knowledge of God.* The movement of theological reflection here is from man to God; man seeks God.

Special revelation, on the other hand, refers to the unique self-revelation of God through his mighty acts in the history of Israel and above all in Jesus Christ, through the Bible which tells us of the God who made himself known in this way, and through the Christian church which bears witness to him as he is proclaimed in the Bible. The knowledge of God derived from this source is called the *revealed knowledge of God.* The movement of theological reflection here is from God to man; God seeks and finds man.

In this chapter we shall discuss the knowledge of God which comes from general revelation. We shall save special revelation until the next chapter. Now we ask, "How can we find God?" In the next chapter we shall ask, "How does God find us?"

The Problem

"Why am I here? Where did I come from? Where am I going? What is the meaning of my life?" We do not ask such ultimate questions every day, but they plague us especially at times of crisis—when we face death, or war, or an important decision which will alter the course of our lives and affect the lives of others. And sometimes such questions crop up in an unexpected way in the normal routine of our lives.

We read the newspaper at breakfast: violence, corruption, injustice, tragedy, ruined lives everywhere. What is it all about?

We drive to work, do the same thing today we did yesterday, drive home—and do it all over again the next day. We make beds, wash dishes, sweep floors—over and over again. And suddenly the question is there: What am I doing here?

We make money, spend money, fulfill our responsibilities, enjoy simple and great pleasures, do what has to be done, look forward to the next weekend or the next vacation. We are alternately happy and depressed, frustrated and successful, resigned to our place in life and hopeful that things will get better. But sometimes at night we cannot sleep because the question comes: Why? Where? What? Who? How?

"The question" is a religious question. It very easily becomes the question, Is there a God? Is there Someone at the beginning and end of my own life and of the world in general who can make sense out of it all? Is there Someone in charge here, who, if I know what *he* is up to, can help me to understand who *I* am, why I am here, and how I can go about living as I should?

Not only Christians but probably all men, in all times, everywhere, have asked these questions. Some have come to the conclusion that there is no God, or that we cannot know whether he exists or anything about him. But others (non-Christians as well as Christians) have come to the conclusion that there is good evidence for the existence of God, some indications of the kind of God he is, and therefore some helpful answers to our questions about the meaning and purpose of our lives. In other words, they say that a "natural knowledge" of God is possible, if only men are open and sensitive enough to perceive his presence in and around them. What, then, are the evidences for the existence of God?

1. **The empirical evidence.** The following answers (sometimes called proofs) have been given by philosophers and theologians through the centuries.

a. When we look around us, we feel that *the world is not self-explanatory*. Where did it come from? What holds it together? There must be a God who is the source and ground of all things. Behind all the change and decay we see around us, there must be an Ultimate Reality which is eternal and unchanging. We are born; we work, love, hate, suffer and die. But we may find comfort, strength and hope from the fact that we do not come from nothing and return to nothing. We come from God, live in a world created and governed by him, and return to him.

b. When we look at the world around us, we not only feel that it must have an origin and ground; we find that *the universe displays a purpose.* There are many signs of order and design in the world of nature. Think, for instance, of the regularity with which the earth turns on its axis, and how it orbits around the sun at precisely such a distance that life is possible on earth. Or think of the wonderful structure of the human body, with all of its parts so exactly coordinated to function together. It cannot be sheer accident that there is order and harmony and not simply chaos in the world. There must be a God with a purpose at work here.

c. The world of *history shows planning and purpose* also. The evil and injustice of men and nations have been defeated again and again throughout history. Decency and justice, law and order, have triumphed again and again as history unfolds. There must be a good God working his purposes out. If we study history, we can discover what kind of God he is, and what he wills for our lives.

d. Not only when we look at the world around us but also *when we look within ourselves, we discover evidences for the existence of God and clues to his nature.* All human beings, in contrast to animals, feel within themselves a sense of moral responsibility. We have a conscience, a sense of right and wrong, a feeling of duty to do what is good and true. Is that not an indication that some great Moral Power is at work in us? We can discover what it means to live as true human beings if we listen to the voice of God directing our lives through our consciences.

e. When we look deep within ourselves, we find not only a sense of moral responsibility, but also *a spiritual awareness of a divine presence.* We are not only rational, moral and physical beings, but spiritual beings as well. An important dimension of life is left out if we ignore the creative presence of a Spirit which we cannot explain, but which we are all intuitively aware of. This awareness of God is more like the knowledge of a poet or artist or religious mystic than the knowledge of a philosopher or mathematician or scientist. But why should it be any less trustworthy? Why should it not be *more* trustworthy?

f. There is a strange agreement between the way our minds work and the structure of the world. We are rational beings, and *the world seems to function in a rational way.* We can formulate in our minds certain logical rules, and we discover that the world of nature operates according to these rules. Must there not be a great Mind behind both rational human beings and a rational world? If we carefully analyze the laws of nature and of reason, we can learn how the mind of the Maker works, and therefore what the world is all about, and how we can live in it meaningfully. If we learn what it means to live as rational men in a rational world governed by a rational God, we will live as genuinely *human* beings just because we live according to the will of *God.*

By way of summary: An analysis of the world around us and of our own lives points to the fact that there is a God. Such an analysis gives us evidence of his eternity, wisdom, power and goodness. It furnishes us with at least a foundation upon which we can discover the answer to those disturbing questions we cannot escape: "Why am I here? Where did I come from? Where am I going? How should I live?"

2. The basic attitudes of Christian thinkers. What shall we make of the knowledge of God to be gained from "the light of nature and the works of creation"? How is it related to the knowledge given to us by God's revelation of himself in "his holy and divine Word"? Christian thinkers have taken three basic attitudes toward the knowledge God gained by general revelation and the relation of this knowledge to that gained by special revelation.

a. The first position is a radical one taken by only a few. It was especially typical of the Deists in the eighteenth century, but it is not unknown today. According to this view, what we know about God from our observation of the world and from a study of ourselves is the *most certain* knowledge we have. Anything else we are told about God must be measured, judged and corrected by this knowledge. There may be a special revelation such as that recorded in the Bible. But anything the Bible says about God can be true only if it does not contradict what men already know by rational or natural religion. If there is a contradiction, it is the Bible which must be rejected, changed or reinterpreted—not our analysis of the world and our experiences in it.

In the same way, the surest guide we have to right living is given to us in our consciences and the natural laws of the world. There may be a specially revealed will of God, but it can be valid only in so far as it agrees with the moral law of the universe any rational man of integrity can figure out for himself. In so far as the biblical ethic does not conform to that, it must be either rejected or corrected.

So, for instance, if I think I have learned what is possible and impossible according to the God-given physical laws of the natural world, and I read in the Bible about a God who breaks those laws and does the impossible, I must automatically conclude that the Bible is wrong in what it says, or explain it in such a way that it only seems to speak of a God who acts in an unnatural way. Would God break his own law—the law we find operating in the world he made?

If my conscience tells me that the segregation of the races is a God-given moral law of the universe, and then I read in the Bible that in Christ God is at work to break down the barriers between men, I must either reject outright what I hear about God in the Bible, or interpret it so that God in Christ does not contradict the moral standards given in my conscience.

If I decide that according to the laws of nature it is unnatural to love my enemies, then I must refuse to accept the biblical claim that God himself is a God who loves his enemies and commands us to do the same. Or perhaps I can interpret the biblical claim so that it becomes only a great spiritual ideal which is not meant to apply to the practical issues of everyday life.

The main stream of Christian thought has, of course, rejected this extreme position that special revelation is to be judged by and made to conform to natural religion. This obviously is a subtle way of man's deciding what God can and must be and do. Man asks himself the questions and gives himself the answers. There is no place for a real revelation at all. Revelation means that something *new* is made known. But this extreme position will hear and accept only what a man already knows, or thinks he knows, or can learn by himself.

How, then, shall we understand the relation between the knowledge of God "by the creation, preservation and government of the universe" and the knowledge of God "by his holy and divine Word"? There are two other possibilities.

b. General revelation cannot dictate what special revelation can and must be, but it can give us a preliminary, incomplete knowledge of God. It can at least show us that there *is* a God, and tell us *something* of his power, wisdom and goodness. This knowledge is not enough in itself. Contrary to the position of natural or rational religion, the knowledge derived from general revelation must be interpreted, supplemented and perhaps even corrected by that derived from special revelation. Nevertheless, we really can know something of God through natural evidences, and this knowledge can at least prepare us to recognize and receive the full knowledge given in Christ, the Bible, and the Christian church. This is the position taken by most Roman Catholic and most Reformed theologians, including Calvin himself.

c. The third position is the denial of any validity at all to the natural knowledge of God. Perhaps it is true that all men have some sense of the existence of God from their observation of nature and history, and from an analysis of their own minds, hearts and consciences. But as soon as we try to say anything about this God, we talk only about our own ideas and feelings, not about God. There is *no* way from man to God, not even a beginning. The *only* way to any true knowledge of God is from God to man through God's revelation of himself in the events recorded in the Bible. True Christian theology must depend completely and exclusively on the grace of God in Christ. This is a position relatively new in the history of theology. It has been taken especially by the Swiss Reformed theologian Karl Barth and those influenced by him.

The Search for a Solution

This issue is more important than may appear at first glance. It was because he rejected all natural theology that Barth was able to speak so effectively as he called the churches in Germany to acknowledge the sole authority of Jesus Christ over their thought and life. The "German Christians" claimed, instead, to find the "will of God" in an ideology of "blood and soil" and in the destiny of a "super race." Not nature but Christ shows us God's will, replied Barth. Karl Barth could write:

> The fellowship of those belonging to the Church is not determined by blood, therefore, not by race, but by the Holy Spirit and Baptism. If the German Evangelical Church excludes Jewish-Christians, or treats them as of a lower grade, she ceases to be a Christian Church.[1]

But we only have to change two words to make the last sentence read:

> If the American Church excludes Negro Christians, or treats them as of a lower grade, she ceases to be a Christian Church.

We can see then that the discussion of the place of natural theology is not a hairsplitting debate of interest only to technical theologians. Important issues are involved here for all Christians. How we understand God and the meaning of our lives, how we relate Christianity to other religions, how we go about evangelism and missions, and even how we stand on political, social and economic issues—every area of Christian thought and life will be influenced by the decisions we make at this critical point.

Let us examine the alternatives more carefully. In what follows, we shall look at the arguments both for and against general revelation, and then suggest some guidelines for making a decision on this issue.

1. Arguments for the natural knowledge of God. The light of nature and the works of creation are admittedly "not sufficient to give that knowledge of God, and of his will, which is necessary unto salvation" (Westminster Confession, I, 1). They do not tell us about the love, grace and forgiveness of God which we know only by his special revelation of himself in the history of Israel and in Christ. Nevertheless, it is important to take seriously what can be known of God in this way for the following reasons.

a. It would be arrogant and blind to argue that no one knows God at all who does not know him through the biblical revelation. Awe, wonder and joy in the presence of a creative Power which a man knows is not drawn from his own resources but is a gift from outside himself; worshipful awareness of a dimension of life which transcends everything men can know by their five senses; obedient response to a Spirit of Love and Justice which frees a man to become a courageous and compassionate human being—all this is no monopoly of Christians. Without any reference to Jesus, the Bible or the Christian church, many philosophers, scientists, psychologists, artists and followers of other religions have convictions about God and the purpose of man's life in the world which are remarkably similar to Christian convictions. How can we deny that, however imperfectly, they have some awareness of the same God we worship—even when they call him by a different name?[2]

b. Some Christians are eager to recognize that a limited knowledge of God is available to all men, because they want to show that nonbelievers are "without excuse" in *not* knowing and serving God. Look at Romans 1:18 ff. to see how Paul makes this point.

c. The knowledge of God's existence which is available to all men furnishes us with a good beginning point in evangelism. We can best help nonbelievers to become Christians when we begin "where they are," pointing to the evidences for the existence of God in their own experience of the world, and in their reason, conscience and spiritual intuition. Having thus helped them to see that belief in God is possible, we can then go on from there to tell them who this God is. He is not just some kind of powerful, wise, good Creator and Ruler of the world; he is the loving heavenly

Father whom we Christians know because he has made himself
known to us in Christ. The natural knowledge of God, in other
words, enables us to lead non-Christians gradually to understand
and accept the full truth of the Christian faith. This is a far more
sympathetic approach, and far more likely to be a successful form
of evangelism, than a blunt, direct presentation of the Christian
gospel with a "take it or leave it" attitude. Look at Acts 17:22 ff. to
see how Paul used this approach in talking about God with nonbelievers.

If there is no connection at all between the God we are able
to conceive from our side and the God who meets us from his side,
how could there be any communication at all between us? We may
expect, then, that the God of special revelation is not totally different from the God we postulate on the basis of general revelation.
Our natural knowledge of God may not get us to our destination,
but it can at least get us to the right station.

d. Finally, we must take seriously what can be known about
God from the light of nature and the works of creation, because
the Bible itself invites us to do so. Look up the following passages
which are cited by those who defend this point of view: Psalm 19;
Acts 14:16 ff.; 17:22 ff.; Romans 1:18 ff.; 2:12 ff.

**2. Arguments against the natural knowledge of
God.** The case against any dependence at all upon general revelation, and for exclusive dependence on biblical revelation, rests on
the following arguments.

a. The arguments for the existence of God are not convincing,
and therefore it is very questionable whether an analysis of the
world and of ourselves leads us even to a preliminary knowledge
of God. It can be argued, for instance, that what we once thought
was the plan and purpose of a divine mind in nature was in fact
only a pattern we falsely read into nature with our human minds.
Again, modern anthropologists have shown that man's sense of
right and wrong varies in different cultures and in different times
and places. Conscience is not the "voice of God"; it simply reflects
the particular environment in which men live and their practical
experience in learning how to live together. All the other arguments

for the existence of God can be criticized in a similar way. The point of such criticisms is not to deny that God exists. The point is that if we are to have any certainty of his existence, we cannot depend on any of the highly debatable arguments for it. They all tell us more about the men who are searching for God than about God himself.

b. The result of looking outward at nature or inward at ourselves is not only uncertainty about the existence of God but also uncertainty about his *nature*. If lovely sunsets and flowers are evidences of a good God, what kind of God do earthquakes and poison ivy point to? If events in history such as the defeat of Hitler's Nazi regime are evidences of the rule of a just God, what kind of God is he who allows the slaughter of six million Jews before the Nazis were defeated? If the miracle of a baby's birth and the laughter of a little child suggest one kind of God, what kind of God is suggested by the suffering of a child born tragically deformed? The natural knowledge we can have of God is contradictory and confusing. And just for that reason, the very arguments which lead men to think about him also lead them to doubt whether he exists at all.

c. The knowledge of God we think we derive from an analysis of the world around us or from our own experience is untrustworthy not only because it is uncertain and ambiguous, but also because it is inevitably distorted by our sinfulness. Real evidences of God may be manifested in his works of creation and in history, but we look at those evidences with hearts and minds clouded by our own corrupt ambitions and prejudices. The result is that instead of discovering the true God and his will, we make for ourselves false gods to lend respectability to our sinful desires and opinions.

For example, we may find evidence of a God guiding the destiny of our nation. But the "God of our forefathers" very easily becomes an idol. We have a tendency to think that instead of our being here to serve God, he is there to serve us. His function is to give success to all our self-chosen economic, political and military enterprises. And if someone suggests that God is not automatically on our side, and may even be against us in this or that enterprise, we suspect that such a man is probably an atheist or communist. Our national idol prevents us from knowing the true God.

Another example: We may find evidence of the providence of God at work in the lives of individuals. But some people make an idol of providence and use it to justify any given social situation, especially when it is to their own advantage. If some men are poor and exploited and if others are comfortable and secure, that is "the work of Providence." Those "on top" should be thankful, and those "at the bottom" ought not to complain or rebel against their divinely appointed position in life. The idol Providence sanctifies the status quo as the "will of God," and prevents men from knowing the true God who might possibly be *against* the status quo.

In short, sinful men use the natural knowledge of God they think they discover in creation to *avoid* being open to hear and accept what God tells us about himself in Christ, through Scripture.

d. A natural knowledge of God based on our own reason and experience is impossible not only because of man's sinful nature but because of God's transcendent nature. According to the Bible, God in his majestic holiness is far beyond and above anything we can think or imagine. He is a "hidden" God, unknowable in himself. We cannot hope to bridge the gap between our finite humanity and his incomparable deity. The God whom we think we can discover for ourselves always turns out to be too little—a God made in our own image, a magnified copy of ourselves. True knowledge of the true God, therefore, can come only from God's side, when he who is unknown and unknowable in himself comes to us personally to "unveil" himself. How is this transcendent hiddenness of God expressed in Isaiah 55:8 f.; Matthew 11:27; John 14:6; 1 Corinthians 1:20–25; 2:9 f.?

Those who want to depend only on special revelation argue that their position is supported and not undermined by the texts which at first glance seem to indicate a general knowledge of God. Psalm 19 says that "the heavens are telling the glory of God and the firmament proclaims his handiwork." But the psalmist was a member of the community of Israel which drew its very life from the special revelation of God to his chosen people. He could recognize God everywhere because he already knew who God was. In Romans, Paul speaks of the knowledge of God in creation "not as a knowledge which men actually have and from which they can advance to further knowledge, but as a knowledge they have lost; for by their failure to act on it they have forfeited it, and ... unable to recover it, they are driven in their blindness to fashion idols (and ideas) as substitutes for the reality. (Romans 1:21–25.) ... Paul appeals to the religiosity of the Athenians as evidence, not of a knowledge of God, but of ignorance of God, for which he calls them to repentance. (Acts 17:22–31.)"[3]

To summarize the whole argument against a natural knowledge of God: All men everywhere may have some idea of God, but what we can know by ourselves is at best uncertain and ambiguous, and at worst a dangerous hindrance to real knowledge of the true God. The only trustworthy and sure knowledge we can have of God comes by his breaking into our lives in a special way which is not at all dependent upon what we can tell ourselves about him.

Some Guidelines for Making a Decision

We have seen that convincing arguments can be made both for and against general revelation and the natural knowledge of God. How can we decide between them? We conclude this chapter with some guidelines for making a decision. Do you agree with them? How would you change or correct or add to them?

1. The use of Scripture. We must take seriously *all* the passages of Scripture which are relevant to this problem. We can never hope to find a true solution if we listen only to those passages which support our personal bias and ignore those passages which do not, or if we twist the passages which cause us difficulty to make them say what we would like for them to mean. Good Christian theology is possible only when we listen with open minds to the *whole* witness of scripture.

2. On the side of those who deny general revelation and the natural knowledge of God:[4] We must take seriously their emphasis on the transcendence of God on the one hand, and on the limitations of man on the other. God's thoughts are not our

thoughts, and his ways are not our ways. In his love, power, goodness and truth he is far beyond even the very best and highest of
our finite human thinking and feeling. We will never know him
and his will so long as we try to limit him to what we can know
of him by our analysis of our personal experience and the world
around us. Moreover, we must never forget the tendency of all
men—Christians as well as non-Christians—to use "God" and the
"will of God" to serve their own sinful prejudices, plans and desires.
We must always be very modest about what we think we know of
God and his will, and constantly subject everything we think we
know to the correction of his "special revelation" of himself. Or
to put it positively: We do not *have* to depend upon the uncertain,
ambiguous and contradictory knowledge of God we can discover
for ourselves. We can live by the promise that God himself comes
to the community of those gathered in the name of the Christ we
meet in Scripture to show us who he is, what he is doing in the
world and what he has for us to do.

      **3. On the side of those who defend general revela-
tion and the natural knowledge of God:**[5] We must take seriously
those who insist that the truth of God makes sense; it is not
irrational or antirational truth we are asked to swallow at the cost
of intellectual honesty and understanding. We must also take
seriously those who insist that Christian truth does not simply
contradict but illumines and interprets our personal experience,
the restless longing of our hearts, and the inexpressible Presence
we sometimes feel in the depths of our being. However unexpected
and surprising it may be, Christian truth does not ignore but really
answers the questions all men ask about the meaning and purpose
of life. Talk about "God" or "Jesus Christ" or "what the Bible says"
or "what Christians believe" should not be just meaningless jargon
or pious cliches. If the Christian faith claims to speak of the truth,
it must have some correspondence with the truth we can learn
from the natural sciences, philosophy, modern psychology, and
the attempts of artists to grasp the mystery of life. It must be able
to acknowledge the insights of other religions into the truth. After
all, we Christians must remember that we too are only finite, sinful

men, and that *our* understanding of God and his will is limited. It would be sheer arrogance to assume that our wisdom and virtue is so superior to that of non-Christians or nontheologians that we can instruct them but have nothing to learn from them. God is not the prisoner of the Christian church. We must expect him to be present and at work also outside the sphere of those who know about and depend on Christ and the Bible.

Is it really possible to follow all three of these guidelines? At the end of the next chapter, after we have discussed special revelation, we shall make an attempt to take all three guidelines with proper seriousness. See the section entitled "The Freedom of God" on p. 84.

Meanwhile, the questions and suggestions which follow are intended to help you get clear in your mind the issues involved as you struggle to formulate your own position regarding general revelation and the natural knowledge of God.

FOR FURTHER REFLECTION AND STUDY

1. How would you as a Christian try to speak meaningfully and helpfully to someone who said to you, "There is no God"? Would you try to prove the existence of God to him?
2. If you tend to agree with the arguments *for* a natural knowledge of God, how would you answer the arguments *against* it?
3. If you tend to agree with the arguments *against* a natural knowledge of God, how would you answer the arguments *for* it?
4. Read Romans 1:16–32 and Acts 17:23 with this question in mind: Does Paul defend, reject, or accept with certain reservations (What are they?) a natural knowledge of God?
5. What difference would the affirmation or denial of a natural knowledge of God and his will make in evaluating as Christians the following statements:
    a. "Whatever your sickness is, know certainly that it is God's visitation." (Anglican Book of Common Prayer, Seventeenth Century).
    b. The lower classes should accept social inequality with humility and patience, knowing that "their more lowly

path has been allotted to them by the hand of God"
(William Wilberforce).[6]

c. "When in the course of human events it becomes necessary for one people to dissolve the political bands which
have connected them with another, and to assume among
the powers of the earth the separate and equal station to
which the Laws of Nature and of Nature's God entitle
them, a decent respect to the opinions of mankind requires that they should declare the causes which impel
them to the separation . . . . We hold these truths to be
self-evident, that all men are created equal, that they are
endowed by their Creator with certain unalienable rights,
that among these are Life, Liberty, and the pursuit of
Happiness" (American Declaration of Independence).

d. "In the long run it is only to the man of morality that
wealth comes. We believe in the harmony of God's universe. We know that it is only by working along His laws
natural and spiritual that we can work with efficiency.
Only by working along the lines of right thinking and
right living can the secrets and wealth of nature be revealed. . . . Godliness is in league with riches. . . . Material
prosperity is helping to make the national character
sweeter, more joyous, more unselfish, more Christlike"
(Bishop Lawrence of Massachusetts, 1900).[7]

e. The statement of the German Christians on page 30
above.

4

How Does God Find Us?

"I didn't see God up there," says a cosmonaut who returned to earth from the heavens. "God is dead," says a theologian, speaking both for himself and for a secular world which not only fails to experience the reality of God, but thinks it no longer needs God because it has learned to answer all questions and solve all problems just as well without him.

"Religion is the opiate of the people," said Karl Marx, speaking also for a long line of people since his time, communist and noncommunist alike, who have seen that "God" is often only an excuse for the rich, the comfortable and the powerful to maintain the social-political-economic status quo, and to persuade or force the poor and exploited to stay where they are.

Consider the following contradictory statements.

There is one only, the true and the living God.

There is no God.

Man cannot be truly human without a God of some kind.

We can achieve a more just, more human world without dragging in God as a sop or as a weapon.

Look around you: There are evidences everywhere of a wise, good, powerful heavenly Father.

Take another look: A world so filled with evil and suffering screams that God does not exist—or if he does he must be either mean or just plain lazy.

These statements present the issues and problems involved in our search for God. They are the issues and problems debated by those who affirm or deny a natural revelation of God in the world and a natural knowledge of God made possible by such a revelation. We have seen in the last chapter that Christians differ among themselves about the results of such a conversation.

But however Christians may differ in their answer to the question how and whether we can find God, they all agree that there is another and more certain way of talking about God. How do we know that there *is* a God, and how do we know what he is like? All Christians agree that in the last analysis we know not because we can prove his existence or because we can show that man needs a God, or because we have searched for him and found him, but because *he* has come looking for *us* and made himself known to us. We know what God is like, not because we have decided what he *can* or *must* be like on the basis of our speculations about him, but because he has *told* us and *shown* us what he is like in a special way. In other words, there is a "special revelation" of God which gives us a "special knowledge" of him and of his will and nature.

How does God reveal himself to us in this special way? Christians give three answers: (1) God revealed himself in *history* —the history which leads up to, centers in, and follows from a man named Jesus. (2) God reveals himself in the *book* which tells us what he said and did in that history and in that man. (3) God reveals himself to and through the *community of people* in all times who listen to and proclaim the message of the Bible. In this chapter we shall discuss the meaning of this special revelation. First we shall try to understand some things it tells us, taken as a whole, about what we mean when we say that God reveals himself. Then we shall try to understand the relation between the three different ways in which this revelation happens.

The Meaning of Revelation

We said at the beginning of our study of the knowledge of God that two factors are always involved in theology at the same time: knowledge of God and knowledge of ourselves. What we think about God influences what we think about ourselves, and what we think about ourselves influences what we think about God. It is especially important in this section to remember this. In what follows, we shall try to keep this question in mind: What new understanding or God and what new understanding of *ourselves* is given in special revelation?

1. The truth of revelation is a Person. God reveals *himself*. Revelation is not the giving of some supernatural information or ideas about God and man and the world. It means that God confronts us with himself, person-to-person. To receive God's self-revelation is not to know something we did not know before, but to know some*one* we did not know before. The revealed truth Christians believe in is not an "it" but a "he." This is most clearly seen in Jesus' strange saying, "I am the truth"—his way of saying that the truth is a *person*. In God's self-revelation we are of course given some new thoughts and ideas about God, but revealed theology differs from natural theology just in that it does not have to do with an explanation of the world, or some ethical laws and principles, or with a philosophy of life, but with a living, personal God. Our next point shows what a big difference this makes.

2. The knowledge which results from revelation is not theoretical but personal. If the content of revelation is the living personal God, then we must have a particular understanding of what the "knowledge of God" given in revelation means. In the Bible, where we learn about the self-revealing God, "to know" God does not mean to know *about* God, to believe intellectually and grasp rationally that there is a God, to have information about him and his will. To know God means to experience him, to have a personal relationship with him, to encounter him. To know God's judgment, for instance, is not simply to believe that there is a God who judges; it is to have his judgment *happen* to you (Jeremiah 16:21; Ezekiel 25:14). To know God's love is not to believe in a theory of his love; it is to experience his loving actions (read Deuteronomy 4:32–40, looking especially for the verb "to know"). To know God is to acknowledge him, confess him, give him honor, do his will.

On the other hand, those who know only theoretically do not

know at all. The sons of the priest Eli (preacher's sons!) "grew up in the church" and knew all about God, yet because they were faithless and disobedient, it is said that they did not "know the Lord" (1 Samuel 2:12, K.J.V.). The People of Israel had all the information they needed about God, believed all the right things about him, and were very careful in their religious practices. But Isaiah said that they did not know God (Isaiah 1:3), and he explained why: Despite their orthodox beliefs and proper religious rituals, they rebelled against God and were guilty in their social and political lives of oppression, injustice, and indifference to the needs of the poor and defenseless. Jeremiah even dared to say that the prophets and priests (the preachers!) who handled the Law did not know God, because their knowledge was only a matter of correct doctrine, not an obedient, thankful, personal relationship with God (see Jeremiah 2:8).

The situation is the same in the New Testament. What is the meaning of "knowledge" in 1 John 2:4; Philippians 3:8–11; Ephesians 3:14–19? Look again at Romans 1:18–23, the passage we discussed before when we were speaking about the natural knowledge of God. Do those who "knew" God but "did not honor him as God or give thanks to him" really know him at all, according to the biblical sense of the word? Does the meaning of this passage become a little clearer if we think of the difference between these men as the difference between those who only know about God and his existence and those who know the living God himself?

3. **The knowledge given with revelation is the knowledge of something (or better: someone) new and unexpected.** The word "revelation" itself suggests that something hitherto hidden or unknown has come to light. Christians who believe in a natural knowledge of God agree that when he makes himself known to us in a special way we learn some surprising new things about what kind of God he is and about how he works in the world and in our individual lives. Our thoughts are not God's thoughts and our ways are not his ways (Isaiah 55:8–9). Therefore, when revelation happens we are confronted with " 'What no eye has seen, nor ear heard nor the heart of man conceived' " (1 Corinthians

2:9). The God who reveals himself to us is so new and unexpected that his truth is sometimes offensive to men who think they already know how God ought to act if he acts like God. Thus in the first century Jesus seemed to the Gentiles folly and to the Jews a stumbling block (1 Corinthians 1:23).

If we today are to know God in his self-revelation, we must be willing to hear and accept something brand-new—even if it contradicts our previous ideas about God. Only then can we learn that the news given us in revelation is Good News. We may learn *gladly* that God is not the Greek god imprisoned by his own spirituality and shut out from the physical, flesh-and-blood world where we live, but is God-with-us and God-for-us *in* the world. We may learn *gladly* that God is not the great heavenly bookkeeper of the Pharisees, but the God who loves and gives himself just for men who are *not* good and deserving of reward. And we may learn *gladly* that God is at work not just where there is success and power and victory, but even in the midst of failure and weakness and suffering.

4. **We know God because he reveals himself in words-with-action and in action-with-words.** We open up or reveal ourselves to one another in two ways: in speaking and in acting. But with us speaking and acting are often unrelated or even contradictory, and the result is that communication breaks down. When our words are not followed by corresponding actions, we lie. Our words do not reveal but cover up what we really are. On the other hand, if we act without corresponding words, our actions are often ambiguous. If a parent disciplines a child, for instance, the action without explanatory words might convince the child that the parent does not love him, when in fact the discipline may have been an expression of love.

God reveals himself to us both in words and in action. He really reveals himself, because his words and actions agree. He *does* what he *says*. And when he acts, he explains what he is doing with an interpretative word. Revelation, then, is not word *or* act, speaking *or* doing, but word-with-act, doing-with-speaking. Thus the central event of revelation for ancient Israel was the deliverance from

Egypt. God *said*, "I will be your God and you shall be my people."
And he *acted* to do what he said: "I am the Lord your God, who
brought you out of Egypt, out of the house of bondage."

This unity of word and act is even more clearly seen in God's
revelation of himself in Jesus. Jesus is himself the Word of God
(John 1:1). What God has to *say* to us is what he *did* among us
and for us in this man. And in his life, Jesus did not just *talk* about
God and his own relation to God (although he also did that); he
demonstrated what he said. He not only spoke about God's love;
he himself loved with the love of God.

We may always expect God's revelation of himself to come
to us both in mighty acts and in spoken words which interpret
these acts. To know God, therefore, is both to *hear* what God has
to say and to *experience* what God is doing. Revelation and the
reception of revelation is a personal encounter in which God speaks
and we hear, God acts in our history and we respond.

**5. God reveals himself and we know him always
in an earthly, worldly, human way.** As you have read what we have
said so far about the meaning of revelation, perhaps you have
thought to yourself, "That sounds right, but it just does not agree
with my experience. God may be a 'person', but I can't really think
of him as a person except when I slip back into a childish view of
an old man with a white beard up in the sky. There may be such
a thing as a 'personal' relationship with God in which God speaks
and people hear, God acts and people recognize him—but God
never spoke personally to me, and I can never be sure in the events
of my life whether he really is at work or not. Maybe I'm just not
a real Christian. Or maybe God revealed himself only in the past,
in biblical times. Or maybe he still speaks and acts personally in
the lives of other people now, and I have been left out."

There is another aspect of God's self-revelation which helps
us with this problem—a problem which any honest person must
admit that he has at least sometimes. (Even Jesus himself could
cry out, "My God, my God, why hast thou forsaken me?")

Let us put it bluntly: God is never *directly* present to us in his
self-revelation, and *no* man (with one exception) ever had a *direct*

personal relationship with God. God comes to us, and we can know him, but we know him only *indirectly*, through worldly means. After all, I cannot know totally and directly even a fellow human being. What he is had to be communicated to me by his words, his acts, his appearance. I know who any person is "on the inside" only through the external means of his acts, words, and expression.

Similarly, I know God indirectly, for God is not a man and even his "personalness" is not the same as human personalness. God is different from us. That is why he is in himself an "unknown God." But God reveals himself. He wants to be God-with-us and God-for-us, to enter into personal relationship with us. How does he do it? Revelation means that he comes down to our level—our human, worldly earthly level. He comes to us in a form which is foreign to what he himself is. He unveils himself to us only as he veils himself in a human, worldly form. He reveals himself to us by hiding himself (or clothing himself). He really reveals himself, but he does it only in an indirect way. Perhaps this difficult paradox will become a little clearer if we look at some of the concrete ways in which God reveals himself.

a. God reveals himself above all *in the man Jesus.* How do we come to know the Creator of heaven and earth? Where do we meet him personally? In a weak, helpless baby lying in a cradle in a barn! In a Jew who was the friend of dishonest business men, prostitutes, social outcasts! In a man sentenced to die by capital punishment between two thieves! What inappropriate places to meet *God!* How unspiritual! But hidden in this peasant baby, in this ancient Jewish carpenter-preacher, in this "criminal"—there is God himself speaking, acting, personally present. Christians believe that when they are personally confronted with this man, they are personally confronted with the sovereign God himself. God is not a man, but in this man God himself is with us. "No one has ever seen God; the only Son . . . he has made him known" (John 1:18). "He who has seen me has seen the Father" (John 14:9).

b. Or again, God made himself known by his *mighty acts in the events of the history of Israel and in the words of the prophets.* But his mighty acts coincided with the mighty acts of heathen kings and armies, which in themselves may be completely explained by the political and economic conditions of the ancient world. And when the prophets said, "Thus saith the Lord . . . ," people in their time as well as in ours could say "I didn't hear the Lord. All I heard was Jeremiah or Isaiah." In the history of Israel God spoke and acted *indirectly*, in a worldly way—in ordinary historical happenings and through ordinary men.

c. God reveals himself *in the Bible.* Christians believe that God himself speaks to us in this book. But he speaks in and through human writers using the original languages of an ancient near Eastern tribe and of an ancient Western civilization. Moreover, the biblical writings reflect their writers' education or lack of education, historical environment and culture, primitive views of geography and physics and astronomy. As God in Christ came to us wrapped in swaddling clothes, so the word of God comes to us wrapped in the words of these men—in this *human* form.

d. In our own time, the living God promises to be personally present, to speak and act, *through his Spirit in the community of people who belong to him.* He still works outside the church, of course, just as he once worked in and through the pagan empires of Babylon, Assyria, Persia and Rome. But he *makes known* what it is he is doing and saying in the world also in our time through the community of people who belong to him. Now we see how seriously we have to take the worldliness of God's revelation! The present-day church is no more worldly than ancient Israel was. Present-day preachers are no easier to believe than the ancient prophets were in their day. The glaring gap between what our church and its members *say* and what they *do* is no more glaring than it was in the New Testament church. But here is where *we* are confronted with the self-revelation of the living, speaking, acting God!

Now, what does all this have to say about the question with which we began? Can this worldly-earthly-human character of God's revelation help us with our difficulty in knowing what a personal relationship with God means? Three things follow from what we have said.

First, we ought not to be surprised that we have no personal relationship with God in which we hear him speak to us directly "out of the blue." We ought not to be surprised that we cannot always positively identify his activity in our lives. We are men and not God. We cannot and should not expect to meet him on his level.

Second, if we want to have a personal relationship with God and hear him and know that he is present and at work in our lives, we should look for him and listen for him and expect him in a disguised indirect form. He comes to us in the world, and if we want to meet him, we must meet him in the world—not in a vain attempt to escape our earthly human existence and to ascend to the heavenly heights. As we listen to the words of a book written in human language, growing out of the experiences of an ancient human people; as we focus our attention on the account of the words and deeds of an ancient Jewish carpenter-preacher; as we participate in the life of an all-too-human community gathered around that book and that man; then as we interpret all the events of our own lives and the history of our society and nation and world in the light of this—*there* God himself promises to reveal himself and be present to us. Indirectly, to be sure—"only" in a book written by men, "only" in a man named Jesus, "only" in a very questionable community of people, "only" in what seems to be the everyday happenings of life. But "only" in these worldly ways, God really reveals himself to us.

How can we have a personal relationship with God? Could it be that God becomes real to us only in and with and through our personal relationships with other *men*—the men who wrote the books of the Bible, the one man who is God himself with us, the men around us in the Christian community, the men we encounter in our daily lives and in world history? Could it be that the *kind* of relationship we have with God is indicated by the kind of relationship we have with these past and present men? Could it be that our openness or closedness to *them,* our acceptance or rejection of *them,* our love or indifference or contempt in relation to *them,* is the worldly indication of what our relation to God himself is? "No man has ever seen God; if we love one another, God abides in us and his love is perfected in us" (1 John 4:12).

On the other hand, if we want to have a personal relationship with *God,* we must be careful that we do not confuse the worldly "clothing" in which he comes with God himself. God comes to us in the man Jesus, but the man himself (his "human nature") is not God. God speaks to us in the Bible, but these men and their writings are not themselves God. He speaks and works through the church, its human creeds, witness and actions—but none of these things is the word and work of God as such. He works through the social and political movements of our times and meets us in our encounters with other men, but no nation or party or movement or program can claim our ultimate loyalty. If we make idols of any of the worldly *means* in which God comes to us and is personally present with us, we cut ourselves off from God himself.

There is no such thing as a personal relationship with God without a personal relationship with our fellowmen. But our fellowmen are not themselves God. *In, with,* and *through* these relationships God comes to us—judging, forgiving, renewing, doing among us and for us what we can never do for ourselves or for one another.

Revelation is the revelation of a *mystery!* Even as the God who reveals himself to us, God remains the God who in himself is beyond all our thinking and conceiving. Even as God-with-us, he still remains God and not a man. Even as the God who draws near, he remains the God who is a Stranger in our midst. So do not be surprised if the paradox of the worldliness of God's self-revelation is difficult to grasp. What is important to reflect on is this: To have *faith* in God means to expect and find and accept and know him where he gives himself to be known: on *our* level, in an earthly, human, worldly way. And to have faith in *God* is to do this without confusing the worldly clothing in which he comes with God himself.

The Word of God

We have seen that God's special revelation of himself happens in three different ways: (1) in the history of his mighty acts which centers in Christ, (2) in the Bible, and (3) in the Christian community today. So far we have put all these ways of revelation more or less on the same level. Now we must talk about how they are alike and how they differ.

One way of pointing to the *unity* of the different ways in

which God reveals himself is suggested by a phrase we have already used in speaking about revelation, "word of God." (When "word" refers generally to God's message or truth or his revelation of himself, it is not capitalized; when it refers to Jesus Christ or to the Bible it is capitalized.) What comes to mind when we hear this phrase? Word of God—that is Jesus himself, the Word made flesh. Word of God—that is the Bible. Word of God—that is what we go to hear on Sunday morning when we go to hear a preacher. It is no accident that the phrase suggests all three to us, because the Bible itself suggests this three-fold interpretation. You can see this if you compare John 1:1–14; 2 Timothy 3:16; 2 Peter 1:19 and Acts 13:44. Moreover, the confessional statements of the Reformed churches also recognized that God's revelation comes to us in this threefold way.[1]

Christ, Bible, preaching—all three are ways in which the one word of God comes to us. But we must obviously make a *distinction* between these three "forms" of the word of God. A word which is identified with historical events and a person is not the same as a word which refers to the written words in a book, and neither of them is the same as a word which Christians speak when they communicate Christian truth. Moreover, there is a certain order and priority among these three forms of the word of God. *First* God revealed himself in his words and actions in history and in a man. *Then,* under his guidance, a written record and interpretation of his speaking and acting was made. *Then* we can speak of God's self-revelation in the words and actions of the Christian community now.

In other words, within the unity of the three ways in which the word of God comes to us, distinctions in *form* and distinctions in *priority* have to be made. Instead of talking theoretically about these distinctions, we shall try to understand them by dealing with two familiar questions, the answers to which clarify the necessary distinctions.

1. Do you believe in the Bible? Strictly speaking, a Christian whose faith is grounded on God's self-revelation has to say *No* to this common question—just when he takes the Bible seriously as the Word of God. Our faith is not in a book, but in

the God we learn to know in this book. God himself, not the
Bible, rules and judges and helps and saves us. We do not
"believe in" Isaiah or Paul or John. We believe in Jesus Christ. He
and he alone is God-with-us in person. The biblical writers are
not themselves God's self-revelation as Christ is. They are *witnesses* to the events and to the person in which God spoke and
acted. We would completely miss the point of what the biblical
writers want to tell us and do them no honor, if we believed in
them. They do not ask us to place our trust and hope and confidence in them, but in the God to whose speaking and acting they
point. We believe the Bible just when we do not believe *in* the
Bible, but in the living, acting, speaking God to whom the biblical writers introduce us.

But, on the other hand, we who are not prophets and
Apostles and were not the direct recipients of the self-revelation
of God which happened in the history of Israel and in the coming of Jesus Christ—we have access to this God only in this
witness, in the words of the biblical writers. So while their witness is not identical with that to which they bear witness, it does
make present to us the personal self-revelation of God. In this
sense—a secondary sense—the Bible is not only a witness to
revelation; it is itself revelation.

There is a *distinction* between the Bible as the Word of God
and Jesus Christ as the Word of God—the distinction between
God himself in our midst and a book about him. But there is
also a *unity* here: We know the personal Word of God only as we
meet him in the written Word of God.

**2. Why doesn't God reveal himself today as he did
in biblical times?** We have already answered this question: God
does still reveal himself. He does it in and through the church.
We learn in the Bible itself that God is a *living* God and that
Christ is a *living* Christ. God lives and acts and speaks among his
people *now* as well as *then*. But the *past* revelation is indispensable
if we are to be able to distinguish between what God is saying and
doing in our time and what is only the speaking and acting of men.

Let us illustrate. Does the church speak and act as if physical human life is cheap and unimportant? To that extent it is not speaking and doing the word of God. For we learn in the Bible that God is the *Creator* who willed and created physical life and saw that it was "very good." The church proclaims the word of *God* only when it speaks and acts to value and preserve the physical needs and welfare of men.

Does the church speak and act as if the alienation of individuals, races, classes and nations from one another is unimportant or even desirable? To that extent it is not speaking and doing the word of God. For the God of the Bible is God the *Reconciler* who is at work in the world to overcome the hostility and alienation of men in relation to each other as well as in relation to himself. The church proclaims the word of *God* only when its speaking and acting is reconciling and healing.

Does the church speak and act as if its task were to serve itself, at all costs to make itself big and influential and successful? To that extent it is not speaking and doing the word of God. For we learn in the Bible that God is the *Savior,* who in Christ, for the sake of others, though he was rich, became poor; though he was strong, made himself weak; though he could have been successful, risked failure; though he was Lord, became Servant. And the church proclaims the word of *God* only when it speaks and acts not to help itself, but to help people—people on the "outside" as well as people on the "inside."

What specifically will the church and individual Christians do and say when they proclaim in word and in action the word of God the Creator, Reconciler and Savior? No program can be outlined or general answer given. That would be again to claim that we have the word of God at our disposal. Christians will be able to speak and do the word of God only when in every new situation they confess they do not have all the answers to every question or know the solution to every problem. Then and only then will they be ready and open to *learn* what God is saying and doing, and to participate in his word and work.

In other words, there will be a *unity* between the word of the church and the personal word and the written Word of God just when, and only when, we acknowledge the *distinction* between the speaking and acting of Christians and the speaking and acting of God. But when we do recognize this distinction, then we may be confident that the same living God, who once made himself known long ago *does* make himself known also in our time.

The Freedom of God

In this chapter we have been speaking about special revelation. Special revelation means that God does not reveal himself just anywhere and everywhere, and that he is not known by just anyone and everyone. Christians believe that for his own good reasons God chose to make himself known in the history of one particular nation among all the nations of the earth. He chose to enter into our world and make himself known in one particular man at one particular time. He chose and guided particular men to record in one particular book this special revelation of himself. And we believe that since the original time of revelation he has chosen a particular community of people among whom he promises to make known what he is doing and what he has to say in every new time and place.

The particularity and exclusiveness of the Christian faith is offensive not only to non-Christians, but to many Christians as well. Why Israel and not also other nations? Why Jesus and not also other holy men throughout history? Why the Christian church and not also other religious communities? Why the Bible and not also other inspired writings? We stumble here upon the mystery of election and predestination, which we shall have to discuss in detail later. But already now at the end of our discussion of the doctrine of revelation we need to make some remarks which will help us to guard against misunderstanding what the particularity and exclusiveness of God's special revelation of himself means. Some of them underline points we have already made in the course of our previous discussion.

1. God is at work even where he is not known. The particularity or exclusiveness of God's revelation of himself in the history of Israel, in Christ, the Bible and the church does not mean that he was and is *at work* only in these particular times and places and people. It means that he is *known, recognized, honored* especially here. The word of God heard in the biblical history and in the church tells us that God is the Creator and Ruler of *all* men. He is at work in the history of *all* nations, in *all* times, to judge and help. The difference between "insiders" and "outsiders" is not that God loves us and works among "us," and does not love and work among "them." The difference is that we *know* about his love and about what he is doing for the good of all men in the world. Because we have heard who God is, what he wills and what kind of God he is, we recognize as others do not signs of his work not only in religious affairs of the church, but also in the secular affairs of the world; not only in the community of believers, but also in the political and social community in which believers and unbelievers are mixed; not only in the "Christian" West but in the communist East.

2. We may not boast. The particularity and exclusiveness of God's special revelation of himself is therefore no ground for Christians to feel superior to other people—chosen while others are rejected, "in" while others are "out" with God. The special knowledge we have is not a call to Christian arrogance, but to a special *task*. If we know about a source of judgment and help and hope which is intended not only for us but for all men, how can we not share the knowledge we have? If we proudly withhold it from other men, do we not deny the very God we claim to know?

3. We are limited but God is not. The particularity and exclusiveness of God's special revelation of himself is a limitation placed on *us* but not on *God*. We are told that in his freedom, God chose to make himself known in the history of Israel, in Jesus Christ, in the Bible, in the church. Therefore, if we want to know God, we are bound first of all to look *here* and no place else. It is true that we learn from these particular sources to recognize his work everywhere around us. But we are not free to look *first* just anywhere and everywhere to discover God. To use an old analogy, we must look at ourselves and at the world through the "spectacles" of the Christian gospel if we want to see clearly what is going on around us. Without these spectacles, we will receive a false image of God and what he is up to in our individual lives and in the world. In this sense, we are limited to the particularity of special revelation: *These* spectacles and no others enable us clearly to see God, ourselves, and the world.

But having spoken so exclusively of God's special revelation of himself in and to a particular nation, a particular man, a particular book and a particular community; and having so exclusively limited the knowledge of God to these particular sources, we cannot end our discussion without an important qualification. God is free! *We* are bound to seek him first of all here and no place else. But God is not bound. The Spirit "blows where it wills" (John 3:8). In his freedom, God can and does make at least something of himself known even where we might never expect it. Not because they have sought and found *him*, but because he seeks and finds *them*, also non-Christians may have insights into his truth. People who do not know Christ or read the Bible or belong to the Christian Church! John Calvin wrote of the "admirable light of truth" shining in "secular writers," from whom we can learn that

> the mind of man, though fallen and perverted from its wholeness, is nevertheless clothed and ornamented with God's excellent gifts. If we regard the Spirit of God as the sole fountain of truth, we shall neither reject the truth itself, nor despise it wherever it shall appear, unless we wish to dishonor the Spirit of God. For by holding the gifts of the Spirit in slight esteem, we condemn and reproach the Spirit himself. (*Institutes*, II, 2, 15)

Or again: ". . . we ought not to forget those most excellent benefits of the divine Spirit, which he distributes to whomever he wills, for the common good of mankind" (*Institutes*, II, 2, 16).

This reminder of the freedom of God to make his truth known whenever, wherever and however he sees fit does not mean that we are free to seek him whenever, however and wherever we see fit. But it is a reminder which can save us Christians from pride and arrogance. Why should we not rejoice when we see also among unbelievers or the adherents to other religions signs of the beauty, truth, goodness, justice and compassion of God at work? And why should we Christians not be willing to listen as well as speak to such men, learn from them as well as instruct them.[2]

We have been talking about how we know God. But who is this God? What is he like? That is what we have to talk about in the chapters which follow.

On "The Meaning of Revelation"
1. Why is it wrong to ask, "What is God?"
2. In light of our discussion of what it means to "know" God, would you say that everyone knows God who believes every thing the Bible and the doctrinal standards of the church say?
3. What new and unexpected things does the Christian revelation tell us about God?
4. How is the meaning of revelation made clear by saying that Jesus is the "Word of God"?
5. How would you teach a child to know God and have a personal relationship with God as a loving Heavenly Father?
6. How would you answer someone who said, "The Bible cannot be a trustworthy source of the revelation and knowledge of God, because it presupposes an outmoded scientific view of the universe"?
7. How could the Bible or the church become "idols" which prevent us from knowing God and having a personal relationship with him?

On "The Word of God"
1. In what sense are true Christians "Bible believing"?
2. What would you say to someone who said, "I don't need to go to church. I had rather stay home and read the Bible than hear some teacher or preacher talk. The Word of God, not the words of men, is what I want"?
3. How does God still reveal himself in our time? Is his present revelation different from his past revelation?

On "The Freedom of God"

1. What is the difference between saying that all men can discover God for themselves by natural revelation and saying that
   God is free to make something of himself known, even to non-
   Christians, whenever and wherever and however he chooses?
2. Do you think Jesus was too exclusive when he said, " 'I am the
   way, and the truth, and the life; no one comes to the Father,
   but by me' "? (John 14:6)
3. Is Christ at work only in the church, among those who know
   him? For help in answering this question, look up Ephesians
   1:16–23 and Colossians 1:15–20.
4. In a conversation between Christians and Buddhists or Mo-
   hammedans, do you think we could learn anything of the truth
   of God from them?

5

Who Is God?

THE DOCTRINE OF
THE TRINITY

"Holy, Holy, Holy! Lord God Almighty . . . God in three Persons, blessed Trinity!"

"I believe in God the Father Almighty . . . and in Jesus Christ his only Son our Lord . . . I believe in the Holy Ghost . . ."

"I baptize you in the name of the Father, and of the Son, and of the Holy Ghost."

"O God, our Father in heaven . . . by the inspiration of thy Holy Spirit . . . through Jesus Christ, our Lord. Amen."

"Glory be to the Father, and to the Son, and to the Holy Ghost . . ."

"The grace of our Lord Jesus Christ, and the love of God, and the communion of the Holy Spirit be with you all."

So we sing, confess our faith, baptize our children, pray—and so we go out into the world to live. It is no accident that the Trinity has such an important place in our worship. It is the uniquely Christian answer to the question who God is, the answer which distinguishes the Christian understanding of God from that of other religious or philosophical views. If we move now from the question of how we know God to the question of who God is, then here is where we have to begin. In this chapter we shall struggle with the mystery of the doctrine of the Trinity as such. But even when we have concluded this chapter, we shall not be finished with it and have it behind us. Everything the whole of Christian theology has to say about God and man and the world is nothing but an attempt to understand what it means to believe in God the Father, Son and Holy Spirit. So we only begin in this chapter what will be the main theme of all the following chapters.

Why This Doctrine Is Important

Many of us have heard a conversation in a church school class or study group something like this:

"Do we *have* to believe all this business about one-in-three and three-in-one to be Christians?"

"Yes, the church has always held that the doctrine of the Trinity is essential."

"Well, what does it mean? How can you put three persons together and get one, or divide one person into three parts and still have one?"

The defender of the faith then blunders through a fuzzy explanation, and concludes hopelessly, "It's a mystery no one can understand. You just have to accept it by faith."

Then some people say, "Well, if you're supposed to believe it, I guess I do—whatever it is." And more honest people think to themselves, "If no one knows what it means, and no one can explain it, it can't really be all that important."

It is true that "three persons in one Godhead" is a mystery no one can understand. Augustine, who wrote a long book about it, said that he spoke of it only in order not to keep silent. And the great contemporary theologian, Karl Barth, has written, "When we have said what is meant by Father, Son and Spirit in God, we must continue, and say that we have said nothing."[1] But this mystery is far too central to the Christian faith either to be unthinkingly accepted because we are supposed to, or to be casually shrugged off because no one can explain it. If it were only a mathematical puzzle or a numbers game, we might either take someone's word for the solution, or simply say we are not interested. But the doctrine of the Trinity is far more than that. It is the church's admittedly inadequate way of dealing with some concrete questions and problems every Christian must face. Only this doctrine, for instance, can overcome the following *corruptions* of what Christians believe about God and his dealings with men. (As with other

Christian doctrines, the church formulated this one first of all in opposition to some *false* interpretations of the Christian faith.)

• 1. God is an angry God who wanted to punish us because we are not good. But Jesus loved us and died to pay for our sins, so God had to let us go free. God would still like to get us, but he can't, because Jesus keeps him from it. Jesus, our Savior who loves us, saves us from God, the righteous Judge, who hates us.

But the doctrine of the Trinity means that the will and action of Jesus is the *same* as the will and action of God. It means that if Christ is for us, *God himself* is for us and not against us.

2. In the beginning there were three Gods up in heaven. At first the Father himself came down to deal with his people. Then he sent the Son. And after the Son went back up to heaven, the Holy Spirit came.

But the doctrine of the Trinity means that Father, Son and Holy Spirit are not a heavenly club, with the members coming and going like the gods of pagan mythology, or like substitutes in a football game. Christians believe in *one* God, not a team of gods.

3. The Holy Spirit makes us to be spiritual people by helping us to be concerned about such spiritual things as prayer, worship and church activities. He has nothing to do with such "worldly" things as sex, buying and selling, paying taxes, playing and voting.

But the doctrine of the Trinity means that the Spirit is the Spirit of the God who is Creator and Ruler of heaven *and* earth. He is the Spirit of the Christ who was a flesh and blood *man,* the same Christ who is Lord over *all* of life. What does a spiritual life mean if the work of the Spirit is not to deny but to *renew* our natural, material life in a world created and governed by the Father and the Son?

4. Those people who believe in Christ are loved by God and helped by his Spirit, but everyone else is left out. Christians belong to God, but the rest of the world belongs to the powers of darkness and evil. That is why we must have missions—to tell people about Christ so that God's sphere of influence in the world may be expanded, and so they may be included in it.

But the doctrine of the Trinity means that the God who is at work in Christ is the same God who is the *whole world's* Creator.

Christ therefore tells us about the love of God not just for the church and for Christians, but for *all* men, *everywhere.* The Holy Spirit is not the exclusive possession of Christians, but the Spirit of the God whose renewing and helping sphere of influence *already* extends throughout all the world. Would our understanding of non-Christians, of the world outside the church, and the task of missions be different, if we learned not to separate but to connect the work of God the Son and God the Holy Spirit with the work of God the Creator?

Who is God? What is he like? How and where is he at work in the world? What does he think about us, do for us, want from us? What are we to think of God's relation to non-Christians and to the world outside the church? All these questions are concrete aspects of the basic question of the relation and distinction between God the Father, God the Son and God the Holy Spirit. At the deepest level they are *trinitarian* questions. The doctrine of the Trinity, then, is not just a matter of hairsplitting intellectual gymnastics. It has to do not only with the mystery of God, but also with the mystery of our own lives in relation to God. We make the effort to struggle with it not just because we have to, or because we are supposed to, but because here we are confronted with some questions and answers which lie at the very heart of the Christian faith.

It has been said that every single heresy in the past and present history of the church is at bottom a heresy about the Trinity. The point is not that the doctrine as such is so important, but that the truth the doctrine attempts to understand and interpret is just that important. Whether or not we think in a truly Christian way about God and men and the world depends upon whether or not we confess and live by faith in the one God who is Father, Son and Holy Spirit.

The Biblical Source of the Doctrine of the Trinity

The Bible does not teach the doctrine of the Trinity. Neither the word "trinity" itself, nor such language as "one-in-three," "three-in-one," one "essence" or "substance," or three "persons" is biblical language. The language of the doctrine is the language of the ancient church, taken not from the Bible but from classical Greek philosophy. But the church did not simply invent this doctrine. It used the language and concepts available to it to interpret what the Bible itself says about God and his dealings with men in the world. (We shall have to ask later whether this language is adequate, or whether we ought to try to find new ways to say it.) While we cannot find the doctrine itself spelled out in Scripture, we can find there the *roots* of the doctrine, some affirmations about God which forced the church to ask questions which led it to formulate the doctrine.

1. One God. "Hear, O Israel: the LORD our God is one LORD" (Deuteronomy 6:4). That was the Apostles' Creed of ancient Israel, its central confession of faith in a time when most people believed in many gods. "*I* am the LORD your God . . . you shall have no other gods before me" (Exodus 20:2–3). That was the first commandment Israel lived by. "I am the LORD, that is my name; my glory I give to no other" (Isaiah 42:8). That was the warning the prophets repeated again and again, as the people of Israel were constantly tempted to fall back into the superstitious worship of other gods.

When Jesus was asked what is the first and greatest commandment, he simply repeated the creed of Israel: " 'Hear, O Israel: . . . the Lord is one; and you shall love the Lord your God with all your heart, and with all your soul, and with all your strength' " (Mark 12:29 f.). The writers of the New Testament said the same thing: " 'There is no God but one' " (1 Corinthians 8:4). There is "one God and Father of us all" (Ephesians 4:6).

"We confess and acknowledge *one* God alone, to whom *alone* we must cleave, whom *alone* we must serve, whom *only* we must worship, and in whom *alone* we put our trust" (author's italics) This opening statement of the Scots Confession of 1560 summarizes the faith of Christians in all times and places.

The biblical faith stands or falls with the affirmation of one God. Christians are by definition people who are freed *from* the superstition, fear and slavery of believing in all kinds of visible and invisible powers and authorities. And they are freed *for* loving and fearing, trusting and obeying the one true God. Under no circumstances can we allow other gods to stand over or alongside him. "Other gods" includes not only the wood and gold idols of primitive people, but the more sophisticated idols of modern men, often called "isms": socialism *and* individualism, communism *and* capitalism, secularism *and* spiritualism. To know the one God who alone is God means that neither do we *have* to nor are we *allowed* to be dominated and controlled by any political ideology *or* by self-interest, by worldly *or* other-worldly concerns, by brute force *or* by ·doormat weakness, by our physical needs and desires *or* by the repression and denial of our physical needs and desires. *No wonder the first Christians were denounced as atheists!* They renounced all the gods other men anxiously or fanatically clung to for the sake of the *one* God who freed them from all the dehumanizing, tyrannical gods, and at the same time made an exclusive, total claim on their lives.

2. God the Son. But who is this one God? The very earliest Christians did not say directly that Jesus *is* God or that God *is* Jesus. First of all they said only that Jesus *does* what only God can do. They did not think in the abstract, intellectual language of "being." They thought more concretely in verbs—in terms of *action.* Here is a man who *acts* like God, who does God's work. He speaks with authority—even more authority than Moses, through whom the people believed God had made his will known (Matthew 19:3–9). He forgives sins (Matthew 9:2). He dares to speak and act as if *his* coming means that the Kingdom of God has come (Matthew 12:28). He speaks and acts as Revealer, Reconciler, Redeemer, Lord and Liberator. It is not surprising that the Pharisees accused him of blasphemy; he claimed to do what only God can do.

During Jesus' life his disciples were confused and uncertain about what all this meant. After his death and resurrection it became clearer to them. But still they did not say it directly, or try to explain it. Now they confess Jesus as Lord—the Lord who is "far above all rule and authority and power and dominion, and above every name that is named" (Ephesians 1:21). That is, they now give him the name and the sovereignty they attributed to God himself. Still without explanation, they began to mention Jesus and God in one breath: ". . . for us there is one God, the Father, from whom are all things, and for whom we exist, and one Lord Jesus Christ, through whom are all things and through whom we exist" (1 Corinthians 8:6). "There is ... one Lord, one faith, one baptism, one God and Father of us all" (Ephesians 4:4–6).

Did these first Christians know what they were doing? Emil Brunner writes:

> These first Christians, who gave him the title "Lord" were no polytheists; that is, they were not people to whom it would be easy to ascribe divine dignity to any human being. They were Jews, men who had recited the Jewish Creed every day of their lives, from their early childhood; "Hear, O Israel! The Lord our God is one Lord,"—Jews for whom there were no demi-gods, no transitional beings between creation and God. When they addressed Jesus as "Lord" in their prayers, they intended to give him the dignity of the one God.[2]

But finally, it was said openly—still without explanation—Jesus *is* God. In the Gospel of John we hear it most directly: "The Word was with God and the Word *was* God" (John 1:1). "Thomas said to him, 'My Lord and my God!'" (John 20:28). "I and the Father are one" (John 10:30). "'He who has seen me has seen the Father'" (John 14:9). In the first chapter of Hebrews, an Old Testament psalm, originally written as a prayer to God, is now addressed to Christ (Hebrews 1:8).

In Christ we have to do with God himself. Christ is not just a man sent from God, or a prophet or an angel. When we meet this man (a *real* man!), we meet God himself—the *Lord.* If you want to know who God is and what God is like, you must look at this man. He is Immanuel—God with us.

But there are obvious problems here. There is only *one* God. He is the Creator of heaven and earth, the Lord of Israel. On the other hand, now we hear that *Jesus* is God with us. If God is *one,* how can we say that he is really present and known in Christ? And if we say that God is really present and known in Christ, how can we avoid saying that there are in fact *two* Gods—one "up in heaven," the Creator and Father, and one down here on earth, the Son? The New Testament does not answer this question. But it does raise it. This is the problem which forced the ancient church to go beyond what was explicitly said in the New Testament to formulate the doctrine of the Trinity. And it is the problem which makes that doctrine still important for us. On the one hand, there is at stake the *oneness* of God, which under no circumstances can we sacrifice; and on the other hand there is at stake the reality of the self-revelation of God in Christ, which we also under no circumstances can sacrifice.

3. God the Holy Spirit. Historically, it was the question of the person and work of Christ which gave rise to the doctrine of the Trinity. But the same problem arises when we see what the New Testament says about the Holy Spirit. Who is God? He is the God who is *over* us as God the Father and Creator, the God who is *for* and *with* us as God the Son—and the God who dwells *in* us ("in our hearts," Galatians 4:6) as God the Holy Spirit. He is the God who not only *was* present and at work among *other men* in the *past,* but who *is* present and at work among *us, now.*

But how are we to understand this "spirit"? On the one hand we hear that he is the "Spirit of God" (1 Corinthians 2:11 ff.; 6:11; 7:40; 2 Corinthians 3:3; Ephesians 4:30). And on the other hand we hear that he is the Spirit of the Son (John 14:16; Romans 8:9; 2 Corinthians 3:17). This raises the problem of the relation between the Father and Son all over again. But it also raises other questions: Have we here in fact a third God? Or are we only talking of a kind of impersonal spiritual power? These are questions just as crucial as those raised by the New Testament claims about Christ. Once again the issue is the *oneness* of God on the one hand, and the real presence of God himself on the other.

4. Father, Son and Holy Spirit. We have seen that the New Testament faith in *one* God and the claims it makes about Christ and the Spirit raise some difficult questions. These questions become all the more pressing when we look at the numerous passages in the New Testament in which the Father (or God),

Christ (or the Lord), and the Spirit are mentioned *together*. Look, for instance, at the following passages: Matthew 28:19; 2 Corinthians 13:14; Ephesians 4:4–6; 1 Peter 1:2; 1 Corinthians 12:4 ff.

The *doctrine* of the Trinity is not found in the Bible. But the Bible does speak of the *one* God who makes himself known and acts in *three* ways. What is the meaning of this "one" and this "three"? Modern as well as ancient Christians must try to understand and interpret it, if what the New Testament tells us about God and his relationship with us is important.

The Development of the Doctrine

The church slowly worked out the doctrine of the Trinity in opposition to *false* interpretations of what it means to say "God was in Christ." Without going into the details of a centuries-long debate, we shall look briefly at some ancient trinitarian heresies for two reasons. First, they *seem* to be legitimate solutions to the problem at hand, and they are solutions, expressed in other words, still held by many in our time. Secondly, it helps us to clarify what we *do* want to say if we can clarify what we do *not* mean.

The problem was and is this: How can we hold to the concrete presence and work of God in Christ (and the Spirit) without sacrificing the oneness of God? How can we believe in one God and still believe that God himself is really present and at work in Christ (and in the Spirit)?

1. **The answer of subordinationism.** One group of thinkers in the ancient church was especially concerned in a polytheistic age to maintain the *oneness* of God—but they did it at the expense of the real *self-revelation* of God in Christ. They were called "subordinationists" because they subordinated the Son to the Father.

One version of this said that Jesus was only a man who was inspired by God and filled with God's spirit so that he was enabled to do miraculous works and live a perfect life. Jesus was not really God himself with us, but a man of God who was so completely controlled by the Spirit of God that we may say he was adopted to be the Son of God.

Another version said in effect that Christ was a kind of half-God. He was created by the Father like all other creatures, but he was created and existed in heaven before anything else was created. Not quite real man and yet not quite real God, Christ is a kind of intermediate being.

But the more seriously subordinationists take the oneness of God, the less seriously they can take his self-revelation in Christ. God remains a hidden God whom we do not really know, a God who either is not able or does not care enough really and completely to identify himself with our human situation and to work in our world. On the other hand, the more seriously ancient or modern subordinationists insist that God is present in this especially gifted man or this half-god, the more they are denying their own concern for the oneness of God and are talking in fact about two gods. But what can faith in Christ mean then except the idolatrous worship of a man, or the superstitious worship of a mythological figure who is neither God nor man? And then the question is bound to come: Why *this* man and not some other inspired leader? Why *this* mythological figure and not some other superman?

An unknown and unknowable, weak or uncaring God; or idolatry and superstition—these are the alternatives open to the subordinationists. And *both* alternatives have been condemned as heresy by the church.

2. **The answer of modalism.** A second group of thinkers were especially concerned to hold on to the real *revelation* of God in Christ, but they could not do it without making questionable the *oneness* of God. They were called "modalists" because they tried to understand the Father, Son and Spirit as modes or ways in which God makes himself known and acts. In order to reveal himself, the one God assumes different forms, or plays different roles. First he acts as Creator and Law-giver, then as Redeemer, then as Life-giver.

But the modalists ran into trouble too. The more seriously they took the real presence of God in these three different roles, the more they could be accused of believing in three different gods.

On the other hand, if they insisted that these are only forms of appearance of God, they seemed to be saying that the *real* God is a kind of fourth Being *behind* these forms. And that raised the question once again: What is God really and truly like? He wears the mask of a loving Father, of a self-giving Son, and of a helping Spirit—but could it be that in himself, behind these disguises, he is a quite different kind of God?

Three gods or a God whose true feelings about us are a great question mark—these are the alternatives open to ancient or modern modalists. These alternatives too have been condemned by the church.

3. The answer of the early church. Having rejected the false solutions of subordinationism and modalism, the church then had to work out its own statement about the Trinity. Its alternative was not really a solution to the problem of how God is one and yet three, three and yet one. All it really did was to affirm both his oneness and his genuine presence and work in Christ (and in the Spirit). The one God makes himself known to us and works in our world and our individual lives in three different ways. But in each of these three ways of his presence and working, we really have to do with the one God himself, not with three gods, nor with a hierarchy of divine beings, nor with Halloween masks which hide who the one behind them really is.

The ancient church said this in the language and concepts available to it at the time. Even then it had no adequate way of expressing what it wanted to affirm; its formulation was open to misunderstanding, and it was often misunderstood. The ancient formula is even more difficult to understand in our time. Not only are the language and concepts of the second and third centuries strange to us; they have actually changed meaning over the years. Part of the confusion and misunderstanding of the doctrine of the Trinity in our time is of course due to the inexpressible mystery it points to. But part of it is due also to our reading into the language of the doctrine handed down to us a meaning it was never intended to have. If we turn now to look more closely at the classical doctrine, therefore, we have two things to do: We have to try to understand its *content,* and we have to translate its *language.* Let us look briefly at what this doctrine affirms.

One God in Three Persons

The Westminster Confession preserves the doctrine of the Trinity formulated by the ancient church with these words: "In the unity of the Godhead there are *three persons* of *one substance,* power, and eternity . . ." (II, 3). The Belgic Confession says the same thing: "God is one in essence, yet distinguished in three persons" (Art. VIII). If we are to understand what the doctrine affirms, then, we must try to understand what it means when it expresses the *unity* of God with the concepts "one essence" or "one substance," and what it means when it expresses the *distinctions* in God and his work by speaking of "three persons."

1. The unity of Father, Son and Holy Spirit. The Father, the Son and the Holy Spirit are of one essence or substance. They have the same nature. This language is misleading today, first of all because it is impersonal, suggesting that God is a neuter something composed of some kind of basic stuff—as we have learned to think that all things in the world are composed of the fundamental elements. The classical trinitarian language seems to suggest a lifeless reality of one kind or another, rather than a living, acting person.

Moreover, in our thinking this language could suggest not a way of expressing the oneness of God, but a way of losing it. The doctrine does *not* mean that Father, Son and Spirit are three different persons who share a common divine essence in the same way that three different men might be said to share a common humanity. That would obviously be a crude tri-theism.

One essence or one substance originally meant that Father, Son and Holy Spirit are the *same* in being or *identical* in being. It meant, as Barth has put it, that in God there are not three divine "I's" but *one* "I."[3] It is a way of saying what we have already emphasized: When we have to do with the Father or with the Son or with the Spirit, we have to do not with a part of God, or someone possessing divine characteristics, or with a different God; we have

*Not descript. of God
(but of how we
understand God*

THE TRINITY   101

to do with the one God himself. The Father is God; the Son is God;
the Spirit is God—all one and the same God, expressing himself
simultaneously in different ways.

2. The distinctions within God and his work.

If the
terms essence or substance are confusing to us today as means of
expressing the oneness of God, the term "person" is disastrous as
an expression of the distinctions within God. In our time "person"
means a self-conscious, individual, autonomous personality. To
speak of God in three persons suggests to us three different
personalities—three different gods somehow combined into one.
The church has *never* intended to say this. But in using the language of the ancient world, it has led many people who are not
technical theologians to assume that Christians are supposed to
believe in three gods, no matter how carefully this is concealed
with double-talk. It is very important to get this straight. *In our
sense of the word, there are not three persons or personalities in
God. God is only one person.* When we speak of God as personal or
as a person, we refer to the *one* person who is Father, Son and Holy
Spirit.

Nevertheless, the fact that we can speak of this one person
only in a three-fold way does mean that there are *distinctions*
within the richness of God's being and work. The classical doctrine
of the Trinity tried to express these distinctions with the Latin
concept *persona.* This concept referred in the ancient world to a
mask worn by an actor in the theater to help him play his role more
effectively. Later it came to refer to the role itself rather than to the
mask.[4] When this concept was used in the traditional doctrine of
the Trinity, it was intended to mean something like "way of being"
or "way of existence." "One God in three persons," then, means one
God who has at the same time three distinct "ways of existence" as
God or "ways of being" God.

To translate *persona* in this way is not to fall back into the
heresy of modalism, (a) so long as we remember that these three
ways of being are not just masks behind which the real God is
hidden, but ways in which God himself lives and works; (b) so
long as we remember that God lives and works in these three ways,
not in temporal succession (as if there were *first* the Father, *then*

the Son, *then* the Spirit), but simultaneously. God always has been, is and always will be the *one* God who both in himself and in his work has three ways of existence.

What are they? The one God lives and works as Father, as Son, and as Holy Spirit. In order to express the richness of God's being and work in these three ways, the church (following the Bible) has attributed different works to each. Without discussing them now, we simply list the different ways different theologians have expressed this. As you read them, do you find disagreements? Do the different ways of saying it help clarify each other?

Calvin: ". . . to the Father is attributed the beginning of activity, and the fountain and wellspring of all things; to the Son, wisdom, counsel, and the ordered disposition of all things; but to the Spirit is assigned the power and efficacy of that activity" (*Institutes,* I, 13, 18).

The Heidelberg Catechism: "God *the Father* and our *creation* . . . God *the Son* and our *redemption* . . . God *the Holy Spirit* and our *sanctification*" (Q. 24).[5]

The Belgic Confession: "The Father is the cause, origin, and beginning of all things, visible and invisible; the Son is the Word, and Image of the Father; the Holy Ghost is the eternal Power and Might, proceeding from the Father and the Son" (Art. VIII).

George Hendry: "In Christ we have God *with* us, and in the Holy Spirit we have God *in* us, without his ever ceasing to be God *over* us."[6]

Karl Barth: "The threeness of Revelation, Revealer and Revealedness, the threeness of God's holiness, mercy and love, God's threeness on Good Friday, Easter, and Whitsunday, the threeness of God the Creator, God the Reconciler, and God the Redeemer . . ."[7] Or in another place: "He is the Speaker, without whom there is no Word and no Meaning; the Word who is the Speaker's Word and the bearer of the Meaning; the Meaning which is as much the Meaning of the Speaker as of his Word."[8]

R. P. C. Hanson: "We know God in three different activities and three different manifestations of himself; we find him and know him as the Father who is approaching us in Christ, as the Son who is God entering human history and human life to save us, and as the Holy Spirit who is God in whom we perceive God's activity towards us and in whom we respond to that activity."[9]

Paul Tillich: ". . . the threefold manifestation of God as creative power, as saving love, and as ecstatic transformation."[10]

Many analogies have been devised to express these distinctions in the life and work of God. None of them is really adequate. The unity and distinction between God the Father, Son and Spirit are absolutely unique, comparable to nothing else. Nevertheless, these analogies can perhaps help us to catch a glimpse of how the one God may exist and work in three different ways at the same time. Father, Son and Holy Spirit are like the sun, the rays of the sun and the heat generated by the sun. They are like the spring, the stream and the lake which as a single whole make up a river. They are like water in the form of liquid, ice and steam. They are like memory, understanding and love which exist in the innermost being of one man. In what ways do you find these analogies helpful? In what ways are they inadequate?

There Is No God But One

Our last word concerning the Trinity must be about the oneness of God. The primary concern behind the formulation of this doctrine is not to call into question the unity of God, but to emphasize and preserve it.

Its purpose is to guard the basic Christian faith that in Christ and in the Holy Spirit we have God himself, and though we have to distinguish between God in himself, God with us, and God in us, it is always the one God with whom we have to do. By the same token, the doctrine guards the unity of the works of God. It is not intended to point to a division of labor within the Godhead, as if God the Father alone were responsible for the work of creation, the Son for salvation, and the Holy

Spirit for sanctification, but rather to stress the fact that, although each of these works is sometimes associated in a special manner with one of the three "persons," each is the work of the triune God, who is wholly present in all his works, and through all of them is pursuing his one eternal purpose.[11]

Whenever we read or hear anything that sets Father, Son and Holy Spirit against each other, or suggests that what one wills and does is different from what the other two will and do—then we can be sure that what we have heard is wrong. Or to put it positively, if we want to know what the Father wills and does, then we have to look at what the Son wills and does; for Father and Son are one God. If we want to recognize the presence of the Holy Spirit in us and among us, we have to look at what the Father and Son are like; for the Holy Spirit *is* the Spirit of the Father and Son, and any "spirit" which contradicts or ignores God the Father in Christ cannot possibly be the *Holy Spirit*.

This brings us back to the very practical questions with which we began this chapter and indicates again how important the doctrine of the Trinity is.

What kind of God is the Creator and Ruler of the world? He is not a God of sheer naked power and unpredictable whims. He is not a dark, threatening, invisible Being before whom we must live in terror and uncertainty. He is none other than the God whom we know in Jesus Christ, the God who is for us and not against us.

What happens to our lives in the world when we are saved and follow Christ? Christ does not change us from earthly creatures into angels or otherworldly saints. His work is to do the "works of my Father" (John 10:37)—the Father who willed and made the *world*. The Christian life, then, is not a replacement or a denial of the creaturely life, but the *fulfillment* of it.

What is all this business about "having the Holy Spirit" or being "filled" with the Spirit? The work of the Holy Spirit is, to be sure, mysterious. But it is not spooky, or some kind of magic which enables us to do supernatural tricks. The Holy Spirit who works in us is none other than the Spirit of the Creator who made us *human* beings, of the Son who reconciles us to God and our fellowmen. The power he gives us is nothing but the power to be what God created us to be, and what Christ was re-creating us to be.

Who is God? Christians say with one voice that he is the *one* God who is Father, Son and Holy Spirit. Everything depends on whether in every part of our thinking about the Christian faith we hold on to and think consistently in terms of this one God in his "three ways of existence."

FOR FURTHER REFLECTION AND STUDY

1. Look at the following passages in which Father, Son (or Lord), and Spirit are mentioned: Matthew 28:19; 2 Corinthians 13:14; Ephesians 4:4–6; 1 Peter 1:2; 1 Corinthians 12:4 ff. What is the significance of the fact that there is no fixed order in which the names appear? What is the significance of the fact that the three names appear together not in the context of theoretical speculation, but in the context of worship (baptism or prayer) or in the context of a discussion of the Christian life?

2. Creation is usually associated with the Father, reconciliation and redemption with the Son, and sanctification or newness of life with the Spirit. With whom is creation associated in John 1:1–3; Hebrews 1:2; Colossians 1:16? With whom is reconciliation or salvation associated in 2 Corinthians 5:18–19; Titus 3:4? With whom is sanctification associated in 1 Thessalonians 5:23; Ephesians 5:26; Hebrews 10:10? What is the significance of this inconsistency?

3. Answer the following questions from the point of view of the doctrine of the Trinity:

   a. Would it be wrong for a parent to teach his child to sing "Jesus Loves Me," and then threaten the child that God will hate him if he is not good?

   b. How would you try to answer a friend who has lost a loved one, or whose home has been destroyed by a storm, if he said, "God must be against me"?

   c. What should be the attitude of a serious follower of Christ toward such "creaturely" things as sexual pleasure, the enjoyment of good food, and play or fun in general?

d. Should a truly "spiritual" person be interested and involved in such a "worldly" program as social welfare?

e. Suppose you went to a church which had decided to exclude some Christians because of their race, and you heard someone say, "The Holy Spirit was certainly with us today." What would you say?

f. How would the revelation of the will of God in Christ help us to evaluate the legitimacy of "speaking in unknown tongues" as a manifestation of the presence and work of the Holy Spirit?

g. Could the Holy Spirit be at work outside the Christian church and apart from Christians—in a communist, for example? How could we distinguish the work of the Holy Spirit and some other spirit when we listen to non-Christians?

6

What Is God Like?

Is God dead? As this chapter is begun, these three words in bright red letters fill the cover page of a popular magazine. Not only technical theological journals but newspapers and magazines everyone reads are discussing the "God-is-dead theology." Perhaps by the time you read this book, this movement will have proved to be a passing sensational fad. But the fact that it exists is symptomatic of the fact that, in our modern secular age, faith in God is difficult even for many Christians. The fact that radical doubt can catch fire even in our "Christian" nation says something about the time in which we live; it raises some serious questions we Christians must answer for ourselves and be prepared to answer as we speak about God to those who do not share our faith in him.

Even though theologians announce the death of God, and many ordinary people are impressed by what they say, that does not say anything about *God,* of course. But it does say something about *us.* Not only unbelievers but many serious Christian people do not experience the presence of a living God in their lives. The church may talk about a God who is near to us, speaks to us, and works in our individual lives and in our world. But many people experience only the distance, silence and absence of God—like the psalmist (and later Jesus himself!) who cried, "My God, my God, why hast thou forsaken me?" (Psalm 22:1). Why does God seem so far away, even dead, in our time? Because we live in a scientific and technological age which no longer needs God to explain everything that happens around us? Because "if there is a God," he seems to do nothing at all about the misery and suffering and injustice in the world? Perhaps these are partial explanations. But could it be that instead of blaming science or God himself, we ought to ask if the fault is not in ourselves? Could it be that we have had some wrong ideas about what God is like, and that some of our old conceptions of him need to die before we can know what he is really like? Could it be that we ought to *welcome* the announcement that "God" is dead, because only as our conceptions of him are challenged can we learn to know what the living and true God is like?

God is dead. *Which* God? The god who was a Great Heavenly Granddaddy: The god who was there to answer all our questions, solve all our problems, protect us from the hurts and hard knocks of life, make our lives warm and safe and comfortable, and get us out of trouble. The god who made no demands of us, but did everything for us. The god who automatically forgave us, no matter how we disobeyed him and ignored or hurt other people. That god is dead. In fact, he never was alive!

God the Great Heavenly Tyrant is also dead: The "sovereign" god who could do anything he wanted to and proved it by unpredictably being sometimes mean and sometimes kind, loving some people, hating some, and simply ignoring others, according to his whim of the moment. The god who was always sneaking around spying on us, trying to catch us doing something bad so he could grab us. The god whose will it was easy to know, because he was always against everything that was fun and pleasant and always demanded of us just what we did *not* like and did *not* want to do. That god is dead. We may rejoice and be thankful that he too never was alive.

Finally, that god is dead who was really only a Great Heavenly Idea, the god some especially educated men thought of not in personal terms, but in terms of big abstract nouns and adjectives: The "Supreme Being." The "Almighty." "Providence." Absolute Wisdom, Power, Justice, Goodness and Truth. That god never did *do* anything. He never was a *living* god. He was just a Big Idea.

Which god is dead? All the gods which really were nothing

but a projection of our own fears, wishes, insecurity, greed, or imagination—all the gods which were idols made in our own image. If all the talk about the death of God in our time exposes our idols and their inadequacy, we may welcome it. The quicker we bury and forget the gods we have made for ourselves, the quicker we learn who the *living* God is.

Who is this living God? Not a Great Heavenly Granddaddy or Tyrant or Idea. As we have seen in the last two chapters, he is the God who as Father, Son and Holy Spirit has made himself known to us and not left us to guess who he is or think of him to suit ourselves. And what is *he* like? That is what we have to talk about in this chapter—in *contrast* to the dead gods we have mentioned.

Even catching a glimpse of what this true God is like will not automatically solve the problems all of us have, at least sometimes, with the silence, distance and "unreality" of God in our own lives, and his seeming absence from the world in which we live. Nor will it enable us automatically to speak convincingly about God to others. But perhaps it will help us to face the difficulties of faith in God in our time as *Christians.* Perhaps it will help us at least to ask the *right* questions about God, and not be disappointed or disillusioned when we do not get answers to *wrong* questions!

The Living, Personal God

God acts, speaks, knows, wills, decides. He reveals himself. He is called "Father," "Son" and "Holy Spirit." He loves, rejoices, regrets. He can be angry, compassionate, jealous, merciful. All such language assumes that God is not something but someone. He is not just an idea or a spiritual force. He is a *person.*

But is this kind of thinking not too anthropomorphic (man-like, giving human characteristics to something not human)? Is it not a very crude way of making God in man's image? Who gives us the right to take the concept of personality, which is clearly our experience of ourselves, and apply it to God?

In answer to this objection, we ought first of all to admit quite frankly that we do speak anthropomorphically when we say that God is a person who has feelings, speaks, acts. This is especially obvious in the Old Testament, which speaks with childlike unconcern of God's arm, mouth, hand, eyes, and ears. We do the same thing when we ask God to watch over us, to hold us in the hollow of his hand, to hear our prayers.

But what other alternative do we have but to speak of God in this way? In order to do justice to the majestic godness of God, most philosophers and many theologians have tried to speak of him in *impersonal* terms. They have usually changed personal categories expressing *action* into purely intellectual categories expressing *being*: God is the Highest Being, or Being Itself. Or they think of God in terms of abstract concepts or ideals such as Love or the Good. But is an impersonal God really higher and greater than a personal one? Is a God "without passions" (Westminster Confession, II, 1) really greater than a living God who feels? Moreover, do we really escape anthropomorphism by thinking impersonally? Is it any less anthropomorphic to apply to God our idea of being, love or goodness than to apply to him our experience of personality? We ourselves are human and we can think and speak only in a human way. *All* language about God, personal or impersonal, is anthropomorphic.

Having said this, we must do everything we can to guard against making God in our own image. The same Old Testament people who spoke so naively of the parts of God's "body" lived by the command to make no images or likeness of anything in the heaven above or in the earth beneath (Exodus 20:4). Question 109 of the Westminster Larger Catechism is certainly correct in interpreting this commandment to prohibit also making any representation of God "inwardly in our mind." We must think of God as a person. But we ought carefully to guard against picturing him, even in our minds, in any human form—that of an old man with a beard or any other. God is a person, but he is not a *human* person, not even a very big or very old or very perfect one.

This brings us to the last thing to be said about God's personalness. The best way of keeping our inevitable anthropormorphic thinking from getting out of hand is to interpret what we are in the light of what God is, and not vice versa. We are made in the image of God, not God in our image. The original and authentic person is God himself. If we want to know what it means to be a real, genuine person, we have to learn how *he* lives and acts in a personal way. *We* can be impersonal. We can depersonalize other people and be depersonalized by them. We can treat other people as objects, and we ourselves are not always freely deciding persons; to a large extent all of us are products of our environment or family background. One of the main goals of every man is to *become* a real person. In the last analysis, then, we do not know what it means to be genuinely personal, and it would be wrong to apply our incomplete, confused ideas about it to God. Difficult as it is, we must be open to learn from him, *the* Person, what it means to be a person and how we may become real persons—in *his* image. An impossible task, this strange reversal in our thinking? Not if we take into account that God has spoken and acted in a person. Not if we let this particular person become the standard and source and goal of our understanding both of God's and our own personalness.

The Loving, Sovereign God

What kind of living person is God? He is not a Great Heavenly Granddaddy who does everything for us and makes our lives smooth and painless and easy. Nor is he a Great Heavenly Tyrant who terrorizes us by his arbitrary, unpredictable, power and glory. Both these gods are dead idols. But both these figments of our imagination have an element of truth in them. The Bible does tell us two things about the living and true God. On the one hand, he is in fact infinite, almighty, sovereign, sufficient in himself, able to do whatever he pleases. And on the other hand, he is in fact a God who draws near to men and makes himself known in an intimate way as the God who wills to help and be their companion. He is neither a Tyrant, nor a Granddaddy, nor a combination of both. But he is in fact a God who is both free from men and yet bound to them; far above, yet with them; distant, yet near; powerful and yet loving, loving and yet powerful at the same time.

Exodus 33:7–23 expresses this profound paradox in a delightfully simple way. God speaks to Moses "face to face, as a man speaks to his friend." But even in this intimate relationship he remains hidden and even terrible. Moses is allowed to see only God's "back" when God's "glory" passes by. In seeming contradiction to

what is said at the beginning of the passage, he is *not* allowed to
see God's face, "for man shall not see me and live."

This paradoxical nearness and distance is characteristic of all
the Old Testament. See how it is expressed, for instance, in Isaiah
55:6–9; 57:15; Hosea 11:9. God is often called the "Holy One" in
the Old Testament. "Holy" means separate, totally different. But
God is the Holy One *of Israel*. He is the God who is free and independent above Israel and all its claims, and yet the God who
graciously makes himself *Israel's* God.

The situation is the same in the New Testament. God is the
God who "dwells in unapproachable light, whom no man has even
seen or can see" (1 Timothy 6:16). Yet Jesus can say, " 'He who has
seen me has seen the Father' " (John 14:9). Jesus is himself the
paradox we have been talking about. In him God is both over us
and with us (the doctrine of the Trinity!), hidden and yet revealed
(doctrine of revelation!). He is just Judge and loving Savior, self-
asserting Lord and self-sacrificing Servant, King and Brother, Almighty God and fellowman—not first one and then the other, not
sometimes one and sometimes the other, but always both at the
same time.

Perhaps we can best summarize the two sides of God with the
beginning of the Lord's Prayer. We may call God "our Father," one
of the most familiar, intimate relationships we know. And yet he is
our Father "who art in heaven"—above us, beyond us, foreign to us,
different from us and what we are.

If we are to think in a Christian way about what the personal
God is like, we must take both sides of the paradox seriously. If we
think of God only as Father, we will end up with a sweet, sentimental Granddaddy who is not the God of the Bible. But if we
think of him only as the God "in heaven" we will end up with an
unknown, threatening Tyrant who is also not the God of the Bible.

The next step we take in thinking about God is more important
than it seems at first glance. In thinking of the attributes or characteristics of God, should we think *first* of God our Father or of God
"in heaven"? Should we *begin* by trying to understand his love, or
by trying to understand his sovereign majesty; God in relation to
us or God in himself?

The Reformed churches have usually thought first of the attributes which point to God's sovereignty, describing him with such adjectives as infinite, unchangeable, eternal, incomprehensible, almighty, free, absolute (see the Westminster Confession, II, 2; and the Belgic Confession, Art. I). Then *in the second place* come the attributes which describe God as our Father: loving, gracious, merciful, patient, forgiving, just. That the first category is considered really the most important is shown by the fact that the Westminster Confession returns to it and deals exclusively with it in the second paragraph of chapter II.

Unfortunately, we cannot follow the Reformed fathers in this approach—just because of what they themselves have taught us! It is fatally significant that these confessional documents can "define" God without mentioning either the biblical history of his dealings with men, or the fact that he is supremely known as he meets us in Christ. Where did they get their information about what God is like? They surely intended to speak of no other God but this one, but the fact that they begin with a very abstract description of God in himself rather than with a biblical description of God-with-us suggests that their concept of God actually came from another source.

The form of the attributes of the sovereignty of God gives away what that source is. They are expressed either in *negative* or *superlative* terms, which suggest that God either is what we are *not* (*in*finite, *un*changeable, *in*comprehensible), or is what we are at our best raised to perfection (*most* wise, free, holy).[1] But when we define God by comparison with ourselves (even by negative comparison), are we really talking about God or only about ourselves? If we think that we can begin talking about what God is in himself, bypassing what he has revealed himself to be in our midst, how can we escape making God in our own image, thus defeating our original purpose of magnifying his greatness?

Moreover, if we begin as the fathers of the church did by thinking abstractly of the sovereignty of God before we speak of his love for us in Christ, can we avoid making him in the image of a human tyrant? Could it be that the one-sided emphasis of the traditional Reformed approach to the doctrine of God's attributes gives

some justification to the popular idea that the God of Calvinists is
a God powerful and majestic, but distant, harsh, cold-hearted?

If we are to speak of God in a biblical way, we must follow the
advice of Calvin himself rather than the example of his followers
who wrote these confessional documents. Calvin said:

> . . . we know the most perfect way of seeking God, and the
> most suitable order, is not for us to attempt with bold curiosity
> to penetrate to the investigation of his essence, which we ought
> more to adore than meticulously to search out, but for us to
> contemplate him in his works whereby he renders himself near
> and familiar to us, and in some manner communicates himself
> (*Institutes*, I, 5, 9).

That is, we must speak *first*, as not only Calvin but Jesus himself
taught us, of the God who has revealed himself as our Father.
Then, in the light of that, we can understand what it means that
this Father is also the sovereign God "in heaven." But we must not
make a separation here, as if we were speaking of two different
Gods. The love of God our Father is *sovereign* love. And the power
of our sovereign God is *loving* power.

Our Father

A fully developed doctrine of God would require that we investigate the subtle differences between many attributes which
describe God's fatherly approach to us. We would have to talk
about his love, mercy, pity, compassion, grace, patience, holiness,
righteousness, and justice. In this brief discussion, we shall discuss
only two of these: love and justice. Love emphasizes God's fatherly
nearness and concern for us. Justice emphasizes that our Father is
the sovereign God who remains true to himself even as he gives
himself. The God who is both loving and just at the same time is
neither a Granddaddy nor a Tyrant. He is our Father—in heaven.

1. God is love. God *is* love (1 John 4:8). He is not
sometimes loving and sometimes unloving. He does not love some
people and hate others. He *is* love, and *everything* he does, *always*,

in his dealings with *everyone,* is loving. Love is his very nature. To say that God is love does not mean that love is God. We do not discover what God is by analyzing and then deifying our ideas and experiences of love. Such a God would obviously be an idol. Rather, we discover that love means by learning to know God in his action toward us. We have only to see how God has revealed himself in biblical history and especially in Christ to see how radically different his love is from what often passes for love among men—even in the church among men who call themselves Christians. As you read the following characteristics of God's love, ask yourself these two questions: "What would my church be like if its members loved each other as God loves us?" "How should the church as a whole and individual Christians speak and act in relation to 'outsiders' and non-Christians?"

a. God's love is universal. He loves, wants to help and wills the best for *all* men, for the whole world. There is no discrimination or exclusiveness about his love. How is this expressed in John 3:16; 1 John 4:14; 1 Timothy 2:4; Galations 3:28?

b. God's love is unconditional. He does not say, "I will love you *if* you prove that you deserve my love and are worthy of it. I will love you *if* you first become law-abiding, god-fearing respectable people." Rather: "Christ died for the ungodly. . . . God shows his love for us in that while we were yet sinners Christ died for us" (Romans 5:6–8). God's love is the love of Jesus, who was the friend not only of the moral and religious and socially acceptable, but also of political revolutionaries (the Zealots), dishonest businessmen (the tax collectors), immoral women (the woman caught in adultery), social outcasts and half-breeds (the Samaritans).

c. God's love is initiating love. He does not wait for men to come asking for his love and acceptance; he makes the first move. He loves *before* they ask or even acknowledge their need. He does not wait to love until men are good enough, until they do what they can to help themselves, or even until they have faith. "For the Son of man came to seek and to save the lost" (Luke 19:10).

d. God's love is faithful. God does not take back his love. Even when those whom he loves are faithless to him, he remains faithful to them. They may desert him, but he never deserts them. His love is "everlasting" (Jeremiah 31:3). Hosea went so far as to compare God's love for his people with the love of a husband who still cares for and remains faithful to a wife who has become a prostitute (Hosea 3:1).

e. God's love is reconciling love. God does not love only those who love him, and ignore or despise his enemies. He loves his enemies too. And his love is not just a feeling he has in his heart. It is active. He *acts* to break down the dividing walls of hostility in order to reconcile men to himself and to each other (Ephesians 2: 11–22; 2 Corinthians 5:19).

f. God's love is costly, self-giving love. He does not love for what he can "get out of it." He does not love only in order to "fulfill himself," to satisfy his own needs, or to possess and control those whom he loves. He is God, rich, full, and complete in himself, "not standing in need of any creatures which he hath made, nor deriving any glory from them" (Westminster Confession, II, 2). He loves not because he needs anything from anyone, but purely in order to give. And what he gives is not a *thing*, not this or that blessing or gift. He gives *himself*—his only Son (John 3:16).

g. God's love is helping, renewing love. He accepts men as they are. He forgives them. But he does not leave them where they are. What kind of love would that be? God's love *frees* men from their self-destroying rebellion against him and alienation from their fellowmen. He sets them on their own feet, so that, instead of only passively letting themselves *be* accepted and helped, they may become strong, active, responsible people growing up into "mature manhood" (Ephesians 4:13), loving God and fellowmen with their whole selves. This helping, renewing love of God sometimes hurts—but then God's love becomes an aspect of his justice.

2. God is just. God is not only loving but just—or righteous, to use the biblical language. He is not sometimes loving and sometimes just. He is not at one moment kind, giving and forgiving, and the next moment strict, demanding and judging. He is always both at the same time. In his justice he is loving, and in his love he is just. This is what we have to try to understand, if we are to understand the nature of the God who is not only our Father, but our Father *in heaven*. As you read the following, ask yourself what it would mean in human relations if we understood love and justice in God's way.

a. In his justice God is loving. With us, justice means an unbiased granting to every man his due. It means that "everyone gets what's coming to him": bad men are punished; good men are rewarded. A strain of this understanding of justice runs through the Bible (see 2 Corinthians 5:10, for instance). But it is not the predominant view. That would lead to the false conclusion that success and happiness are automatically signs of God's favor; failure and misery, automatically signs of his disfavor. But as a matter of fact, God was usually *against* Israel just when it was most powerful and successful, and *for* Israel just when it was weak, threatened, and aware of its guilt. It was the *obedience* of Christ which led him to the suffering and defeat of the cross. We cannot understand the deepest meaning of God's justice when we think of him as a heavenly Policeman or Administrator or blind Judge, who metes out what we deserve.

Even if we have not done anything, we tend to dread the thought of being brought to justice or of having to stand before a judge. The thought of justice in general, and especially of God's justice, is something at best unpleasant and at worst terrible. But Israel yearned and prayed for God's justice! Notice the ecstatic joy with which the righteousness of God is mentioned in Isaiah 45:8; Psalms 36:5–6; 98:7–9; 111:1–10. For Israel, God's justice did not bring to mind the thought of a fearful Policeman or impartial Judge, but the thought of a *Savior*. It meant that God was unconditionally and passionately on the side of the weak, the poor, the threatened, the oppressed, the defenseless. God's justice meant that he was for the lowly who were denied or deprived of their right, and against the proud, comfortable and secure who held their privileged position at the expense of others (Psalms 72:12 ff.; 82:1 ff.; Isaiah 3:13 ff.; 11:5 ff.). In this respect, God's justice is anything but impartial; it is quite biased. Nowhere is this typical bias expressed more radically than in Mary's song when she learned that she was to be the mother of the Messiah. See Luke 1: 46–55.

If the Old Testament view of God's justice sounds politically subversive, the New Testament translation and deepening of it sounds theologically suspicious. Here God's righteousness or justice expresses itself not just in favor of the economically and politically poor and threatened, but in favor of the *morally* poor and threatened—sinners guilty of breaking his own law. God's justice or righteousness does not mean that he rewards good men and punishes bad men, but that he condemns all the goodness of men and saves sinners. God is righteous in becoming man to *help* rather than to condemn poor helpless men trapped in the consequences of their lawlessness. That is what justification through faith instead of by works is all about. Romans 3:21–26 says it explicitly and unmistakably. When it dawned on Luther what these verses meant, the Reformation started.

That is how different God's justice is from that of some human policemen and judges. His justice is not to be avoided, dreaded and feared. It is to be received with joy and thanksgiving, because it means help and hope precisely for those who have no rights and are not in the right with their fellowmen or with God. It is not a terrible alternative to the love of God in Christ; it *is* the love of God in Christ.

b. In his love, God is just. We have emphasized how completely and unreservedly God loves precisely in the exercise of his justice. But this does not mean that he is a soft, indulgent God who is there for us to manipulate and use to serve our own interests. In giving himself to us and for us, he does not stop being the sovereign, righteous God. In being true to us, he remains true also to himself. He does not wink at our disobedience or good-naturedly shrug off our hurting other people whom he loves as much as he loves us. He is not indifferent to our guilt and injustice. The Bible speaks often of God as a righteous Judge who will not tolerate individual or social-political disobedience to himself or individual or social-political injustice among men. His wrath burns against sinful individuals and societies. He punishes, overthrows, tears down, condemns, and destroys. It *is* a terrible thing to fall into the hands of the righteous God. There is no point in denying or overlooking the fact of God's severity and judgment because we do not like to think of him that way. Nor is there any point in trying to argue that only the God of the Old Testament is a God of wrath, while the God of the New Testament is a God of love. The Old Testament speaks just as radically of God's self-giving love as does the New Testament, and the New Testament speaks just as radically of God's demanding and punishing justice as does the Old Testament.

The important question is not whether, but *why* God can also be an angry God. Because we tend to think of his justice and wrath as well as of his love in human terms, we tend to think that if he acts as such a God, it must be because he is short-tempered, vengeful and mean—or at best because he is a cold-blooded, unconcerned Judge bound to uphold the law even at the expense of human life and welfare. But the Bible does not tell us of a revenge-seeking Tyrant or of a Judge helplessly trapped by his responsibility to inforce an impersonal law of his own making. It tells us of a faithful Father.

That can only mean that God exercises his justice, lets his wrath burn, and punishes *because* he loves. It is for our own good that he will not tolerate our rebellion against him, our hurting one another, our consequent imprisonment by our own rebellious and unloving spirits. He judges and punishes *in order to* help, *in order to* free us from our sinfulness, *in order to* bring us back to himself and thus back to our own true selves. The very fact that he can become angry means that he cares about us. If he did not care, he would simply let us "stew in our own juice." But he cares so intensely that he can be hurt and moved by what we are and do. He cares so much that he will not let us get by with the chaos and self-destruction we bring upon ourselves when we refuse to live as the genuinely human beings he created us to be. His law and his demands are intended to help us live creative, meaningful, human lives. And he thwarts and punishes our disobedience in order to call us back from the inhuman ways we have chosen against him and our fellowmen and therefore against our own best interests. God's punishment is like a surgeon's knife that heals by hurting. It is like the discipline a good parent exerts on a child who disobediently plays in the dangerous street. His wrath, in other words, is the burning of his love.

How do we know? Because that is the way God himself explains and demonstrates the meaning of his justice. "You only have I known of all the families of the earth; *therefore* I will punish you for all your iniquities" (Amos 3:2). The Lord disciplines and reproves those whom he loves (Proverbs 3:12; Hebrews 12:6; Revelation 3:19). But it is especially in the death of Christ that we see both how serious and how loving God's justice is. "The wages of sin is death" (Romans 6:23). That is how strict God's justice is. And he executes his sentence. But he does it in such a way that his death sentence brings life to us. He takes it on himself, comes to stand with us and by us even in the death we bring upon ourselves when we contradict his life-giving will. Later we must try to understand in more detail the meaning of Christ's death as God's judgment against us and at the same time his love for us. But we cannot talk about God's loving justice and his just love without mentioning it now as the clue to the whole problem we are discussing. There above all we see in one and the same act what it means that, as our Father in heaven, God is not only just in his love, but loving in his justice.

In Heaven

We come now to the point at which most of our Reformed fathers began, and at which they spent most of their time, when they spoke of God. God is our Father *in heaven*. "In heaven" does not mean "up in the sky" (see 1 Kings 8:27). It means that God in himself is infinitely superior to us and our world, far beyond us and all our thoughts about him, not to be identified with anything human and earthly. If we discuss now some of the big words Christian theology has used to try to express this majesty of God, we must keep in mind Calvin's advice not to speculate theoretically about the essence of God (How could we, if he really is so infinitely superior to us and our thoughts?); we can only "contemplate him in his works." So, if we had constantly to remind ourselves that, as our Father, God is free to exercise his love and justice in *his* way, now we must constantly keep in mind that the majestic God "in heaven" is no other than the God who has made himself known and acted as our Father. The God *over* and *beyond* us is no other than the God who in Christ is God *with* and *for* us.

1. **God is *omnipotent*.** He is almighty, all-powerful, sovereign. He is not limited by anything outside himself. He can do anything he wills. But it is as our Father who loves us that he is so powerful. God's sovereignty does not mean that he can do literally anything and everything. It means that he can do anything and everything consistent with his own goodness and love. God *cannot* do evil. He *cannot* contradict his own nature. He *cannot* be an arbitrary, unpredictable tyrant. His power is not unlimited brute force. It is the power of his love. It is his unlimited ability to do whatever his sovereign *love* requires and allows—and *only* that.

Moreover, God's power is not a prison, as if he were a king who could not escape his majestic office. God is so powerful that he can accomplish his will in weakness as well as in strength, in defeat as well as in victory, in the form of a lowly Servant as well as in the form of an exalted Lord. If we know about the accomplishment of his will in the little insignificant people of Israel, and in a man dying on a cross, how can we think that he can be powerfully at work only where we see glorious success and triumph? How can we limit him by thinking that he can accomplish his will only in the heights and not in the depths, in happiness and not in sorrow, in great and not in small things, in success and not in failure? Could it be that we often look for Almighty God in the wrong places? Do we look up when we should be looking around?

2. **God is *omnipresent*—infinite, not limited by space.** God is everywhere, we teach our children. We have to be careful that we do not think that this means that God is vaguely everywhere in general and no place in particular. "Everywhere" in this sense very easily becomes "nowhere." God's omnipresence means that he is never bound to any one particular place, and that there is no particular place where he is not and cannot be. And if he is a *personal* God (not just an impersonal Force or Spirit), must that not mean especially that God is present everywhere we have personal encounters with other *people*?

Who is this "everywhere" God? Not a great heavenly Snooper we would like to escape if we could, but our Father who is loving in his justice and just in his love. Where in particular is he? In the church and among Christians, of course. But "the Most High does not dwell in houses made with hands" (Acts 7:48). He is not the prisoner of the church, nor the private property of Christians. He is present and at work among non-Christians as well as Christians; with those who do not know him as well as with those who do; with "bad" as well as "good" people; in communistic as well as democratic countries; with men of *all* races, *all* economic and social classes, *each* level of civilization. He is *everywhere*. There is *no* place—not even hell itself—where he is not present, this God who is sovereign in his love and loving in his sovereignty. Notice with what joy and comfort this is said in Psalm 139.

3. God is *eternal*, not limited by time. This does not mean that God is timeless, "outside" or excluded from time. It means that there is no time when he was not, is not, and will not be God. He was God "before the foundation of the world." But with the beginning of time, he did not retire from the scene and become simply an onlooker God passively watching history unfold like a spectator at the theater. God was *in* the play (the main character!) in the history of Israel and in Christ. Nor did he then retire, as if he had said all he had to say and done all he had to do. The God whom we meet in biblical history is the *living* God, who also since then has been present and at work in the drama of time. In *every* time: the "good old days" and the present when "everything is going to the dogs"; during both Republican and Democratic administrations; when the Herods and Hitlers as well as when the Washingtons and Churchills determine the course of history. "Eternal" means that "*my* times are in thy hand" (Psalm 31:15). It means that in every moment, from beginning to end of world history and from beginning to end of *my* history, God is our Father in heaven. Now and forevermore. Everything else comes and goes, but God remains or endures (Psalm 102:26). He is eternal.

4. God is *invisible* and *spiritual*. But that does not mean that he is limited to the invisible and spiritual, excluded from the visible, material, and physical. How could we limit God in this way—especially in light of the fact that his power and majesty are

so great that, without sacrificing his divine dignity, he could dwell among us in a flesh and blood man? God's invisibility and spirituality do not mean that he is trapped in heaven and locked out of the world, that he can be concerned about souls but not bodies, that he can be involved in our religious but not in our secular activities. That the sovereign God is a Spirit means that he can and does enliven, renew and make creative the material, physical, worldly lives and activities of flesh and blood men.

5. God is unchangeable, immutable, immoveable,

That does not mean that he is unchangeable as a timeless truth. God is not timeless but eternal, not a "truth" but a living person. Nor does it mean that he is immoveable like an idol of wood or gold which neither hears, nor sees, nor feels, nor acts. He is our Father in heaven. In different times and places and situations, he acts in different ways to express his fatherly concern for us. In this sense he *does* change. But in all his actions, he wills and does only what is consistent with his fatherly concern. In *this* sense he is unchangeable—dependable and faithful just because his compassion, grace, justice and goodness are new and relevant to every new and fresh situation. God is unchangeable in the same way as Christ, who is the "same yesterday and today and for ever" (Hebrews 13:8), yet who meets every individual with just what he needs in his particular time, place and situation.

We began this chapter by referring to the fact that faith in our time is difficult (was it ever easy?)—so difficult that many people can speak of the absence or even death of God. We suggested that part of the trouble may be that we have some wrong ideas about what God is like. We have tried to identify the God who is our living Father in heaven in contrast to the God who is an idolatrous Granddaddy, Tyrant, or Big Idea. But now at the end we cannot avoid returning to the question with which we began. Suppose that we have caught at least a glimpse of the true God. Is *he* real to us? Or have we only been (hopefully) biblically and theologically correct, without speaking of a reality in our own individual lives and in the world in which we live? Is this God alive for *me*? What difference does he make in my life? In the Christian church? In the world? The questions which follow are intended to help you answer for yourself.

FOR FURTHER REFLECTION AND STUDY

1. Do you think it is correct and meaningful to speak of God's having "passions" or feelings?
2. What does it mean to say that God is a "person"? What does it mean for *us* to be genuinely "personal"?
3. How would you try to speak of God to a child so that he would not think of God as a great big man up in the sky?
4. How would it affect our human relationships if we took seriously God's love in his dealings with us? Do you think that sincere Christians, being human beings, could or should love other people as God loves us?
5. In what ways could the hurt and suffering in our own lives and in the world around us be signs of God's love?
6. Is it correct to say that God's justice is biased in favor of the weak, oppressed and helpless?
7. What does God's wrathful, punishing love teach us about the way good earthly parents should love their children?
8. In light of what we said about God's omnipotence, how would you answer someone who argued that God is absent or dead wherever we see misery and suffering and defeat? Does 2 Corinthians 12:7–10 help here?
9. Has your understanding of God changed as a result of reading this chapter? How?
10. Make a list of what you consider to be the inadequacies, mistakes and unanswered questions in what this chapter has said about God. Save the list, and check the following chapters of this book by it to see if they offer help and clarification—or perhaps only make matters worse!

7

What Does God Want With Us?

THE DOCTRINE OF
PREDESTINATION

"I've had the absolute conviction—it's much more real than anything one can see or touch—that God and his world exist. And everyone can enter in and find their rest. Except me. I'm infinitely far away for ever. I am alone and apart and infinitesimally small—and I can't come near."

... "Could there be a world, Ralph, in which God existed —but with some people in it who were never allowed to believe?"

"It would be a tragic world?" said Udal.

"Why shouldn't it be tragic," Roy cried, "Why shouldn't there be some who are rejected by God from the very beginning?"[1]

That is the problem of the doctrine of predestination, expressed in the words of a tormented man in C. P. Snow's novel, *The Light and the Dark*. Is God for some people and against others? Has it been decided in advance that some are included and others excluded, some destined now and forever to life in the fullest sense and others now and forever to loneliness and death? Is it a tragic world we live in—for some people at least? In this chapter we shall wrestle with this complex problem which reaches to the heart of everything we believe about God, ourselves, and the world in which we live.

Before we begin, we need to define the problem precisely. Properly understood, the doctrine of predestination does not have to do with any and everything that happens. It has specifically to do with the "history of salvation"—with God's plan and work for our relationship with him and with other people. It has to do with who we are and what we may become in these relationships. Belief in predestination is not the fatalistic belief that "what will be, will be." It is not the deterministic belief that everything that happens, good or bad, is the will of God. It would be wrong to think of predestination, for instance, if it rains on the day of the picnic, or all the traffic lights are against me on the way to town, or I have a stroke of luck in my business. We may believe that all the trivial or momentous events in our lives are not outside the providence of God. But predestination as such has to do with the more limited question of the covenant relationship between God and men: with his choosing (or not choosing) to be their God, his choosing (or not choosing) them to return his love, to reflect it in their dealings with one another, and to find the wholeness of life that goes with loving and being loved. The doctrine of predestination is thus synonymous with the doctrine of election. In this chapter we shall think of it only in this limited sense, which is suggested not only by Snow's novel but by the way the Bible deals with the problem.

This will be our procedure: We shall investigate both the advantages and disadvantages of the three classical ways in which Christians have spoken to the desperate situation of Snow's character. Then we shall see what conclusions we can draw for ourselves.

Three Classical Interpretations

1. Double predestination. Some are included and some are excluded. This interpretation of predestination is often considered the one position you are supposed to believe if you are a good Presbyterian or Reformed Christian. Calvin himself taught it, and it is strongly affirmed in the Westminster Confession and the Canons of the Synod of Dort. But other genuinely Reformed confessions, such as The Scots Confession, the Second Helvetic Confession, The Heidelberg Catechism and the Cumberland Confession, do not teach it. It is only one of several possible views in the Reformed tradition.

According to the Westminster Confession: "By the decrees of God, for the manifestation of his glory, some men and angels are predestined to everlasting life, and others fore-ordained to everlasting death" (III, 3). There is thus a double predestination, one negative and one positive, one to life and salvation and one to death and damnation. God is for some men (about 20 percent, Calvin estimated), and against the others. According to God's eternal purpose, therefore, Christ died only for the elect. Only the elect are given the gift of faith, forgiveness for their sins, and the ability to live as sons of God. The nonelect are rejected or "passed by." Christ did not die for them. God "withholds his mercy" from them. They are ordained to "dishonor and wrath for their sin" (Westminster Confession, III, 7). God has decreed to "leave them in the common misery into which they have willfully plunged themselves" (Canons of the Synod of Dort, Art. XV). It is not unjust of God to choose to be for some men and against others, because *all* men have willfully disobeyed his commandments and deserve his wrath, judgment and condemnation. If God damns the nonelect, he only gives them their just reward. If he decides to love and help some, he does so not because they have any more claim on him than the nonelect, but out of his free grace and good pleasure.

a. Several points can be made in favor of this interpretation of predestination: (1) It emphasizes the sovereignty of God. (2) It emphasizes the fact that God's love is not earned or deserved but freely given. (3) It tries to take seriously both the justice and love of God. (4) It emphasizes that salvation comes from God alone, and that men contribute nothing to it. Even faith is a gift of God, not a self-achieved way of earning God's acceptance. (5) It seems a logical explanation for the fact that the vast majority of men always have been and still are unbelievers, while only a relatively few are believers. (6) It tries to take seriously some difficult biblical statements which seem to suggest a double predestination.

In Romans 9–11, one of the key sections of the Bible with respect to predestination, Paul tries to understand why the Jews, God's chosen people, have not accepted Christ but remain "outside." He seems to suggest that it is because God has rejected them, as he has in general determined that some men will know only his wrath and destruction. Look at the hard words of Romans 9:14–23.

b. On the other hand, there are serious *objections* to the doctrine of double predestination:

First, the Bible does speak of God's hardening or blinding men, but it never says that he does so forever. When we read all of Romans 9–11, instead of lifting a few verses out of context, we learn that God has "by no means" rejected even unbelieving, hard-hearted Israel who rejected Christ (Romans 11:1). On the contrary, his plan is to graft even these broken-off branches back into the tree (Romans 11:17–24). The Bible does teach that God has mercy on whomever he wills (Romans 9:18), but it also teaches that he wills to "have mercy upon *all*" (Romans 11:32). It warns of God's wrath and judgment, but nowhere are we taught to separate his justice and love, so that we may think he is sometimes, to some people, loving, and at other times, to other people, only just. Such a separation in God's dealing with men would mean an unbiblical division in God himself, the denial of his oneness and unchangeableness. Despite some statements which seem to point in that direction, the Bible never speaks of an eternal negative decree by which from beginning to end some men are rejected or left out.

In the second place, the word "predestination" itself suggests and is interpreted according to the doctrine double predestination to mean that once a long time ago God planned everything that would ever happen to everyone who would ever live. Does not world history and the history of every individual then become simply the predetermined, unalterable unwinding of a long film made before the creation of the world? And does that not imply that once the world began, God simply retired from the scene and became a passive, helpless observer of a pre-fixed world process in which he himself can no longer be involved? Does it not in addition mean the end of all human freedom and spontaneity?

But the Bible tells us of a living, active God, who is at work *in* the history of the world and the lives of individual men, demanding and making possible real human decisions, bringing *new* things to pass. A Christian doctrine of predestination, therefore, cannot refer to a rigid, mechanical plan of God made "before time." God is always "before" us, to be sure, but he is before us as the cloud and pillar of fire which every new day and night went before Israel in the wilderness, leading the people to the "destination" he had planned for them (Exodus 13:21 f.).

Double predestination speaks of what God willed and decided in the distant past, but does it leave room to ask what he *is* willing and deciding and doing *now?* It speaks of an already worked-out plan for our lives, but does it leave room for any free, active participation on our part in what he is doing in our lives? We may speak of an eternal plan of God, in other words, but if we interpret that to mean only a plan made "before time," do we not do violence to the biblical understanding of eternity (see our previous discussion on p. 122)?

A third objection is that the doctrine of double predestination is sometimes based not only on a particular interpretation of Scripture and a particular theological interpretation of the meaning of eternal, but upon an observation of the world around us. We can see that some people are in the church and some outside. Some people hear the Christian message and believe. Others hear it and do not believe. Millions never even have a chance to hear and believe, simply because they were born in the wrong time or place. Some, like the man in Snow's novel, desperately *want* to believe and enter in but cannot. How shall we explain that? The doctrine of double predestination jumps to the conclusion that those whom we observe to be "insiders" are chosen and loved by God, while the "outsiders" are rejected or passed over. But is that a legitimate conclusion? Is it God or theologians who choose and reject in this case? Who gives us the right to make such judgments? How do we know that those who seem to be "out" to us are not "in" with God? How do we know that some who seem to be in to us are not out with God? Is it not arrogant presumption to conclude that God's choosing or rejecting corresponds to the differences we observe between insiders and outsiders?

All the objections we have mentioned can be summarized in this way: Is the source of the doctrine of double predestination really God's revelation of himself and his will, or is it not rather illegitimate speculation on the basis of our own ideas of how God can and should act if he is really sovereign? Even when this doctrine appeals to the Bible, does it not just use the Bible to lend subsequent authority to a position arrived at apart from the biblical revelation? Even when it acknowledges that God has "made known to us in all wisdom and insight the mystery of his will, according to his purpose which he set forth *in Christ*" (Ephesians 1:9), could not everything double predestination asserts about God and his will for men be said without reference to Christ? Is not Christ at most the "instrument" of a divine will and purpose which in itself either is completely unknown or is discernable without Christ? Can such a doctrine be a biblical, Christian understanding of predestination?

One final point: It is clear in any case that double predestination turns the Good News of Jesus Christ into bad news at least for some men. The "mystery" of God's will of which Paul speaks with unqualified joy and thanksgiving in Ephesians 1:3–10 and Romans 11:32–36 becomes a doctrine so gloomy and threatening that it must be treated with extreme caution (Westminster Confession, III, 8). Anyone who accepts this doctrine can only speak of the Good News of God's love with open or secret reservations: "God loves you—maybe. Christ died and lives for you—maybe. You may believe and have newness of life now and forever—*if* you are one of the elect."

Let us return to the problem with which we began this chapter. In answer to the tortured man in Snow's novel, those who believe in double predestination would have to answer: "Yes, it is a tragic world—for some people, anyway. Some *are* rejected from the beginning. They cannot and never will be able to enter in and find rest. They are doomed to be infinitely far away forever. Perhaps you *are* one of them. But if so, you have no right to complain. God owes you nothing. You deserve only his wrath, and you will get only what you deserve."

Is that a Christian answer?

2. Universalism: Everyone is included. One alternative to double predestination is the view that God loves and is gracious toward *all* men. He chooses all and rejects none. Even if some are alone and apart and cannot find rest now in this life, they are destined *ultimately* to life and joy and peace with God, with fellowmen and with themselves. Salvation is universal.

a. Although this view was condemned as heresy early in the history of the church and has never been accepted as an orthodox position, it cannot be too quickly dismissed. It is not simply the result of wishful thinking. Nor is it simply the result of abstract speculation about what God must do if he is love (as the doctrine of double predestination tends to be speculation about what God can and must do if he is sovereign). There are many biblical passages which suggest universalism. God is our Savior, "who desires all men to be saved and come to the knowledge of the truth" (1 Timothy 2:4). The Lord is "forbearing toward you, not wishing that any should perish, but that *all* should reach repentance" (2 Peter 3:9). God sent his Son into the world, "not to condemn the world, but that the *world* might be saved through him" (John 3:17). Jesus is the "Lamb of God, who takes away the sin of the *world*" (John 1:29). "As in Adam all die, so also in Christ shall *all* be made alive" (1 Corinthians 15:22). "... As one man's trespass led to condemnation for all men, so one man's act of righteousness leads to acquittal and life for *all* men" (Romans 5:18). "For in him all the fulness of God was pleased to dwell, and through him to reconcile to himself *all* things, whether on earth or in heaven" (Colossians 1: 19–20). God wants *all* men for himself—the *world*. And in Christ he himself was and is at work to achieve his will. How can Almighty God not have what he wants? How can his work be ineffective and without result?

Such passages as these emphasize as strongly as the doctrine of double predestination that salvation comes by God's free grace. It could be argued that they emphasize even more strongly the power of God. Is it not a far greater triumph to reconcile and renew than to condemn and destroy? There is no doubt that universalism understands predestination as glorious Good News we can joyfully and thankfully proclaim to everyone in the whole world, without any reservations.

b. But an unqualified universalism is nevertheless a heresy. (Remember that heresy is not a total falsehood but a perversion of the *truth!*)

In the same way that the doctrine of double predestination

ignores or tends to explain away universalistic biblical texts, universalism tends to ignore or explain away those texts which speak of God's wrath and judgment. It tends to overlook those texts which warn that rebellion against God and indifference to fellowmen have eternal consequences. Look at Matthew 25:31–46, for instance. We ought to note that Jesus' threat of "eternal punishment" here is not directed against people who have never heard of God and who are sinful, unbelieving outsiders. It is directed against those who, like the Pharisees, piously claim to know and believe in God, but prove that their claim is a lie by not caring for their fellowmen in need. That is typical of Jesus: gracious invitation and promise of new life to sinful outsiders, serious warning and threat of judgment against complacent insiders. But the warning about the separation of the sheep from the goats is there. Universalism is unbiblically one-sided in assuming that everyone will automatically turn out to be a sheep and no one a goat.

Furthermore, if double predestination has trouble with God's unqualified love, universalism has trouble with his justice. The one has justice without love (for some people at least); the other tends toward love without justice. In the first, God looks too much like an arbitrary tyrant: in the second, he often looks too much like a sentimental granddaddy. It certainly is not good news to say, "God is for you—maybe." Is it much better to say, "It doesn't matter what you are and do. God will be for you"? Does that really help men trapped in hostility, rebellion and alienation?

Finally, God treats men as persons. That means he wants a two-way relationship. He speaks and he wants an answer. He loves and he wants to be loved in return. He commands and he wants obedience. But universalism tends as much as double predestination to think one-sidedly of God's relationship toward us and to do less than justice to our response. In double predestination some men do not even have a chance to say "yes" to God because God has said "no" to them. In universalism, eventually no one can say "no" to God even if he wants to. It is almost as if the father in the story of the prodigal son went out and *forced* his son to abandon his self-destructive life. Is a benevolent manipulation of men for their own good any more helpful than an impersonal or hostile manipulation? Does not good news become bad news when it says, "You *will* love God and your fellowmen and reach self-fulfillment, whether you want to or not"?

In answer to the agonizing question of C. P. Snow's character, the universalist would answer: "Don't worry. You are not really alone and apart and outside. You only imagine that we live in a tragic world. God is in his heaven and all is right with the world— or will be eventually. So buck up. Everything is going to turn out fine for you, whether you believe and enter in or not."

Is that the Christian answer?

3. Pelagianism: It's up to you. A third way of understanding predestination is called Pelagianism because it was first articulated by Pelagius, a theologian against whom Augustine first formulated the doctrine of double predestination in the fifth century. A modified form of Pelagianism became the official doctrine of Roman Catholicism and has cropped up again and again within Protestantism, most notably with Arminius and his followers, who were condemned by the orthodox Reformed churches in the seventeenth century. Nevertheless, it is still a popular position with many Protestants, including men who consider themselves Presbyterian or Reformed. It has been said, in fact, that all Anglo-Saxons are by nature Pelagians.

In the several different ways it may be expressed, Pelagianism says basically that God chooses those who choose him. If you turn to God, he will turn to you. His love, help and life-renewing power are *available* to all, but *effective* only for those who ask for it. Or, to put it in another way, Christ achieved *potential* salvation for all men, but it becomes *real* salvation only for those who decide to believe in him, depend on him and follow him. In other words, it is up to every individual to decide for himself whether he wants to be "in" or "out." God, who knows all things, knows how everyone will decide, but predestination is only a matter of this foreknowledge, not of an active divine plan and purpose.

a. There are some things to be said in favor of this position. It obviously emphasizes very strongly something the Bible also emphasizes: the importance of man's decision about his relationship to

God and other people, the importance of faith and obedience. Was it not emphasized in the Old Testament covenant that "it will be righteousness for us, if we are careful to do all this commandment before the LORD our God, as he has commanded us" (Deuteronomy 6:25)? Did not the prophets promise God's favor "if you are willing and obedient" (Isaiah 1:19)? Does the New Testament not teach that " 'whoever calls on the Lord shall be saved' " (Acts 2: 21)? Not only does Pelagianism seem to have many such texts on its side; it also avoids the danger in the doctrines of double predestination and universalism of thinking that God does everything, while man can and is required to do nothing.

b. But there are some disastrous consequences of this interpretation. Pelagianism makes questionable the sovereignty of God. The Bible does speak of God's demanding a response from men, but it never suggests that God will or can do nothing in the lives of men until and unless they ask for his intervention. In biblical history it is God, not man, who initiates the saving events of the Exodus from Egypt and the coming and victory of Christ. God carries out his judging and saving plan for Israel and in Christ for all men *despite* all opposition. In the last analysis, Pelagianism puts men in control of God. We say it openly and unblushingly when we speak of "*letting* God be God" or of "*making* Christ the Lord of our lives" or of "*bringing in* the kingdom of God." As if God could be God only by our permission! As if the risen, triumphant Christ could be Lord only if he gets the majority of our votes! As if the rule of God in the world depended on the support of Christians and their little church! Are the advantages of Pelagianism worth making God dependent on our asking, seeking, believing, working? Are they worth having to think that the course of world history depends on the genuine faith and complete commitment of Christians? That would hardly be Good News!

Pelagianism also makes questionable the love of God. What kind of love is it that says, "I will love you if you first love me"? According to Jesus that is not real love even among men: " 'For if you love those who love you, what reward have you? Do not even the tax collectors do the same?' " (Matthew 5:48). " 'But I say to you, love your enemies' " (Matthew 5:43). How could we ever be sure that God loves any of us, if we thought that his love depended on the certainty of our faith, the constancy of our seeking him, the completeness of our obedience? With its "*If* you do so and so, I will love you," Pelagianism turns the Good News of God's love for unworthy, undeserving people (such as all of us are) into a mechanical business deal. God our Father in heaven becomes the great heavenly Bookkeeper who pays off for credit earned.

Finally, Pelagianism is based on confidence in the free will of men. It assumes that men are free either to believe in, love, trust, depend on, turn to, serve God—or not. Their destiny depends on their free decision one way or the other. Now there is no question but that we are free to do or not do many things. But are any of us really free when it comes to the fundamental decisions about what kind of people we are and can become? Are we really free when it comes to decisions about our relationship with God and our fellowmen?

To trust in God, for instance, means "do not be anxious about your life" (Matthew 6:25 ff.). But who of us can simply decide to be free of anxiety?

Again, are we free to love or not love as we choose? Can a person gripped by fear, bitterness, prejudice or self-centered pride simply decide to love either God or other people, and let himself be loved in return? *Can* a white supremacist love a Negro? *Can* an estranged husband and wife just make up their minds to love each other? *Can* a modern man who sees no signs of God at work in the church, the world, or his own life simply decide to believe in God? Are not all of us caught in the same trap Paul was caught in: "I do not understand my own actions. For I do not do what I want, but I do the very thing I hate . . . I can will what is right, but I cannot do it. For I do not do the good I want, but the evil I do not want is what I do" (Romans 7:15 ff.)? We might like to think that we are free, but are we really? Is not this the most agonizing problem of our lives—how can we who are *not* free *become* truly free, free for God, free for other people, free to be our own true selves? Is not the free will that Pelagians believe to be the answer to the problem of predestination the problem itself?

In answer to the desperate man in Snow's novel, the Pelagian would answer, "You just have to try harder. You can believe if you really want to. If you feel alone and apart, it is your own fault. All you have to do is make up your mind to turn to God, and then he will love you and help you. But you have to make the first move."

Is that a Christian answer?

How to Approach This Doctrine

We have seen that each of the three main interpretations of predestination has legitimate insights into what the Bible tells us about God's plan for our lives. No one of them can be called *the* Christian doctrine of predestination. Nor can all three be reconciled and combined into a neat system which could be called the one true Christian doctrine. God's purpose for us and how it is fulfilled remain a mystery. But while we cannot solve all the problems connected with this mystery, there are at least some things we can say about it with confidence. In this last section we shall gather up some of the results and implications of what we have learned in our study. First we shall describe three basic rules for approaching the doctrine of predestination as Christians. Then we shall discuss three consequences of these rules.

First, it is clear that *we must take into account the total biblical witness*—even when some passages do not fit easily into a nice, logically consistent doctrinal scheme. We shall never understand predestination so long as we refer only to those passages we like and ignore or try to explain away those we do not like. This means that we can take just as seriously as the universalists those biblical passages which tell us that God is for *all* men, the whole world. But we must take just as seriously as do those who believe in double predestination the clear biblical warnings to outsiders *and* to insiders that God will not let men get by with rebellion against him, their hostility or indifference toward other men, and the self-destruction which always goes along with these broken relationships.

Secondly, while we must not forget God's wrath and judgment and the possibility of eternal punishment, *our primary emphasis, if we follow the biblical pattern, must be positive*. The Bible never speaks of a plan of God before the foundation of the world for some men to be left out or rejected. It does speak of a plan "to unite all things in him, things in heaven and things on earth" (Ephesians 1:10). Predestination in the Bible is always *good* news. It does not point to joy *and* terror, salvation *and* damnation, a Yes of God *and* a No. "For the Son of God, Jesus Christ . . . was not Yes and No; but in him it was always Yes" (2 Corinthians 1:19). In Romans 9–11 there seem to be many contradictions and hesitations as Paul wrestles with the problem of predestination. But his final word too is not Yes and No but only Yes: "For God has consigned all men to disobedience that he might have mercy upon all" (Romans 11:32). Predestination in the Bible does not include what Calvin called a "horrible decree." It is the summary of the Good News of Jesus Christ. In this respect, those Reformed confessions which speak only in a positive way of predestination are more biblical than those which speak also of an eternal negative decree.

Finally, it follows that *when Christians think of predestination, they think of God's plan for themselves and for non-Christians in the light of his revelation and execution of his plan in Christ.* We must think of it *only* in this light, not first of all or even secondarily in light of our own opinions about what God wills for us and for others.

Now, these three basic rules give us a foundation for some concluding observations about a Christian doctrine of predestination.

Light on the Mystery of His Will

1. The freedom God wills for all men. We have encountered several times a persistent problem connected with the doctrine of predestination. It seems to force us to choose between two equally unacceptable alternatives. On the one hand, if we believe in the plan and work of a sovereign God in the history of the world and in our own lives, we seem to be forced to deny the significance of human decisions and actions. What meaning can human freedom have if God shapes our destiny for us? On the other hand, if we insist on man's freedom to choose and determine his own destiny, we are forced to deny the sovereignty of God in history and in our own lives. What significance can a plan and purpose of God have, if it is dependent upon man's decision about his own destiny? God's sovereignty *or* man's freedom—that seems to be the choice we have to make.

So long as we think theoretically and abstractly about this problem, there is no solution to it. But what if we think about it from a biblical point of view?

First, we have to admit that men are not and cannot be free in themselves—not in the deepest sense. We Americans do not like to hear this. But both our own experience and the Bible tell us that it is so. Experience tells us that most of our decisions and actions are in fact determined by where and when we were born. We think and act, whether we want to or not, whether we are aware of it or not, with the biases of Southerners or Yankees; with the prejudices of rural, suburban or urban dwellers; with the mentality of the poor, middle-class or rich; with the point of view of the educated or the ignorant; with the advantages or disadvantages of a healthy or crippling, religious or irreligious, family background. Moreover, all of us are compulsively motivated to one degree or another by fear, anxiety, pride, greed, and lust. (Think of the various psychological motives exploited by advertising and television commercials to manipulate us into buying cars and cosmetics.) And the Bible tells us the same thing about ourselves: we are "slaves" of sin (Romans 6:17), free neither to love God nor our neighbors, nor even to love ourselves properly. The blunt, brutal fact of the matter is that we are *not* free. Attractive as it is, the Pelagian position is simply not realistic. We desperately need to be *made* free.

But that is just what predestination is all about. According to the Bible, God is our Savior, "who desires all men to be saved and come to the knowledge of the truth" (1 Timothy 2:4). Another way of saying this is to say that God desires all men to be free. The truth God desires us to know is Christ, and he is the truth that makes men free (John 8:31, 36). The sovereign plan of God is not a threat to the freedom of man; it is the *source* of man's freedom. Predestination is not an *alternative* to human freedom; it *brings* human freedom. Once we see it in the light of the Bible and a realistic evaluation of the human predicament, the Christian doctrine of predestination becomes sheer good news. What God desires for all men, what he foreordained for them before the foundation of the world, what he accomplished in Christ, and what he is at work to accomplish in the twentieth-century world and in all our individual lives—is the gift of genuine freedom! God's sovereignty, then, is not just an unfortunate necessity, which we reluctantly and regretfully have to acknowledge at the expense of our own human willing and doing. His sovereignty is the sovereignty of his love, a sovereignty which frees us *from* slavery to our environment and the destructive relationship-breaking forces within us; and frees us *for* genuinely human decisions and actions—that is, for God and fellowmen.

Predestination *or* human freedom? No, predestination and *therefore* human freedom. ✳

2. The Christian attitude toward non-Christians. We have said that when Christians think of predestination, they think of God's plan and purpose for non-Christians as well as for Christians in the light of his revelation and execution of his will in Christ. What does it mean to think also of non-Christians in the light of Christ?

a. First of all, let us emphasize the negative point we have touched before. If the meaning of predestination is seen only in Christ, then we cannot speculate about how God should or must treat outsiders according to our ideas of sovereignty, justice or love. What would be Christian about a doctrine of predestination which is deduced from the way *we* think God ought to act? Moreover, as our intellectual speculations about the nature of God cannot be the foundation of a Christian doctrine of predestination, neither can our observations of the world around us. That would be a doctrine of predestination based on our own observations, not on God's will and decision. It would not be God but we ourselves who were choosing or rejecting. We cannot conclude that God's choosing or rejecting simply corresponds to the differences we observe between insiders and outsiders.

b. More positively, if we look at non-Christians in the light of God's plan for men in Christ, we are permitted and we are required to assume that God is for them too, desires their salvation too, is at work to make them free men too. It may be true that they do not yet believe, or no longer believe, or only partially believe. Perhaps they never believe. Such men do not live as those who are loved, chosen and freed by God. But that does not mean that we may decide that God is against them. We do not judge what God's attitude toward them is by their lack of faith and obedience. We judge by what we know and believe about them, even if they do not know and believe it themselves: God desires *all* men to be saved—them too. Christ died and lives for all men—them too. How can Christians take non-Christians' unbelief more seriously than we take what God himself has told us he has planned and willed for them?

c. On the other hand, it is true that there is opposition to the love of God in the world—and not only among non-Christians! Where this opposition does not break down, even the love of God must be destructive. *Because* he loves, God cannot and will not let men get by with their self-destructive insistence on living in slavery rather than in freedom. So long as this insistence endures, God's love must express itself as judgment and wrath. This means that although we cannot believe that some men are rejected by God from the very beginning (as double predestination believes), neither can we say that God *must* eventually save all men (as universalism believes). But even when we take this into account, we are neither allowed nor required to judge whether any man or whether whole groups of people are finally saved or damned. God and God alone is Judge. He has not turned the decision about the destiny of men over to us. He is quite competent to decide for himself. Meanwhile, we may be sure that in dealing with non-Christians as well as with Christians his decision will be not only just but also loving. Instead of following Calvin's example of deciding that only a few will finally be saved, we would do better to follow the example of the Second Helvetic Confession: "And although God knows who are his, and here and there mention is made of the small number of elect, yet we must hope well of all, and not rashly judge any man to be reprobate" (Chapter X).

d. Finally, while we are not permitted to judge for ourselves who is "in" and who is "out," there is one clear responsibility we do have to "outsiders." That is to tell them the Good News of the God who desires that they too be saved and has planned and willed in Christ that they too should receive the gift of freedom to be human in the fullest sense.

Why should we tell them? Not so that God may come to love them *if* they believe and obey, but so that they may believe and obey because God *has* loved and *does* love them. Not only so that they may go to heaven when they die, but so that they may receive the gift of freedom *now*.

How do we tell them? Not by words only, but by demonstrating in the life of the Christian community and in our individual lives the freedom for God and for fellowmen we ourselves have received.

If there are some who never hear and see, or hear and see only a perversion of the Christian gospel, who will be responsible? Will God ask them accusingly, "Why did you not believe and obey and accept the gift of a free life?" Or will he turn to *us* and say, "Why did you not tell them? Why were your lives such that all your fine words were unconvincing? You who talk about the love of God for guilty, lost, helpless men, why were *you* so unloving toward them? You who talk about God's justice, why were *you* so indifferent to injustice? You who talk about the gift of freedom, why were *you* so bound by social conventions or pious legalism or inner compulsions? Why were you so afraid of real freedom in others?"

Instead of worrying theoretically about what God thinks of the "people in Africa" or the people around us who are not Christians, could it be that we ought to worry more about what he thinks of *us* when he sees such men who are still outsiders because of what *we* say or do not say, do or do not do?

3. The meaning of predestination for Christians.

We Christians interpret the meaning of predestination also for our own lives in the light of God's revealed and executed will and plan in Christ. What does that mean?

a. If we see in Christ the basis for our election to be God's people, we will not dream of looking for its reason in ourselves. If we are insiders, it is not because we are morally better, wiser, more pious or more deserving than those who seem to be outsiders. God did not choose us and he does not love us because we are superior to other people in any way. If Christ was the friend of sinners and died for the ungodly, that means God loves and chooses men who in themselves deserve only his rejection. We will understand the good news of predestination only when we recognize that we stand not above but in solidarity with all those outsiders who have nothing to bring as a claim on God's love and help. In the words of Karl Barth, therefore, as we have to proclaim to unbelievers their unmerited election, so we have to remind believers (ourselves) of their merited rejection.[2] Our predestination to life and freedom is sheer grace. If we know that, we can hear of our election only with joyful thanksgiving, without the slightest trace of smug self-congratulation as we look at non-Christians.

b. But how can I be sure that God is for me and not against me? How do I *know* that his plan for my life is to give me freedom to serve him and to love other people, and therefore freedom to be my real self? The answer is that, as we see in Christ the *reason* for our election, we see in him also the *assurance* of our election.

Some people look for assurance in the external condition of their lives. They interpret sickness, trouble and tragedy as signs that God is against them; comfort, prosperity and success as signs that God is for them. But the Bible tells us that it is often the "wicked" who prosper. And it is often those especially beloved by God who suffer most. Our happy or unhappy experiences in themselves tell us nothing about what God thinks of us and plans for us. To look there for assurance is to look where real assurance is impossible. Christians are not those who are sure God is on their side if or because they *escape* "tribulation, distress, persecution, famine, nakedness, peril or sword." They are those who know that *in the midst* of all these things "nothing will be able to separate us from the love of God in Christ Jesus our Lord" (Romans 8:31–39).

Some Reformed theologians have suggested that we may find assurance of our election in our faith and obedient lives. Are not faith and new life the gifts that come with God's choosing us? If we examine the *results* of predestination, can we not discover whether the *cause* is there? But we must be very careful in thinking this way.

Whose faith is certain enough, whose life pure enough, to give him the assurance that he is one of the elect? Who can find certain evidence of his election in the extent of his freedom from all the external and internal pressures and drives which keep us from being free for God and fellowmen? Will not self-examination as such always lead us to doubt rather than to be certain that God is for us? Certainty of our election comes from hearing again and again what God himself has said and done to reveal his will for us, not from what we can guess of his will by analyzing ourselves, the state of our faith and the condition of our lives.

On the other hand, it is true that predestination or election means the plan of God to give us faith and freedom for a new life. Once we know the "mystery of his will" in Christ, why should we not find courage and take hope when we can see signs occasionally that our faith is a little stronger, our lives a little freer, than once was the case? Perhaps we can sum it up this way: When faith wavers, our lives are a mess, and we feel cut off from God, other people and ourselves—then we may find assurance in Christ that despite everything God has not abandoned us. But when (perhaps only now and then) faith is strong, our lives are right, and we can see in ourselves some progress toward the freedom we have been promised—then we may be thankful for these signs that our confidence in God's will for our good has not been misplaced. See 2 Peter 1:5–11.

c. If we interpret the meaning of predestination in light of Christ, then we must think about it in connection with the *church*, for that is where the will and work of God in Christ are visibly accomplished in the world. In the Bible election is never a matter simply of a private relationship between isolated individuals and God. It is first of all a community which is the center of the biblical discussion. God chooses and makes covenant with the whole people of Israel. In Romans 9–11, Paul is concerned primarily with the relationship between the Jewish and the Christian communities. In his discussions of the problem in Ephesians 1 and Romans 8, he addresses what he has to say not to private individuals but to Christian congregations. Individuals are of course loved and chosen in the Bible, but only in connection with the whole community of those who are God's people.

This aspect of the biblical view of predestination means first that we cannot understand the meaning of predestination so long as we make it a self-centered concern about me and my life and my salvation. The doctrine of election has to do not just with "I" and "me," but with "we" and "us." It is not just a matter of "me and God," but of God and the life, freedom and welfare of all his people.

Secondly, it follows that to be chosen by God means to live freely and responsibly in a social context—to forgive, love and help other men as we have been forgiven, loved, and helped by God. To say that it is first of all and primarily a community of people whom God loves and chooses is to underline what we have said about the gift of freedom that goes with predestination: I am truly free to be myself when I am free from my obsession with my own present and future security and become free for thankful obedience to God and sensitive concern for other people.

Finally, the biblical connection of predestination and community throws more light on the problem of the assurance of our election. We cannot say that membership in the church is automatic proof that God is for us and not against us (just as we are not allowed to judge that God is against and not for outsiders). But participation in the community of God's people is a *sign* of our election. God is at work also outside the church for the good of all men. Christ is loving and powerful Lord over the world as well as over the church. But the church is the community of people who seek and acknowledge the will and plan of God in Christ for all men. This is the community where faith and the freedom of new life are especially promised by God and especially expected by men. We will never be assured of our election so long as we think abstractly of predestination as a timeless, spaceless, unknown will of God for an unspecified number of solitary individuals. But we can be assured of it when we remember that the predestinating, electing God is the God who has gathered together a visible earthly "family," committed himself to it and invited all men to become a part of it. As we participate in the life of this family whom God himself instructed to pray, "Our Father in heaven," we can be sure that he is also *my* Father.

d. We conclude this chapter with a final word about what it means to understand predestination in the light of the revelation of God's will and plan for us in Christ. It is one of the most important—and most neglected—factors in what it means to be loved and chosen by God.

To be one of the elect is a high honor and privilege. Predestination is the gift of what matters most in all the world: freedom to live both now and forever the genuinely human life God wills for us. But it is the honor and privilege and gift of being the *servant* of God and fellowmen. Christ, *the* "Chosen One" of God (Luke 9:35), God's "beloved Son" (Matthew 3:17), was chosen to be the Suffering Servant of God. Life for him meant the sacrifice of his life in obedience to God and in love for other men. Freedom meant freedom from the temptation to make himself a great political ruler, freedom to fulfill his destiny to be the Savior of the world by dying a criminal's death.

For us too, then, to be chosen "insiders" who receive God's gift of life does not mean the occasion for a feeling of pride or superiority in being God's elite. It is no occasion for us insiders to look at outsiders with contempt or pity or indifference. That was precisely the mistake by which Israel misunderstood her election: "God is for us and against them, and therefore we will have nothing to do with all those sinful outsiders." It was the mistake of the disciples who wanted the first place for themselves in the Kingdom. We never will understand the meaning of predestination so long as we think of it only as getting and enjoying something others do not have, perhaps even being thankful that we are "not like other men" (Luke 18:11).

Or to put it positively: If we interpret our election in the light of Christ, we will know that it means not only a gift but a command, not only life passively received from God but life actively lived in obedience to God. God chooses us not so we can sit around and enjoy our election, but get to work. And the work he gives us is the work of participating in his plan and will to give life and freedom to *all* men—outsiders as well as insiders, our enemies as well as our friends, social outcasts as well as respectable solid citizens, black as well as white, immoral as well as moral.

That means trouble, of course. It is dangerous and costly to be loved and chosen by God. It means to become a follower of Jesus in caring for the "wrong" people, upsetting the political and social and maybe even the religious status quo—and suffering the consequences. That is the warning that goes with the good news of being predestinated to belong to the people of God. Be careful if you want to be an insider! It does not mean escape from the dirty, guilty, painful world; it means you will be sent into the very middle of its life. For you have been given the gift of freedom—freedom to obey the God who loved the world and gave his own Son for it; freedom to follow the one who said, "The Son of man also came not to be served but to serve, and give his life as a ransom for many" (Mark 10:45).

But those who are willing to accept their election on these terms will also learn the promise that goes with it and the secret of the deepest meaning of the doctrine of predestination: " 'For whoever would save his life will lose it, and whoever loses his life for my sake will find it' " (Matthew 16:25).

FOR FURTHER REFLECTION AND STUDY
1. Read chapters 9-11 of Romans straight through. Then answer the following questions as you study this passage more carefully:
    a. Romans 9:19–24 is a passage often used to argue for double predestination. It is said specifically that God has "prepared beforehand" some people to be "vessels of mercy"? Is it said that God has made some "vessels of wrath"? The image of God as a potter occurs also in Jeremiah 18:1–11. What does the potter do with the pot that is spoiled? Do you agree that this passage teaches double predestination?
    b. Does Paul teach that the Jews are rejected by God? What is God's plan for the Jews?
    c. What is Paul's own attitude toward unbelieving Jews?
    d. What warning is given to Gentiles and what promise to Jews in Romans 11:13–24?
    e. Do you think Paul's conclusion in Romans 11:30–36 is consistent with the rest of his discussion?

2. Read Ephesians 1:3–14 and Romans 8:28–37. Do these passages teach universalism? Double predestination? Pelagianism?
3. Do you believe that all men have free will? Do Christians have it?
4. Why should the church and individual Christians be involved in evangelism and missions?
5. Do Christians believe that God helps those who help themselves?
6. Does God love only those who love him first?
7. How would you answer someone who asks you whether those who never heard of Christ are going to hell?
8. Are you certain that you are one of the elect? Explain your answer.
9. Dietrich Bonhoeffer, a young German theologian who was killed by the Nazis, once wrote, "When Christ calls [that is, chooses] a man, he bids him come and die."[3] What did he mean? Do you agree?
10. How would *you* answer a man who said to you what the man in Snow's novel said?

GOD
THE FATHER
and
CREATION

PART III

GOD THE FATHER
and
CREATION

Christians believe in God the Father, God the Son and God the Holy Spirit. He is the one God who is the Creator, Reconciler and Savior of men. The Apostles' Creed, most Reformed confessions and many Christian theologians organize the exposition of what Christians believe according to the threefold work of the triune God. Following this traditional pattern, we come now to the first article of the creed: "I believe in God the Father Almighty, Maker of heaven and earth."

At first glance it seems that the doctrine of creation is the easiest part of the Christian faith to understand and accept. Even people who have trouble with the doctrines of revelation, the Trinity, or the miraculous birth and resurrection of Christ find it easy to speak of God as the Almighty or Creator, and of man as a creature. But to say "I believe in God the Father Almighty, Maker of heaven and earth" is just as much a confession of faith as to say "I believe in Jesus Christ His only Son our Lord." In fact we cannot understand and believe what Christians mean when they confess God as Creator unless we understand and believe what they confess about Christ. What we believe about the Creator and his creatures is not the result of our observations of the world and ourselves and of our reflections about where we came from. It is the result of what we know about God, his will and his work, in his Son. To know God the Father Almighty is to know him first of all as the almighty Father of Jesus Christ. In other words, when we talk about God the Creator and his creation, we are not talking about something that comes *before* Christian theology—as if this were a doctrine which says what everyone can figure out for himself, whether he is Christian or not. The doctrine of creation is a *part* of Christian theology. It will become clear as we go along what a big difference it makes whether we deal with it in this way or not.

In the chapters of this part of our study, we will deal with the following questions:

Chapter 8: "What Are We Doing Here?" How shall we understand the meaning of our lives in the world of nature and history from the perspective of our faith in God the Creator? (The doctrine of creation.)

Chapter 9: "Why Doesn't God Do Something About It? If it is his world, why is there so much suffering and injustice and misery in the world? (The doctrine of providence and the problem of evil.)

Chapter 10: "Who Are We?" How shall we understand ourselves, if we are creatures made in the image of God? (The doctrine of man.)

Chapter 11: "Why Don't You Be Yourself?" How can we explain the contradiction in ourselves between what God created us to be and the way we actually live? (The doctrine of sin.)

8

What Are We Doing Here?

THE DOCTRINE OF CREATION

About 4,000 years ago God decided to create the world. In six days he made the world with all the kinds and species of things that were ever to exist in it. He made the earth like a flat disk with all the mountains and valleys we see, and the sky like an inverted bowl over it. Below the earth and above the sky were oceans of water. He put the sun and moon and stars in the bowl. Then, somewhere near what we call Mesopotamia, he made all the plants and animals with which we are familiar, and finally man. That is the picture of creation and of the created world we are given in the Bible.

About 4,000,000,000 years ago our planetary system developed out of a disk-shaped mass of gas surrounding the sun. The earth is only one of millions of stars in a universe where distance is measured in light years (a light year is approximately 6,000,000,000,000 miles and most of the stars are more than 100 light years away from the earth). Most of the forms of life which exist on the infinitesimal speck that is our earth did not formerly exist at all, and many of those which used to exist no longer do so. The human race is at least 100,000 years old, though it is not certain just how this form of life originated and developed. While there are many theories and unanswered questions about details, this is the general view of the world and its origin which has emerged from the actual measurements and research of modern science. (See the articles on earth, evolution and man in a good new encyclopedia.)

When the contrast between the biblical and scientific under-
standings of the world is put this way, it is no wonder that Christians have often seen science as a threat to biblical faith, and scientifically educated people have often thought the biblical doctrine
of creation an incredibly naive relic of primitive pre-scientific
mythology. One must choose either to "believe the Bible" or to be
a modern man.

But to compare the two views in this way is like comparing
apples and oranges and arguing that apples are inferior because
they do not yield orange juice, or oranges worthless because they
cannot be made into cider. The Christian doctrine of creation and
the scientific description of the origin of the world answer different
kinds of questions. They are not alternative truths, but different aspects of truth. Rather than being enemies, as a matter of fact, science has helped (and sometimes forced!) Christians to discover
the real meaning of the biblical doctrine of creation; on the other
hand, it has been precisely that doctrine which has created in
Western civilization an understanding of the world which encouraged the development of science.

Astronomy, biology and geology ask how the world and its
present forms of life came to be as they are. They ask about the
observable character, structures, processes and facts of the given
world and its development in history. Science does not and cannot
study the event by which the whole process came into being. Nor
does it try to say what the meaning and purpose of the process is.[1]

Now, included in the biblical story of creation and view of the
world there is also a kind of primitive science. It is not unique to the
biblical writers. They borrowed more than one ancient myth in
order to bear witness to God the Creator, and they shared many of
the presuppositions of the ancient Near East in general about the
structure of the world. But the purpose of the biblical writers was
not to instruct their readers in astronomy or biology. The primitive
science included in their message was not their message itself, but
only the means they used to get the message across. What they had
to say was something that neither ancient nor modern science can
tell us. They bore witness to the God who is the ultimate source
and ruler of everything that is. They spoke about the meaning and
goal of man's life in the world. They were not so much concerned

with the details of *how* we got here as with *why* we are here and κ
how we can realize our destiny in the world.

We can be grateful to modern science for forcing us to distinguish between the vehicle of the biblical doctrine of creation and its primary message, because now we can concentrate on what is really important and unique. The Bible is not a science textbook, and we will miss what it has to tell us if we treat it as such. We can confidently leave all our factual questions to be answered by scientific inquiry: How old the earth is, what physical factors produced it, how big it is, what is "up there" in the sky, how plant and animal and human life develops biologically. The scientist and not the preacher or theologian is the expert in these matters. Christians can and should respect him as such and be thankful for all he can tell us about the mystery and greatness of God's creation.

What, then, is the unique content of the Christian doctrine of creation? Three truths which we can learn nowhere else and which will furnish the basis for our study in the rest of this chapter: (1) The God of Israel, Father of Jesus Christ, is the ultimate Source and Ruler of the world. (2) Therefore the world and our life in it are good. (3) We need fear nothing in the world, nor can we give ultimate loyalty to anything in the world. The truth of none of these statements is obvious. Quite the opposite; they are confessions of faith made despite much evidence to the contrary: I *believe* in God the Father Almighty, Maker of heaven and earth . . .

God the Creator

The Christian doctrine of creation does not begin with an analysis of the world and then try to deduce what the Creator is like. It begins with the Creator and understands the world in the light of what he has revealed himself to be. The doctrine tells us three things about the Creator which determine how we are to understand his creation and our life as a part of it.

1. God creates in the beginning (Genesis 1:1; John 1:1). That suggests to most of us that God's creative activity took place in the distant past, back there at the beginning of time when the world came to be. This interpretation is certainly suggested by the Bible. We need not try to date the beginning. We need not try to say *how* the creative process took place. And there is no point in even trying to answer the impossible question of where God was and how he "spent his time" before the beginning, since space and time are themselves a part of the created world. We cannot even imagine before time or outside space. But Christians do believe that whenever and however it took place, and however he existed before then, God the Creator is the source of all that is.

But we would miss the most important meaning of "in the beginning" if we thought that it means only "back there." The Bible does not say only that God *was* but that he *is* Creator. His creative activity is not limited to the distant past, as if a long time ago he did everything he was going to do, then retired from the scene (a view called "deism"). Even now he is the God who "gives life to the dead, and calls into existence the things that do not exist" (Romans 4:17). He who once was Creator of heaven and earth will one day create a "new heaven and a new earth" (Revelation 21:1). In confessing that God is Creator, Christians confess that he is *continuously* making new beginnings, opening up new possibilities, initiating new events.

This biblical idea of God's continuous creative activity helps us to interpret theologically the discovery of modern science that the universe did not come into existence in its present form all at once, but developed gradually over countless years. We need not be surprised or shocked to learn this, if we know that the living Creator God is constantly at work creating afresh. We may in fact *expect* new things from him!

Even more important, the interpretation of "in the beginning" as meaning in *every* new beginning tells us something about ourselves. God is also the Creator at *my* beginning. The psalmist does not say, as Emil Brunner points out, "Thou hast created Adam and from him I am descended," but "Thou didst knit me together in my mother's womb (Psalm 139:13).[2] In his Small Catechism, Luther says that to believe in God the Father Almighty, Maker of heaven and earth means "I believe that God has created *me* and all that exists." The Heidelberg Catechism says it means "That the eternal Father of our Lord Jesus Christ, who out of nothing created heaven and earth ... is ... *my* God and my Father" (Q. 26).

Now the psalmist, Luther and the authors of The Heidelberg

Catechism all knew the "facts of life" about "where babies come from." But just as the scientific description of the world cannot tell us the whole truth about the world, neither does the sexual process of procreation tell us the whole truth about who we are and why we are here. Once again without even attempting to explain how, a Christian believes that God is also *my* Creator and Father. No one of us is simply the product of a cause-and-effect process. Whatever his heredity or environment, each human being is an individual person with unique significance and possibilities. I believe that in *my* beginning and throughout *my* life God the Creator was and is and will be creatively at work. And if I believe it for myself, how can I not believe it also for other men—including those who are usually not seen as unique persons but only as insignificant or hopeless examples of psychological, social, racial, economic or political categories?

2. **God created *out of nothing*.** This classical statement of the meaning of creation points first of all to the absolute uniqueness and utter inconceivability of the creative work of God. Every act of creation we know is the shaping of some given material: A carpenter makes a chair out of wood, or a musician creates a sonata out of tones. Creation from nothing is completely beyond all our experience. That is why Christians make no attempt to explain how it happened. The only "explanation" the Bible gives is that it happened by the sheer expression of God's powerful will by his word: God *said*, "Let there be light"; and there was light. "He spoke and it came to be" (Psalm 33:9. See also John 1:1 ff. and Hebrews 11:3).

Secondly, the claim that God made everything that is out of nothing is a protest against all forms of "dualism." This is an understanding of the world characteristic of most non-biblical ancient religions. It crept into the early Christian church from its Greek environment. The New Testament writers fought it, and Christian theologians ever since have had to fight it.

In many different ways, dualism has taught that there are *two* fundamental, eternal principles of reality: Spiritual and Physical, Mind and Matter, Soul and Body. They are as eternally opposed to each other as Good and Evil, Light and Dark. In most ancient mythologies creation is a struggle in which the superior Good Spirit conquers and tames some inferior monster or principle of chaos which represents unformed nature. All history then becomes a war between the two.

To say that God made *all* things and that he did it out of nothing is to say first of all that there is no eternal reality alongside or apart from God. Even those forces and powers which oppose him are not rival gods. They also have their source in him, are dependent upon him, and cannot ultimately thwart his will. Secondly, this statement says that the physical, material, bodily and natural are not enemies of God or inferior realities. He himself willed and created them. Therefore they are just as real and good as the spiritual and intellectual (which are themselves only the creation of God, no more "divine" in themselves than the natural-physical-bodily).

Do you see what radical consequences this has for our understanding of the world and our lives in it? We shall have to talk about it in detail presently, for dualism is a heresy dear to the hearts of many American Christians—including some who consider themselves "orthodox" precisely in this heresy.

3. God creates for his own glory ... and for man's sake. To say only "for his own glory" could be misleading, taken by itself. It could suggest that God simply wants to show off his creative ability, prove that he can run things to suit himself, congratulate himself on how great he is. But this picture changes as soon as we see that the glory of God Almighty is the glory of God the *Father* Almighty. His glory is the glory not only of his eternal wisdom and power but also of his *goodness* (Westminster Confession, IV, 1). That means, as Calvin put it, "God himself has shown by the order of Creation that he created all things for man's sake" (*Institutes* I, 14, 22).

How dare we say that the Creator of heaven and earth (the immense universe science tells us about) wills all things for the sake of *man?* We can say it because the powerful Creator God who is behind the world and everything in it is the same God who in Christ entered into that world and acted with loving power and powerful love for our sake.

An ancient heresy (the Marcionite) which is still not too uncommon today makes a split between God the Creator and God who meets us in Christ, the God of the Old Testament and the God of the New Testament, the God of power and the God of love, the God who made the world and the God who saves it. Such a split is unbiblical, and it contradicts everything the church has taught about the unity of Father, Son and Holy Spirit in the Trinity. The truth is that it is the same God who creates and saves. Although he accomplishes his will in different ways, what he wills as Creator is exactly the same thing he wills as Savior—to be God for man's sake.

God the Father Almighty, Maker of heaven and earth—all things for man's sake. If we believe that about God, how shall we understand the world he made and the meaning of our lives in it? That is what we have to talk about next.

God's Good Creation

"And God saw everything that he had made, and behold, it was very good" (Genesis 1:31). The created world is good, and life in it is good. They are good because God made and willed them.

It is true that men rebel against their Creator, misuse his good creation, make themselves and other men miserable by refusing to live according to its order. Immediately after the creation story comes the story of the temptation and fall of man. But neither the Bible nor genuinely Christian theology says that God's good creation has become a bad creation. The evil which invades the world and the hearts of men is not stronger than the Creator. It cannot change the essentially good structure of his world. So before we try to understand the evil which is an intruder in the world, we must try to understand this truth and hold on to it even when we come to the problem of evil: Despite everything, the created world we live in is a good world, and it is good to be alive in it.

This means in general that, unlike some other religions and unlike a common perversion of Christianity, the Christian faith is a world-affirming and not a world-denying faith. Christians do not affirm the world because they are optimistic about the world as such, or unrealistic about all the suffering and injustice in the world. They affirm it because God says Yes to it. He willed and made it in the first place. Even when evil invaded it and seemed to gain control over it, he did not abandon it and turn against the men who had turned against him. In the life and death of his Son he himself entered the "fallen" world, and in his very judgment against it he was at work to save it. In the resurrection of his Son he reclaimed what already belonged to him and asserted again his powerful and loving lordship *over* the world, *for* the world. At the end he plans not only a new heaven but also a new *earth*. Christians, then, are world-affirming because they believe in a world-affirming God. To deny the world is to deny both his power and his love. To seek escape from the worldly life and worldly responsibilities and pleasures is to seek escape from God himself. An otherworldly religion may seem very pious but it is not Christian. It is pious rebellion against God the Father Almighty, Maker of heaven and earth.

Let us look more specifically at some of the characteristics of the worldly Christianity which follows from the Christian doctrine of creation.

1. Bodily-physical life is good. Dualistic religions and a falsely spiritual Christianity have always been suspicious of the body, even to the point of finding the origin of sin there. They understand the religious life as the denial of and escape from physical needs and desires. In contrast, a biblically oriented faith is shockingly materialistic.

Part of what God made and pronounced very good was man's sexuality. Maleness and femaleness are in fact connected directly with man's being created in the image of God (Genesis 1:27). Throughout the Old Testament, the sexual image of husband and wife is often used to describe the relationship between God and his people, and Paul used it to speak of the relationship between Christ and the church (Ephesians 5:21 ff.). In the Song of Solomon there is included in the Word of God a "sexy" love song. The biblical writers know that we may misuse our sexuality and that our affections and desires may need to be purified, but nowhere do they suggest that sex is not nice. On the contrary, it is to be thankfully and joyfully received as a good gift of God himself.

Again, the creation story tells us that the plants and trees were created by God for food. In the Lord's Prayer Jesus invited and instructed us to pray for "our daily bread" even before we pray for the forgiveness of our sins and deliverance from evil. In his Small Catechism, Luther interprets this to be a petition not only for bread but for "all that pertains to the nourishment and needs of the body" —food, clothing, shelter, money, property, family, good government, health, education, honor. Earthly possessions may become a source of greed and lust, but if God himself invites us to pray for them, then it certainly is his will that we work for them and be concerned about them.

Some Christians have thought that it is legitimate to be concerned about creaturely *necessities*, but not about creaturely *pleasures*. Sex is all right for the propagation of the race, but not for fun. We should eat only the simplest foods and do so merely to nourish our bodies. In general we ought to give up all luxuries we can do without. But this austere view is, in the words of Calvin, "far too severe. For they would fetter consciences more tightly than does the Word of the Lord—a very dangerous thing" (*Institutes*, III, 10, 1).[3] The Creator gives us not only water to quench our thirst but "wine to gladden the heart" (Psalm 104:15—"to make us merry" as Calvin says in his commentary on this verse). Jesus was no ascetic, but went to parties (John 2:1 ff.) and in general came "eating and drinking," so that he was accused of being a "glutton and a drunkard" (Matthew 11:19). The Song of Solomon certainly does not suggest a love only to propagate the race. In the passage just mentioned and in other places, Calvin also mentions as good gifts of God fragrances, colors, music and beauty in general, none of which are useful and good *for* anything. (It is not necessarily true that Protestants identify virtue with ugliness!)

We may add here that the right to satisfy our creaturely necessities and enjoy the creaturely pleasures of life is not our right alone. God is not only our Creator; he is the Creator of all men. His good gifts are intended for everyone, not just for ourselves and our kind of people. To deny these gifts to any man or group of men is rebellion against the Creator himself. To be indifferent to the physical needs and earthly misery of others, and to claim that the church and individual Christians should only be interested in their spiritual welfare, is to deny our own confession of faith in the God who made *all* men and pronounced the physical-bodily life of *all* men very good.

2. Intellectual life is good.

We live in the age of science and technology. Many Christians are deeply suspicious of the technological revolution. Are not automation, the birth control pill, and the loosening of family control through mass media of communication a threat to what God intended the realms of work, sex and family life to be? Does not the growth of psychology and psychiatry undermine our faith in God and the Bible as the solution to our emotional problems? In every area of life more and more problems are solved and questions answered without needing to talk about God. Must not people become less Christian the more scientific they become?

But, seen in the light of the doctrine of creation, the technological revolution is no threat to the Christian faith in God. On the contrary, to a large extent it has been made possible by faith in a Creator God, and Christians can understand it and its accomplishments as one of his good gifts and one of the ways he himself is at work in the world "for man's sake."

It is no accident that the development of modern science took place in the Western world. Neither the ancient Greeks (who, along with the Hebrew-Christian religion, were the main source of Western civilization) nor the Eastern religions believed that the physical-material world is real and good and intelligible in itself. They looked for meaning and truth behind or above the empirical world, the world which they observed and experienced. Only men who believed that truth and meaning can be found also *in* the physical-material world because it is the orderly creation of God— only they could believe that the world as such is worth investigation. Even when modern science has forgotten its own origins, Christians can welcome it as consequence of faith in a Creator and his good creation.

The technological revolution is not only a legitimate consequence of faith in the Creator; it is his specific command. "And God . . . said to them, '. . . fill the earth and subdue it; and have dominion over the fish of the sea and over the birds of the air and over every living thing that moves upon the earth' " (Genesis 1: 28–29). If science opens up and controls the secrets of the world around us, masters the space above us, and learns to understand and deal with the psychological depths within us, then it is only doing the will of the Creator, whether it knows it or not. We need not be afraid of anything scientists may discover, because what they are learning to understand and subdue is God's good creation, made precisely for man's sake. Like God's good gifts of sex, food and pleasure, men may of course misuse the good gift of his intellectual ability. Technology can enslave as well as free, destroy as well as serve. But it is not only permitted but expressly commanded by the Creator. Not to do what we can to have dominion over our world would be disobedience.

Finally, we may add that dependence on scientific achievement is not necessarily incompatible with dependence on God. If it is the will of the Creator for man to have dominion over the earth, and if he made man and the earth so that his will can be fulfilled, why should we not see the work of God in and through the work of men? Is it less the healing work of God if a medical doctor or psychiatrist rather than a preacher makes sick people well? Is it less the fatherly protection of God if the engineering achievement of a dam rather than prayer for the weather to change controls flood waters? Whether God or science gets the credit, Christians who believe in a Creator God and his good creation know that *every* good and perfect gift comes ultimately from him—including those that more immediately are the good results of man's intellectual achievements in science and technology. Belief in God *or* in science? No, *because* we believe in God the Father Almighty, Maker of heaven and earth, *therefore* respect and thanksgiving for science.

3. **Temporal life is good.** Life in time has always been a problem for men. The ancient Greeks thought that the life of every man and the history of the world is a hopeless, meaningless repetition of birth, decay and death. There is no point in being concerned about the things of this world either for myself or for other people. Serenity and meaning can be found only by being indifferent to what happens in the world, stoically accepting the futility of

historical existence, contemplating only eternal and unchanging truths now, and hoping to escape to a better world when we die.

Into this pessimistic Greek world the Hebrew-Christian faith came declaring the good news that the history of the world and of every individual *does* have meaning. It is true that men are born, grow old, suffer and die. It is true that empires rise and fall. But it is also true that there is a God who stands at the beginning and end of time. He is the powerful and loving Creator of all things, the God whose creative purpose at the beginning and for the end of history we can know because he is working his purpose out *in* history. The Creator of the world not only was and will be, he *is* at work in the world to overcome evil and establish justice, minister to the sick, free those who are enslaved. His purpose will finally be fulfilled only at the end of history, but already now within history he is fulfilling it. Despite all the forces in the world which sour and defeat life, Christians confidently and courageously live by the truth that life here and now is good. They do not run and hide or try to escape the world. They thankfully receive life in the world as the good gift of God the Creator.

This biblical view of time has shaped the whole of Western civilization. Confidence that history is "going somewhere" and that progress is possible and therefore worth fighting for in our individual and our institutional lives—this is the legacy of the Judeo-Christian faith. It is true that the Western world in general gradually forgot the original reason for this confidence and came to believe in man's goodness and potential for progress as such. The result has been a new wave of deep hopelessness and despair in our time. The consequence of our faith in history as such (rather than in the God of history) is the brutality of modern warfare, the suffering of racial and economic minorities, the fact that some lives are comfortable and prosperous but empty, while others are poverty-stricken, disease-ridden and hopeless.

But what shall we do in this situation? The Christian answer is not to give up on this life, withdraw from our troubled world and return to the otherworldly religion of the Greeks. The Christian answer is, "I believe in God the Almighty, Maker of heaven and earth!" That means to throw ourselves with renewed confidence and courage *into* the secular world and to fight for economic development, social welfare and political justice *in* the worldly communities which shape our own and other people's lives here and now. We *can* do it and we *must* do it, because the struggle against poverty, ignorance, disease, inequality, war and oppression is not our fight alone; it is the fight of the Creator himself. He is the God who not only saves us at the end of time, but invites and commands us creatively and responsibly to participate in his own creative work, here and now, in secular history, for the good of all men.[4]

Good But Not God

We have emphasized as strongly as possible the goodness of everything God has made. The doctrine of creation makes us free for a thankful, joyful, responsible *worldly* life. We do not qualify but only underline what we have said when we now emphasize just as strongly that although the created world is good, it is not God. This seemingly obvious statement has two consequences which are not so obvious: (1) Nothing in the world is to be feared, (2) Nothing in the world is to be worshiped.

1. Nothing in the world is to be feared. Since the whole world and everything in it depends on God for its very existence, nothing in all creation can have absolute and undefeatable control over us. We see what good news this is when we consider the fact that Christian tradition has interpreted the phrase "heaven and earth" to mean "all things visible and invisible."

There are many visible things in the world which, though good in themselves, can be misused so that instead of being good gifts of the Creator they become terrible threats. Political authority, ordained by God to preserve justice and peace, can become a dreaded instrument of terror and oppression. Wine, given to "make us merry," can become a cruel tyrant which makes us haunted slaves. So also food, sex and the achievements of science and technology can become things that use us instead of good gifts to be used by us. But to believe that God is the Maker and Ruler of "all things visible" is to believe that no visible thing, however powerful and destructive it may become, is stronger than God. How could the creature be stronger than the Creator?

The same is true of the invisible world. When the Bible and

the ancient church confessed that God is Creator of the "heavens," they did not mean only the sky. For ancient men, the heavens were the realm of all kinds of invisible demonic powers which controlled the fate of men. In confessing that God is Creator and Ruler of this realm also, Christians did not deny the existence of such powers, but they did deny final and absolute authority to all the invisible "principalities, dominions and powers" (Romans 8:38; Ephesians 1:21; Colossians 1:16). They, too, are only creatures, not rival gods.

Now, whether or not we modern men believe that this is a world "with devils filled," this ancient confession still has meaning for us. It means the end of all talk about the invisible power of fate ("It's written in the cards," "a bullet with my name on it"). It means the end of all superstitious dependence upon luck, all fear of ghosts or the supernatural. It also means that, without denying their reality, we do not have to surrender hopelessly to the invisible powers the modern scientific world has taught us to dread—the psychological power of the unconscious or subconscious, the biological power of heredity, the sociological power of environment. Powerful though they may be, even these invisible scientific powers do not have the last word about what we are and may become.

God the Father Almighty is the Maker of heaven and earth. He is the God who creates and rules *all* things, always, for man's sake. Therefore we need not live in anxious dread before anything in all the world, visible or invisible. This does not mean that we can sit back and let God take care of everything, confident that everything will work out all right in the end. It means the end of the paralyzing fear of all the very real tyrannies that have invaded God's world, and the confidence to take courage to challenge and fight them—whether they be the tyranny of political oppressions, alcohol, sex, food, bad luck, psychological depressions and compulsions, hereditary defects, environmental handicaps, or any other tyranny.

2. Nothing in the world is to be worshiped. The doctrine of creation is a great warning and battle cry against all forms of idolatry. Idolatry is by definition giving absolute loyalty to something that is only a creature rather than to the Creator. When the good gifts of God are made substitutes for God, they become demonic, enslaving and destroying even as they promise to help and fulfill. We see how this happens, and how faith in God the Creator both condemns and frees us from all idols, when we think of the gods modern men worship as absurdly as ancient men worshiped images of wood or gold.

National identity, good in itself, becomes demonic when a nation becomes a god demanding total, unquestioning loyalty and obedience, whether it is right or wrong, just or unjust. International wars between the "gods" and domestic tyranny are the inevitable result. Faith in God the Creator means " 'We must obey God rather than men' " (Acts 5:29). This faith, by its protest against national arrogance abroad and injustice at home, helps to restore a nation to its proper role as servant rather than god of the people.

Racial distinctions are not bad in themselves, but they become demonic when people begin to speak of white or black "supremacy." Christians, who know that only God is supreme and that he is God the Father Almighty of *all* men, refuse to worship the god of race. They work to free both themselves and others from the arrogance, fear, bitterness and inhumanity which result from serving such an idol.

Sex, one of the essential characteristics of humanity in the image of God, becomes a dehumanizing demon when it becomes a god worshiped for its own sake. Then we turn other people into things to be used instead of recognizing them as persons to be loved and make the sexual relationship an obsession rather than a joy. Faith in the God who creates and rules not only for his own sake but for man's sake rejects the self-destroying, other-destroying worship of sex as such, and restores it to a genuinely free, personal relationship of mutual giving and receiving.

And so it is with all creaturely realities. The protection of our national interests and the rights of the individual, the welfare of the whole community and my own economic security, the demands of racial minorities and of racial majorities, our physical and our spiritual needs—none of these finite, partial realities is to be given absolute priority in our lives. We rebel against the Creator and hurt both ourselves and other people when we make gods of any of them. But to say that we must love and serve God above all is not to deny and reject the creaturely world with all its various needs and pleasures. On the contrary, just by insisting that everything in it is only the creature of God and not a substitute for him, we make possible the real fulfillment of every legitimate creaturely need and desire.

"I believe in God the Father Almighty, Maker of heaven and earth." That means at once freedom *from* the world (as the home of all idols) and freedom *for* the world (as God's good creation).

FOR FURTHER REFLECTION AND STUDY

1. Read the first two chapters of Genesis with these questions in mind and make a list of your answers: (a) What are the characteristics of God the Creator? (b) Why did he create the world? (c) What are the characteristics of man? (d) What is man's purpose in the world?

2. Read John 1:1–3; Colossians 1:15–16; Hebrews 1:1–2. What are we told about the meaning and purpose of the world when we are told that it was created in, through and for Christ?

3. How does modern science help us to understand the Christian doctrine of creation? How does the doctrine of creation help us to appreciate science?

4. If a child should ask you, "Where did I come from?" how could you answer in a way true both to faith in God the Creator and to the biological facts of life?

5. Read through the whole book of the Song of Solomon. Do you think this book ought to be in the Bible? Should teen-agers be encouraged to read it?

6. Is luxury sinful? Should we Americans feel guilty because we have so many material comforts, while other people in the world are poor and hungry?

7. Can Christians believe in progress?

8. Should a Christian talk about having bad luck, or wish other people good luck?

9. How would you answer someone who said that everything a man is or can become is determined by heredity and environment?

10. How does faith in God the Creator make a "social gospel" necessary?

Why Doesn't God Do Something About It?

THE DOCTRINE OF PROVIDENCE AND THE PROBLEM OF EVIL

When Christians confess "I believe in God the Father Almighty, Maker of heaven and earth," they affirm three things: (1) God is loving and just; (2) God is powerful; (3) the world and life in it are good because they come from and are ruled by such a God.

That sounds very nice—for children in church school, kindly preachers, and people standing up to confess their faith in quiet sanctuaries with stained glass windows and inspirational organ music. The only trouble is, this is a world in which we find cancer, insanity, deformed children, hurricanes, bloody wars, starvation, persecution of minorities, and grinding poverty in city slums. Life as we experience it *outside* the sanctuary is filled with sorrow, suffering, brutality, just plain emptiness and pointlessness—and death. How can Christians be so sentimental and naive about the world? Given the kind of world we really have to live in, must we not conclude that if there is a God at all, he must be *either* loving and just but not powerful enough to do anything about it; *or* the almighty source of everything that is and therefore an unloving and unjust God who is the *cause* of it all? Must not God be *either* willing to prevent evil but not able, *or* able but not willing? And if we insist that he is both able and willing, then how can we explain all the terrible evil in the world?

That is the problem we must deal with in this chapter. It is a strange one, because we shall see that:

The reality of evil in our world is at once the greatest intellectual threat to the convincing power of Christian theology, and
the single characteristic of our human existence which gives to
Christian faith its continual meaning and creative power in
men's lives. On the one hand ... everything that Christians say
about God and their life seems contradicted by this pervasive
fact of evil. And yet on the other hand, it is true that everything Christians believe about God and human life, provides
the only force strong enough to conquer the radical power of
evil over men's minds and hearts.[1]

The Reality of Evil

Since the fact of evil is such a threat to what Christians affirm
about God and his good creation, it might be expected that the
Bible and Christian theology would try to solve the problem by trying in one way or another to explain away its reality. Various ways
of trying to do this have been suggested by some philosophers, and
some Christian thinkers have been tempted by them. But genuinely
Christian thought has rejected all the easy answers.

Some people try to deal with the evil around them and in their
own hearts and lives by pretending that it isn't there. They always
look on the bright side of things. If they can't say something good
about other people and events, they don't say anything at all (like
the three monkeys who see no evil, speak no evil, hear no evil).
They cheerfully remember that April showers bring May flowers
and in other ways practice the power of positive thinking. Sometimes such Pollyanna sentimentality has crept into the church, but
the main stream of Christian tradition has rejected it. Some of the
worst injustice and suffering in the world results from the fact that
sometimes "good" people simply refuse to acknowledge that an
evil even exists and therefore do nothing at all to challenge it.

Another solution to the problem might be called the omelet
theory: Eggs have to be broken if you want to make an omelet. Evil
is one step on the way to good and is, in the long run, not really evil
at all. A war which slaughters millions can bring peace. To compromise the Christian gospel of God's love for *all* men can make the
church big and successful. Dishonesty in filling out income tax

forms enables me to give my children more advantages. Communists use the omelet theory to justify aggression. Americans use it to "explain" thousands of permanently maimed human beings in Hiroshima. But even if good does sometimes come from evil, does that make evil good? What kind of God would create a world in which wrong and the infliction of suffering is the law of progress toward right? Christians cannot dispose of the problem of evil as easily as that.

Against all attempts to explain evil away in one way or another the Christian faith is uncompromisingly realistic. Immediately following the biblical story of the good God and his good creation comes the story of the Evil One and his satanic work. The new heaven and new earth we look forward to will not be the climax of gradual progress in history in which there is less and less evil and more and more good. According to the New Testament, they will come only after a final cataclysmic battle between God and the powers of evil. There will be wars and rumors of wars, nation against nation, famine, earthquakes, suffering, false leaders, injustice, hatred, persecution of the righteous—in other words, *evil* (Matthew 24:3–14).

This unflinching realism about the reality of evil despite what we are told in the very same book about the love, justice and power of God and the goodness of his world, becomes even more intense at the event which is the very center of the Christian faith, the cross of Christ. God himself was with us in Christ—and he was killed. Evil is so strong that it seems not just the enemy of God but the victor over God. Good is defeated and evil triumphs. Hatred overcomes love. God's world becomes Satan's world.

That is not the end of the story, of course. But it is an inescapable part of it. The same cross which is the symbol of the Christian faith in God the Father Almighty—that same cross is the symbol of the terrible reality and power of evil.

If then we talk about the problem of evil as Christians gathered around the cross, no trivial, easy answers regarding either the evil in the world around us or in our own hearts will do. The Christian faith is not an escape from the problem of evil; it *raises* the problem "to the nth degree."

The Dark Side of Creation

It will help us to get to the heart of the problem we are discussing if we discuss first what is called natural evil, that which comes from natural causes not influenced by human motives, decisions and actions.

A woman develops cancer and, after a long, agonizing illness, dies, leaving a family without wife or mother. A storm rips through a town, leaving ruined homes, mangled bodies, hunger and disease in its wake. Parents who have eagerly awaited their first child take him home from the hospital, knowing that he is hopelessly deformed physically or mentally. And we ask, "If there is a God, why does he let this happen—or did he actually *make* it happen?"

Several things can be said which help us to understand such misfortunes (although nothing can be said to take the hurt away).

1. Being finite creatures. There are hard experiences in our lives which are simply a part of what it means to be finite creatures. It is a part of our creaturely existence that in life there is decay as well as growth, age as well as youth, loss as well as gain, pain as well as pleasure, sickness as well as health, death as well as birth. Creaturely life at its best is fragile and temporary. In itself that is no evil. It only means that we are men and not God. Real evil enters the picture when we refuse to accept our own finiteness, complain that we are not God, and futilely try to make ourselves into gods.

Death, for instance, is not an evil in itself. But fear of death, a bad conscience in facing our own or another's death, frantically clutching life at all costs—that is evil. It means lack of trust in God and his power over death and an obsessive concern for myself to the exclusion of concern for other people. What is evil is not the fact that the life of every created being comes to an end. It is our American worship of youth, fear of old age and pagan refusal even to admit that people die (instead of "passing away").

The first thing to be said about natural evil, then, is that we must bluntly acknowledge that there is a dark side to God's good creation. The vulnerability and mortality of our lives are painful and hard to bear. But they are an intolerable problem only for those who cannot or will not accept the fact that they are creatures and not gods.

2. Natural law.

Modern science has learned that the laws of nature are not as mechanically fixed and absolute as we once thought. Nevertheless, part of the goodness of creation is that our world is not an unpredictable chaos, but at least a relatively ordered, intelligible system of interrelated parts. Man has been able to subdue and have dominion over the world because it functions in a relatively constant way. But this very regularity of nature which helps human life can also hurt it. Given certain conditions, living cells which grow according to their dynamic structure as cells become malignant cancers. Under certain conditions, the structure of meteorological forces, which make our weather predictable and usually favorable to human life, can also bring tornadoes, destruction, famine and death.[2]

Is God responsible for the suffering which results from natural causes? Yes and no. Yes, in the sense that he willed and created the orderly structure of the world, gave it a relatively independent existence of its own, and for our own good does not constantly interfere with it. No, in the sense that he is not directly responsible when that same structure works to our disadvantage. Perhaps this situation can help us understand how The Heidelberg Catechism can so calmly acknowledge God's responsiblity also for the dark side of creation, without doubting his goodness: "The almighty and ever-present power of God whereby he still upholds, as it were by his own hand, heaven and earth together with all creatures, and rules in such a way that leaves and grass, rain and drought, fruitful and unfruitful years, food and drink, health and sickness, riches and poverty, and everything else, come to us not by chance but by his fatherly hand" (Q. 27).

3. Human negligence and intelligence.

Many so-called natural evils are at least partly caused and can be partly remedied or controlled by men. If a plane crashes, should we ask why God let it happen, or why safety measures were not enforced?

When sickness comes, is it partly the psychosomatic result of guilt, or perhaps disregard for the rules of health? Is it partly caused by unhealthy living conditions resulting from an unjust economic structure? Human negligence, selfishness and unconcern for the welfare of other human beings can cause many forms of evil we like to blame God for. And human intelligence and good will can remedy many forms of evil we sometimes think God ought to do something about.

4. No final solution. But when we have said all that, we still have not solved the problem of what often seems to be needless, meaningless pain and suffering. There is no final solution. The Christian doctrine of providence says that God not only creates but upholds the world. That does not mean the cheap promise that all hardships and difficulties will be smoothed away for us, that there is a silver lining to every cloud, and that everything will always turn out fine. There *is* a dark side to God's good creation, and it would be dishonest, superficial and unfaithful if we Christians denied it or promised any escape from it. What we can say is this (And the decision to be a Christian or not may depend on whether we decide that it is enough.): As the Father of Jesus Christ, the God who is the almighty Creator of heaven and earth, understands our pain, grief, loss and agony in the face of our own death and that of others we care about. He has been there himself and shared it! That is what Good Friday is all about. Besides that, we can say what The Heidelberg Catechism says about what it "profits" us to know that God has created and by his providence still upholds all things. With simple dignity, not evading the facts of creaturely life, the catechism affirms: ". . . that we are to be patient in adversity, grateful in the midst of blessing, and to trust our faithful God and Father for the future, assured that no creature shall separate us from his love, since all creatures are so completely in his hand that without his will they cannot even move" (Q. 28).

Is that enough? Can we believe it? If we can, it will not solve all our problems, but we will be able to face them without bitterness or despair.

The Power of Darkness

Terrible as it can be, the worst form of evil is manifested not in natural misfortune that happens to us, but in what we do to each other. It appears not in pain, suffering and death as such, but in the pain, suffering and death we inflict on each other. Misfortune is far easier to bear than guilt.

The evil that men do to each other has three dimensions. It is always rebellion against God and the order of his creation. It is always enmity against our fellow creatures. And it is always the self-destructive contradiction of what we ourselves were created to be. The worst form of evil, in other words, is revealed in sin.

But evil is more than sin. When we sin, we come under the spell of a power greater than ourselves and our ability to resist, a power from which we cannot free ourselves. We *do* evil, but when we do, we are trapped and controlled *by* evil. It dwells in us, yet somehow has an existence of its own outside us. There are some people in our country today, for instance, who generally are God-fearing, neighbor-loving men. But in the area of race relations, they are overwhelmed and trapped by a blind, irrational, dark power which is completely indifferent to what God commands and neighbor-love demands, and which therefore literally destroys their own humanity. They cannot free themselves from this demonic spirit, nor can they even *want* to be free, no matter what rational or Christian arguments they may hear.

Even when we do set out to combat the power of evil, we often find that we are mastered by it. A soldier fights tyranny in order to free others from the pain and suffering it causes—and finds that to do so he himself must cause horrible pain and suffering. A community establishes a program of urban renewal so that poor people may have better homes—and in tearing down slums, it deprives some poor people of any home at all. We fight evil and discover that we are not only its victims but its instruments.

When we ask about evil, we ask about this hypnotic, enslaving, mysterious power which takes possession of decent people and perverts even the good they do try to do. We are asking *why* good men sin, *why* they cannot and do not even want to stop sinning, *why* even their efforts to destroy evil perpetuates rebellion against God, enmity against neighbor, and self-destruction.

Where does this evil come from, and what is the nature of this dark power which has invaded God's good creation? In what follows, we shall look at some of the various answers men have given as they have wrestled with this universal problem, and try to evaluate these answers from a biblical point of view.

1. An evil god? One of the most ancient explanations of the existence and power of evil is to say that besides the good God there is an evil god—an eternal principle of evil which opposes an eternal principle of good. There is in fact a kind of relative dualism in Scripture. Against God there is Satan, who can be described as "the god of this world" (2 Corinthians 4:4) or the "ruler of this world" (John 12:31; 14:30; 16:11). But in the last analysis the Bible and Christian tradition reject the dualistic explanation of evil. God would not be God if there were another god beside him who could finally thwart his will and his work. Before the world was, there was only the one true God. And we do not have to look forward to a dreary, never-ending battle between a god of light and a god of darkness. Whatever Satan is, he is not really a second god (How do the passages in John just mentioned make this clear?). Christians do not believe in a powerless or only partly powerful God. We believe in God the Father Almighty, who alone is God and who alone will be triumphant in and over the world.

2. God himself? Another explanation of the existence and power of evil is that it comes from God himself. One could reason logically that if God is the Creator of all that is, and if he is in control of everything that happens, then he must also be the source of "moral" evil too. This answer also has always been rejected by Christian theology—and most vigorously just by Calvinistic theologians themselves, who could most easily be tempted by it (and who have always been accused of implying it because of their insistence on the sovereignty of God). The Bible teaches uncompromisingly that God is good and that he is *against* evil. How

could he will or cause resistance and opposition to himself when he
created men precisely for the purpose of fellowship with himself,
when he gave his own Son to *overcome* man's resistance and opposition and to *reconcile* them to himself? How could God will or
cause man's enmity against fellowman, when he created men for
the mutual helping of one another, when he himself became a man
just to reconcile them also to each other? How could he will the
self-destroying inhumanity that goes with the evil men do, when
he created men to be human and entered into the human sphere
himself to re-create them to be genuinely human beings? We shall
see that God is powerful enough to use evil and turn it to his own
purposes. He can make good come out of evil. But we cannot say
that God is the author of evil. Evil is by definition what God does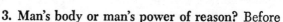
not will and does *not* do. There is no secret identity between God
and the Devil!

 3. **Man's body or man's power of reason?** Before
Christianity ever came on the scene, many ancient Greeks thought
that evil is basically sensuality, that the needs and especially the
pleasures of man's body are a drag on his higher nature. They lead
him to sin and captivity to evil. Despite the fact that this theory of
the origin of evil very early crept into the Christian church and has
probably influenced all of us, it is unbiblical and un-Christian. It is
wrong, first of all, because it traces evil to something God has
willed and made, and thus dishonors the Creator, making him ultimately the cause of evil. Our bodies may of course be the *instrument* of evil, but nowhere does the Bible suggest that they are evil
in themselves or the source of evil.

Secondly, this explanation is inadequate, because it implies
that evil can be overcome if we develop our rational capacities so
that they subdue and control our bodily desires. But reason too
can become evil and the servant of evil. The rational man is not
necessarily the good man. The coldly rational, calculating man can
in fact do far more harm than the man driven only by his passions,
for he is far more imaginative in devising subtle forms of evil. It
was not sensual, lusting "animal" man, but highly educated, reasonable man who developed nuclear warfare. The point is not that

reason in itself is any more evil than body (and certainly ignorance is not the same thing as innocence or virture). Reason also is a good gift of the Creator. The point is that we must look deeper than either body or mind to discover the origin and nature of evil, which can possess both but arises from neither.

4. Society? A more modern explanation of the origin and nature of evil is that it comes from some form of economic or political structure. The root of all evil (depending on one's personal bias) is said to be communism or capitalism, the Democrats or the Republicans, segregation or integration, labor or management. All such political-economic explanations are inadequate for two reasons: (a) They cannot explain how evil social structures which are supposedly the *source* of evil, came into being themselves. (b) They always look for evil only in the "other guy" and ignore the fact that, when a class or party which has no power manages to gain control of power, the oppressed always become the oppressors. Evil does not end; it only changes managers and forms of expression. Could it be that evil does not reside in and work through any one class or party or group as such, but that it somehow has hold of *people—all* people: communists *and* capitalists, poor *and* rich *and* middle-class, "foreigners" *and* Americans, Republicans *and* Democrats, white *and* black?[3]

5. Free will? Perhaps the most common way of explaining the origin of evil is to say that it comes from the freedom God gave us when he created man. God gives us freedom of choice between good and evil. How could we choose good, if evil were not an alternative? But logical as this sounds at first glance, it is neither logical nor biblical. How could the good creature of God choose evil? If he was created good, his will was also good, and a good will can by definition only will and choose good. If, as a matter of fact, we prefer evil, we must already have had rebellious, hostile, self-destructive thoughts and desires in our hearts *before* we made the choice. But where did *they* come from? Not from God, for God is good. Not from the heart of man, for the heart of man is God's good creation. According to the Bible, it is not free will *in* ourselves but temptation *outside* ourselves that leads us to choose evil. We do choose it. No one forces us to do so. But in choosing it we do not exercise our freedom. We voluntarily *give up* our freedom to the enslaving power of evil. Freedom in the Bible is by definition freedom *from* evil, freedom *for* God and fellowman and therefore also for the realization of our own humanity. Freedom for evil is a contradiction in terms.

6. Fallen angels? As soon as we mention temptation from outside ourselves, we run into another possibility for explaining the origin of evil. If it can come neither from God, nor from a second God, nor from the man whom God created, is there not still another alternative? According to the Genesis story, it was the *Devil* who put evil desires into the heart of man and tempted him to choose against God, against his fellowman and against his own true humanity. We need not fall into the error of dualism and think of Satan as a second god. We might conceive of him also as a creature of God—not a human creature but an angelic creature of some kind. He, and perhaps other angelic creatures with him, rebelled against God and then corrupted God's good creation. The idea of Satan and his minions as fallen angels was common in the ancient church, but it is hinted at only in texts on the outermost fringe of the New Testament canon: 2 Peter 2:4 and Jude 1:6. Even if we took these texts literally, they still would not explain the origin of evil. They only push the problem back one step, and leave unanswered all the same questions we have asked about attributing the origin of evil to God's human creatures. How could God's angelic creatures rebel against their Creator, when *all* that God creates is good by definition?

Just when we are driven finally to the biblical statements about Satan, we are driven at the same time to the conclusion that there *is* no explanation for the origin and fact of evil in God's good world. The Genesis story is very profound in its simplicity at this point. It makes no attempt to explain where the tempter came from, or how he could exist at all in God's world. Satan is a hideous intruder who does not belong in the picture, but nevertheless he is there. Logically, evil is impossible in a world created and ruled by

God, for it is just what God the Father Almighty did *not* create and does *not* will. That is just the parasitical power of evil in our world and in our own lives. It is not the truth about what we are and what the world is like; it is a *lie,* a *contradiction* or *denial* of the truth. That is why it is so dangerous. Evil is the lie that leads us to the futile, self-destructive attempt to live without God, against God, when the truth is that it is God's world. It is the lie that leads us to the futile, self-destructive attempt to live without and against our fellowmen, when in fact we can only be ourselves when we live with and for them. It is the lie that leads us to the futile, self-destructive attempt to seek self-fulfillment in living like animals or gods, when the truth is we can find self-fulfillment only as *human* beings. Evil is the Big Lie which is so destructive and terrible just because it convinces us that the truth is not the truth.

The real problem of evil is not how we can explain the intellectual problem of its origin. It is whether and how the death grip this lie has on our world and on our own lives can be broken. That is what we must talk about next.

The Light Shining in the Darkness

We have ended up where we began. We believe in God the Father Almighty, Maker of heaven and earth, and therefore we believe that the world and life in it are good. But that very faith confronts us with the unexplainable, logically impossible fact of the power of God-hating, brother-hating, self-destroying evil in this "good" world and in our own "good" lives.

Is that all we can say? No, because while Christians (along with everyone else) are not able to explain the source of evil, we do know that it does not have the last word. We conclude our discussion by drawing some conclusions about what we have learned to this point, then by adding the truth that *is* the last word.

1. **We must take evil seriously.** We began by speaking of the reality of the power of darkness in the world. Because the cross of Christ stands at the center of the Christian faith, we must take evil with dead seriousness as a real threat to God himself. Christians are divided in their understanding of what this

means. Some think it means that we must believe in the existence of a personal Devil and invisible demonic powers. That is a possible answer, so long as the powers of darkness are not interpreted as eternal, rival gods in opposition to the one true God, and so long as no non-biblical mythological speculations are made about when and how angels fell from heaven.

Other Christians believe that we ought to demythologize or depersonalize the Devil and his demonic forces. They are said to be only a primitive way of expressing the truth that in God's world there is not only order but chaos, not only truth but lies, not only humanity but inhumanity—not only God but evil. We may still believe everything the Bible tells us about the reality and power of evil without thinking literally of personal demons and devils running around getting into people. Even without that, can we not speak, in all loyalty to biblical truth, of the "demonic" or "satanic" power which can take possession of individuals and whole nations, changing ordinarily decent people into brutal, bloodthirsty mobs —or simply coldly indifferent observers of injustice, need and suffering?

Whichever interpretation you take, it is important to emphasize that Christians do not "believe in" either a personal Devil or an impersonal principle of evil. We believe in God the Father Almighty, in Jesus Christ his only Son our Lord, in the Holy Spirit. But no Christian creed contains a profession of faith in the Devil or evil. That would not be strict orthodoxy, as some have thought; it would be plain idolatry—*worship* of evil! Christians do not believe *in* but *against* the powers of darkness in God's good creation.

2. **The Devil is a gentleman.** To take Satan and his powers of darkness seriously means (whether we think of them personally or not) to expect them to be at work just where we do *not* expect them. We hear in 2 Corinthians 11:14 that Satan "disguises himself as an angel of light," and that his servants "disguise themselves as servants of righteousness." It was not to the political subversives, prostitutes, social outcasts and dishonest businessmen, but to the moral, God-fearing law-abiding Pharisees that Jesus spoke of "your father the devil" (John 8:44). The Devil once

found his support for putting the Son of God out of the way among the "good church people." So let us take warning. It is not only in atheists and godless totalitarian societies that Satan is at work. He is also at work especially where pious men try to use God to maintain their own security, prosperity and well-being, instead of letting themselves be used by him. He is at work not only where men hurt other men and destroy themselves by lust, drunkenness and immorality of various kinds, but especially where one's own morality, respectability and law-abiding piety become more important than the needs of fellowmen and an excuse to reject or ignore them. To take evil seriously is to remember that the Devil can assume the form of the perfect gentleman—even a Christian gentleman.

3. But we ought not to take evil *too* seriously. Thinking and talking about the Devil too much is like looking at a coiled snake too long: One can easily be paralyzed, hypnotized, mastered and finally destroyed by it. It is better immediately to destroy a poisonous snake than to gaze at it in terrified fascination. Satan and his forces should not become the positive center of our attention, so that slowly and unconsciously we begin to look at them with secret respect and admiration. As Christians we are called to make theology, not demonology; to concentrate on the love which casts out fear rather than on fear itself; to serve and proclaim the power of God, not the power of evil. When we talk too long, too loudly and too exclusively about evil, it is not surprising that people begin to think that it is really evil we honor and respect, really evil to whom we believe the world belongs. How pleased the Devil must be when people leave the church supposedly gathered in the name of *Jesus Christ* under the impression that *sin* was the main theme of the worship and preaching!

4. The message of Good Friday and Easter. This brings us to the final answer of the Christian faith to the problem of evil. It is not an answer which after all resolves the problem and explains it away. Evil remains a contradiction of everything we believe about the love and power of God and the goodness of his world. It remains an unexplainable intruder in God's good crea-

tion, a threat to God himself. We can never leave behind the ugly truth revealed on the cross: This is a world in which evil can triumph over good, Satan over God. So there can be no glib and easy explanation that now suddenly answers all questions, solves all problems and brings this chapter to a nice happy ending.

What the Christian faith does have to say is not an explanation but a confession of faith: Jesus Christ is risen! It is not Good Friday but Easter which is the last word about ourselves, our world, and the place of God and the powers of darkness in it. Christ is the victim of evil, but also the victor over evil. However strong evil may be and however inadequate we are to overcome it, it is not finally stronger than God. It is a terrible reality which resists and opposes God, but in the last analysis it is always overcome by *his* opposition and resistance. If the cross means that we can never treat evil lightly, the resurrection means that we can never treat it with ultimate fear and despair. Even since Easter, of course, the powers of darkness are still at work among us. But those who know about Easter and believe what they have heard know that however powerful these dark forces may be, however much damage they still do, they are only usurpers doomed to failure in their attempt to take a throne that does not belong to them.

Is the Christian faith, then, optimistic or pessimistic? We cannot be optimistic, because Good Friday and the cross are a symbol of the dark power of evil which is still at work in the world around us and in our own lives. But we cannot be pessimistic, because Easter and the empty tomb are a symbol of the power of God the Father Almighty who "has delivered us from the dominion of darkness and placed us in the kingdom of his beloved Son" (Colossians 1:13), who "disarmed the principalities and powers and made public example of them, triumphing over them in him" (Colossians 2: 15). Notice that these passages do not speak only of a victory that some day *will* happen, but of a victory which *has* happened. The cross keeps the resurrection from leading Christians to a falsely optimistic view of the world, and the resurrection keeps the cross from leading them to a false pessimistic view of the world. Could it be that a faith symbolized both by a cross and an empty tomb is the only *realistic* answer to the problem of evil?

We may add that this realistic attitude toward evil says something also about how Christians ought to live in a world in which there is so much suffering caused by individual immorality and by political, economic and social injustice. We can have no optimistic hope that we can gradually stamp out all evil if we try hard enough, changing the world into a utopia and individual men into saints. But on the other hand, we cannot hopelessly abandon the world to the forces of evil, passively waiting for a better world to come. If we live from an Easter faith and believe that there is a Power at work in the world stronger than all the powers of darkness, we *must* and we *can* join in the fight against them, confidently expecting signs of the truth that "the light shines in the darkness and the darkness has not overcome it" (John 1:5).

5. Evil must serve God. We conclude with the hardest thing of all to understand about the power and reality of evil on the one hand, and the power and reality of God on the other. God is so powerful that evil must serve him whether it wants to or not. God does not will evil. Evil is what he does not *will*. But nevertheless God can and does *use* evil for his own purposes. This, too, we learn from the cross and resurrection of Christ. All the political and religious leaders and, in their own way, even his own disciples rejected Christ. And in rejecting him, they rejected God himself, rejected their own brother and fellowman, and rejected their own humanity. But it was precisely their rejection which made the salvation of the world possible. Where evil seemed to triumph most completely, just there it served the powerful love of God for the good of all men. This is not to say that evil is secretly good, or that we should do evil that good may come of it, or that evil is not so bad after all. It is only to say that *nothing* can separate us from the love of God in Christ, and that in *everything*, even the worst manifestations of evil, God is at work for the good of those who love him.

FOR FURTHER REFLECTION AND STUDY

1. Does a good end justify evil means (a) in the case of a war to bring peace? (b) in the case of excluding some people for

the sake of the peace and the numerical and financial security of the church? (c) in the case of lying on income tax reports for the sake of my family's welfare?

2. Is death evil?

3. The whole book of Job wrestles with the problem of suffering, and especially why God allows good men to suffer. Finally, after hearing all Job's complaints and questions, God answers him in chapters 38–41. What is the gist of the answer? How does Job respond? Do you think this is a satisfactory solution to Job's problem? You will find a stimulating study of Job in the youth booklet, *Is God Cruel?* (Richmond: The CLC Press, 1964).

4. How would you answer a friend or loved one dying of cancer who asked you, "Why does God let this happen to me?"

5. Albert Camus, a French novelist and philosopher, and one of the most sensitive and compassionate men of our time, once said that he could not believe in God because this is a world in which innocent children suffer and die from the brutality of war. As a Christian, what would you say to him?

6. Do you think educated people are less likely to be evil than uneducated people?

7. Do you think it is important to believe in a personal Devil?

8. In what ways do you think Satan might be at work today in his disguise as an angel of light or as a gentleman?

9. Before you read this chapter was it your impression that the Christian faith is pessimistic or optimistic about the world? What do you think now?

10. Would you say that the Christian understanding of evil results in more or in less active involvement in the affairs of the world?

11. Read the following texts with this question in mind: Who was responsible for the evil of the cross? Acts 2:22–36; John 13:2; Mark 14:10–11. Can these texts be reconciled with each other?

10

Who Are We?

THE DOCTRINE OF
MAN

Suppose you were a long way from home, got involved in a conversation with a total stranger whom you instinctively liked, and he (or she) suddenly asked, "Who are you, anyway?" Stop now and make a list of ten or more things you would say to identify yourself. (Why is it easier to be honest about ourselves with people we never expect to see again?)

When you have finished that, ask yourself more directly, "Who am I?" Add to the list as many more things as come to mind—including those things too "close to home" to tell even a stranger.

After you have finished your whole list, go through it and underline what you think are the most important facts or characteristics.

Now analyze your list with the following questions:

1. Do the most important things come first? Last? What is the significance of their place on the list?

2. How many items on your list identify your public and private image of yourself in terms of *personal relationships* (married, single, parents, children, participation in various groups or classifications of people)? How many items are not relational (purely intellectual or physical)?

3. Which of the following categories are emphasized, and which are left out: *politics* (nationality, party, conservative or liberal convictions), *economics* (business or profession, indications of financial status and needs), *religion* (church affiliation, refer-

ence to God), *physiology* (sex, state of health, physical characteristics, age), *culture* (degree of education, indication of artistic or
intellectual interests), *psychology* (expressions of happiness or un-
happiness, loneliness, loving and being loved or not, fears and anx-
ieties, hostility)? What is the significance of your emphases and
omissions?

4. Are there *contradictions* in your list? Items which express
not so much what you are as what you *wish* you were, or think you
ought to be?

5. Which of the items would you say are essential to your
basic humanity? Which are incidental? Which are *destructive* of
your basic humanity?

If you were honest (or at least if you are like all the rest of
us), the analysis of your list probably yields two basic conclusions:
First, all of us tend to understand ourselves primarily in terms of a
few areas of our lives, and to forget or ignore the very important
influence of other areas. That means a dangerously limited understanding of ourselves. Moreover, it is very difficult to fit even the
various facts about ourselves we *are* aware of into a unified picture.
In fact, the more different factors we take into consideration, the
harder it is to know who we really are. Secondly, as soon as we try
to explain who we are, we run into the problem of some disturbing
self-contradictions. Why can't we *be* what we know we are? Why
is there such a gap between what we know about ourselves deep
down, and the way we actually live and experience life? Is our real
self revealed in the way we actually live, or in what we know we
should be, would like to be, and somehow think we really are basically?

We shall deal with the first of these problems in this chapter,
and with the second in the next chapter. Meanwhile, save your list
to see whether you would change it when you have finished these
two chapters.

Our problem now is: What is man? What were we talking
about in previous chapters when we spoke about living as *human*
beings? More directly: Who are we? Who am *I*?

Before we begin discussing the Christian doctrine of man,
which tries to answer these questions, we need to be clear that this

doctrine is not a substitute for what we can learn about ourselves from all the various sciences which study human nature and behaviour. A physician or sociologist or psychiatrist can obviously tell us very important things about ourselves that a preacher or theologian cannot. The Christian doctrine of man does not deny or try to replace all the essential information the various sciences give us. It tries rather to get behind it to ask what it *means*. Christian doctrine tries to *interpret* and *integrate* all the fragmentary, unrelated, partial bits and pieces of information we can learn from the study of economics, political science, cultural anthropology, sociology, psychology, and so on. *Why* is the data of no one area of our lives adequate to explain the whole picture? What is our purpose in learning all we can from the various sciences? How can we fit what they teach us about man as a brain with a central nervous system and a given anatomical structure, man as a social animal, man as a sexual being, man as the product of environmental and hereditary influences, man as an economic entity—how can we fit that all together to understand man as a *human being*?

Christians believe that in entering into the life and history of men, God reveals not only who *he* is, but also who *we* are. While our faith does not replace (but in fact needs) all we can learn about ourselves from all kinds of other sources, it does add a dimension to our self-understanding which we can discover no place else. Our task in this chapter, then, is to learn what we can about this dimension, which Christians believe gives them a unique perspective on all the other dimensions.

In the Image of God

Like all other animals, man is born, breathes, eats, sleeps, eliminates, fights a losing battle with death, and returns to dust. What is it that makes him a distinctively *human* being, uniquely different from all other animals? All Christian theology has answered that it is man's being created "in the image of God" (Genesis 1:26). But different Christians, in different times and different theological traditions, have given different answers about what that means. Very often, instead of asking how the Bible itself understands this concept, they have simply read into the Bible what they already thought to be the distinctive essence of humanity.

1. Three theological interpretations. We shall first look at some of the most important of these inserted views of the image of God, then try to discover what the biblical writers themselves meant by it.

— a. Western civilization in general has followed the ancient Greek belief that man's *rationality* is what makes him uniquely human. It is not surprising, then, that many Western Christians have assumed that "image of God" means ability to reason and to act in accordance with what is reasonable. (Whatever you may think theoretically about this, did it occur to you to say, "I am a rational animal," when asked who you are?) But, while the Bible does not deny that we are thinking beings and shows no contempt for the intellect, nowhere does it suggest that this is the key to our humanity. On the contrary, it knows what modern psychiatry has also taught us—that a man may be completely rational and logical and yet diabolically or pathetically inhuman.

— b. Another explanation of the image of God is to identify it with the *spiritual* side of man's nature, or with his *soul*. This view also comes from the ancient Greeks, who believed that man's soul is divine, of the same essence as God himself, and that the body is only the prison of man's truly human (basically divine) self. Popular as this view has been in the Christian church, it is not biblical. (Did it occur to you to answer "I am an immortal soul" when asked who you are? What is popular theoretically is not always a part of our real lives.) The creation story does make a distinction between body and soul. God made man "of dust" and then "breathed into his nostrils the breath of life" so that man became "a living being" (Genesis 2:7). But on the one hand, it is not suggested that this breath or "spirit" (the same word in Hebrew) makes man inwardly divine or even similar to God. All the birds and beasts have exactly the same "breath of life" (Genesis 1:30). And on the other hand, the Bible does not have the Greek contempt for the body. Man's physical nature as "male and female" is directly connected with his being created in the image of God (Genesis 1:27). In short, we cannot understand the biblical doctrine of the image of God in terms of a body-soul split. In the Bible, man is not essentially spiritual *or* physical. Whatever his basic humanity is, it is something that has to do with his *whole* being, spiritual and physical, soul *and* body, not with just a part of him. Strictly speaking, in fact, man's soul or spirit is not even a part of him, something located somewhere within him. It is simply the livingness of his body, that which makes him a "living" being. (Look up the words "man," "spirit," "soul" and "image of God" in one or more of the various theological word books.

c. Still another possibility is to identify the image of God which comprises man's distinctive humanity with his *capacity to make moral judgments*. Sometimes this is the interpretation given to the statements in the Reformed confessions which identify the image of God with the "righteousness" or "holiness" or "goodness" man originally possessed. (See the Second Helvetic Confession, VIII; The Heidelberg Catechism, Q. 6; Belgic Confession, Art. XIV; Westminister Confession, IV, 2.) We shall have to return presently to what this "original righteousness" does mean. Now it is important to say that in the Bible it does *not* refer to an independent moral capacity of man to know right and wrong and to act accordingly. On the contrary, man is *forbidden* to eat of "the tree of the knowledge of good and evil" (Genesis 2:17). It is the temptation of the Devil and rebellion against God to desire to be good and know the good for himself (Genesis 3:5). To want a righteousness of one's own is to be ignorant of the righteousness that comes from God (Romans 10:2 f.). Like Paul when he was still the persecutor of the church and thus of Christ himself, one can be "blameless under the law" and still be the enemy of God. The legally moral man is not necessarily genuinely human and Godlike. Sometimes it is just the most "moral" people who are the most inhumanly unforgiving, unloving, insensitive to the needs of others, and unwilling or unable to let themselves be loved, forgiven and cared for. To be a morally responsible agent does not in itself make a man a human being in the image of God.

2. The biblical definition. All three of the interpretations we have discussed try to impose some presuppositions we already have about our humanity on the biblical concept of the image of God. These interpretations are inadequate because it is wrong to expect the Bible simply to confirm what we already

know. But more than that, they are inadequate because we are all
cut off from our own basic humanity. When we analyze ourselves,
we do not see the human beings God created us to be. We see
fallen humanity—human life at odds with itself. (Remember the
contradictions that came to light if you were honest when you
tried to identify yourself?) We look at ourselves with minds and
hearts that are sinful, so that we cannot see ourselves clearly and
understand ourselves correctly. "I do not understand my own actions. For I do not do what I want, but I do the very thing I hate"
(Romans 7:15).

a. Where, then, can we see a man who, without self-contradiction, lives a really human life as man in the image of God? We
do not really see him when we look at Adam. The story of Adam
is the story of man in rebellion against God and his own true
nature. For an answer, we have to go to the New Testament. There
we hear of a "Second Adam," who was "the man" Jesus Christ
(Romans 5:15 ff.; 1 Corinthians 15:45 ff.). *He* is the man who is
the "image of the invisible God" (Colossians 1:15), "the likeness
of God" (2 Corinthians 4:4), "in the form of God" (Philippians
2:5). Jesus is the only man who has ever been true to his own
humanity and thus demonstrated in his life what it means to be
man in the image of God. He is the only man who ever was in fact
what the first man (and every other man since him) refused to be.
Pilate spoke more truly than he himself knew when he looked at
Jesus and said, "Here is *the* man" (John 19:5).

And what is the decisive thing about Jesus' humanity? Not
his rationality; those who saw him only as a wiser teacher than
other teachers missed the point completely. Not a spiritual life
lived despite or apart from a worldly, bodily life; he was the Word
who became *flesh*, who fulfilled his task as a flesh and blood man
among men. Nor does the New Testament emphasize his moral
integrity (though he was, of course, a moral man in the deepest
sense); he refused to let men call him "good" (Matthew 19:17),
and he scandalized the highly moral Pharisees by being utterly unconcerned about conventional morality, and about whether his
friendship with immoral people would damage his own reputation
(Mark 2:15–22).

The unique thing about Jesus was not something he had, or some attribute or quality within him. It was the way he lived. He was the one man who ever lived who lived (1) completely for God and in complete obedience to God, (2) completely for fellowmen and in complete identity with them. As such, Jesus was not the weak, passive, selfless man we sometimes make him. Just in holding without compromise to doing the will of his Father, and in standing with and for his fellowmen, was he a strong, active, self-asserting man. Neither the political and religious leaders nor Satan himself could force or scare or bribe him into turning away from doing what he had to do.

What we learn from Jesus, therefore, is that to be truly human, to be man in the image of God, is not to possess some intellectual or spiritual or moral qualities in oneself, but to be *man-in-relationship, man-in-community,* or *man-in-encounter.* We cannot be human by ourselves, in ourselves, independently and self-sufficiently. Only as we discover our very existence in relatedness to God and to fellowmen can we be truly human. But just then we discover that this does not mean the sacrifice of self, but being true to self. This understanding of the image of God in terms of personal relationships is at least hinted at in the Westminster Confession when it connects the "original righteousness" of man in the image of God with "communion with God" (VI, 2. Would "communion" with fellowmen have been omitted if the writers had thought about this from a New Testament point of view?)

b. Perhaps we can understand better what all this means if we now look again at the Genesis story, which says the same thing in a different way.

In the first place, God himself does not exist in lonely isolation, in himself and for himself, as far as the Bible is concerned. It never describes in any detail what God was or did before the creation. In the creation story itself and throughout the Bible, God is a God with and for men—a "covenant-making" or community-creating God.

Since God himself is not alone, it is not surprising to hear that he said (according to the second creation story), "It is not good for *man* to be alone; I will make him a helper fit for him" (Genesis 2:18). So (according to the first creation story), "God created man in his own image . . . male and female he created them" (Genesis 1:27). To be a human being in the image of God is first of all to have something in common with all the other animals—sexuality. Every human being *is* a male or a female. Sex is not just something we "have," but something we *are*—as creatures in the image of God. (Perhaps it is worth noting here that the *only* distinction mentioned as fundamental to man's humanity is the sex distinction. We hear that *animals* are created according to "kinds" or "species," but not man. The attempt to find some essential distinction between men in terms of race or "kind" is to dehumanize and make animals out of both ourselves and other men.)

The point in connecting man's maleness or femaleness with the image of God is to say that no human being can find the fulfillment of his humanity in himself, for himself. As man is made for woman and woman for man, so human beings can be human only in relationship with an "other" outside themselves. Human beings differ from animals in that this orientation toward others is not purely instinctive or automatic but personal. That means, according to the Genesis story, a twofold relationship. On the one hand God *speaks* personally to man and creates man so that he can *answer*. God commands and man can obey. God gives and man can receive. And on the other hand, as God himself is spontaneously and freely with and for men, so he creates human beings to be like himself—spontaneously and freely with and for one another.

In its primitive way the Genesis story of the creation of the first Adam says the same thing as the New Testament account of the Second Adam about what it means to be a human being in the image of God. Nothing is said about being intellectually gifted, about physical strength and attractiveness, about spiritual piety and religiousness or about a strict and moral integrity. Nothing at all is said about what a man is in himself. Everything turns on how we use whatever intellectual, spiritual, physical or moral powers we have in encountering God and other people. Only as man-in-relationship, man-in-community, man-existing-in-love, are we truly human.

For the rest of this chapter we shall investigate what this means in more detail.

Man and God

We have already summarized everything that can be said about a proper relationship with God when we say that Christians pray to "Our Father in heaven," and believe in "God the Father Almighty, Maker of heaven and earth." A right human relationship with God is a relationship of the thanksgiving and obedience a good son gives a good Father. In the present context, we emphasize only two aspects of this relationship.

1. **Our total dependence.** To say that we are *creatures* is to emphasize our total dependence on God. The doctrine of creation is a constant warning against all human arrogance. None of us is or can be a self-sufficient, independent, "self-made" man. Everything we have and everything we are comes from God, including the breath of life itself. If God were not the kind of God he is, our dependence on him could be a threat to our "life, liberty and pursuit of happiness." If he were concerned only about his own majesty and power, if he were stingy or simply indifferent, we might still have to admit our dependence, since he is "bigger than we are," but we could only do it grudgingly. But God is the God who created the world for man's sake and gave us everything we need to achieve life, liberty and happiness. Our dependence on him is therefore not a reason for resentment but for thanksgiving. It is not a threat to, but the source of, our freedom as human beings. Acknowledgment of total dependence—with thanksgiving: That is the first characteristic of a right relationship with God.

2. **Our creative activity.** But dependence is only one side of a right relationship with God. Faith in God is not just a matter of receiving, and depending on him for everything. A dog has that kind of relationship with his master! By emphasizing too exclusively our total dependence on God, the church has sometimes given the impression that to be a Christian is to be a weak, passive pet waiting to be fed. By talking too exclusively about why people "need God," we have encouraged the whining or belligerent question, What can the church do for me? We have nourished

the attitude that being a Christian means only going to church to
ask God for what we need and to thank him for what he has given
us. No wonder strong, healthy people are bored with such a religion.

The creation story and the Bible in general do remind us of
our dependence, but they also teach us that to be a human being
created in the image of God means strength, creative activity, a job
to do. Be fruitful! Multiply! Fill! Subdue! Have dominion! Prayer,
"waiting on the Lord" and worship are each an essential part of
faith in God the Creator, but another equally essential part is to
tend to the world he gave us. That means that God does not intend
for us to think about him, religion and church activities all the
time. We cannot devote full time to such things if we live obediently in a world in which he himself has put "all things" under our
supervision (Psalm 8:6 f.). We can live as human beings created
in the image of God only when we concentrate most of our time
on living an active, "secular" life. The purely passive, receiving
person who finds his relationship with God only in the church and
religious activities is a *disobedient* person who surrenders his own
humanity as he refuses the worldly task God gave him to fulfill.

In answer to such questions as, Why should I be a Christian?
or, What can the church do for me? perhaps we ought not to
begin too quickly making promises about what people can "get
out of it." Perhaps we ought to tell other people and remind ourselves that God has something for us to do in the world. He created
and he commands us to live a faithful, responsible, active life in
our "non-religious" intellectual, sexual, business, political and
social relationships. That is the way we fulfill our humanity in his
image.

Thankfully receiving *and* actively obeying, religious *and*
secular activities, worship in the church *and* work in the world—
all are included in a right relationship between man the creature
and God the Creator.

Man and Fellowman

To be man in God's image means to be man-in-relationship or
man-in-community not only with God but also with fellowmen.

The man who is against or merely neutral toward his fellowman, or who wants to escape into a life of secure independence and isolation from his fellowman, denies his own humanity. To be man *is* to be "fellow-man."[1]

We could talk about this as existence-in-love. But now we shall speak about it in terms of some basic forms of human encounter which must take place even before love can become a reality.

1. Seeing and being seen. The most basic form of human encounter is looking one another in the eye. How can we be with and for one another if we do not first *see* one another? There are many ways we deny our own and other's humanity by not seeing. Sometimes we do not bother even to look (as when we cannot remember which waitress in a restaurant is ours, though we have spoken with her). Sometimes we deliberately avoid seeing (as when we carefully do not see the people in the slum section we drive through to work every day, or in the section where the maid lives when we take her home). Sometimes we do not see concrete people but only abstract categories (Negroes, Catholics, Jews, foreigners, females or males, conservatives or liberals).

But just as dehumanizing as not seeing is not letting ourselves *be* seen. Instead of being open enough to let other people see us as plain old human beings, we "act like" the Business Man, the Mother, the Preacher—or whatever role we assume and image we try to project. We all have functions to fulfill. But when we use the function as a mask to hide behind, we make it impossible really to do what our function requires, just because we avoid genuinely *human* relationships.

To see and let ourselves be seen can be painful. We have to get involved. We have to admit our own fallibility and vulnerability. It is easier and safer to have eyes but not to see, and to retreat behind our mask. But we do so at the great price of our own and other men's humanity.

2. Speaking and listening. Important as they are, looks can be deceiving. To know another person by sight alone is not yet really to know him. To judge by appearance alone is often to gain a false impression. Real human encounter does not take place until speaking and listening are added to seeing. A purely anthropological as well as a theological study of man indicates the importance of words and language in distinguishing human beings from beasts. When we speak to each other, we are saying, "Let me explain myself to you, and let me tell you my impression of you. Let me share with you something you do not know." We say that we take each other seriously enough to share ourselves and what we know, and to try to understand one another. "I have nothing to say to him" or "We are not speaking" means a deliberate denial of the very thing that makes us human beings instead of animals.

Speaking is useless without listening. Willingness to listen to what another is saying (not just waiting for him to get through so I can talk) says, "I do not know you really, but I want to. I want to give you a chance to correct the false impression I may have of you. I believe you have something to tell me that I need to learn." Listening is perhaps even more important than speaking as a way of taking another person seriously. "He has nothing to say which could possibly interest me" or "I wasn't listening" or "Shut up!" means the refusal to accept another person as a human being—and therefore the denial of our own humanity.

Words, of course, may be dishonest words, simply empty words, or nothing but propaganda. They can prevent as well as establish real communication. But there can be no complete communication *without* words. In any case "human relations" means willingness to *speak* (with the intention of clarifying and not concealing or clouding the truth) and to *listen* (with the openness to change my mind as a result of what I hear). Speaking and listening are an absolute prerequisite for every genuine human community —between husbands and wives, black men and white men, political powers (*especially* when they are enemies), labor and management, teachers and students, and in all other forms of human encounter. It is no accident that the one man who ever lived out a genuinely human life in the image of God was called "the Word."

3. Helping and being helped. How we act is the final test of whether we see and let ourselves be seen, and speak and listen, in a really human way. We have not really seen or heard each other unless we understand and respond to our encounter as a mutual call for assistance. When we recognize one another's humanity, we learn that to be human is to depend not only on God but on one another. As human beings we need each other's help.

All helping is not human. Sometimes when we help others we are only playing God. We go to our neighbors in need as superior to inferior, wise to foolish, strong to weak, good to sinful. We think we are competent to give them good advice, and we are confident that what they need is to become like what we are—thrifty, clean, trustworthy, courteous, helpful, kind, virtuous, etc. And then we are angry because those we have helped are not properly grateful for the patronizing or contemptuous help by which they know we have only used them to build up our own ego!

Sometimes we are kind to other people only to get them in our debt, so we can make them pay off in one way or another for services rendered, or manipulate them into being and doing what we want.

At other times, we are only buying off our own guilty consciences when we help others. What is important is not so much their need as our own peace of mind and the warm glow we get from having done a good deed.

There are two prerequisites for genuinely human help of another. First, we must recognize that the help we can give anyone is very limited. We cannot heal the deepest hurts, relieve the torments and consequences of guilt, wipe out the permanently crippling effects of wrongs suffered and inflicted. Most of the time we do not really know ourselves what is good for others. The most we can do is stand by them in their need, giving them what support we can, aware that we too are only human beings who cannnot be the saviours of men.

Secondly, our help of others will be genuinely human when we know (and do not try to hide the fact from those whom we help) that we too need the help and support of other men. Perhaps we are better off than others financially, morally, in physical and mental health, as responsible citizens and parents. But we are needy too. Perhaps not for money, but for something to fill our empty, meaningless, comfortable lives. Perhaps not to be freed from immorality but from our coldly unloving and unforgiving attitude toward those who have been immoral. Perhaps not to be cured of the diseases that some other people have, but to be cured of our own peculiar sickness—greed, fear, bitterness, a compulsive lust for prestige and social success. Perhaps some of the social nonconformists who need to learn from us how to bathe and dress properly could teach us what it means to have a sensitive and courageous concern to fight injustice. Perhaps some of the people we want to teach to be responsible providers for their families could teach us that it is equally important not to be so busy "getting ahead" that we have no time to give our families the love and attention they need more than anything else.

Every one of us in his own way needs to *be* helped, to have others stand by and with him in his own need, to learn from others. Only when we are not "too proud" to acknowledge and ask for the help *we* need, only then will we be able to give others the help they need.

"Then the LORD God said, 'It is not good that the man should be alone; I will make him a helper fit for him'" (Genesis 2:18). To be a human being in the image of God means to help and let ourselves be helped, recognizing our mutual dependence on one another.

Me, Myself and I

We have emphasized as strongly as possible that human life in the image of God is life in community. A man cannot be human by himself but only in a twofold relationship with God and fellowman. This means that Christians must stand firmly against all "rugged individualism." The individualistic desire to be independent, self-sufficient and self-centered is inhuman.

But having said that, now we must add finally that the doctrine of the creation of man in the image of God preserves *individuality* just as strongly as it condemns *individualism*. A genuine relationship between myself and another is possible only where there is a distinction between us in which I remain myself and the other remains himself. To attempt to do away with my own or the other's unique individuality is to make a real relationship between us impossible—and is just as inhuman as individualism. There is a kind of Christian talk about self-denial, self-sacrifice or selfless service which is profoundly inhuman and unchristian. And there is a kind of talk about self-assertion and self-affirmation, often regarded by Christians with suspicion, which is genuinely human and Christian.

Think first of the man-God relationship. Mysticism is a kind of religious expression in which a man seeks such complete unity with God that he literally "loses himself" in God. By giving himself totally to prayer, meditation and devotional exercises he seeks so completely to deny and rise above his existence in the world and in the body that there is no longer any self-awareness but only God-awareness. But this intense spirituality means not only that he has abandoned his fellowmen in his exclusive (and paradoxically self-centered!) concern for unity with God, but that any real relationship with God is impossible. It is far better like Job or Jeremiah to "get mad" at God, complain to him, argue with him, express my thoughts and desires in opposition to him, than to be so spiritual that no dialogue or confrontation is possible either from his side or mine, since I have in fact withdrawn myself from him by trying to pretend that there is no difference between us, who we are, what we think and desire.

Or take the husband-wife relationship. Sometimes a husband or wife thinks that to love the partner means to sacrifice all one's own desires, likes and dislikes, interests and concerns for the sake of the other. One simply dissolves himself into the other, becoming his carbon copy. But that is not love. It means really that one partner withdraws himself from the other, making both real loving and being loved impossible. How can one love the "other" when the other is only a reflection of himself? How can one expect to be loved if he or she is not even there any more as a distinct personality? To make a marriage, it takes two clearly distinct individuals, neither of whom sacrifices or denies his self, each of whom remains himself. There can be no "we" unless there are two "I's."

A political or social community which tramples individual rights (including the right *not* to conform as well as to conform to conventional patterns of life) is no more a genuine community than

one in which the insistence on individual rights is really an excuse
for social irresponsibility and anarchy (so that "my rights" means
in fact the denial of others' rights). As individuals exist only in
social relationships, so societies can exist only when the variety
and uniqueness of individuals are not only allowed but protected.
There are no individual rights apart from civil rights, and no civil
rights without individual rights.

"Christian relations" (as in ecumenical discussions) and
"Christian service" (as in ministering to the sick and needy) are
not genuinely Christian when they mean only a sweet, loving acceptance of every claim and demand of others and the surrender
of one's own unique responsibilities, tasks and convictions. How
can a doormat or an echo have a personal relationship? Might
not a permissive acceptance of others sometimes mean indifference
to them, not wanting to be bothered by them? And might it not
mean that we take them seriously and are really concerned about
them just when we take the time and trouble to assert our own
desires and opinions and convictions against them? Cannot a self-
asserting *opposition* sometimes be the sign of genuine relationship,
and self-denying surrender the sign that there is no relationship at
all?

The proper balance between individuality and community is
difficult to understand and even more difficult to achieve—as all the
examples we have given indicate. The life of every one of us is the
story of the struggle with just this problem. Who of us knows the
solution to it?

What we can say is that the clue to this puzzle is found in the
fact that God created all men with a common humanity, but he
also created them as unique individuals. We cannot understand
one without the other, for it is just as they are explained in connection with each other that man achieves his humanity in the
image of God. As male is created for female, and female for male,
so in general we cannot fulfill our humanity without our fellowmen. But as there can be no genuinely human sex relationship except when the distinction between male and female is maintained,
so we cannot be human unless we remain true to our unique individuality. As Jesus was the man who was totally and unreservedly

for other men, yet fulfilled his task just by uncompromisingly sticking to his own particular task, so we can fulfill our humanity as man-in-community only as we struggle to discover, gladly affirm and unapologetically assert who we are as the particular individuals God intended us to be.

Who are we? Who am I? We are human beings created in the image of God. And what does that mean? We can summarize everything we have said in this chapter by saying that it means: " 'You shall love the *Lord your God* with all your heart, and with all your soul, and with all your mind . . . . You shall love your *neighbor as yourself* " (Matthew 22:37–39; author's italics).

FOR FURTHER REFLECTION AND STUDY

1. Communism understands man primarily in terms of the satisfaction of his bodily needs—hence its materialistic emphasis on the economic means of production. Some Christians say that a materialistic concern about bodily needs and the economic structures which influence their satisfaction are unimportant; as Christians we are only concerned about man's soul and its eternal destiny. Which view is more accurate in light of the biblical doctrine of man in the image of God?

2. In what ways can morality be a contradiction of what man is in the image of God?

3. Is the "self-made man" who "asks no favors from anyone" but "makes his own way" and "owes nobody anything" what God created man to be?

4. In the light of Genesis 1:28 and Psalm 8:5–8, how would you answer the common charge that the Christian faith is mostly for women, children and weaklings who turn to God because they cannot face the world as it really is?

5. In what ways do we show by our dealings with the following that we do not really see people as persons but only as categories: (a) Catholics, (b) "foreigners" who live among us, (c) Jews, (d) men or women we meet, (e) conservatives or liberals.

6. Do you think it would be all right for your minister to own a red sports car? Participate in the civil rights movement?

Belong to a country club? Do everything you consider legitimate for yourself?

7. As a Christian, do you think America should have diplomatic relations with such atheistic countries as Russia or China? What light does this chapter throw on this question?

8. Can you think of any ways slum dwellers might "help" people who live in middle-class suburbs?

9. What is the difference between respect for individuality and individualism?

10. Read the description of marriage in Ephesians 5:21–33. Does this first-century idea of a Christian marriage help us to understand a twentieth-century marriage in which there is both individuality and community?

11. What is the relation between individual rights and civil rights?

12. Look at the list you made at the beginning of this chapter. Would you change it now?

11

Why Don't You Just Be Yourself?

THE DOCTRINE OF
SIN

I'm sorry. I didn't mean to say that. I'm just not myself today.

He's not really a bad boy. He's just trying to find himself.

Why don't you stop being so mean, and just be yourself?

He's not even human; he's just an animal.

You have to get hold of yourself, or you'll just go to pieces. Pull yourself together.

That guy thinks he's God Almighty.

All these everyday expressions we use to talk about ourselves and other people acknowledge the self-contradiction that plagues all our lives. "I am not myself" says illogically but realistically, "I am not what I am." Trying to "find" or "be" or "get hold of" myself is admitting the illogical but true predicament we are all in: I am somehow separated from my inmost, truest self. A human being by definition is not and cannot be animal or God, yet all of us sometimes act as if we were what we are not and cannot be.

This self-contradiction which makes life so hard to understand and live is the symptom of what Christian theology calls *sin*. This is what we are going to talk about in this chapter.

We have already indirectly defined what sin is. In the last chapter we learned that to be a human being means to be created in the image of God. And that means: (1) life received from and lived for God in a relationship of thankful dependence and active obedience; (2) life with and for our fellowmen in a relationship of mutual openness and help; (3) life that is self-affirming and self-fulfilling when we live as man-in-relationship with God and fellowmen. But the more concrete we became about what it means to be man in the image of God, the clearer it became that no man (with one exception) ever lived such a life. In various ways, all of us try to live without or against God and our fellowmen, and in so doing we deny our own humanity. That is what lies behind the self-contradiction expressed in the daily recognition that we need to "be" or "find" or "get hold of" ourselves. Our basic problem, to use the strong language of The Heidelberg Catechism, is that though we are our true selves only in community with them, we are prone to *hate* God and our neighbor (Q. 5). This is the sin we have to try to understand.

Is it not putting it a little too strongly to say that our trouble in finding and being ourselves is that we *hate* God and our fellowmen? After all, we are Christian, not atheists, communists, Nazis, heathen, or criminals! *Why* do we have such trouble being ourselves—or even knowing for sure what we would be if we were? *Why* do we sometimes try to live like animals or play God? These are the specific questions which will concern us.

Before we begin, we must be clear about where we stand when we speak of sin from a Christian point of view. We must take sin very seriously, but not too seriously. Contrary to the impression we are sometimes given, sin is not the main theme and central emphasis of the Christian faith. We see this both when we look at the doctrine of man in the image of God and when we look at the doctrine of Christ.

In the first place, from the point of view of the doctrine of man, we must talk with dead seriousness about man (ourselves) as sinner, but we must not suggest that this is the basic truth about what man is. The basic truth is not that we are sinners, but that we are human beings created in the image of God. Sin distorts, twists, corrupts and contradicts this truth, but it does not change into something else this human life God made. Sin is not stronger than God. In the Bible, even sinful man is still recognized as man in the image of God (Genesis 9:6; James 3:9). We may disobey God, and we may turn against our fellowmen, but we cannot really escape either. By our very nature we are dependent upon and responsible to God and bound to our fellowmen. We may refuse to acknowledge, but we cannot escape, the relatedness of our lives as human beings. Sin may become "second nature" to us, but it is never really "natural." What we are naturally is what God created us to be. All men are sinners, but their sinfulness is something *unnatural*.[1] That is why our sinfulness is such a problem. We keep trying to be what we are not, but we can never bring it off. No matter how hard we try, no matter how we ruin our own and other's lives in the attempt, we can no more really live without God and our neighbor than a chicken can turn itself into a duck and learn to swim. We may kill ourselves trying, but we cannot turn ourselves from the human beings God made us into animals or substitute gods.

We can express the same thing by pointing out that in the Bible the very word "sin" itself has only a negative meaning. It means *departure* from what is normal, to *miss* the real and true way, to get lost or miss the goal. Dangerous and destructive as it is, sin is not the truth about man, but the distortion, twisting or denial of the truth. (It would be helpful here to look up the word "sin" in one of the theological word books.) Humanity and not inhumanity, the meaning and realization of a *right* relationship with God and fellowmen—that is what Christians are primarily interested in.

We see the same thing from the point of view of Christian faith in Christ. It is no accident that, when we confess our faith in the Apostles' Creed, sin is mentioned only when we say that we believe in the *forgiveness* of sin. Although he certainly reckoned with its reality, Jesus himself never speculated about sin as such or even explained what he understood by it. And the followers of Jesus do not "believe in" sin. We believe that "Jesus Christ died for our sins" (1 Corinthians 15:3). Paul did not come preaching the bad news of sin but the *good* news of the Christ who loves and helps sinners (1 Corinthians 2:2). We must talk about sin in order to understand the forgiveness of sin, Christ's death for our sins, or the good news that in him God was and is at work in the world and in our lives to overcome and free us from sin. But the fact remains that sin is neither the first nor the last nor the most important word

about who we are. We give sin too much honor when we give it
such a central place.

So if we have to talk about sin now, we do it only "in passing"
—in passing from the humanity God gave us in creation to the *new*
humanity he is restoring in us, in passing from the work of God the
Father who made us in his own image to the work of God the Son
who *renews* in us that image (Colossians 3:10).

Three Basic Forms of Sin

We can best understand the meaning of sin as self-destructive
breaking of relationship with God and fellowmen by looking at
some of the forms in which sin appears.

1. Sin as disobedience. Most of the Reformed confessions, following one emphasis of biblical thought, define sin as
disobedience to the law of God. If we are to understand sin as disobedience correctly, however, we must be very careful to understand the law of God in the radical sense in which Jesus interpreted
it, and not in the way moralistic, legalistic thinkers since the Pharisees have always understood it. What the law of God requires is
ourselves (our hearts, to use the biblical terminology), not just certain external actions. And what it forbids is the withholding of ourselves, not just the doing of certain bad things. The intention of the
whole law and of every part of it, in other words, is the commandment that we love God with our whole being and our neighbor as
ourselves. Doing things which in themselves may be quite proper,
but doing them without love; or *not* doing these things which love
requires—this is disobedience to the law of God.

In relation to God, sin as disobedience is not just being irreli-
gous or breaking the Ten Commandments. Disobedience can also
take very pious, religious forms. Sin is obeying all the commandments, perhaps very strictly, not because we love and trust God, but
to get something out of him. It is treating our relation to him as a
business deal, trying to use him for personal success and happiness
(tithing because you get a good return on your investment) or
seeking only to save ourselves when we die (see Matthew 16:25).
Sin is not just making graven images of wood or gold, but

trying to make God himself into the image of a white, middle-class American and thus worshiping ourselves even as we pretend to worship him.

Sin is taking the Lord's name in vain not only by cursing, but also by making it trivial. It is using "God" or "God's will" only to justify our own personal, social or national prejudices and ambitions—or, on the other hand, claiming to be Christians whose lives belong to God, but saying that religion has nothing to do with practical matters.

Sin as disobedience in relation to our fellowman is not only the external act of adultery. It is *wanting* to commit adultery (Matthew 5:27). It is living in a legally "pure" marriage without love and compassion for the partner. It is being legally faithful, while in fact only using the partner to satisfy one's own needs, pleasure, comfort, desire for social status, or quest for security.

Sin is not just lynching or shooting Negroes or killing six million Jews. It is having contempt for any human being (Matthew 5:21–24). It is not only actively murdering other people, but simply letting them starve to death physically and emotionally because we decide social welfare and foreign aid are "money down a rathole."

Sin is not just robbing banks. It is also stealing other people's money by false advertising. It is not just taking advantage of people and leaving them lying in a ditch. It is also "passing by on the other side" when we see people in city slums helplessly at the mercy of unscrupulous landlords and indifferent politicians.

Sin, to sum it all up, *is* disobedience to the law of God. But it is not just something those immoral, unbelieving outsiders do. It is something *we* do. More than that, they and we do not just *do* sinful things; we *are* sinners—"in our hearts." Sin as disobedience means that we as well as they must confess, "*I* am by nature prone to hate God and my neighbor." Whoever cannot say that honestly has not yet learned what disobedience to the law of God is.

2. Sin as sensuality.

When most of us hear the word "sin," we think first of all of "worldly" or "fleshly" pleasures— wine, women and song. While the Bible knows that sin may express itself in this form, it is by no means the center of the biblical doctrine of sin. Why then do we automatically think first of all along these lines? There are probably two main reasons. First of all, adultery, drunkenness and other physical lusts are "safe" sins to talk about in the church. They are more prevalent (or at least more visible) among people outside the church, and no one is offended so long as we are talking about other people's sins. It is easier to talk about sexual immorality and liquor than about the sin of social injustice, which is emphasized just as strongly in the Bible. Secondly, the emphasis on sin as sensuality enables us to blame sin on our bodies, to tell ourselves that though the "flesh" tempts us to do bad things, our "heart is in the right place," or we "mean well." We may *do* sinful things, but we are not "basically" sinful. Once again we run into the classical Greek idea that man's lower (evil) physical self is a drag on his higher (good) spiritual nature.

We can learn the true meaning of sin as sensuality only on three conditions.

a. We must not forget that it is only *one* form sin can take. If we are better off than some others in this respect, that does not mean we are less sinful than they. It would be hard to argue that the moral, law-abiding Pharisees were less sinful than the prostitutes, wine-bibbers and tax collectors—especially in the light of Matthew 21:31–32 and Luke 18:10–14 (not to mention the part the Pharisees played in the crucifixion of Christ).

b. We can think correctly of sin as sensuality only when we remember that the source of *all* sin is the "heart." We must look for the root of sexual immorality, drunkenness, gluttony, and so on, not in the body but in the *self*. When the New Testament speaks of "sinful flesh" (Romans 8:3) or living "according to the flesh" (Romans 8:12), it is not referring to the body alone, but to the whole personality of sinful men. Thus the "works of the flesh," according to Galatians 5:19 ff., include physical sins: immorality, impurity, licentiousness, drunkenness, carousing and the like. But "works of the flesh" are also such nonsensual sins as idolatry, enmity, strife, jealousy, anger, selfishness, dissension, party spirit and envy. And Paul does not suggest that one kind of "fleshly" sin is worse than the other. The point is, man's body is no more sinful in itself than his heart, soul or spirit; and his heart, soul or spirit are no less sinful than his body. *I* am sinful—not just my body.

c. Finally, it follows from what we have just said that we can understand the sinfulness of physical immorality only when we think about it in *personal* terms. The act of stuffing too much food in the stomach or swallowing too much alcohol is not in itself sinful. Extra-marital sexual intercourse is not sinful just because two bodies are joined. "Petting" that refrains from "going all the way" can be just as sinful as the act itself. On the other hand, a sexual union that is "legal" is not necessarily free from sin.

The important question is *why* one becomes a glutton or a drunkard. Does one drink or eat too much because he makes himself into a god through inordinate self-love—or because he makes himself into an animal by thinking only of physical pleasure? Why does he want to escape his humanity in one way or the other? Is it self-love or self-hatred? How does drunkenness or gluttony affect a person's relationship with God and with wife or husband or children?

With regard to sexuality, what is the *meaning* of any particular sexual union, whether outside or inside a legal marriage relationship? Is it a wrong kind of self-love which only uses the other, as if I were God and the other my possession? Or is it idolatry that makes a god not of myself but of the other? ("He worships the ground she walks on." "She adores him.") Or is it genuinely *human* on both sides? What kind of personal relationship with God and the partner does it express?

Sin expresses itself in wrong sensuality of various kinds. But we will never understand it so long as we think only about liquor or calories or sex instead of *people* who are what they are in their personal relationships.[2]

3. Sin as the desire to be good. *"The Lord God* commanded the man, saying, 'You may freely eat of every tree of the garden; but of the tree of the knowledge of good and evil you shall not eat, for in the day that you eat of it you shall die' " (Genesis 2:16–17). "But the *serpent* said, 'You will not die. For God knows that when you eat of it your eyes will be opened, and you will be like God, knowing good and evil' " (Genesis 3:4–5).

What is the sin of Adam (which means "man")? Disobedience? Yes, because he does what God commanded him not to do. Sensuality? Perhaps. Nothing is said of sexuality as the root of sin. But it is said that "the woman saw that the tree was good for food, and that it was a delight to the eyes" (Genesis 3:6). But the deeper meaning of the story is that man wants to be *like* God. He is not content to be a *human* being in the *image* of God; he wants to be *divine*, God himself. Why? Several answers can be given—an indication of how profound this story is. We could say that the root and essence of sin is *pride*: Man wants to be more than he is. He is not content to be dependent on God, to let himself be loved and cared for by God. He wants to be self-sufficient and independent, to do whatever he pleases, and to know everything so that he does not need to ask or learn or receive anything. Or we could say that the root and essence of sin is *unbelief*: Man does not believe that he can trust God to give him everything he needs and to tell him how he should live, so he tries to do for himself and give himself what only God can do for him and give him. He does not believe that he is really safe and secure under the care and command of God, so he tries to take care of himself, tell himself how to live. Pride and unbelief go hand in hand.

But the point we want to emphasize now is that the concrete expression of sin in this story is man's desire to "know good and evil." The desire to tell ourselves and know for ourselves the difference between good and evil is *sin*. According to the Adam story, the root and essence of *all* sin! How can that be true? Is not the whole purpose of going to church school and church, reading the Bible, praying, and living a Christian life to know just this, and to be good and not evil? No wonder some thinkers have said that the fall of Adam was a fall *upward*! Does not a man *make progress* when he learns to distinguish between good and evil?

But the Genesis story traces the desire to be like God in this way to the Devil. This desire is the essence of sin in all three of its basic forms.

a. The desire to know good and evil is *rebellion against God*. God alone is good, and he alone knows what is good and not good. To want to know and be good by ourselves (to "establish our own righteousness," as Romans 10:2 puts it) means that we do not want to depend on God, to learn afresh every new day, in every new decision and situation, what is good and what is not good. We want to know for ourselves, by ourselves. And as soon as we think we *do* know, then we begin to feel competent not only to dictate to other people but to dictate to God himself what he must be and do and say *if* he is really good. Nor do we want day by day constantly to receive from him the ability to *do* what is good and avoid evil. We want to have the ability in ourselves. And as soon as we think we do have it, then we become certain that "good" is by definition what I, and those who are like me, want and do. We no longer need to be judged and corrected by God; we ourselves have become the infallible judges of good and evil—*in place of* God. And that is sin—the sin of good people!

b. The desire to be like God, knowing good and evil, is *enmity against our fellowmen.* Who is more dangerous than the man who is sure he knows both for himself and for everyone else what is good and what is not good? Who is more inhuman than the man who is sure he is in a position to judge other men but does not need to be judged himself? What crimes against fellowmen have been and are committed by "good" men who are sure of their own superior wisdom and virtue and therefore sure that anyone different from them is evil and foolish and must therefore be "helped" to be good like themselves—by force, if necessary. How demonic are people who think they are *like* God, *knowing* good and evil!

c. The desire to be like God, knowing good and evil, is *self-destructive.* The man who is sure he has arrived in knowing and being good is just the man who has cut himself off from the very relationship with God and fellowman in which his own humanity consists. In his independence from needing to learn and be helped by God and by fellowmen, he does not become really free. He becomes the slave of his own self-deception, arrogance and inhumanity. He does not become like God; he becomes like Satan. Who knows but what the man dehumanized by his pretended knowledge of good and evil is not worse off than the man dehumanized by liquor or sex. The "good" man does not even know that he has destroyed himself in trying to be like God.

We can sum up everything we have been trying to say about

what sin is by going back to what we said at the beginning of our discussion. Whether expressed in terms of disobedience, sensuality, pride or unbelief, sin always means broken relationships. It means not being what we are as human beings in the image of God, human beings who are ourselves only as we live for God and for our fellowmen. Or in short, *sin is not loving and not being willing to let ourselves be loved.* Only when we get beyond thinking of sin as immorality or irreligiousness and understand this can we know what we are saying when we confess that there is "no health in us." Only when we learn that, however moral, law-abiding and religious we are, we are still "miserable offenders"—only then will we understand the power of sin in our lives.

Original Sin

A mother says to herself at the breakfast table, "I'm going to do better today. I won't get impatient with the children as I did yesterday." But when she goes to bed that night, she feels guilty, knowing that, despite her good intentions, today was yesterday all over again.

"I'll be more understanding, more forgiving, more open, more courageous in standing for what I know is right—more Christian." Who of us has not decided that over and over again, only to discover over and over again that we *should* but *can't*—or *could* but *don't?*

What we are up against is "original sin." The problem lies in two apparently contradictory truths: (1) *Sin is inevitable.* All men, everywhere, always, have lived in self-contradiction to their true being in the image of God. (How is the universality of sin expressed in Romans 3:10–12; Genesis 8:21; Psalm 143:2?) But if *all* men are sinners, then *every* man must be a sinner. There is no man who can *not* sin. (2) Nevertheless, *every man is responsible for his sinfulness.* No one forces me not to love God and my fellowmen. It is *I* who sin, and I know that I am guilty, even if I do not want to do it, and cannot help doing it. All of us are caught in the trap William Faulkner so accurately describes when he has a character in *Requiem for a Nun* say paradoxically about sin, "You ain't got to. You can't help it."

Christian theology has tried to understand this predicament

of our inevitable yet responsible guilt by connecting it with the sin of Adam. Read Romans 5:12–21 and 1 Corinthians 15:22 to see how Paul makes the connection. We shall consider two ways in which the relation between Adam and "all men" has been interpreted within the Reformed tradition.

1. Inherited sin. The classical explanation of why all men are sinners, and cannot *not* be sinners, was first formulated by Augustine. Most Reformed confessions follow him. The first man Adam sinned and his "sinful nature" has been passed down to all other men as a "hereditary disease, wherewith infants themselves are infected even in their mother's womb" (Belgic Confession, Art. XV). We are connected with Adam and his sin by our biological descent from him.

a. This explanation has some things in its favor. It seems logical and even "scientific." We know that some characteristics are inherited. Why not sinfulness also?

It also seems to have a biblical foundation. Did not Paul say that sin came into the world through one man and spread to all other men? Does not Psalm 51:5 say, "I was brought forth in iniquity, and in sin did my mother conceive me"?

b. But there are some *disadvantages* also. For one thing,

If this view is correct, how can anyone be held any more responsible for his sinful nature and sinful acts than for the fact that he inherited blue eyes or insanity? The doctrine of inherited sin is not consistent with the biblical view that every man is accountable for his own sin. The Bible does teach, "You can't help it." But it also teaches, "You ain't *got* to."

Furthermore, in the background of the doctrine of inherited sin is the unbiblical idea that sex is the root of all sin, and that sexual intercourse is responsible for the spread of sin from parents to children.

Another disadvantage is that, while the Bible does connect the sinfulness of all men with Adam, it says nothing at all about a cause-and-effect hereditary connection. Even Psalm 51:5 means only that I have been a sinner since my birth. In the Bible sin has to do with personal relationships. It is not a medical problem of genes and chromosomes, semen, and the prenatal period.

Finally, the biological explanation of the connection between Adam and us tends to distract attention from the one way in which sin and guilt are transmitted from person to person, generation to generation—not by sexual intercourse but by the fact of social solidarity. By their bigoted attitudes and practices, for example, parents can pass on bigotry to their children. Members of a society which deliberately or by negligence deprives some people of economic, religious and educational opportunities share in the guilt if those people become criminals. This *social* solidarity of sinful men is far more biblical than the strangely mechanical view that the solidarity is only *biological,* because the social view understands man not as an animal but as man in community.

2. **Adam as the representative man.** Another interpretation of the connection between Adam and all men works not with biological but juridical or legal images. It says, in the language of classical theology, that Adam is the "federal head" of the human race, and that God "imputes" his sin to us (see Westminster Confession, VI, 3). Expressed in contemporary language, this view says that Adam is not just the first man at the beginning of history. The word "Adam" means simply "man" in Hebrew. The story of Adam is the story of *every* man. What Adam did, every man does. What he was, we all are. The meaning of all history, including our own, is revealed in his history, for men in all times simply repeat over and over again Adam's rebellion against God, with the same consequences. If I want to understand who I am and what I am like, I have to look at him. I *am* Adam.

a. These are the advantages of this interpretation. It avoids the fatalistic, deterministic view of the doctrine of hereditary sin. Adam has not poisoned the human race or passed down an inescapable disease or infection. No one *has* to be Adam. "You ain't *got* to"! All men do repeat Adam's sin, but they do so on their own responsibility, by their own choice. Sin is not a fate forced on us; it is what *we* are and do.

Second, this interpretation understands sin personally. It is an interpretation of Adam's and our relation to God and fellowmen. It is the truth about *us,* not about an impersonal disease or defect.

Third, this interpretation is also biblical. It maintains Paul's

understanding of all men in connection with Adam, without looking for an artificial, nonbiblical connection between us in terms of
heredity. Moreover, we can accept this "representative" interpretation whether we think of Adam literally as the first man in history,
or as a parable about all men.

b. From one point of view, of course, the representative view
of Adam has a big *disadvantage*. It does not explain, as does the
biological view, *how* or *why* it is that all men, everywhere, always,
do what Adam did. It simply states that this is the predicament we
are all in: "You ain't *got* to. You can't help it." We can't blame
Adam or anyone else for the fact that over and over again, in all the
many variations we have discussed, we rebel against God, turn
against our fellowman, and contradict our own true humanity. No
one forces us to be Adam. But on the other hand, we can't help it.
We *are* Adam. No matter how good our intentions, how often we
"turn over a new leaf," how firmly we set out to "get hold of ourselves," we *cannot* love God with our whole being and our neighbor as ourselves, not even when we believe that it is the key to real
self-fulfillment. As soon as we overcome sin in one form (immorality, for instance), it crops up in another (an unforgiving attitude
toward those who are not as "good" as we).

"You ain't *got* to. You can't help it." That is an illogical, contradictory, impossible statement. But that's the way life is. That's
the trap we are in. And the real problem is not how we can explain
the intellectual puzzle of our responsibility for sin that is inevitable. The real problem is whether and how we can get out of this
trap.

The Consequences of Sin

We can summarize the results of this chapter and catch a
glimpse of where we go from here by discussing the meaning of
two consequences of Adam's (our) sin—total depravity and death.

1. **Total depravity.** The man who "falls" from his
humanity in the image of God as man-for-God and man-for-
fellowman is, according to the Reformed confessions, "unable to do
good, and prone to evil" (The Heidelberg Catechism, Q. 7). He is

"wicked, perverse, and corrupt in all his ways" (Belgic Confession, Art. XIV). He no longer has the "free will" to do good, but has become a "slave to sin" (Second Helvetic Confession, IX; Belgic Confession, Art. XIV; Westminster Confession, XI).

We must be very careful how we interpret such statements about this "total depravity" of all men if we are not to confirm the idea of many people that Calvinists are cynical, sour people who believe in sin more than anything else, refuse to see any good anywhere, always look around suspiciously for the real evil under every apparent good, and especially denounce any good that non-Christians accomplish.

All men (including those who are moral and religious) are sinners. But that does not mean that there is no difference between an Albert Schweitzer and an Adolf Hitler. It would be absurd to say that since, according to Jesus, a man who lusts is guilty of adultery, there is no difference between a "girl watcher" and a rapist. Or that there is no difference between a man who is angry with his neighbor and a man who shoots his neighbor. The extreme statements in the confessions do not mean that all men are monsters or devils, or that all men are equally "bad."

Nor do the statements in the confessions about the inability of sinful men to do any good mean that there is no progress in history, and that it is useless for Christians to have anything to do with the attempt to make the world a better place to live in. The abolition of slavery, the gradual realization that women are human beings and not property, the achievement of a democratic government, the reforms to make treatment of prisoners and the mentally sick more humane—such achievements are certainly progress, progress sometimes made by unbelievers and mere humanists without the help, and even despite the opposition, of Christians who said that nothing can or should be done in this hopelessly sinful world!

Total depravity, correctly understood, means that although both Christians *and* non-Christians can do much good, no part of any man's being (body, mind, soul or spirit) and nothing he does (including very moral, heroic or religious acts) are free from the corruption of sin. It means that although there may be all kinds of progress in history, man himself stays monotonously the same. (We are no longer savages who cruelly throw hundreds of our enemies to the crocodiles. Now we are savages who neatly kill hundreds of thousands with a bomb developed through scientific progress.)

We are obviously "free" to do many things: to go to church or stay home, to be honest or dishonest in our business relations, moral or immoral in our sexual relations, just or unjust in our political relations. And it makes a great deal of difference how we use this freedom. But "total depravity" means that we are *not* free to be and do what matters most. We are not free wholeheartedly, without reservation or qualification, to love and let ourselves be loved by God and the people with whom we live. But that means that we are not free really to be ourselves. In this sense, good and bad people alike, we are "slaves to sin"—slaves trapped by the anxiety, the division within ourselves and the self-contradictions which result from the twisted relationships in which we all live. And this is a trap from which we cannot free ourselves, no matter how hard we try.

2. **Death.** That is the second consequence of sin. "'In the day you eat of it you shall die'" (Genesis 2:17). The "wages of sin is death" (Romans 6:23). What is meant here is not just physical death, which in itself is only a sign of the fact that we are finite creatures. It is the death Paul speaks of when he speaks of being "dead through the trespasses and sins" (Ephesians 2:1). It is the death John refers to when he says, "He who does not love remains in death" (1 John 3:14). Sinful man—that is, man who does not or cannot love, who hates, who because of pride or fear refuses to "get involved," who avoids genuine encounters with God and other men by using them only to serve himself—that man is *dead*. He is dead even though he may still be walking around and acting as if he were alive. He is "dead inside," as we express it in everyday language.

To say that the sinner is dead in his sin is to say first of all that just as a dead man cannot make himself alive again, neither can we help ourselves out of our self-contradictory inability to live in real community with God, our families, our associates, other nations, races or classes. The power of sin over us is as strong as the power of death itself.

Secondly, the point of saying that the "wages" of sin is death is not so much a warning about what God will do to us as a warning about the self-destruction we bring on ourselves when we contradict our humanity in his image. As a matter of fact, the whole Bible bears witness to the truth that from his side God still loves and is still faithful even to the men who are no longer faithful to him. The Bible does not end with the Genesis story of the fall of man and the death it brings. That is only the beginning!

Proneness by nature to hate, slavery to sin, separation and alienation, living death, inhumanity: Such subjects have been the main theme of this chapter. But this theme is not the main theme either of the Bible or of the Christian faith. The main theme is one who brings love, freedom, righteousness, real community, life—humanity! Precisely to *sinful* men! We cannot understand the joyful main theme apart from the tragic secondary theme. But we must not peer too long into the darkness, lest we come to love darkness rather than light. It is time now that we turn to the light which shines into the darkness.

FOR FURTHER REFLECTION AND STUDY
1. Is sin "doing what comes naturally"?
2. Read Exodus 20:1–17. Stop after you read each commandment and ask yourself whether you could honestly respond with the words of The Heidelberg Catechism, "By nature I am prone to hate God and my neighbor" (Q. 5).
3. Is it legitimate to be a Christian because it "pays off" in happiness, success and peace of mind?
4. "My husband has been a Methodist all his life, but if it comes to choosing between being a Methodist and an American, he'll be an American every time."[3] Do you consider this a sinful statement? Why? Why not?
5. Is a loveless marriage as sinful as adultery?
6. Read Romans 14:1–23 and 1 Corinthians 8:1–13. Do these passages give us any guidance about how Christians should deal

with the problem of drinking? What about sex ethics?

7. Remembering the basic meaning of sin, do you think hard work motivated by greed is less sinful than laziness motivated by irresponsibility?

8. "Hell is the home of honor, duty, justice, and the rest of the seven deadly virtues. All the wickedness on earth is done in their name."[4] Do you agree with G. B. Shaw?

9. "You ain't *got* to. You can't help it." Do you think these words of Faulkner about sin are an accurate description of the human predicament?

10. Do you think it is proper to speak of "inherited" sin? Does Paul teach it in Romans 5:12–21?

11. Is "total depravity" a misleading description of man's sinfulness? Why? Why not?

12. Read 1 John 3:14–18. How would you explain John's statement, "He who does not love remains in death"?

GOD
THE SON
and
RECONCILIATION

PART IV

GOD THE SON
and
RECONCILIATION

"I believe in God the Father Almighty . . . ; And in Jesus Christ his only Son our Lord." Conceived, born, suffered, crucified, dead, buried, descended, rose, ascended, sitteth at the right hand, from whence he shall come—these words of the "second article" of the Apostles' Creed suggest three things we must keep in mind throughout our study of God the Son and his work.

1. When we come to this part of Christian theology, we do not come to just one doctrine among others. It is no accident that the part of the creed dealing with Christ is the longest part. This is the one doctrine which gives meaning and content to all others. All the doctrines of the Christian faith are related to Christ as spokes to the hub of a wheel. We could not talk about who God is, how we know him, what he is like and what he wants with us, without talking about the revelation of himself, his will and his work in Christ. Nor could we talk about what it means to be human beings in the image of God, and sinners who contradict their own humanity, without talking about the man Jesus. We shall see that the same holds true in the parts of the Christian faith that are still before us. It is only by looking at Christ that we know who the Holy Spirit is, what the church is all about and how the present and future of the world can be understood. We stand here at the very center of the Christian faith. Everything else Christians believe stands or falls with what they believe about Jesus.

That means we must proceed very carefully here. And very

modestly. For we come now to a mystery no man can grasp and
master. No one ever reaches the point at which he can say, "Now I
understand. Now I have it." Whoever thinks that he understands
everything here, has it neatly wrapped up in a nice system, and no
longer needs to listen and let what he thinks he already knows be
corrected only proves that he understands nothing. This does not
mean that we must not try to understand as best we can who Jesus
Christ is and what he means. But it does mean that we never reach
the end of our attempt to understand. When you have finished this
part of our study, you will have been successful if you can say,
"Now I understand a *little* better and see a *little* more clearly."

2. What do we believe? When the church confesses its faith,
it does not say, "I believe in the virgin birth, the substitutionary
atonement, and the empty tomb." We believe in "Jesus Christ his
only Son our Lord"—in a *person*. The doctrines concerning his
birth, death and resurrection are necessary if we are to articulate
our faith. But they are not themselves the object of our faith. Our
trust, hope and confidence are in him and him alone. We must take
doctrines *about* him very seriously, but we must never confuse even
the most orthodox doctrine with genuine Christian faith. We may
in fact be comforted by the fact that faith in him can be real, even
though our ability to express that faith in words is always imperfect
and fallible. As we begin our study of "Christology" (the doctrine
of Christ), we must keep constantly in mind that our main concern
is with Jesus himself, not with our ideas about him—not even our
right ideas.

3. Who is this person who stands at the center of the Christian
faith? It is significant that the Apostles' Creed speaks of him with
verbs: born, crucified, rose, ascended, and so on. It does not give
us an explanation of his nature or a theoretical discourse on his
deity and humanity. It simply tells a story. It says who he is in
terms of some things that happened. We learn who Jesus *is*, in
other words, by looking at what he *does*. This is also the way the
New Testament talks about him. It tries to understand who Jesus
is in terms of various "titles" which describe how he acts: Lord,
Son, Servant, High Priest, Shepherd, Messiah, and so on. All these
titles describe *functions* which Jesus fulilled. This action-oriented

way of talking about Jesus in the Bible and in the creed is more important than it may seem at first glance. Who is Jesus? We cannot answer that question by speculating about his "essence" or his "nature." We can only answer by looking at what he has *done* and what has *happened* to him. He is one who speaks with authority, heals, serves, loves, obeys, commands, forgives, judges, prays, suffers, triumphs, rules. Consider the meaning of these *actions* and you will learn the secret of who he *is*. This means that we cannot separate the "person" of Jesus from his "work," as theologians have sometimes done in the past. We can only learn who the person is *from* and *in* his work. As we go about our study of Christology we must keep in mind that it is not an intellectual puzzle we are working at but an interpretation of history.

The question before us, then, is, Who is this person who stands at the beginning, middle and end of everything Christians believe, and whom we come to know in the story of his life and works? We shall try to answer this one question by asking three different questions.

Chapter 12: "Where Is God?" The Christian answers this question by affirming that God is "with us" and by trying to say what this means with the doctrine of the incarnation.

Chapter 13: "Is God Against Us?" The Christian answers that "God was in Christ reconciling the world to himself" and tries to explain what this means with the doctrine of the atonement.

Chapter 14: Who's in Charge Here? Christians answer, "God has made him both Lord and Christ, this Jesus whom you crucified" (Acts 2:36), and try to explain this with the doctrine of the resurrection.

12

Where Is God?

"Conceived by the Holy Ghost, born of the Virgin Mary."
"Round yon virgin mother and child."
We say it and sing it in church. Once a year we even blast it
over loudspeakers in drugstores and supermarkets. Non-Christians
shake their heads in amusement or amazement over this "primitive
mythology." Christians, especially theologians and preachers,
sometimes fight bitterly over it. But what does it mean? Why all
the fuss? In this chapter we are going to talk about who Jesus is and
what the incarnation means in light of the Christmas stories in Matthew and Luke and of the church's doctrine of the virgin birth
which depends on them. This is not the only way we could do it. We
shall see in a moment that other biblical writers can talk about who
Jesus is without mentioning his miraculous birth. But we shall take
this as our point of reference because the classical creeds and confessions of all churches confess it, because it is important that we
know what we are saying when we repeat the creed, and because
both those who defend and those who reject the virgin birth often
do so for the wrong reasons.

Some Christians in all sincerity confess, "I believe in Jesus
Christ his only Son our Lord," but do not think it necessary to confess that he was "conceived by the Holy Ghost and born of the Virgin Mary." They point out that the story of Jesus' birth is recorded
only in Matthew and Luke. It is not mentioned in Mark or John.
Paul never mentions it in any of his letters, nor do any of the other

New Testament writings. It is not mentioned in the earliest summaries of the Christian gospel and of the first Christian preaching in 1 Corinthians 15:3 f. or Acts 2:22–36. (What *is* mentioned in these texts as the center of the Christian faith?) Does this not indicate that many of the first Christians, including Paul himself, could be real Christians without talking about (perhaps without even knowing about) the story of Jesus' miraculous birth? Were not the birth stories of Matthew and Luke added later to try to explain how or prove that Jesus is really the Son of God? And do they not fail to prove what they are supposed to prove, since they both trace the genealogy of Jesus to Joseph rather than to Mary?

Other Christians defend the birth narratives by suggesting that they could have been such common knowledge that it was unnecessary for the other biblical writers to mention them. Is it not significant that after the birth stories, Joseph is very seldom mentioned, whereas Mary is mentioned fairly often? It could be argued that the genealogies intend only to show that, through Joseph, Jesus had a legal but not a natural connection with the line of David.

After we have listened to all the arguments on both sides, it is hard to argue that "one cannot be a *real* Christian without believing in the virgin birth." Why could not a person, without knowing about or accepting the birth narratives, believe that in his life, death and resurrection Jesus is really God himself with us, our Lord and Savior? What concerns us now, however, is not to argue this point but to ask about the *meaning* of these stories. Some Christians have trouble with them because they do not understand what Matthew and Luke and the Christian tradition following them really meant to say. Other Christians, as we have already said, vigorously defend the virgin birth for the wrong reasons. In what follows we shall try to understand what we are saying when we confess "conceived by the Holy Ghost, born of the Virgin Mary." Our purpose, remember, is not to understand the doctrine for its own sake, but to learn from it who Jesus is.[1]

Real God and Real Man

Whatever else they may mean, the birth stories of Jesus emphasize the Christian belief that "God with us" (Matthew 1:

23) is not just a beautiful idea or an abstract theological truth. It *happened!* John also tells us that it happened when he says that the "Word" (God's self-communication, the Word which was God himself) "became flesh and dwelt among us" (John 1:1–14). But Matthew and Luke tell us more specifically that it happened at a particular time, in a particular place, in connection with a particular mother: "In the days of Herod the king," "when Quirinius was governor of Syria," in Bethlehem, of Mary. When we speak about God's presence and activity in the world, in a man dwelling among us, we are not talking only about a "spiritual presence" or a "feeling" of God's nearness or God "in our hearts." We are talking about *geography:* He was born in Palestine. We are talking about *politics:* He was born when a census was being taken, when there was danger of political revolution, and he himself was expected to be a political revolutionary (Luke 1:51–53; Matthew 2:3–5, 16). We are talking about *economics:* He himself was poor, born in a barn, and he came to help the poor (Luke 1:53; 6:20 ff.). In short, we are not just talking about religious ideas and doctrines; we are talking about *history.*

It is obviously a history which cannot be proved or verified. In the first place, not only the birth stories but the story of *all* Jesus' life is preserved for us not by objective historians but by people who believed in him and who wrote in order to convince other people to share their faith. They were prejudiced witnesses who did not just stick to the facts but *interpreted* what they had heard and seen in the light of their faith. Even if some unbiased newspaper reporters with TV cameras and tape recorders had been there at his birth and during his life, still we could not prove that in this helpless baby, this itinerant preacher, this dying man, God himself was at work reconciling the world to himself. Even if we had a medical report, not just the word of believing witnesses, to prove that he really died and lived again, we still would not have proved that God raised him and made him Lord over all things.

Nevertheless, the stories of the birth of Jesus (to limit ourselves now to this part of the history) tell us that it is into the real world of flesh and blood men that God comes—whether it can be proved and verified or not. The Christmas story is anything but the sentimental, harmless, once-a-year occasion for a "Christmas spirit" that lasts only a few days before we return to the "facts" of the "real world." Christmas is the story of a radical invasion of God into the kind of real world where we live all year long—a world where there is political unrest and injustice, poverty, hatred, jealousy, and both the fear and the longing that things could be different. John tells us that when Jesus comes "the light shines in the darkness" (John 1: 5). Matthew and Luke tell us just what the darkness is into which the light shines. It is the same darkness in which *we* live. John tells us that the "Word became flesh." Matthew and Luke emphasize that it is the same flesh we know—that of a man who came into the world the same way and lived under the same threatening conditions we do. John says it happened. Matthew and Luke say that it did not happen only in sermons or in Christmas plays at church; it happened also *outside* the church, in the *world.*

The incarnation of God in the man Jesus does not mean that Jesus is half God and half man. To put it bluntly, "conceived by the Holy Ghost" does not mean that the Holy Spirit is a substitute for the human male in the conception and birth of Jesus. The church has never held that the Spirit is the "father" of Jesus. There are many pagan mythologies about gods having intercourse with human females, producing half-breed offspring which are a combination of both. But the biblical accounts of the virgin birth are not examples of such mythology. Neither Matthew nor Luke tells us about a Jesus who is somehow superhuman but less than God, a combination or mixture neither quite human nor quite divine.

Some people who insist on the importance of the virgin birth do so because they have just this pagan mythological understanding of Jesus. Probably the most common idea of his deity and humanity in our time is that he had a human body but a divine soul or mind, will or spirit. "Outside" he was a man, but "inside" he was God. This kind of half-and-half Jesus is not the Jesus of the Bible or of Christian theology. This understanding of him, sometimes mistakenly considered orthodox, is a heresy (Apollinarianism) condemned by the church long ago in the fourth century.

"Conceived by the Holy Ghost" really means not that the Spirit is the father of Jesus, but that according to his human existence

Jesus had no father at all. This phrase is not a biological explanation of the two natures. It means that there *is* no biological explanation, that the Word became flesh purely by the will and word of God. God spoke, and Mary heard and responded: " 'Let it be to me according to your word' " (Luke 1:37). The proper analogy here is not the physical process of conception and birth but God's creation of all things at the beginning when he simply spoke and it was done.

Those Christians who cannot in honesty accept the stories of Jesus' miraculous birth should acknowledge in any case that the church has never understood the doctrine of the virgin birth to be an *explanation* (much less a proof) of what happened and how it happened when God came to us in a man. The doctrine is only a way of stating the mystery that it did in fact happen. On the other hand, those Christians who do accept the doctrine must be careful that they do not interpret it to mean a half-and-half Jesus who is neither really one of us nor really God himself in our midst. Of what interest or help could such a half-breed be?

A Real Man

Christians most anxious to defend the virgin birth often do so primarily in order to insist on the divinity of Jesus. We shall see presently that this is proper in itself. But it can be done properly only when we first understand how this doctrine preserves the real *humanity* of Jesus. Those who do not understand this invariably use the doctrine to support the very heresy it was used to defeat in the early church. We shall first describe the heresy and then see how the doctrine of the virgin birth guards against it.

The heresy is called "Docetism," from the Greek verb which means "to seem." It is a heresy which threatened to destroy the Christian faith almost as soon as it was born and is just as popular and dangerous in the twentieth century as it was in the first. Docetism asserts very strongly that Jesus was divine, but denies that he really was human. He only seemed to be a man. Actually he was God only *disguised* as a man. His human nature was only a mask behind which his true divine self was concealed. Jesus was not a real man, but only a spiritual being who looked like a man, acted like a man, seemed to be a man, but was not really subject to all the limitations and problems of earthly human existence. In him God was only pretending to be with us in the midst of our sinful, suffering, creaturely existence. His purpose was not to help us *in* the world but to help us escape *from* the world.

Already in the New Testament period the church began a 2,000 year struggle against this spiritualistic heresy. Its apparently very pious insistence on the deity of Jesus was really a denial of the very good news that makes the Christian faith Christian—the good news of God really with us. John 1:1–14, for instance, was written precisely as a protest against Docetism.

Another way the early church fought this faithless spirituality with its contempt for fleshly existence was to insist that Jesus was "born of a woman" (Galatians 4:4), flesh and blood of his mother. In this respect he was just like any other man. He—the Son of God! —was born as we all are. He was a helpless baby who had to be fed, whose diapers had to be changed, who had to develop and mature slowly. The Apostles' Creed asserts that Jesus was "born of the Virgin Mary" not only to emphasize that he came from God, but, in deliberate opposition to Docetism, to insist that he came into the world in the same way every other man does. He did not just appear out of nowhere like a ghost or a "heavenly body." The creed puts Jesus' birth in a line with other marks of real human existence: born, suffered, dead and buried.

In short, the birth narratives of Jesus are just as important to protect his real humanity as to protect his real deity. The doctrine of the virgin birth is misused when it is used consciously or unconsciously to ignore or deny his humanity.

In this connection, we may go on to mention some of the ways Matthew and Luke, with the other New Testament books, emphasize against all Docetic views that this man "born of a woman" was a real human being:

1. **Jesus was a *Jewish* man.** Not a heavenly ideal man, not "man" in the abstract. He was a *Jew*—one of that group of men who from the first century to the present have been laughed at and joked about, when they have not been excluded and perse-

cuted. Although the New Testament shows no interest in what
Jesus looked like, we may be sure that he was not the blond, blue-
eyed, soft-complexioned figure of much Western religious art and
of Hollywood productions. Men of the Near East look neither like
Anglo-Saxons with long hair or like all-American boys! Moreover,
if Jesus was in fact what he was expected to be according to Isaiah
53:2, he was an *ugly* man, even by standards different from ours.

**2. Jesus was a "real man"—a man of strength and
determination.** Although he was a genuinely gentle and kind person, he was far from the "sweet Jesus, meek and mild," we have
sometimes made him. He called the pious religious leaders "blind
fools" (Matthew 23:17) and a "brood of vipers" (Matthew 23:33).
He was a nonconformist who dared to break all the religious and
social conventions of his day. He openly announced that he came
to "disturb the peace" (Luke 12:49–53; Matthew 10:34–39). We
might say that this man from God came as an "outside agitator"!
No one could be kinder and more compassionate in his relation to
obvious sinners and outcasts—but no one more fearlessly revolutionary in opposing sham, hypocrisy and injustice. He was a *man!*

**3. Jesus experienced every human need and ap-
petite.** He was completely human in *all* aspects of his life. We have
learned to accept this with respect to his physical life. It is no longer offensive as it once was to think that the man who was the Son of
God could be hungry and thirsty, need rest and sleep, suffer and
die. But many Christians are still hesitant to accept Jesus' humanity
with respect to his spiritual and mental life. Like any other man,
Jesus was limited also in his knowledge. He had to *grow* in wisdom
as well as in stature (Luke 2:52). He himself admitted that he did
not know everything (Mark 13:32). He was not just God pretending to be a man; he was a real man—a man of the first century.

The same holds true for his spiritual life. We hear often that
he prayed, without any suggestion that he was only talking to his
own inner self. Especially when he was in the garden and knew he
was about to die, we hear of his inner wrestling with himself and
with God. Like any other normal man, he did not want to die

(Matthew 26:36–39). Then in his prayer on the cross we hear that he felt completely separated from God, *doubting* God's presence with him. There is no stronger proof of his genuine, total humanity than those agonizing words of Matthew 27:46.

Physically *and* intellectually *and* emotionally *and* spiritually Jesus lived the same life we all live. He hurt. He played. He had to learn. He could be afraid as well as self-confident. He could feel lonely and deserted not only by other men but by God. He was one of us—a human being.

4. Jesus was tempted to sin, just as every other man is. What were the temptations he faced in Matthew 4:1–11? Do we experience the same kind of temptations within the possibilities open to us? While all of us may experience such temptations on our level, these were "messianic" temptations especially related to the peculiar task Jesus had to fulfill as the one sent from God.

More relevant to our situation are the amazingly strong words of Hebrews 4:15: He is one who "in every respect has been tempted as we are." What are *your* everyday temptations—the ones so dark and shameful you never speak about them to anyone and hardly admit them to yourself? Jesus faced the same kind of temptations. He was not just God pretending to be a human being. He was a man subject to all the same pressures, doubts, fears, and desires we are. If he was not, how could he be God with *us*? How could he "sympathize with our weaknesses" (Hebrews 4:15)?

5. Jesus was without sin—perfectly fulfilling his humanity. He was tempted in every respect as we are, "yet without sinning" (Hebrews 4:15). Could he still be human if he did not sin? Yes, because, as we have already learned, sin is not a part of what it means to be human. It is the *corruption* or *contradiction* of true humanity. It is not "natural" but unnatural. Jesus was "real" man not only in the sense that he shared our human condition in every respect, but also in the sense that he was true man, a human being who perfectly fulfilled his humanity. In what sense was he without sin, and how should we understand his sinlessness?

In the present context, when we are asking about the significance of the stories of Jesus' virgin birth, we need to say first of all
what it does not mean. Protestant theology does *not* teach that the
explanation or cause of his sinlessness was the fact that his mother
was a virgin. Behind this view is the unbiblical idea that sexuality
as such is sinful and the source of all sin. In the background also is
the unbiblical view that "original sin" is "inherited sin," so that the
biological connection of all men with Adam must be broken if the
stain of sin is to be removed. Once one accepts this idea, the logical
consequence is the doctrine of Mary's "immaculate conception,"
which says that Mary too had to be born in a miraculous way so
that she too was not corrupted by inherited sin and could not pass
it on to the child. Protestant theology must reject from the very beginning any biological explanation of Jesus' sinlessness, and that
means that we cannot trace it to the virginity of his mother.

How then should we understand what it means to say that this
man was "without sin"? The key lies in what we said at the beginning of this chapter about how the New Testament writers, including Matthew and Luke, try to understand who Jesus is: not in
terms of his nature or essence but in terms of his *actions*. He is sinless, not because he escaped a biological defect everyone else has,
but because he *lived* without sin. And to understand what that
means we must go back to what we learned in chapters 10 and 11.
Jesus was sinless because, unlike Adam and every other man, he
fulfilled and did not contradict his true humanity in the image of
God. He lived always, without exception, as man for God, and as
man with and for his fellowmen.

How did he live this life of perfect relatedness and therefore
sinlessness? *He was sinless because he was the friend of sinners!*
" 'This man receives sinners and eats with them' " (Luke 15:2).
Jesus' sinlessness was anything but obvious or provable. The sign
of it was not heroic moral purity but a life that called his purity into
question. His friends and associates were not the good church
people of his day. *They* were his enemies (not because he rejected
them, but because they rejected him). His friends were the political revolutionaries (the Zealots), dishonest businessmen who were
also traitors to their nation (the tax collectors), immoral women

(the woman caught in adultery), social outcasts and half-breeds (the Samaritans). People in his day said just what we would say now: "A man is known by the company he keeps." "Birds of a feather flock together." But it was just this morally suspicious life which was the sign of Jesus' sinlessness. Just in this way he was man with and for other men as they really are—guilty, needing forgiveness, acceptance and help. Moreover, it was just in being the friend of the "wrong" people that Jesus was obedient to God and fulfilled the task God had given him to do—not to minister to well people who do not need a doctor, but to sick people who do; not to call the righteous but sinners (Matthew 9:12 ff.). His sinlessness is his willingness to be sent "in the likeness of sinful flesh" (Romans 8:3 f.) in order to overcome the broken relationship between God and men, men and men. It is the willingness of one who "knew no sin" to be "made sin" for our sake (2 Corinthians 5:21). Jesus was sinless because, in perfect obedience to God and perfect love for his fellowmen, he was willing to risk his "good name" and his "moral reputation" in being not against but with and for undeserving, unworthy, *sinful* men.

The Son of God

In this real flesh and blood man, Jesus of Nazareth, God himself was uniquely present in the world. This man was not just a great teacher of profound truths about God, man, the world and the secret of a happy, peaceful, successful life. He was not just a great moral hero for us to imitate as best we can; nor just a very Godlike religious personality, the model of a truly spiritual life; nor just the founder of a religious club later called the church, where religious people with a common interest in him come together to admire him and admire themselves for admiring him. To know this man is not just to know a very great, very good, very wise man. It is to know God himself. His very name is "Jesus," which in Hebrew means "God helps" or "God saves" (Matthew 1:21). He is called "Emmanuel," God with us (Matthew 1:23). He is the "Christ," the Messiah, the "Anointed One" of God. And his miraculous birth is a sign of the fact that where he comes from, who he is, and what he does cannot be explained in terms of the ordinary process of human life and history. This man comes from God, not from men. He is the "Son of God."

Before we try to understand what this title means, we must speak of the connection between it and the Christmas story and doctrine of the virgin birth. Jesus' virgin birth did not make or prove him to be the Son of God. Even if it could be proved that his mother was a virgin, that would only prove that his birth was a medical anomaly (a deviation from the common rule). Christians do not believe that Jesus was the Son of God because he was born of a virgin. On the contrary, because they have already come to believe that he was the Son of God, therefore they listen to the stories of his miraculous birth. The way goes from faith in Jesus to the virgin birth, not vice versa.

This is the way it is in the New Testament itself. When Jesus spoke during his life, people did not say, "Here is the Son of God who was born in such a miraculous way. We'd better listen to what he has to say." They said rather, "Is not this Jesus, the son of Joseph, whose father and mother we know? How does he now say, 'I have come down from heaven'?" (John 6:42; Luke 4:22.) Even those who followed him did not follow him because they first knew who he was and the secret of his origin. Only after they had been with him, listened to him, watched what he did, and especially only after they had seen his death and experienced his presence as the Risen One—only then did they understand who he was. For the earliest Christians, then, "suffered under Pontius Pilate, was crucified, dead and buried and rose again" came before a true understanding of "Christ his only Son our Lord." Their deepest faith came not with the beginning but with the end of Jesus' life on earth, not with his birth but with his resurrection. Had they not experienced his presence as the living, risen Christ, they would simply have dismissed him as another martyred prophet and never have understood who he was and where he came from.

Is not this the way faith comes also to modern men? How many people first believe that Jesus is the Son of God, born in a miraculous way, and then for that reason consent to listen to the story of his words and actions, his death and resurrection? Is it not so that also today most people are confronted first of all with the man Jesus, his teaching, his deeds, his suffering, and his living presence, and then finally confess him as the Son of God, God himself with us? What does this have to say about the way we ought to talk about Jesus to non-Christians? Is "talk" enough to confront them with the reality of the Son of God?

What we have been suggesting is the same thing we said at the beginning of the chapter, and later with reference to the sinlessness of Jesus: Men do not come to believe in Jesus as the Son of God by speculating about his "divine nature" or his origin. Faith comes by seeing, hearing and experiencing what he *does*. Also Matthew and Luke, along with the rest of the New Testament, tell us the meaning of Jesus' birth not by theorizing about it, but by telling us the story of what happened *after* that. Jesus is the Son of God, God himself with us, because throughout his life he does what God does.

What, then, does the title "Son of God" mean in the light of these considerations?[2]

In the first place, "Son of God" is obviously a title of majesty. How is this made clear in the announcement of Jesus' birth in Luke 1:32–33? Throughout his life Jesus spoke with authority and acted with power. Even when he did not talk about himself, he claimed to be one with God by daring to put his own teaching on the same level with Scripture. "You have heard it said . . . But *I* say to you" (Matthew 5:21 ff. See also Matthew 7:28.). Moreover, he backed up his words with actions. He performed miracles of healing and forgave sins (Mark 2:5–12). And the people got the point! Read the debate between Jesus and the Jews in John 10:19–39. What is their objection to Jesus? How does he answer their objections?

Why is Jesus the Son of God? Because he speaks with the authority of God himself and does mighty works which are *God's* works. "Son of God" expresses his oneness with God and his consequent divine majesty and power.

But that is not all. The title "Son of God" was a common one in the ancient oriental world. Many ancient rulers were called "son of God" because their majesty and power supposedly proved that they were the offspring of the gods. In the New Testament period one could meet everywhere men who called themselves "son of

God" because they claimed they had miraculous divine powers. Some of them called themselves "savior" for this reason. Perhaps we meet such people in the New Testament in Acts 8:9–11 and 16:16. The fact that Jesus was a miracle worker and spoke with authority was not in itself unique. If he had only been a son of God or a savior on the basis of the miraculous powers he demonstrated, he would have been nothing unusual, certainly not *the* Son of God.

The unique thing about *this* Son of God, that which set him apart from all the many "sons of God" and set the Christian religion apart from other ancient religions, was not first of all his strength but his weakness, not his majestic power but his suffering, not his authority and rule but his obedience. He was a *lowly* Son of God. We see this at several decisive points in the life of Jesus.

Think first of all of the birth stories themselves. An insignificant little colony of the Roman Empire. A stable. The wife of a common laborer. Who would expect the Son of God under these circumstances? What an inappropriate way for God Almighty to make himself known!

In the temptation story in Matthew 4:1–11, the tempter says, "*If* you are the Son of God. . . ." And his temptation was that Jesus should use his divine power to care for his own needs, gain popularity by miraculous deeds, and become a great world ruler. Jesus proved himself the true Son of God by *refusing* to be what all the other "sons of God" were or wanted to be.

In Matthew 16:13–20, Peter confesses that Jesus is "the Son of the living God." But when Jesus began to teach the disciples that as such he must *suffer* and *be killed,* Peter protests. And Jesus says to him, "Get behind me Satan, for you are not on the side of God, but of man." The idea that the Son of God is to be great and powerful on earth is the idea of the devil—even if it is expressed by Peter.

Finally, it is when the centurion sees Jesus dying on the cross between two criminals that he confesses, "Truly this man was the Son of God" (Mark 15:39). Precisely in failure and defeat God's presence and work in Jesus is recognizable.

What is the meaning of all these texts which reverse what "Son of God" meant to everyone in Jesus' time—and to many Christians in our time? We can answer this question by reflecting once again on the Christmas stories and the doctrine of the virgin birth. They point to a strange "switch" which takes place when the Word becomes flesh and dwells among us. Christmas means the *deity of the man Jesus:* He is God himself with us. But it also means the *humanity of God:* God stoops to identify himself with the cause of humanity by himself becoming man.[3] To put it in the language of traditional theology, Christmas and the doctrine of the virgin birth point to the "exaltation" of man and the "humiliation" of God.

1. The exaltation of man. God did not make himself known to us as an angel or a superhuman spirit, but as a *man*. In so doing he puts his divine stamp of approval on human life. Christmas means that what God wills and accomplishes in the world is not the creation of religious men but the creation of *human* men; not just the salvation of our souls but the renewal of our flesh and blood humanity; not the ability to escape from our human existence but the ability thankfully to accept and courageously to live a fully human life both now in this world and in the new heaven and earth to come. God's coming to us as a man means that he himself supports and participates in every religious *and* secular movement, cause and revolution which helps make human life more fully human and helps free men from all the forces within and without which enslave and dehumanize them. Ever since the first Christmas, whoever is against *man* is against *God*. For in Jesus God took up the cause of men in order to judge, help and renew *human* beings.

2. The humiliation of God. If Christmas means that God affirms and exalts the cause of man in the world, it also means that he is not too good, too holy or too proud to "lower" himself to man's level to participate in earthly human life. He does not sacrifice but exercises his divine power, goodness and holiness by doing so. Christmas means that unlike all false gods, the true God is not the prisoner of his own spirituality, unable to be God in the realm of the nonspiritual. It means that unlike all false gods, the true God can accomplish his will in weakness as well as in strength, by sacrificing himself as well as by asserting himself, in the nonreligious as well as the religious sphere. It means that to identify himself with sinful man in a sinful world does not compromise his goodness and holiness; that *is* his goodness and holiness. Christmas means the Creator "humiliating" himself to become a creature. It means the Righteous One humiliating himself to stand with and for the unrighteous. It means God with *us*. But just in this self-humiliation he proves himself to be *God* with us. Whoever will have God only in heaven, or in church, or in religious affairs, or where there is success and happiness; whoever will not look for him or accept him in the everyday world, among ordinary men, participating in secular human affairs, present also in human struggle and failure—that man will never know God at all. For he is the God who gives himself to be known in the man Jesus who was born in a stable, tried and condemned in a courtroom, executed at public execution grounds.

If you want to know what it means to be a human being and to stand for the humanity of man—look at Jesus Christ. If you want to know God—look at Jesus Christ. That is what we confess when we say "I believe in Jesus Christ his only Son our Lord, who was conceived by the Holy Ghost and born of the Virgin Mary." *How* it is that in this one person we meet both genuinely human man and God the Father Almighty, the church has never been able to explain. All its attempts to explain it have finally only affirmed *that* it is so. He is at once true man and true God, God with *us* and *God* with us.

FOR FURTHER REFLECTION AND STUDY

1. Read the Christmas stories in Matthew 1:18—2:23; Luke 1: 26–56; 2:1–20. Make a list of all the names or titles given to Jesus. What information do the two stories have in common? What information is peculiar to each? Do you find contradictions between them? In what sense do you think these stories are history?

2. How would you answer someone who said that the story of Jesus' birth is just another example of the many myths in ancient religions about gods coming miraculously to earth in human form?

3. John of Damascus, a theologian of the eighth century, said that Mary's ear was the bodily organ of the miraculous conception of Christ. What did he mean? Do you agree?
4. Do you think Jesus could have thought that the earth is flat?
5. In what sense, if any, could we say that when Jesus died, God himself died?
6. The great Greek writer Nikos Kazantzakis wrote a novel, *The Last Temptation of Christ*, in which he suggested that Jesus was troubled by sexual temptations. Do you think the book should be condemned?
7. Do you agree that Jesus was sinless just in being the friend of sinners? How would it influence our daily lives if we followed him? How would it influence the life of the church?
8. If a Christian is successful in his business, is that a sign that God has blessed him? If his business is a failure, does that mean that God has not been with him?
9. Read the "Magnificat," Mary's song before the birth of Jesus, in Luke 1:46–55. Does this explain why some people have called Christmas a dangerous revolution?
10. We sometimes speak of Christianity as God-centered or Christ-centered. In the light of Christmas, is there a sense in which we ought to say that it is *man*-centered?
11. In the light of the Christmas story, what is the relation between "secular" and "religious"?
12. If you had to explain who Jesus is to someone who had never heard of him at all, how would you begin?

13

Is God Against Us?

Once upon a time a boy went to a revival meeting. He had grown up in a Christian home and in the church, but he heard something that night he had never heard before. The preacher held up a very dirty water glass.

"See this glass? That's you. Filthy, stained with sin, inside and outside."

He picked up a hammer.

"This hammer is the righteousness of God. It is the instrument of his wrath against sinful men. His justice can be satisfied only by punishing and destroying sinners whose lives are filled with vileness and corruption."

He put the glass on the pulpit and slowly, deliberately drew back the hammer clinched in his fist, took deadly aim, and with all his might let the blow fall.

But a miracle happened! At the last moment the preacher covered the glass with a pan. The hammer struck with a crash that echoed through the hushed church. He held up the untouched glass with one hand and the mangled pan with the other and made his point.

"Jesus Christ died for your sins. He took the punishment which ought to have fallen on you. He satisfied the righteousness of God so that you might go free if you believe in him."

When he went to bed that night, the boy could not sleep. Meditating on what he had seen and heard, he decided that he was terribly *afraid* of God. But could he *love* such a God? He could love Jesus, who had sacrificed himself for him. But how could he love a God who wanted to "get" everyone and was only kept from doing it because Jesus got in the way? The thought crossed the boy's mind that he could only hate such a hammer-swinging God who had to be bought off at such a terrible price. But he quickly dismissed the thought. That very God might read his mind and punish him.

Some other thoughts also troubled the boy. Despite what the preacher said about the righteousness of God, is it really right to punish one person for what other people do? And granted that he was a pretty bad boy sometimes, was he really all that bad? Did he really deserve to *die*? Was he really so sinful that God had to *kill* Jesus to make up for what he had done?

Finally, he wondered what good it had all done in the end. The glass had escaped being smashed to bits, but nothing had really changed. After the drama was over, it was still just as dirty as it was before. Even if Jesus did save him from God, how did Jesus' sacrifice help him to be a different person?

Something was obviously wrong with the preacher's object lesson and with the boy's theology based on it. But what? What would you say to the preacher? How would you try to help the troubled boy? Our purpose in this chapter is to discover the true meaning of Jesus' death for us, to bring back into focus the popular but twisted doctrine of the atonement we have described, and to answer as best we can the questions we have raised.

We do not approach this problem as something brand-new, of course. The work of God in Christ on Good Friday has thrown light on what we have said about the nature of God and man, the relationship and broken relationship between them, and the meaning of God-with-us in the birth and life of Jesus. We do not really take up a new topic now, but only concentrate on a topic that has run through everything we have been saying from the beginning of our study.

First we shall look at the various biblical images which describe the work of Jesus for us. Then we shall try to understand the underlying truth all these images seek to describe in their different ways.

The Biblical Images

When Jesus died, a dream died in the hearts of his followers. They had hoped that he was the Messiah, the chosen one of God who would free their country from the political rule of a totalitarian foreign government and establish it not only as a free nation but as one which would be the center of power, virtue, wisdom and glory in the whole world. They expected to be rewarded for their loyalty to him by receiving positions of honor and authority in the new government. Is it not clear that those who stick with the one sent from God will finally be rewarded? But Jesus was a failure. He did not defeat his enemies; he was defeated by them. He did not free his nation; he was executed as another of many unsuccessful revolutionaries. His death meant nothing but disappointed hopes, tragedy—the end.

Only after Easter morning and their experience of the presence of the risen Christ did the first followers of Jesus begin to understand that his death was good news and not just a tragedy. In order to interpret its positive meaning, they used various images or pictures or analogies already at their disposal from everyday life. If we are to understand the significance of these images, we need to remember two things about them.

First, the early church did not have a "theory of the atonement" or a "plan of salvation" which they forced upon the life, death and resurrection of Jesus so that he would fit their theories. They did not first reason that if God is God, and if he wants to save the world, he must do so and so, and such and such must happen to Jesus. They had been forced to *give up* all their theories and plans. God did not work according to their schedule and calculations. They took up the various pictures and images only as they reflected on what actually did happen to Jesus.

Secondly, it is no accident that in the New Testament *several* images or pictures are used to interpret the meaning of Jesus' death. The early church knew that no one of them was sufficient in itself. Any one of them has its limitations and needs the emphasis of the others for a grasp of the total picture.

The images serve the event, not the event the images. No one
image is adequate by itself. We must remember both things if we
are not to fall into the error of taking one or another of them too
literally and too exclusively and forcing the death of Jesus to fit
our theories rather than letting our theories be limited and corrected by what actually happened.

Although they often overlap and run into each other, we can
distinguish four main images used in the New Testament to interpret the meaning of Jesus' life and death.

1. The financial image. The scene is a slave market or a prison camp. There are men who have lost their freedom.
They are being sold into slavery, or they sit as captives of the
enemy. But a man steps up and pays the price or gives the ransom
money to purchase their freedom or to redeem them. We are the
slaves or prisoners. Jesus is our Redeemer. The ransom price is
high: his life for ours. But he pays it for our sake.

This image is used in Mark 10:45; 1 Corinthians 6:20; 7:23;
1 Peter 1:18; Titus 2:14; Romans 3:24; Galatians 3:13. It is not the
main image used in the Reformed confessions, but it does appear
in them—as when the Westminster Confession (VIII, 8) says that
Christ has "purchased redemption."

To whom or what, according to the texts mentioned, are we
captives? A more difficult question naturally arises: Do the texts
suggest that the ancient church was right in saying that since men
are captives of the devil, Jesus is God's payment to him to buy
man's freedom? Do they suggest that it is God himself who is
bought off by Jesus so that men might be free?

This image describes us as trapped people who cannot free
ourselves. It describes Jesus as one who at great cost to himself
makes us free. We ought not to try to make the image say any
more than this. We push it too far when we ask to whom the ransom is paid, for there the analogy breaks down.

2. The military image. The scene is a battlefield.
God and the Devil are at war for possession of men, whom the
Devil has stolen from the Kingdom of God and carried off to his
kingdom of darkness. Christ is the warrior of God who invades

the realm of the Devil to bring them home again where they belong. It is a deadly, real battle. On Good Friday Jesus gave his life in the fight to free men, and the powers of darkness and death were victorious. But on Easter morning God triumphed over the enemy and delivered men from death to life, from darkness to light.

This military image appears in Mark 3:23–27; Colossians 1:13; 2:15; 1 Corinthians 15:24–28. It has never been especially emphasized in the Reformed churches, but the Eastern Orthodox Church and the Lutherans have leaned heavily on it. A vivid example is Luther's hymn, "A Mighty Fortress."

Does this cosmic battle between God and the devil sound too mythological to you? If it were thought of not literally but as an image or picture to describe what happened, do you think that even such "mythology" could make sense to modern men?

This dramatic image of the work of God in Christ emphasizes the seriousness of both man's predicament and God's love. Man cannot free himself from the evil forces which dominate him, but God cares so much for man that he himself enters into a costly struggle to rescue and help him. The disadvantage of this image—and of the financial image as well—is that men are only a prize to be bought or fought over. The ransom and battle imagery explain the difference in man's *status* as a result of the work of Christ, but they say nothing of a change *in man himself*. The sin to which we are slaves or prisoners is not only something outside us but something *inside* us. Is the dirty glass we spoke of at the beginning any less dirty just because it is moved from one place to another, or from the possession of one person to the other? How are *we* any different, any freer for God and for our fellowmen, any freer to be our true selves, because of the work of Christ? Other images are necessary to deal with this question left unanswered by the ransom and battle images.

3. The sacrificial image. The scene now is a religious place with a bloody altar where sacrifices are offered. Men are guilty before God and deserve his wrathful punishment. But a priest comes forward who is the mediator between God and men.

He makes a sacrifice to atone for the people's sin. Blood is shed—
a life is offered up. It is a sign of the people's sorrow for their
disobedience, of their offering of their own lives to God, and of
their cleansing from the stain of their sin. But this priest is different
from all other priests in that he sacrifices not the life of an animal
but his own life. He lets his own blood be shed in order to make
peace again between the people and God. He is himself the "lamb"
which is slain. He suffers for the sake of sinful men, as their representative, so that they may be reconciled with God.

This imagery occurs throughout the New Testament; see for
instance Mark 14:22–24; Romans 3:25; John 1:29; 1 Corinthians
5:7. Especially the book of Hebrews interprets the work of Christ
as that of our "Great High Priest." See Hebrews 2:17 and 8–10.
The image of Christ's work as a sacrifice occurs often in the Reformed confessions. Chapter 9 of The Scots Confession is perhaps
the clearest example.

When the New Testament was written, the sacrifice of animals was a familiar part of worship, so it was natural to interpret
the death of Jesus as the atoning shedding of blood. We no longer
worship in this way, and it is hard for us to understand what the
sacrificial system meant to the people who practiced it. Many
people in our time find a "blood" theology primitive and repulsive.
That is perhaps the main disadvantage of this imagery for us. But
if we can overcome our aversion to the bloody rituals of the ancient Jews, which are so strange to us, we can see that this imagery
says something very important. It also points to man's guilt and
need for forgiveness, his estrangement from God and his need for
reconciliation. And the shed blood of Jesus emphasizes in a radical
way his unlimited love for guilty men and the cost he was willing
to pay to help them.

One danger of the sacrificial imagery is that the significance
of Christ's work can easily be corrupted in the same way the
sacrificial system of the Old Testament was corrupted. It easily
becomes a kind of bargaining with God. A sacrifice has been
offered to satisfy his demands and appease him—so now we are
free to go on being and doing anything we like without interference from him. How did the prophets protest against such a

perversion of the sacrificial system? See Isaiah 1:10–31; Amos 5:21–24; Hosea 6:6; Micah 6:6–8. Is the prophetic protest against the misuse of sacrifices relevant also to our understanding of the sacrifice of Christ? Would the prophets allow the split we sometimes make between preaching concerned with social action and preaching concerned with salvation from sin?

4. The legal image. The scene is now a courtroom. God, the just Judge, sits behind the desk, and men who have broken the law stand in front of it to be tried. They hear the verdict: Guilty. They receive the sentence: Death. But a righteous man who has obeyed the law perfectly comes and stands beside the accused, takes the death sentence upon himself, and suffers the consequences of their guilt in their place. Those who were enemies of the law (and thus of the Judge also) are now acquitted and reconciled. Order is restored. They no longer have to fear the Judge, but are free to go out to begin a new life.

This legal imagery is especially characteristic of Paul; see Romans 5:6–11; 2 Corinthians 5:16–21; Colossians 1:19–20. It is used more than any of the other images throughout the Reformed confessions. In the texts mentioned, is God reconciled to men or are men reconciled to God? Who does the reconciling?

Judge, law, guilt, verdict, sentence, justice, reconciliation— these are all concepts which, unlike the sacrificial imagery, are part of *our* everyday vocabulary and experience. It is perhaps the easiest to understand of all the pictures we have described. But what is said here is basically the same thing said with the other images. Here too we hear about the desperate situation of men and the unreserved love of Christ for them.

The danger of this legal imagery is that it is easily twisted to become just what Paul so vehemently fought against: a legalistic concern to satisfy God's honor and justice so that we may escape punishment without inward change. We saw an example of this legalistic thinking in the object lesson of the preacher at the beginning of this chapter. The legal imagery also raises the same question we raised then: "How can my guilt be transferred to another? Even if he takes the punishment I have deserved, am I not still guilty? Is it fair to punish another for what I have done?

Now that we have the language of the New Testament in mind and have seen the main thrust and the problems involved in its images, we shall try to understand the one gospel it proclaims in these various ways.

God Versus the Gods

One way to get at the meaning of the Christian doctrine of the atonement is to contrast it with what reconciliation and atonement meant in other ancient religions.

Men of primitive religions lived in terror before their gods. They knew that the gods were easily offended by man's disobedience and were quick to seek revenge and retribution. In order to live in peace and security, therefore, men had to do what they could to appease, placate, or satisfy the angry gods. The gods had to be "buttered up" and bought off in one way or another so that the people could stay in good standing with them and earn their favor, support and help. Prayers, good deeds devoted to their service, and above all sacrifices were the means by which people could atone for their sins and ease their guilty consciences. And at the same time these religious rituals and moral achievements were ways of manipulating the gods into giving supernatural help to the people. It was basically a "do it yourself" religion. How the gods acted depended on what men did. It sometimes cost men a great deal. But with their piety and sacrifices *they* paid the price and *they* won the salvation.

Now the situation of estrangement and need for reconciliation we have described is not unrecognizable. That is perhaps the reason why biblical religion can be so easily twisted into superstitious paganism in our own time. But the God of the Bible is different from the gods, and the Christian doctrine of atonement is different from that we just described. We can see the radical difference in three ways:

1. **The love of God.** Christians also believe that men are alienated from God. It is man's fault. He has disobeyed and put himself in the wrong with God. He has broken the re-

lationship. God is the offended party. His law has been broken; even worse, his love has been rejected. But strangely enough, it is not the guilty but the injured party who acts to restore the broken relationship. God does not demand that men first do something to "make up" for what they have done before he reluctantly agrees to forgive and love them again. He himself makes the first move. Directly contrary to the procedure in pagan religions, it is not man but God who reconciles, not God but man who is reconciled. It is not man who makes peace with God, but God who makes peace with man. That is what the death of Jesus is all about.

It is more important than it might seem at first glance to emphasize this point, because it is called into question by one classical view of the work of Christ which has strongly influenced all of Christianity, including the Reformed churches (Belgic Confession, Art. XXI; Westminster Confession, VIII, 5). We refer to the view of Anselm (1033–1109), who reasoned that man's sin has offended God's honor and righteousness. God cannot be reconciled to man until something is done to satisfy his justice and pay for the sins man has committed. By his obedience and sacrifice Jesus fulfilled God's requirement, restored his honor, paid the price of his justice, and therefore made it possible for God to forgive and love man. Jesus thus changed God's mind toward us and purchased his love. This is called the "satisfaction" theory of the atonement.

Despite the great influence of Anselm's view on both Catholicism and Protestantism, it is unbiblical. Nowhere does the Bible use the word "satisfaction." Nowhere does it suggest that Jesus came to *change* God's mind; on the contrary, he came precisely to *express* God's mind.[1] Nowhere does it suggest that reconciliation is purchased *from* God; it is the work *of* God. What Jesus does is not done over against God; he *is* God with us, and what he wills and does is what God himself wills and does.

The Bible does not teach that *if* certain conditions are fulfilled either by or for man, *then* God will love him. Nor does it say that *if* man's sins are atoned for in one way or another, *then* God will forgive him. What kind of love or forgiveness is it that is bought or wrung out of another? What the Bible does teach is that "God shows his love for us in that *while we were yet sinners* Christ died for us" (Romans 5:8). It teaches that "he first loved us" (1 John 4:19). Jesus died not so that God could begin to love us, but because he already loved us. Calvin, quoting Augustine, puts it this way:

> For it was not after we were reconciled to him through the blood of his Son that he began to love us. Rather, he has loved us before the world was created, that we also might be his sons along with his only-begotten Son—before we became anything at all. The fact that we were reconciled through Christ's death must not be understood as if his Son reconciled us to him that he might now begin to love those whom he had hated. Rather, we have already been reconciled to him who loves us, with whom we were enemies on account of sin . . . . Therefore, he loved us even when we practiced enmity toward him and committed wickedness (*Institutes*, II, 16, 4).

This change from paganism's concern to reconcile the gods to man to Christianity's faith that God was in Christ reconciling man to himself obviously affects the meaning of the images which express the work of Christ in the New Testament.

The *financial* image does not mean that God is "bought off" by Jesus. What is "purchased" is sinful man (1 Corinthians 6:20; 7:23)—not *from* but *for* and *by* God. To be saved or redeemed is not to be saved or redeemed from an angry God seeking revenge. It is to be saved or redeemed from the sin which separates us from the God who loves us and wills only good for us, even when we are sinfully alienated from him.

When the New Testament used the *sacrificial* imagery, it does not suggest that Jesus' sacrifice produces an effect on God either in satisfying his justice or changing his attitude toward men. Rather it speaks of the effect of the sacrifice on those for whom the sacrifice is made (Hebrews 9:9, 14; 10:10, 14; 13:12).[2] Even in the Old Testament, the sacrifice is not something that comes from man to pacify an unwilling God; it is given by God himself, because *he* desires reconciliation (Leveticus 17:11). Romans 3:25 says in a much debated statement that Jesus' blood is a propitiation or expiation, but even there is it explicitly said that *God* "put forward" Jesus. A sacrifice is made to set things right, but if Jesus is God himself with us, then God himself makes the sacrifice. Here we come to the heart of the Christian gospel: The offering up of Jesus' life is not a way of *buying* God's love; rather, "God so loved the world that he gave . . ." (John 3:16). Jesus' sacrifice is not a way of manipulating God to be on our side; it is God's way of winning us to *his* side.

The same is true of the *legal* imagery. Jesus does take the punishment for sin upon himself, but not to satisfy the justice of a Judge who is against man. Jesus is himself the Judge (2 Corinthians 5:10; Acts 10:42). If he is judged and condemned for us, then that means that the Judge gives *himself* to be judged for us, in our place. If we speak of "satisfaction" at all, we must say not that in Jesus God's justice is satisfied by another, but that in him God satisfied his own just requirements by taking the sentence and punishment on himself.

In summary: In contrast to ancient paganism and Anselm's legalistic view, the biblical doctrine of the atonement teaches that it is *God* who initiates the reconciliation between himself and sinful men. He is the *subject,* not the *object,* of what happens on Good Friday. His desire is not to crush us "dirty glasses" with the hammer of his wrath, so that we have to turn to Jesus to keep him from doing what he would like to do to us. He is "God our Savior, who desires all men to be saved" (1 Timothy 2:3–4). The death of Jesus is his *own* action (not action taken against him) to fulfill that desire. "All this is from God, who through Christ reconciled us to himself" (2 Corinthians 5:18). That means that the doctrine of reconciliation should awaken in us first of all not terror of God's wrath but joyful thanksgiving for God's love.

2. Costly love. If God loves and forgives us already, why atonement at all? Why did Jesus have to sacrifice himself to "pay the price"? Why did not God just say, "I forgive you," and let it go at that?

We can catch a glimpse of the answer with an analogy in human relationships.[3] Suppose I have done something that deeply hurts a friend, and he says to me, "That's OK. It doesn't make any difference. Forget it." Has he forgiven me? What he has really said is: "I don't really care enough about you to be tcuched by anything you say or do. You are not that important to me." Not only that; he leaves me alone with the awareness of my guilt. He lets me "stew in my own juice," refusing to help me by letting me know that he suffers not only because of what I have done to him but because he knows how I feel and can share with me my shame and guilt.

Good-natured indulgence and broad-mindedness, in other words, are not forgiveness and love but indifference and sometimes even hostility. Real love and forgiveness mean caring enough to be hurt, caring enough to put oneself in the other's shoes and sharing his guilt as if it were one's own. Real love and forgiveness are *costly*—not in the sense that the guilty must squeeze them out of the injured, but in the sense that the injured freely participates in a guilt not his own.

Why did Jesus have to die? Why atonement? Because God cares for us too much to dismiss our sin and guilt with a casual, "It doesn't matter." Because words were not enough; *action* was necessary to prove that his love and forgiveness were genuine. Because he wanted to stand with us and share the loneliness and alienation we bring on ourselves when we separate ourselves from him and our fellowmen. Because it is just when he comes to our side that our loneliness, alienation and guilt are overcome. In the cross, God says to us, "Yes, it's true. You *have* hurt and offended me. You have done it just by hurting your fellowmen whom I love. You *are* guilty. But I still love you. Therefore I will make your guilt and its consequences my own. I will suffer with you—*for* you."

3. The wrath of God. Only in light of the love of God, so unqualified that he is willing to pay the *cost* of loving, can we understand what the Bible means when it speaks of the wrath of God (see, for instance, Romans 1:18; 5:9; Ephesians 5:6; Colossians 1:5–6). In primitive pagan religions the wrath of the gods

was an *alternative* to love. Their wrath meant the desire to "get even" for their offended dignity and power. Atonement was necessary to change their hostility into love. But if the God of the Christian faith *is* love, then his wrath cannot be an alternative to his love; it can only be one means by which his love is expressed. The doctrine of the atonement shows us how this is so in at least three ways.

a. The death of Jesus for sinful men does point to the wrath of God against the faithlessness and disobedience of men. But the very fact of his wrath means that he is interested in men and cares enough to be offended and hurt by what they do. It would not be love simply to ignore and shrug off sin. That would be simply indifference. God's relationship with us is not like that of a husband and wife who never fuss or fight with one another because they live together as politely uninvolved strangers. Nor is it like that of a parent who does not care enough about a child to become angry and take measures to correct the child's self-harming disobedience. God can be angry *because* he loves. In this sense, the wrath of God is part of the Good News of Christ: He *cares!*

b. Secondly, God's wrath is an expression of his love because it means that he cares so much that he will not let us get by with our sin. God loves us so much that he must act to save us from our sinful humanity. When we refuse to love him with our whole being and our neighbor as ourselves, we not only sin against God; we hurt ourselves, denying our own humanity. If his wrath burns against us, it is not because (like the petty gods) he vindictively seeks revenge and satisfaction. It is to call us back to order again for our own good. The cross of Christ "for us" means that he judges and punishes *in order to* help, to put an end to the inhuman, self-destructive road we have chosen, and to set us on the right road again. His wrath is *constructive, loving* wrath.

c. Finally, God's wrath is an expression of his love because he gives vent to his wrath in such a way that he himself bears its consequences. This brings us in full circle back to our starting point. The wrathful Judge looks over the desk and pronounces the verdict: Guilty! But in the man Jesus, he himself goes around to the other side of the desk and takes on himself the sentence of death. He rules with harsh, uncompromising justice that the debt

to the law must be paid—and then pays the fine himself. The holy
God thunders that a sacrifice must be made to atone for man's
guilt—then he sacrifices *himself*. If the object lesson with which
we began this chapter were to be used in any way similar to what
really happened, the preacher would have to put his own hand
over the dirty glass to receive himself the blow or the deadly
hammer. He would hurt himself, of course—but then that is just
how God executes his wrath!

Must we talk about the wrath of God? Yes. But his wrath is
not that of the gods. It is the wrath of the God who was in Christ
reconciling the world to himself. We cannot understand the depth
of the love of this God without talking about his wrath. But neither
can we understand his wrath without talking about his love.

Were You There?

We have been thinking about what the death of Jesus means
from God's side: His loving us guilty men so much that he takes
the initiative and bears the cost of reconciling us to himself. But
it takes *two* parties for reconciliation to happen, the reconciled
as well as the one who reconciles. If we are to understand the
meaning of the cross, then, we have to ask how *we* are affected
by what happened on Good Friday. To believe that Jesus died for
us is not only to have a radical new understanding of God, but to
have a radical new understanding of ourselves. More than understanding. It means to *be* different. But *how* are we different?

In a sense, all the rest of this book will be an attempt to answer this question, but we must begin to answer it now. In doing
so, we must pick up the questions we have kept raising about our
involvement in the atonement: Are we really so bad that only
Jesus' death could make things right between ourselves and God?
Is it fair for another to "take the rap" for us? Does it really help?
Are we not still the same old "dirty glasses" we were before?
Words are inadequate to express what Christians experience and
believe at this point. But we can list at least four things that the
cross tells us about ourselves and does to and for us.

1. **The cross convicts us as sinners.** "Were you
there when they crucified my Lord?" Yes, we were there. What

they did then, we still do. The cross of 2,000 years ago exposes what kind of people *we* are.

We were there with *Judas* who sold out, probably because Jesus refused to serve his military and political goals for his nation. If it comes to a choice between Christ and our nation's political and military interests, it is clear which we must choose.

We were there with the *disciples* who deserted him and fled when they discovered that loyalty to him meant being rejected by both the political and religious authorities, put in jail, and perhaps killed. Why be a Christian if it does not pay off? Who wants to follow a loser—especially one who gets us into trouble with the authorities?

We were there with the pious *leaders of the Jews* who were out to get him because he did not act as the one sent from God ought to act. He criticized good people and made friends with bad people. He thought human beings were more important than moral and religious rules and conventions. Who can tolerate such a threat to our way of life?

We were there with *Peter* when he denied him. When it is safe and words are cheap, we too confess, "Thou art the Christ, the Son of the living God." But when we are among outsiders, we too are afraid to be different. Better be silent, and if necessary deny him, than to get into trouble by having convictions, standards and attitudes different from everyone else.

We were there with *Pilate* when he made the decision to let the mob have him, although he knew the defendant was innocent. Better to sacrifice Jesus than to go against the will of the people. What can you do when the choice is between justice which upsets the prejudices of the people, stirs up riots, and makes you lose your popularity, and injustice which preserves peace and order and your own security?

We were there with the *soldiers* who played games while he died. While we enjoy all the pleasures of American affluence, within a few blocks of most of us (not to mention across the world), hungry children go unfed to bed at night, "strangers" are excluded not only from the benefits of our civil society but also from our churches, sick people are untended, prisoners sit alone in darkness.

According to Jesus himself, when they suffer he suffers. What we do or neglect to do with them, we do or neglect to do with him. We were there. The cross of Jesus exposes not just their but our sin—the essence of sin. For when we reject Jesus, we reject God himself, reject our fellowman and brother, and reject our own humanity.

Whoever is willing to let himself be told this will not even think of going on with moralistic, defensive questions and arguments about whether he is as bad as some other people or so bad that the atoning death of Christ was really necessary. He can only ask, "How can I be changed from the person I am to a new person? Is it possible that only the *death* of what I am can make a new life possible?"

2. The cross enables us to live as forgiven sinners.

Is it fair for one person to suffer for what another has done? No, of course it is not fair. In one sense it is even impossible. If I have committed a crime, no court would allow an innocent man to go to jail or be put to death instead of me. Even if he did take the punishment for me, I still would be guilty for the crime I have committed. Guilt and punishment for guilt are not transferable. My guilt cannot be removed or made up for by anyone else.

But the legal and sacrificial imagery of the Bible does not intend to picture a kind of legalistic transaction in which our guilt is transferred to Christ and paid for so that we do not have to pay. This unheard-of act, in which the Judge takes the verdict and sentence on himself and the Priest sacrifices himself, moves far beyond what is merely fair or necessary if justice is to be done. When we talk about *this* Judge and Priest, we have to do not so much with the legal demand that debts must be paid as with love that *forgives* debts. Jesus taught us to pray, "Forgive us our debts." The cross says to us, "Your debts *are* forgiven." What does that mean?

First, it means the recognition that we are still debtors. We are still guilty. Everything has not been stamped "paid" so that the books are in order and we can go complacently on our way. We *have* been disloyal to God. We *have* hurt other people in all kinds of ways. We *have* been inhuman. Christ does not take away our guilt so that all the damage we have done to others and to ourselves is undone. We *are* guilty. We have just said that the cross *exposes* it.

But to know that we are *forgiven* debtors means that we do not have to circle round and round ourselves, arrogantly defending or anxiously questioning ourselves, blaming and condemning ourselves, or trying to think up excuses to make our guilt seem less than it is and therefore easier to bear. We have been *forgiven!* God himself forgives us. We no longer have to spend our lives with tormented consciences, desperately trying to work off our guilt, or desperately trying to convince ourselves that we are not so bad after all. To be forgiven means to be free to put behind us what we have been and have done. It means to be free for a new beginning with God and our fellowmen. If God himself has forgiven us, without demanding that we "pay up," then we can forgive ourselves. We can forget what lies behind and press forward to what lies ahead.

A legalistic view of the death of Christ which says that he has paid God off so that we are no longer guilty and in debt makes us complacent in our sinfulness: Since he has satisfied the judge, we can go on as we were. Or it makes us miserable, because we know that in truth we have not really been helped even if we do escape the wrath of God: We are still caught in the trap of guilt that we know is ours and that no one else can bear for us. But to believe that Christ died "for us" and "in our place" means *forgiveness—* that is, realistically to acknowledge what we have been, and to be made free from a preoccupation with our guilt (that is, with *ourselves*), free for God and for fellowmen, free to be ourselves.

3. The cross means the death of sinners.
We have said that we were there on Good Friday with all the people around the cross because we do the same things they did. But the New Testament teaches that we were there also in another sense. We were there *on* the cross. What happened to Christ has also happened to us. When he died for us sinners, we were put to death with him. How is this said in 2 Corinthians 5:14–15; Galatians 2:20; Romans 6:1–14? What do these texts mean to you personally?

Here we encounter a way of thinking that was familiar to the ancient Semitic mind but is very strange to us. In our time probably only those with the very deepest Christian faith and experience can understand it—and even they cannot explain it to those who have not shared the experience. What can it possibly mean to say that "one has died, therefore all have died," or, more intimately, "I have been crucified with Christ"?

The ancient Jews believed that one person could represent or "stand for" other people so completely that what happened to him actually happened to them also. It did not happen to him *instead* of to them. Rather his experience *was* their experience. Perhaps we can get a vague idea of this complete identity in some of our own experiences. A mother can love a child so much that, when the child is sick and suffering, the mother literally hurts with the child. A husband can identify himself so completely with his wife that when she becomes pregnant, he has the symptoms of pregnancy. A wife can love her husband so much that if he dies, she can say, "Something in me died with him." A man can be so totally wrapped up in a political or social cause that its victory or defeat can mean life or death itself for him. More superficially, some people can be so involved with football players who represent them on the field that defeat or victory of the team is a bitter loss or a triumphant gain for them personally. Something like this losing and finding one's own existence in someone or something outside himself is meant by the Jewish concept or representation, which is expressed in Paul's statements about dying with Christ.

But even if these examples dimly echo the kind of identity Paul says Christians have with Jesus, there is still the big difference that Jesus lived a long time ago. How can we say that what happened to him back then happened also to us? Following is an attempt to answer this very difficult question. You will have to decide for yourself whether it is true to what Paul intended.

To believe in Jesus is to believe that, when I hear about him, at the same time I learn who *I* am. He is the man who lived a truly human life and reveals to me what my own true humanity is. Yet the contrast between us exposes the fact that I have not fulfilled my own humanity: I have denied it by not loving God with my whole being and my neighbor as myself. But then I hear that this

Jesus was the *friend* of sinners—people like me who are alienated from God, from other people, and from themselves. He stood with and for us so completely that he suffered the death which is the consequence of *our* sin. He even "descended into Hell"—the hell we all sometimes experience, the utter loneliness which cries, "My God, why hast thou forsaken me?" From him I learn that in order to achieve true humanity in community with God and my fellowmen, my self-destructive inhumanity must be "sacrificed" and put out of the way. I do not learn this only intellectually; I learn it in my own experience. This Jesus who lived so long ago is so much a part of me and the way I understand myself, and I am so closely connected with him, that when I hear about his dying, I die too. My old self is "crucified" with him, I experience the new and genuine humanity which he himself represents and which I receive in his company.

How does Jesus' death affect me? Not just as somthing that happened to him *instead* of me, but as something that happens also to *me*. On that Good Friday so long ago was revealed the truth about *all* men in *all* times, including me. As I believe in the one who died then, what he was and did and what happened to him determines my own life. I discover, in short, that "I have been crucified with Christ; it is no longer I who live, but Christ who lives in me; and the life I now live in the flesh I live by faith in the Son of God, who loved me and gave himself for me" (Galatians 2:20).

Is this putting to death of our "old" (inhuman) selves and the birth of "new" (human) selves through our identity with Christ even conceivable for us today? Can we give ourselves so completely to him? These are questions that the doctrine of the atonement itself does not answer. The answer lies in the doctrines of the Holy Spirit, justification and sanctification, which still lie ahead of us.

For the present, it is enough to say that when we begin to wrestle with this way of looking at the meaning of Christ's death we are a long way from the tin pan crushed instead of a dirty glass. From our present point of view, the cross means that we "dirty glasses" *are* destroyed when we meet God in Christ. To be a

Christian is not an escape from this shattering encounter. Escape would mean only escape into the hell of continued existence in lonely separation from him, from other people, and from our own true selves. The Christian way is not the way of *escape* but of *death*. For only as our old inhumanity is painfully given up can we hope for a genuinely human life. "For whoever would save his life will lose it; and whoever loses his life for my sake, he will save it" (Luke 9:24).

4. The cross changes our relationship with other people. Our emphasis until now has been on how the death of Jesus affects our relationship with God. But our discussion would not be complete if we did not emphasize finally how it affects our relationship with other people. This is perhaps the last thing to be said about the significance of the atonement, but it is the last thing which is the test of whether everything else we have said is only pious talk.

If the cross really enables us to understand and live by the Good News that our debts are forgiven, and if it means that our old selves are killed, then we will be reconciled not only with God but with our fellowmen. At the same time that Christ breaks down the "walls of hostility" between us and God he also breaks them down between us and other people (Ephesians 2:14). If we know that God has loved us at such great cost, we will love one another (1 John 4:11). If we believe and follow the Jesus who "took the form of a servant, humbled himself and was obedient even unto death," we ourselves will have the "mind of Christ," looking not only to our own interests, but to the interest of others (Philippians 2:3 ff.). The New Testament makes this unmistakably clear: *There is no such thing as reconciliation with God without reconciliation with our fellowmen.* Hostility toward them—*any* of them—always means hostility toward God. Peace with God always means peace also with them—all of them.

Morever, the way God reconciles us with himself determines *how* reconciliation with other people happens. The *offended* takes the initiative—not just with words but with action—to go to the side of the other. There can be no question of, "*If* you pay for what you have done, *if* you make up for your offences and prove yourself worthy, *then* I will forgive you." There will be no suggestion that our acceptance, forgiveness and love have to be earned, bought, or squeezed out of us. This does not mean that disobedient children, for instance, or law-breakers should not be punished. It does mean that punishment will not be administered vindictively seeking revenge; it will be given in order to help. It does not mean that Christians are sweet, passive doormats who excuse all injustices and offences with a gently suffering smile. There is such a thing as legitimate anger at offences to ourselves and—especially—at injustice to others. Such anger is the honest acknowledgement of the hostility, alienation and wrong that in fact exist. But legitimate anger (i.e., anger which reflects the wrath of God) will not express itself in a concern to "get even" or to beat down the "enemy." It will express itself as a concern to *heal* broken relationships and injustice for the good of *everyone*.

We are not concerned now to say in detail how this can be done. We are concerned only to say at the end of our discussion of the atonement that to believe that "God was in Christ reconciling the world to himself" means inevitably and inescapably to seek to learn how *we* can reflect God's way of freely *initiating* reconciliation in all the human relationships in which we live: parents and children, husbands and wives, rich and poor, nation and nation, Christians and non-Christians. Here we learn at the very heart of the Christian faith, at the cross of Christ, what we have seen at every other point in our study: The Christian faith never has to do only with the "religious" sphere of life and our "spiritual" relationship with God; it always includes *every* dimension of our lives, secular as well as religious, life in the world as well as life in the church.

FOR FURTHER STUDY AND REFLECTION

1. Which of the biblical images describing the atonement is most helpful to you? Which would be most helpful in expressing the meaning of Christ's death to a non-Christian in your neighborhood, office, or club?

2. Ancient men believed they could pacify the gods and buy

their support by sacrificing animals. How do modern men try to pacify God and win his support?

3. Not all theologians agree with the position defended in this chapter that God does not need to be reconciled to sinful men, but that sinful men must be reconciled to God. Do you agree? Support your answer with Scripture.

4. Can forgiveness and love be earned?

5. Is it harder to forgive or to accept forgiveness?

6. What is the difference between tolerance and love?

7. In what concrete ways could a parent let a guilty child know that he participates in and shares the child's guilt?

8. How could a husband or wife show genuine forgiveness by sharing in the guilt of the other who has been unfaithful? Or should there be forgiveness at all?

9. Would the most healthy marriage be one in which the partners never became angry with one another, or one in which they expressed hostility toward each other?

10. How would you answer the question of how the death of Christ 2,000 years ago can affect us today?

11. There are three major theories about the reason for punishing criminals: prevention of further crimes, retribution or expiation for the crime, and rehabilitation to be a useful member of society. In light of the doctrine of the atonement, which of these do you think Christians should support? Does the doctrine of the atonement help us to decide whether Christians should support capital punishment?

12. Read Matthew 18:23–35. What light does this parable throw on the connection between reconciliation with God and reconciliation with other people?

14

Who's in Charge Here?

"The third day he rose again from the dead. By this he declared himself the conqueror of death and sin, for by his resurrection he swallowed up death, broke the fetters of the devil, and destroyed all his power (1 Peter 3:22)." That's what Calvin said in Question 73 of his Geneva Catechism. That's what the Bible says. That's what we sing with full organ and trumpets at Easter: "Hallelujah! The Lord God omnipotent reigneth . . . The kingdom of this world is become the Kingdom of our Lord and of his Christ, and he shall reign for ever and ever."

But that's not what the newspapers say: Another bloody purge in Red China . . . Reports of Viet Cong atrocities against civilians and captured Americans . . . An American soldier triumphantly holds up the severed head of an enemy soldier and wins the case of scotch promised by his commander to the first to kill with a hatchet . . . Pictures of an American soldier horribly burned by napalm accidentally dropped on our own troops, and another of a woman blinded by American fire, holding her mutilated baby . . . Almost 3,000 killed in an earthquake in Turkey . . . Man in Detroit in utter despair kills his wife, three children and self . . . Evidence to support the prediction that, with the growing perfection of computers, machines will eventually control our civilization, and that the main function of men will be to produce and tend machines . . . Hungry children refused surplus food because county administrators are against "government handouts" . . . Statistics showing that mental illness now touches as many as one in four Americans ... Reports of squalor, misery and riots in city slums across the country.

By the time you read this, the news will be different. But it will still be the same. Death and sin and the devil will *not* be conquered. They will still be making the headlines—or hidden on the inside pages, or not mentioned at all, depending on where they are at work.

Is Easter only for people who close their eyes to the cold facts of life and seek escape in fairy stories, baby bunnies, spring flowers and loud music? Is there any connection between the news and the Good News, between the "kingdom of this world" and the Kingdom of our Lord and of his Christ? That is what we have to discuss in this chapter as realistically and as faithfully as we can. First we shall look at the stories of the New Testament about the resurrection and ascension of Jesus. Then we shall begin the task of trying to understand what that event of ancient history means for us today.

On the Third Day

If we can say that any one aspect of the Christian faith is more important than any other, the resurrection is it. Without faith that Jesus rose from the dead there would be no Christianity. It was not the ethical teachings of Jesus or his noble death that gave birth to the Christian church and made it spread. It was the news of his resurrection. We have already seen that it was only because they first believed in a risen Christ that the first Christians looked back to ask about the meaning of his birth, life and death. Paul wrote: "If Christ has not been raised, your faith is futile and you are still in your sins. ... We are of all men most to be pitied" (1 Corinthians 15:17–19). The earliest confession summarizing the whole faith of the first Christians was, "Jesus is Lord"—a title conferred on him because of his resurrection.

Sometimes the church has made the cross the center of its faith. (The Belgic and Westminster Confessions, for instance, give careful attention to the meaning of the cross, but hardly mention the significance of the resurrection.) This is not totally wrong, of course. The risen, triumphant Lord is none other than the Suffering Servant who gave himself for us. But the cross is an appropriate symbol for the Christian faith only if it is an *empty* cross. The foundation and center of the Christian faith is not death but life; not a tragedy but victory beyond tragedy; not a gloomy, world-denying fascination with a dead sacrifice, but a triumphant, world-challenging faith in a living Lord; not a passive, breast-beating moaning about how sinful the world is, but an active, joyful moving out of sinfulness to obedient fellowship with him. He is risen! That is where the Christian faith begins, and for Christians it is the one event in history which gives meaning to all of history, including our own.

But can we believe it? What is actually supposed to have happened, and what evidence is there that it really did? Let us look at the story. We find five different versions of it: Matthew 28:1–20; Mark 16:1–19; Luke 24:1–51; John 20:1–21:25; I Corinthians 15:3–8. You will find suggestions for a comparative study of these texts at the end of this chapter. Here are some of the results of such a study.

1. Emphasis: the risen Christ. Many people witnessed the crucifixion, but no one saw the resurrection. No one was there when it happened, and no attempt is made in the New Testament to describe it. The resurrection stories are not really accounts of the resurrection itself, but of the appearances of the risen Jesus. This ought to warn us against any speculation about what happened in the tomb, about how a dead man came to life again. Christian faith, strictly speaking, is not faith in the empty tomb or in the resurrection, but in the risen Christ.

2. A question of faith not proof. There is no proof that Jesus rose from the dead. Even if the tomb were in fact empty, is it not more in accord with what we know about the scientific laws of nature to assume that Jesus was not really dead in the first place, but only in a coma? Or that his disciples stole the body (see Matthew 28:13)? Moreover, even if he really died and really lived again, and even if there were medical reports to confirm it, that still would not prove that *God* raised him, or that his resurrection meant his victory over all the powers of sin and evil. It would only prove that a medical wonder happened. The empty tomb, in short, is no proof of anything.

Critics have argued further that the different accounts of the resurrection do not jibe. The sequence of events on the first Easter Sunday and the following days is different from one story to the next. The accounts differ in reporting to whom he appeared and when. They contradict each other in details: How many angels were there, for instance, and where were they? It is very difficult, if not impossible, to harmonize the various resurrection stories. Does not their conflicting witness throw doubt on the truth of what they are supposed to report?

Finally, it has also been pointed out that only *believers* ever saw the risen Christ. Is it not significant that no unbiased observer ever saw him? Were not the appearances of the risen Jesus in fact only hallucinations of those who could not accept the fact that he was really dead? Or is it not possible that they simply made up the stories to try to convince other people that they had not been wrong in believing Jesus to be the Messiah?

The criticisms we have mentioned can be partially answered. We have already pointed out that the faith of the first Christians was not founded on arguments about the empty tomb but on their encounter with the risen Christ. It was not from the tomb but from *him* that they learned what it was all about.

Secondly, it is true that the reports cannot be harmonized in detail. Why should we be surprised, considering the fact that they were first written down a generation or more after the event? Besides that, however they differ in details about *how* it all took place, they are all agreed on the essential point *that* the same Jesus who died on Good Friday, lived again and appeared to his followers.

Again, it is true that only believers saw him. But all the reports emphasize that the women and the disciples did not expect to discover that he lived and were anything but eager to believe it. They were worried, afraid, skeptical even after they saw him. See Matthew 28:17; Mark 16:8; 11:13; Luke 24:11, 36–39; John

20:24–28. It was not just a matter of convincing others; their own unbelief had to be overcome. It was not a matter of wishful thinking and wanting to pretend to themselves that he was alive; their own certainty that he was dead, buried and gone from them forever had to be overcome.

These answers do not prove that the reports are true, of course. There *is* no proof. Doubts and questions about the whole thing are inevitable. Jesus' own closest disciples, people who were there when it happened, had trouble believing it. But faith does not come only where there is proof without doubt or question. It comes in the midst of doubt and questioning. For us that means to listen, without any proof at all, to what we are told about this absolutely unique, "unscientific" event. Why should we listen? Not so that we may believe the witnesses as such, but so that we may know the risen, living Christ to whom they bear witness. Not so that we may believe that it really happened, but so that we may know him to whom it happened and, knowing him, share with him a new life.

3. The nature of the resurrection. Before we move on to ask what the resurrection means, there are two aspects of these stories which can help us to avoid wrong paths some Christians have taken in trying to understand it.

First, it is important to note that according to the New Testament God raised Jesus from the dead (1 Corinthians 1:4; Philippians 2:9). He did not raise himself. The New Testament does not speak of the resurrection as the result of an inner divine power within Jesus which survived death and enabled him to live again. He really was dead—*totally* dead. The resurrection is the story of God's giving life to a dead man, not of the immortality this man possessed in himself.

This must be emphasized, because Easter is often understood after the analogy of trees and flowers that "come to life" again every spring after passing through the "death" of winter. This analogy of death and an afterlife is common in pagan mythologies. But the story of the resurrection is not such a myth. It does not describe the possibility we have in ourselves to survive after death, or an automatic "immortality of the soul." The New Testament does not teach that either about Jesus or about us. It is much more realistic and serious about death than that. Jesus' and our own deaths are not just a "passing over" or rebirth after winter. Death is really the *end* of us.

The doctrine of the resurrection is not a sentimental assurance that death is not so bad after all, since our inmost selves do not really die. It is the radical good news of the powerful love of God which is stronger than death. It is good news about what *God* does, not about what we can do for ourselves or what happens automatically. We shall return to this later when we speak about our own death and eternal life. But it is important now as we begin to speak of Jesus' resurrection that we do not let it become a kind of cheap happy ending which takes neither his death nor his resurrection seriously. The resurrection means far more than a doctrine of immortality in which many men have believed without even knowing about or believing in Jesus.

The second aspect of the resurrection stories which can keep us from a wrong doctrine of the resurrection is the emphasis the New Testament places on the *physical, worldly* reality of the risen Jesus. It is true that there was a mysterious difference between the Jesus the disciples had known before the crucifixion and the risen Jesus. How is this described in John 20:14–17, and Luke 24:13–16, 30–31? Nevertheless, the biblical writers go out of their way to emphasize that the risen Jesus is the same one they had known before. He walks, talks, eats and can be touched. The risen Jesus is no ghost or phantom! He also has to do with flesh and blood men in this world. Even when he ascends to the Father, he takes our humanity with him (to use the church's language). We shall speak later of what it means for us to believe in the resurrection of the *body*. Now the important point is that when we begin to speak about the meaning of the resurrection, we must not spiritualize it so that it has only an otherworldly significance for the next life. The resurrection happened in *this* world. For Jesus himself it meant not escape from his own humanity and the human existence of other men, but the *renewal* of his own and other's humanity. The resurrection, in other words, does not have to do only with the significance of Jesus for us after we die and leave this world. It has to do also with the lives of flesh and blood men, here and now.

The Lord and His Kingdom

According to the New Testament the resurrection of Jesus meant that he who gave himself as the Suffering Servant of God is now revealed to be the triumphant Lord. He who came preaching the Kingdom of God is now seen to be the King of the Kingdom. Lord, King, Kingdom, victory, rule, authority, sovereignty—these are the concepts which characterize biblical faith in the risen Jesus. And these are the concepts we must try to understand.

We begin with some comments about the terminology of resurrection theology. Words like Lord, Ruler, King and kingdom sound strange to us. They sound so archaic—so *undemocratic!* Should we not translate this outdated political language, taken from the environment of the ancient world, into language that makes sense in our time? Several things need to be said in answer to this legitimate question.

First, it is no accident that the New Testament uses *political* images to speak of the meaning of the resurrection. We shall see that this is not just a matter of language but of essential content. Any translation we made, then, would have to be made into corresponding political imagery.

Second, the meaning of the resurrection *is* undemocratic. Jesus is not Lord by our permission, or because he wins enough votes to get in office. *God* made him Lord and Christ, without any support or cooperation from the side of men—in fact, despite the unwillingness and hostility of men (Acts 2:36). Like the sovereignty of God, the lordship of Christ has nothing to do with the will of the people. So any modern imagery we might choose cannot come from the democratic form of government. The risen Christ is no president or chairman of the board or elected representative.

But what political imagery do we have to express the absolute authority of Jesus? Tyrant? Dictator? Boss? None of these will do, because they all suggest unjust or arbitrary power. The good news about the power of *this* Lord is that, unlike all other unlimited power we know, his power is the sovereignty of love. He is the Lord who gave his very life for us. And he exercises his power in such a way that it does not destroy our freedom and humanity, but grants and nourishes genuinely free human life. He became Lord without our support, despite our opposition. But as Lord, he is for us and not against us. He is not for us in a paternalistic, condescending way as a master cares for a dog, keeping him weak and dependent. Rather, he is for us as one who shared and still shares our human existence and helps us to grow up into strong, free maturity of our own.

What title or name is appropriate for such an authority? There is no political office and no political officer comparable to what he does and who he is. Even "lordship" and "Lord" are really inappropriate. This language was originally borrowed partly from ancient Jewish religion and partly from ancient pagan emperor worship. In the first century it was loaded with heathen connotations. Who Jesus is and what he does are so unique that he cannot be fit into *any* human thought patterns, ancient or modern. If we stick to such archaic terminology as "Lord" and "lordship" it is not because this language is especially sacred in itself, but because in our time it may suggest the uniqueness of this political figure and his government over against all the politicians and forms of government that are part of our daily experience.

But if we do this, we must take extra-special care to see how the risen Christ himself touches every area of our lives in the world today. This brings us back to the question with which we began this chapter: What does the good news of Easter have to do with the real world we read about in the newspapers? In light of the way life really is, how can we seriously confess that Jesus is Lord—a Lord who rules over the world with absolute power and at the same time with freeing, humanizing love? In order to answer this question, we shall look at the various ways Christian thinkers have tried to understand the meaning of his lordship and the reality of the Kingdom of God which challenges and defeats the "kingdom of this world"—the kingdom of sin, death and the devil.

1. The Kingdom as an ideal to be realized. One way of dealing with the contradiction between Christian claims about the risen Christ and the nature of the "real" world is to say that Jesus did not bring the reality but the *ideal* of God's Kingdom of justice, love, freedom and humanity. To be a Christian is to get to work to make the ideal a fact. By our loyalty to Christ, and by our Christian obedience, preaching and teaching, we may hope gradually to overcome the forces of evil in the world and "bring in" the Kingdom.

This is probably the most common idea of the lordship of Christ or the Kingdom of God in our time. We speak of "letting" Christ be the Lord of our lives, or of "making" him Lord. Especially when we take up the offering, we talk and pray about our money being used to "spread" the Kingdom. We speak of applying Christian principles or ideals to our individual, business or social life so that Christ may reign through us. All these expressions are ways of saying that Christ is not Lord but *ought* to be, that the Kingdom of God is not a reality but a goal to strive for. It is up to us to realize the ideal.

This way of thinking has the advantage of taking into account the great gap between the way things really are and the Easter faith that "the kingdom of this world is become the Kingdom of our Lord." And it sees that belief in the lordship of Christ means active obedience on our part. But it is not a biblical solution to the problem. This idealistic understanding subtly changes the Kingdom of God into the kingdom of pious men and makes them instead of Christ the real ruler. If Christ can be Lord only insofar as we let him be or make him Lord, who really is in control? If the Kingdom can become a reality only insofar as *we* bring it in or make it spread, whose kingdom is it really? Suppose we did collect enough money to build churches everywhere and expand the program of the church beyond our wildest dreams—would the successful kingdom of the church automatically be the same as the Kingdom of God? Suppose Christians got in control of everything—would a world run by Christians be the same as the reign of God? What about the injustice, faithlessness and self-centered inhumanity *within* the church and us Christians?

According to the New Testament, it is God and God alone who makes Christ to be Lord, who brings in the Kingdom. While he invites and commands us to acknowledge and participate in his

Kingdom, it in no way depends upon our help and cooperation, nor is it identical with our efforts and achievements. What *bad* news it would be if we had to think that the Kingdom of God could be real only to the extent that we Christians and our church really believe in it and worked for it! How terrible if God's freeing, humanizing justice and love were no greater or more effective than ours!

To relate the kingdom of the world and the Kingdom of God as reality versus ideal is a denial of the truth of the resurrection. The resurrection means that not Christians but Christ is the hope of the world. It means that the reality of the Kingdom of God depends not on what *we* may one day succeed in doing if we try hard enough, but on what *God* has done, is doing and will do.

2. The Kingdom as a future hope.

Another solution to the contradiction between the kind of world we live in and the claims of the Easter message about the victory and rule of Christ is to push the Kingdom of God and the lordship of Christ into the future. Christ may not yet be the Victor and Ruler, but he *will* be when he comes again. The Kingdom of God has not yet replaced the kingdom of this world, but it *will* do so at the end of this age. Easter is the proclamation not of a present reality but of a future hope.

This solution is like the idealistic one in that it understands the Kingdom of God only as a future reality. But it is different in that it believes that not man but God will "realize" the Kingdom, and that this will happen not by a gradual process of changing the world, but by a sudden, catastrophic judgment and destruction of the world as we know it.

Unlike the idealistic view, this apocalyptic understanding of the rule of God in Christ has some biblical justification. During his life Jesus himself sometimes spoke as if, far from becoming gradually better, the world would become worse and worse until finally at the "last day" God himself would step in in a terrible way to establish his Kingdom. How is this expressed in Matthew 24:3–35; Mark 13:1–37; Luke 21:5–36? When do these passages suggest that the end will come?

There is also some justification for the futuristic understanding

of the lordship of Christ in the New Testament's interpretation of
the resurrection and ascension of Jesus. Throughout the letters of
the New Testament we find the expectancy that the risen Christ
will come again to judge, save and claim the world which belongs
to him. Some passages interpret the time between the resurrection
and the end of the world as being for Christ a time of waiting *until*
his enemies are defeated. See 1 Corinthians 15:25 and Hebrews
10:13.

It is clear, then, that there is a futuristic aspect of the Christian
belief in the lordship of Christ and the Kingdom of God. If that
were all there is to it, the problem we are considering in this
chapter would be solved. Or rather we would deny that there is
any problem. We may *expect* injustice, hatred, godlessness and inhumanity in the world. The world *does* belong to sin, death and the
devil. There is nothing we can do about it, and there is no point in
even trying. All we can do is sit, wait, hope and pray for the end
of the world, when the Kingdom of God *will* come and Jesus *will*
be Lord.

This solution has often been accepted as the correct one by
some Christians. It has led to two results. On the one hand those
Christians who accept it have said to the victims of injustice and
evil, "There is no use complaining or trying to better your condition. That's the way it is in this evil old world. Just be patient and
believe, and someday you will be saved." It was just this kind of
Christianity that Karl Marx called an "opiate" to keep the victims
of injustice passive and submissive.

On the other hand, this futuristic view has sometimes been
made a pious excuse for Christians not to participate themselves,
and to criticize those who do participate, in any efforts to combat
injustice and evil and to make the world a better, more human
world. Occasionally it can even lead to a perverse rejoicing at the
triumph of evil: The greater the evil and misery around us, the
more people will give up confidence in all worldly "do-goodism"
and will "turn to Christ."

A purely futuristic way of understanding the lordship of Christ
does see one side of biblical teaching, and it does take seriously the
power of sin and evil in the world. But it conveniently listens only
to one aspect of biblical teaching and ignores another. In so doing

it finally denies the good news of Easter. While the New Testament
writers do look forward to a final triumph of Christ at the end, they
do not tell us only that Christ will one day triumph over sin, evil
and death. They tell us that on Easter morning he *did* triumph.
They do not say that sometime in the future he will be Lord over
the world and our individual lives. They say that he *is* Lord. How
is this triumphant Easter faith expressed in 1 Peter 3:22; Acts 2:36;
Philippians 2:9; Colossians 1:15–20; 1 Timothy 6:15; Revelation
17:14? What is the significance of the verbs in the past and present
tenses in these texts?

Moreover, the same Jesus who spoke of the future coming of
the Kingdom could also say that with his presence, the Kingdom
has come. See Luke 10:17; Matthew 12:28; 28:18.

If this is true, then we do not *have* to, nor are we *allowed* to,
sit and wait, doing nothing until the end of the world. To do that
would be to say in effect that Easter is not true, that power of God
in Christ is not really stronger than the power of sin. If we believe
that all the "principalities and powers" are *already* subject to
Christ, then we can and we must confidently throw ourselves into
the fight against the evil in our own lives and in the world around
us, knowing that we do not fight alone but with the one who has
already triumphed over the forces of evil. If we believe that all
authority in heaven and on earth has already been given to him,
then it is faithless and disobedient to tell others that nothing can be
done and to excuse ourselves from doing anything because the
world is hopelessly ruled by sin, death, and the Devil.

We must return presently to what is legitimate in the futuristic
view of the Lord and his Kingdom. In any case, taken by itself, it
cannot be accepted as the Christian solution to the problem of the
conflict between the Kingdom of God and the kingdom of this
world.

3. The Kingdom here and now. The idealistic and
the futuristic interpretations of the lordship of Christ and his Kingdom try to sidestep the problem of the clash between the facts of
life in the world and the claims of the Easter message by pushing
the Kingdom of God into the future, either to be gradually brought
in by men, or to be suddenly brought in by God himself. Both solu-

tions deny the Easter message that in Christ God has *already* triumphed over the powers of injustice, hatred, slavery and inhumanity, so that the Kingdom of justice, love, freedom and humanity is *already* here.

Now we come to a third position which emphasizes just this missing element in the first two positions we have discussed. Instead of an "idealistic" or "futuristic" eschatology, it defends a "realized" eschatology. (Eschatology is the study of last things or end things, and is the technical theological name for the consideration of when, how and where God's plan for the world is finally fulfilled.) Realized eschatology, citing such texts as we mentioned in criticising futuristic eschatology, holds that the coming of Jesus itself and especially his resurrection mean that the Kingdom of God and the lordship of Christ are a *present* reality—here, now, in *this* world.

This position is a much needed corrective to the one-sidedness of the other views. But it can also be criticized. It neglects the New Testament texts which tell us that the final victory of Christ over the powers of evil in the world lies in the future. If futuristic eschatology must be criticized by realized eschatology, the reverse is also true. Can we really do without the expectant *hope* that the Kingdom of God *will* one day triumph finally, once and for all, over the kingdom of this world? This question becomes all the more acute when we look at the way realized eschatology in its turn also sidesteps the obvious contradiction between the way the world really is and Easter claims about the lordship of Christ.

Those who defend this position are not so unrealistic that they deny the fact of evil in the world. In order to be realistic about the world and at the same time hold that the risen Christ has already triumphed over sin, death and the Devil, they *narrow the extent* of Christ's lordship and the Kingdom of God. The resurrection means not that Christ rules over the whole world, but that he rules in the hearts of individual believers, or in the church. The world at large may still be gripped by the powers of darkness, but that power is broken in those who acknowledge and obey the lordship of Christ. *They* experience the present reality of the freedom, love, joy, peace and goodness of the Kingdom of God.

Now the New Testament does of course teach that the risen Christ is the Lord of individual Christians and of the church, and that his renewing power and help is especially among them. But it will not do to limit his authority and work to individual believers and the spiritual realm. To do so is again to deny what the New Testament explicitly teaches about the meaning of the resurrection: *"All authority* in heaven *and* earth has been given me" (Matthew 28:18). God has put him "above *all* rule and authority and power and dominion, and above *every* name that is named" (Ephesians 1:21). He is Lord of *all* lords, king over *all* kings (Revelation 17:14). According to the New Testament, therefore, to confess that Jesus is Lord is to confess that is Lord not only of believing individuals, not only of the church, but of the whole world—including the secular and political authorities of the world.

Narrowing the lordship of Christ as it does, realized eschatology tends to make obedience to the Lord only a matter of individual ethics and religious service. But if Easter is really true, and if Christ is really Lord over *all*, then we cannot exclude *any* area of our lives from responsibility to him. There is *no* part of the world and of our lives which belongs to ourselves, or to the devil, but not to him. The resurrection faith means that Christ is Lord, and that we are called to obey him, in individual *and* social-political, religious *and* secular affairs. For all their emphasis on the lordship of Christ here and now, the adherents of realized eschatology, with their tendency toward individualism and spiritualizing, tend to become as passive and irresponsible as the adherents of a futuristic eschatology when it comes to confident, obedient service of the risen Christ in the world.

Our conclusion is that, like the other two views of the Kingdom of God we have considered, the view of realized eschatology is partially correct. But it is too one-sided either to do justice to the Easter confession that Jesus *is* Lord, or to solve the problem of how we can believe that his loving power and powerful love are in control of our kind of world.

4. The Kingdom "between the times." We come now to a view of the lordship of Christ and the Kingdom of God which tries to put together all the partial truths of the other views. It is not so simple to understand as they, but then we are not dealing with a simple problem.

We begin at the most perplexing point. We have seen on the one hand that the New Testament writers take so seriously the power of sin, evil and death in the world that they expect them to be at work as long as the world exists. Christ's final victory over these "enemies" will not come until the history of the world itself ends. On the other hand, the New Testament writers take so seriously the victory of Christ at his resurrection and ascension that they confidently assert that the enemies are already subjected and defeated. In other words, both things are said to be true: the Kingdom of God it *not yet* here, but it is *already* here. Christ is *not yet* unchallenged Ruler of the world, but he is *already* the Ruler of the world. Is that not an outright contradiction? How can both things be true at the same time?

Many contemporary theologians have used what has become a familiar analogy to explain how both this "already" and this "not yet" are true,[1] and how the relationship between them is one important clue not only to the meaning of the doctrine of the resurrection, but to all the theology of the New Testament.

This is the analogy: In every war, there comes a decisive battle which makes unmistakably clear what the final outcome will be. The battle following "D Day" in World War II is an example. Mopping up operations may be necessary. The enemy may make a long, desperate, last-ditch struggle. Many lives can still be lost and much damage can still be done before the enemy finally surrenders and peace is declared. But the one decisive battle still determines the outcome of the war. The war is already won even if it is not yet over.

The winning of the decisive battle is Christ's victory over all the powers of sin, evil and death at Easter. The final victory is the final triumph at the end of all history of the justice, love and genuinely human life he brings. "Between the times" (i.e., between Easter and the end) he is already Lord but his enemies have not yet admitted their defeat and surrendered. His Kingdom is already surely established, but there is still fighting to do before it is acknowledged.

Let us look at some of the implications of this view of the lordship of Christ and of the Kingdom of God to see how it includes
what we have found to be correct about the other views we have
considered.[2]

a. We must take evil seriously. This is no sentimental, optimistic view which piously explains away evil, or cheerfully pretends that things are not really so bad after all. It realistically
admits that injustice, hatred, godlessness and inhumanity do and
will continue to ravage our individual lives and our world. There is
no naive confidence that the goodness in man will gradually triumph over the evil in him, or that Christians can bring in the Kingdom of God if they work at it hard enough. Evil is so powerful that
not men within history, but only Christ at the end of history, will
finally overcome it.

b. We must not take evil more seriously than God. If faith in
the lordship of Christ "between the times" is not optimistic, neither
is it pessimistic. It is true that this is a world in which there is and
always will be evil of all kinds. But Jesus Christ is risen! Evil may
be stronger than men (including *Christian* men), but it is not
stronger than God. It does not and will not have the last word.
The resurrection means that God has already challenged the
powers of darkness, and that even now he is already at work in the
world and in our own lives to bring reconciliation where there is
hostility, freedom where there is slavery, life where there is death,
humanity where there is inhumanity. Knowing the power of evil,
Christians are not surprised or disillusioned when they see it crop-
ping up over and over again in all kinds of places—including the
Christian church and the lives of individual Christians. But knowing the resurrection victory of God in Christ, Christians cannot be
ultimately pessimistic and gloomy about the world, the church and
themselves. No matter how hopeless the situation may seem, they
know of a power at work—*here* and *now*—greater than the power
of evil. In the midst of the very worst of evil, Christians live in hope
and not in despair. " If you have heard the Easter message," writes
Karl Barth, "you can no longer run around with a tragic face and
lead the humourless existence of a man who has no hope."[3]

c. We can and must fight against evil. We saw in our criticism
of a purely futuristic eschatology that Christians who believe that

Jesus is Lord cannot sit around wringing their hands over how evil the world is, passively waiting for God to do something about it. Now we can see more clearly why this is true.

All of us could be tempted simply to give up in despair when we take a hard look at the world around us and the mess we make of our own lives. The hostility between the white and colored races throughout the world; the never-ending international conflicts with the constant threat of nuclear warfare; the terrible, ever-increasing misery and turmoil of inner-city slums; the depersonalization, manipulation and exploitation of human beings in and by the business world; the fearful superficiality and inadequacy of the church; the conflicts in our personal and family relationships; the anxiety and insecurity which in one way or another seems to master all of us—in the face of all that, what use is it even to try to do anything? But if we can believe that since Easter the powers of evil are fighting a losing battle and that the one who has already conquered them is still at work to finish what he began, then we can take heart nevertheless to keep fighting, however powerful the enemy without and within may seem.

On the other hand, if the past victory of Christ makes it *possible* for us to keep struggling, the fact that the final victory has not yet been won makes it *necessary.* There is still work to be done. The goal has not yet been reached. The confession that Jesus is Lord does not mean that we can sit back with a sigh of relief and tell ourselves that everything is all right now. The powers of evil around us and within us have not yet admitted defeat. He himself is still finishing the work he began, and to call him Lord means obediently to throw ourselves into the battle with him.

At this point Christians can learn from the communists, who give themselves with such passion to the battle for their ideology just because they are so absolutely sure that history is going their way. Their certainty that capitalism is doomed and communism destined to prevail does not result in their sitting and waiting for the wheels of history to turn in their favor. On the contrary, it means freedom from all hesitation and despair, no matter how powerful the enemy may seem. It means both the courage and the demand to get to work and fight for the cause just because they are so sure their cause is right and certain to win. Christians have (*should* have?) the same action-inspiring confidence and sense of command—not because of a theory of history or an economic ideology to which they are committed, but because of a particular historical event of the past which they believe illumines the meaning of *all* history, present and future.

Go back and read again the introduction to this chapter, where we tried to put as bluntly as possible the problem of the conflict between what the Good News of Easter on the one hand, and the daily news on the other, tell us about the world and our lives in it. Do you agree that the concept of the Kingdom of God "between the times" is realistic about both? Does it take seriously enough both the New Testament claim that the risen Christ is already Lord and the brutal facts of life? Does it really overcome the inadequacies of the other views of the Kingdom of God and the lordship of Christ we have discussed?

Many questions still remain even after we have begun to understand the meaning of the lordship of Christ "between the times" and the Kingdom which is "already" but "not yet" here. *How* is this Lord present and at work in the world between the times? How can we have such faith in the truth of the Easter message that we actually enter and participate in his Kingdom with the confidence, joy, freedom and courageous obedience we have so glibly said Christians have? If he is Lord over the world as well as over the church, what is the difference between church and world, between those who acknowledge and accept his lordship and those who do not even know about it or refuse to accept it? Our task for the rest of this book will be to answer these questions.

Meanwhile, we conclude this chapter by pointing out that the very fact that we must spend so much time dealing with such questions is proof of how central to the Christian faith are the resurrection doctrines of the lordship of Christ and the Kingdom of God. The earliest Christians knew what they were doing when they summarized the whole of their faith with the apparently simple confession, "Jesus is Lord." The whole of the Christian faith depends on our learning what it means that individual Christians, the church and the whole world are on the way between "the third

day he rose again from the dead" (a historical event in the past)
and "he shall come again to judge the quick and the dead" (a
historical event in the future). The clue to what is going on in
the lives of every one of us, in the church, and in the whole world
is the confession that the one who died on Good Friday, rose on
Easter Sunday and will come again is the "Lord" who "sits at the
right hand of God the Father Almighty" (the meaning of history
in the present).

FOR FURTHER REFLECTION AND STUDY

1. Compare the versions of the Easter story in Matthew 28:1–20;
   Mark 16:1–19; Luke 24:1–51; John 20:1–21:25; and I Corinthians 15:3–8:
   a. What is the sequence of events in each story?
   b. How many angels were at the tomb, and where were
   they?
   c. Who saw the risen Jesus first? In what order did others
   see him?
   d. What were the reactions of those who saw him?
   e. What material is unique in each account?
   f. What conclusions would you draw from a comparison
   of these accounts if you were not a Christian? What are
   your conclusions as a Christian?
2. Is it important to believe that the resurrection happened
   literally? Would it be enough to believe that Jesus lived on in
   the memory of his followers, or continued to be very real in
   their hearts?
3. Why is it wrong to make an analogy between the resurrection
   and the rebirth of the natural world at springtime?
4. Do you agree that the archaic title "Lord" is a meaningful way
   of talking about Jesus in our time? If you had to translate this
   title into modern terminology, how would you do it?
5. Is your church a democracy? Should it be?
6. Which of the four views of the Kingdom of God best describe
   what you thought about the lordship of Christ before you
   read this chapter? Have you changed your mind?
7. Was Jesus mistaken in his predictions in Mark 9:1 and 13:30?

8. How would you answer Karl Marx's charge that religion is the opiate of the people?

9. On the basis of the New Testament understanding of the lordship of Christ and the Kingdom of God, defend or criticize the following statements:

    a. We ought to make Christ the Lord of our lives.

    b. Christians ought to give their money and their talents to help bring in the Kingdom of God.

    c. It is useless for us to try to correct social and political injustice, because the world is controlled by sin.

    d. We cannot hope for a better society and world until individuals are converted and turn to Christ.

    e. It will make people lazy and irresponsible if we say that Christ is already Lord of the whole world.

    f. The Kingdom of God is present in the hearts of believers.

    g. Considering the way the world really is, it is absurd to say that all authority in heaven and on earth has been given to Christ.

    h. When we accept Christ as Lord, the inner turmoil and struggle of our lives will be overcome.

10. What do we mean in the Lord's Prayer when we pray, "Thy Kingdom come," and then end by saying, "For thine *is* the Kingdom, the power and the glory"?

GOD
THE HOLY SPIRIT
and
A NEW LIFE

PART V

GOD THE HOLY SPIRIT
and
A NEW LIFE

"I believe in the Holy Ghost." The repetition of "I believe" when we come to this part of the creed suggests that we have come to a new turning point. Something new is about to be said. The new thing is that men—we ourselves—become a part of what Christians believe. "I believe in God the Father Almighty" confesses God *over* us. "And in Jesus Christ his only Son our Lord" confesses God *with* us and *for* us. "I believe in the Holy Ghost" confesses God *in* us. The first article speaks of a movement of God toward men. The second speaks of God among men. Now the third speaks of a movement of men toward God. We now reach the purpose and goal of everything else we have said to this point. "I will be your God" is what the the first two articles tell us. Why? The work of creation and reconciliation take place so that "You shall be my people." That is what the third article tells us. The first two articles speak of God in relation to men. Now the third speaks of men in relation to God.

Another way of expressing the significance of the statements connected with the Holy Spirit in the creed is to say that they are the subjective part which follows the objective part. The first two articles speak primarily of who God is and what he has done, without much reference to our response to him. But now we come to speak about ourselves—the community of us Christians, the forgiveness of *our* sins, the resurrection of *our* bodies, *our* everlasting life. How do we come to say not only God and Father, but *my* God and Father; not only Lord, but *our* Lord? How does what God did "back there" touch *us* and affect *our* lives? How do *we* fit into the picture—we who live "between the times," *after* the reconciling death and victorious resurrection of Christ, but *before* his final victory over all the forces of alienation, hostility, slavery and death around us and in us? These questions have concerned us all the way along in our study, of course. But now they become the central theme when we begin to speak of the work of God the Holy Spirit.

Still another way of saying where we are going at this turning point in our study is to put it in the language of the outline of Calvin's *Institutes*. We have spoken of "The Knowledge of God the Creator" (Book I) and of "The Knowledge of God the Redeemer in Christ . . ." (Book II); now in the third place we have to talk about "The Way in Which We Receive the Grace of Christ: What Benefits Come to Us from It, and What Effects Follow" (Book III).

Once again we see that Christians cannot talk only about God, nor do they believe only in God. If we are talking about the God of the Bible, the Father of Jesus Christ, then we must talk about men too. If we believe in him, then we can also believe in men (ourselves!), insofar as they are men who come from God, among whom God himself dwells, *in* whom God himself is at work. Sometimes Christians have spoken and acted as if it must be *either* God *or* man, God to the exclusion of humanity or humanity to the exclusion of God. But to love God—this God—does not mean to have contempt for man and his life in the world. The love of God is the source of respect for and the achievement of true humanity. We learn that already when we call him our Father and his Son our Lord. But when we come to know him as God the Holy Spirit, then we come to know *how* it happens that, when God is with men, their humanity is not cast aside or destroyed but given a new honor and dignity. That is what we have to try to understand in the following chapters.

In chapter 15 we shall talk about who the Holy Spirit is—*how* God works in our lives "between the times." There is no better way of doing that than to ask, "What's New?"

In chapters 16 and 17 we shall talk about how Christian

individuals enter into and live in the Kingdom "between the times." Christian theology has traditionally spoken of justification and sanctification to deal with this question. We shall consider these doctrines under the title, "Are You a Christian?"

In chapter 18 we shall discuss the Christian *church* and its task in the world "between the times." In our time the Body of Christ is in such trouble that we shall talk about it under the title, "Living or Dead?"

Finally, in chapter 19 we shall ask, "What's Going to Happen to Us?" Here we shall deal with the question of our future as individuals and of the future of the church and the world, as we look forward to the final victory of the Lord at the end.

15

What's New?

If you had to choose between them, which one of the following statements best expresses what you would like more than anything else to get out of being a Christian?

"I want a faith that changes my life, gives me a sense of inner power, awakens and inspires in me a true spirituality, makes me feel happy, free and enthusiastic about being a Christian, and leads me to challenge the evil of the world."

"I want a faith that gives me sound, authoritative biblical doctrine, enables me to have a sure knowledge of the truth of God, and helps me to stand firm against all attempts to water down or compromise that truth."

"I want a faith that can reconcile Christians with one another, stop their endless quarreling and petty bickering with each other, and make them a united Christian community so they can participate effectively in the Christian mission to the world."

Vitality, authority and solidarity (or life, truth and community)—*all three* are important aspects of the Christian faith and life. All three ought to belong together, for they are all gifts of the same Spirit of God. In the Apostles' Creed the Spirit is associated with the "holy Catholic Church" and the "communion of saints" (solidarity). In the Nicene Creed the Spirit is called "Lord" (authority) and "Giver of Life" (vitality).[1]

But as a matter of fact, not only individual Christians but whole denominations tend to emphasize one aspect at the expense of the others. The result has been one-sided Christians, denominational division—and a misunderstanding of the Holy Spirit and his work.

Those Christians who emphasize *vitality* tend to have a religion only of the heart. Intensity of feeling and the emotional experience of sinfulness, conversion, judgment and renewal are what count. These Christians tend to be impatient with what they call a coldly intellectual emphasis on doctrine and truth. And because their religion is so personal and internal, they tend to be individualistic—indifferent or even antagonistic toward the organized church with its "dead" structures, and toward other church members who do not share the personal religious experiences of the few "real" Christians.

Those who emphasize *authority*, on the other hand, tend to have a religion only of the head. Orthodox doctrine and fighting against heresy are what count. These Christians tend to be impatient with "mere" emotions, subjectivism, and "empty" activism. They also tend to be suspicious of the church at large, because it contains too many people who do not think as they do. They would rather split the church and start a church of their own than compromise what they are sure is the truth—*their* truth.

Those who emphasize *solidarity* tend to want unity at all costs. Intense enthusiasm, unique personal experiences and individual feelings are all right so long as they do not disturb the order and stability of the church. Truth is important, but what it is should be decided by the church as a whole and accepted by all members without question. Or at least Christian truth should be interpreted so that division is avoided and room is made for everybody.

How has it happened that three gifts of the same Spirit have led to three conflicting kinds of Christianity? Something is obviously wrong with a Christian experience which is indifferent to truth and to community. On the other hand, how can truly Christian truth be cold, dead and destructive of community? And how can there be genuine community if it is not based on a strict concern for truth, realized in people with a genuinely life-renewing Christian experience?

Where the Holy Spirit is at work there is new life *and* truth *and* community. Could it be that a study of the doctrine of the Spirit could help us to overcome the one-sidedness every one of us has in one direction or another? Could this be a central doctrine in resolving the conflicts within our own denomination and between denominations? This doctrine has been generally neglected in the old-line Protestant churches and left to the sects. (In the original version of the Westminster Confession, for example, there was no chapter on God the Spirit. What would you think was the reason for this omission?) Many theologians today believe that, as the church concentrated on the person of Christ for centuries, we in our time, with our problems, need to give special attention to the Spirit.

That is what we are going to do in this chapter. In light of the problem of the relationship between life, truth and community we shall first ask, "Who is the Holy Spirit?" and then, "What does he do?"

Who the Holy Spirit Is

The foundation of the biblical doctrine of the Holy Spirit, and the basis for preserving this doctrine from corruption and one-sidedness in one direction or another, is the simple fact that the Holy Spirit is none other than God himself. He is "God coming to man in an inward way to enlighten and strengthen him."[2] Once we understand this one thing, everything else will fall into proper perspective. There are at least three important aspects of this one basic truth.

1. **The Holy Spirit is a person.** If the Spirit is God himself, he is Some*one*, not some*thing*. A common error is to speak of the Spirit as a neuter: "When *it* is at work in our hearts" or "When *it* controls us." We have a tendency to think of him as an impersonal power or some energy which somehow gets into men. A frequent but badly mistaken analogy is to think of the Spirit's being like electricity: If we can somehow be plugged in to God, a power will flow into our lives which makes the light shine in our hearts, or which recharges our batteries. Such an analogy is wrong because it is impersonal. It depersonalizes the Spirit himself and it

depersonalizes men. The Holy Spirit of God is not a kind of spiritual electrical current, and human beings are neither light bulbs to be turned on nor batteries to be recharged. He works *personally*, treating us not as objects to be manipulated but as conscious, thinking, willing persons. We can avoid all kinds of magical, superstitious, fanatical ideas about the Holy Spirit if we keep this in mind.

2. He is the Spirit of the God we know. He is the Spirit of God the Creator (Genesis 1:2). What he wills and does is what God the Father Almighty wills and does. He is the Spirit of Christ (2 Corinthians 3:17; Galatians 4:6; John 14:18), and what he wills and does is what God the Son, our Lord, wills and does. The Holy Spirit is God at work in a new and different way —*in* us instead of only over us and for us, *now* and not only in the past. But he is not the Spirit of an unknown God who may say and do all kinds of totally unpredictable things. He is the Spirit at work in our lives to enable us to be human creatures in the image of God, sinners reconciled to God, to our fellowmen and to ourselves.

The fact that the Holy Spirit is the Spirit of the God we know gives us a criterion for recognizing him and his work. Just because he works inwardly, it is easy to confuse the Spirit with our own subjective ideas, wishes and feelings. A preacher, for example, once told his congregation that the Spirit told him that they should buy him a motorboat. Psychologists tell us (and they are confirmed by the history of religious movements in which spiritual experience is exaggerated) that the ecstasy of religious experiences of the "Spirit" is sometimes thinly veiled sexual ecstasy. It often happens in war that both sides feel the presence and support of the "God on our side" as they go out to slaughter the enemy. Sometimes teachers or preachers claim authority for their own peculiar ideas and doctrines by claiming that they are Spirit-inspired. Sometimes a group of Christians claims that it is the only true church because their unique beliefs and practices are proof that they are "Spirit-filled." How can we tell when it is *the Holy Spirit* and not simply some kind of team or national or group spirit—or perhaps simply our own individual human spirits?

Scripture warns us not to "believe every spirit" but to "test the

spirits to see whether they are of God" (1 John 4:1). How can we
do that? What criterion do we have? We can ask always, "Is what
you claim to be a revelation and work of the Spirit consistent with
what we know of God's will and ways in the Bible?" We can ask
ourselves, "Is the desire or feeling or idea I have consistent with
what I have been told about God's desires, feelings and ideas in
Christ?"

Whether it is a question of *truth* supposedly inspired by the
Spirit, or a new kind of *life* supposedly given by the Spirit, or a
community supposedly formed and held together by the Spirit—
this is the test we must make. If it is really *the Holy Spirit*, he may
say and do new and unexpected things, but they will always be a
new and unexpected work of the same Father and Son we know
in Scripture. The seemingly theoretical doctrine of the Trinity,
with its talk about the oneness of Father, Son and Holy Spirit, helps
us with some very difficult *practical* problems when we begin to
speak about how and where the Holy Spirit is at work among us.

         3. The Holy Spirit is Lord. If the Holy Spirit is the
Spirit of God the Father and God the Son, then he too is Lord.
This is said expressly in 2 Corinthians 3:17. This tells us something
about *where* we may expect to find the Spirit at work. Like God
the Father Almighty, and like the Jesus Christ who is Lord over
the whole world, the Holy Spirit is not the prisoner of the church,
nor an exclusive possession of Christians. "The wind [Spirit] blows
where it wills" (John 3:8). He is *Lord*. He works wherever, whenever and however *he* chooses. He is especially promised first to
the church and then to individual Christians within the church. But
he is not limited to work only in the Christian community and the
hearts of believers. We never "have" him in the sense that he is
our private property. Nor can we control him. On the contrary,
we expect—and we may be *glad!*—that the life-giving, truth-
inspiring, community-building work of the Spirit is going on
everywhere in the world. Wherever we see new life achieved, new
truth discovered, new community overcoming old divisions and
hostility, there we may thankfully recognize the work of the Holy
Spirit.

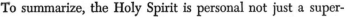

    To summarize, the Holy Spirit is personal not just a super-

natural power. He is not just any spirit, doing and saying just any unusual thing, but the Spirit of the God whose will and ways we know in biblical history and especially in Christ. He is the Spirit who is free to work in outsiders as well as insiders, in the world as well as in the church. With these three marks of identification, we may now move on to speak in more detail about what he does and how his work is distinguished from all the other spirits at work in us and among us.

The Holy Spirit and Life

For many young people life is something in the future, something not yet begun, which they go to school to prepare for. For many of us adults life seems somehow to be something in the past which has passed us by. We know what it means to want to live and yet to feel that we are not yet or no longer really alive. What is this life which we all so desperately want and yet find so illusive? Christians answer that it is what happens to us when the Spirit of God comes into us. He is a "life-giving" Spirit (2 Corinthians 3:6; 1 Corinthians 15:45; John 6:63). He so radically changes a person who experiences his presence that that person can be said to be "born anew"—to have a brand new, fresh life (John 3:1–8).

But what kind of life is that? Because the New Testament often expresses the difference between the "new" and "old" man in terms of a contrast between "spirit" and "flesh" (John 3:6; 1 Corinthians 15:45–46; Romans 8:1–17), some Christians have thought that to be born again of the Spirit means to experience a renewal which is purely inward, private and religious. Spiritual life has to do only with prayer, worship and feeling the presence of God when we withdraw from the everyday, ordinary world. It has to do with church and devotional activities and with the life after death, but it does not have anything to do with sex, business, politics and the like. Again and again in this book we have run into this kind of spirituality which identifies the Christian life with indifference toward, or contempt for, or escape from, the physical and this-worldly. Now we have to argue against this kind of spirituality precisely in order to take seriously what the New Testament tells us about the Holy Spirit.

We have already learned that when flesh is contrasted with

spirit in the Bible, it refers not only to man's physical life in the world, but to the sinfulness which includes *all* of him—heart, mind and spirit as well as body (look again at the "works of the flesh" in Galatians 5:19–21).

To be born again of the Spirit, therefore, does not mean to escape from the physical and this-worldly into a purely religious, otherworldly life. What the Holy Spirit does in a man is to change and renew not just one segment of his life, but all of it. The charactor of his sex life as well as of his prayer life is changed and renewed. His business affairs as well as his Sunday worship become truly spiritual. His social as well as his internal private life is converted.

Another way of saying this is to say that the spiritual life which is the work of the Spirit is nothing but a genuinely *human* life. If flesh in this context means sin (not just physical); and if, as we have learned, sin means the denial of our own humanity by breaking the proper relationship with God and fellowmen; then the Spirit's overcoming the flesh means his overcoming our inhumanity. The new life the Holy Spirit gives us is not the life of angels or of religious personalities. It is the life of genuine human beings.

We can see more clearly what all this means by relating the new life the Spirit brings to two other gifts mentioned in the New Testament. In relation to God, new life means the gift of *sonship*. In relation to fellowmen, it is the gift of *love*.

1. The new life of sonship. When the Holy Spirit comes into our lives, we come to know God as our Father and ourselves as children of God. How is this said in Romans 8:12–17 and Galatians 4:6?

There was a time when even people who did not believe "all that stuff about Jesus" nevertheless spoke confidently of the "fatherhood of God" and of the fact that "after all, we are all children of God." Even if you did not believe anything else, you could at least believe that! But that time is gone. It is no longer self-evident to many people that there *is* a God, much less that he is our Father who cares for us. It seems much more realistic to modern men to understand themselves purely as products of psychological, sociological and economic factors.

Perhaps it is clearer now than it was even a few years ago that *ugh* faith that God is our Father and that we are his children is a *gift*, not a certainty everyone has automatically. We cannot tell ourselves this; only God can tell us and make us sure that it is true. How does he do it? Not by treating us as his special pets and giving us Christians preferred treatment with miraculous proofs which make our lives smooth and easy. The "sufferings of this present time" all remain for those who are the children of a Father God (Romans 8:18). He convinces us that he is our Father and we his children by his Spirit's "bearing witness with our spirit" (Romans 8:16). It is the work of the Spirit now, "between the times," to enable us to *believe* what we cannot see and to live by that faith, despite all the evidence to the contrary. Meanwhile, Christians are those who *in the midst* of the "sufferings of the present time" wait confidently, with eager longing, for the "revealing" of the sons of God. Because we already know that it is the truth, even if we cannot see it, we live in hope and wait with patience (Romans 8:19–25).

What difference does it make, this gift of God's Spirit that enables us to be sure that God is our Father and we his children? How does that mean a "new life"? It means among other things that we do not have to live in "fear" (Romans 8:15) or as "slaves to the elemental spirits of the universe" (Galatians 4:3). We need fear neither that there is no God nor that God might be against us. We need not live in fearful slavery to other gods. The elemental spirits Paul refers to were invisible demonic forces which ancient men believed controlled their destinies. We might translate this mythology to mean something like this: If we know that the last word about our lives is that we are under the care of a powerful God who wills the best for us, we need not live in the servile fear that who we are, and what we can become, is finally dictated by such modern elemental spirits as psychological forces (i.e., the damage parents do to their children), sociological forces (race or class prejudice and exploitation), economic forces (the stock market), or political forces (creeping socialism or creeping fascism). To live in *hope*—would that not mean new life? What a tremendous gift and what a great life to be able to believe and live by Paul's words in Romans 8:31–39, at the end of his discussion of the work of the Holy Spirit. Is not that kind of certainty of God's love for his children *in* "tribulation, distress, persecution, peril and sword" a far greater gift than the kind of spirituality which promises escape from the difficulties and struggles of life? The man who receives from the Spirit the assurance of his sonship no longer *needs* a weak, fearful, escapist religion. He can live a strong, courageous life as a child of God *in* the world.

2. The new life of love. Chapters 12–14 of 1 Corinthians mention other gifts of the Spirit. Paul mentions among others such sensational gifts as the ability to speak in unknown tongues, to work miracles and to heal—gifts which some Christians consider the highest and most impressive evidences of the working of the Spirit in men. But then Paul goes on to say that there are still "higher gifts" than these, a "more excellent way." What spiritual gift could be greater than the ability to heal the sick, or work miracles, or speaking in tongues? Love! That is the theme of 1 Corinthians 13. Without love, speaking even the language of angels (the greatest ecstatic spiritual experience) is just plain noise. Without love, the most profound knowledge of all the mysteries of God (the greatest orthodoxy) is nothing. Without love, even the most devoted service and heroic self-sacrifice ("giving oneself for others") are worthless. The gift of love is even greater than the gifts of faith and hope we have just discussed.

What does it mean to have the Spirit of God come into our lives? Perhaps it does mean tremendous emotional experiences in prayer and worship services for some people. And why should it be inconceivable that the Spirit of God should enable some men to accomplish miracles? But even more important than that: The presence of the Spirit means a new relationship with our fellowmen. What greater miracle and what greater healing than the ability to put aside "bitterness, wrath, anger, clamor and slander, and malice"; and to be "tenderhearted, forgiving one another, as God in Christ forgave you" (Ephesians 4:31–32)? What greater "fruit of the Spirit" can be imagined than "love, joy, peace, patience, kindness, goodness, faithfulness, gentleness and self-control" (Galatians 5:22–23)?

Perhaps the best way to "test the spirits" and to discern a true spirituality in our own lives and in the lives of others is to ask whether our prayer and devotional life, our religious feelings and convictions and experiences, are accompanied by an openness and sensitivity to all the people we live with every day. No matter how intensely pious or moral or orthodox we are, we have not yet known the presence of the life-giving Spirit of God in our lives until the love he brings shapes the relationship between employers and employees, rich and poor, educated and uneducated, husbands and wives, whites and Negroes. Where love is not at work, the Holy Spirit is not at work. Where real love is, there is present the Spirit of the God who is himself love. To be really spiritual people in the New Testament sense means that along with immorality, impurity, licentiousness, drunkenness and carousing, also such "works of the flesh" as enmity, strife, jealousy, anger, selfishness, discension, party spirit and envy (Galatians 5:19–21) begin to disappear in all areas of human life—including the church community (which is not immune to the works of the flesh!).

3. The gift of life. Everything we have said about the Spirit's gift of new life in relation to God and to other people raises the question of how we can have this gift. How can we have the faith, hope and love which offer not escape, but the transformation of our daily lives? We cannot answer this question completely until we discuss the other gifts of the Spirit but we can begin to answer it now.

In the first place, if new life is a gift of the Holy Spirit, we cannot give it to ourselves. We cannot simply decide to have faith, to live with hope and to love. Not only the New Testament but also our own experience tells us this. Sometimes when we most desperately want to believe that there is a God who cares, or to have hope for the future, or to love another person, we find that we simply cannot.

Secondly, there is nothing we can do to force the Spirit of God to come to us and give us faith, hope and love. We cannot manipulate him to work according to our schedule and desires. There is no more guarantee that he will come with his renewing power if we turn off the lights and sit in the dark than if we sit in broad day-light. He is no more bound to come in a church sanctuary than in a restaurant. He is no more summoned by jazzy hymns and highly emotional preaching than by sixteenth-century chorals and color-less preaching—or vice versa. He is free to work when, where and how *he* chooses. *He* takes the initiative and not we.

But that does not mean that we can do anything we please or do nothing at all, excusing our lack of faith, our hopelessness or our unloving attitudes by complaining that the Spirit has not chosen to come to us. We have been told who he is, and where and how he is promised. Although we cannot control his coming and going, we can at least place ourselves in the kind of situation in which we know he accomplishes his work.

We cannot expect to receive the gift of the faith and hope which come in the midst of the hardships and difficulties of life if we fearfully seek escape from the disturbing, painful realities of the world around us. So long as Luther, for example, thought he could find God by retreating from the world into a monastery, he was tormented by doubts and despair. His faith and hope be-came sure only when he left the security of the monastery and threw himself as a Christian into the confusion, insecurity and danger of involvement in the worldly "orders" of family, vocational and political responsibility. If we really want the gifts of the Spirit, we must have the courage to sacrifice the self-protecting safety of a withdrawn religious life. We must risk throwing ourselves into the kind of costly involvement in the needs and problems of the world which are so frustrating and threatening that it is im-possible to trust and depend on ourselves and our own strength.

Again, we cannot hope to receive the gift of love if we refuse to have anything at all to do with some people whom we Christians should love, or if we avoid getting involved with those around us by building an impenetrable wall of mere politeness around our-selves. If we cannot love because we are afraid to risk the hurts and disappointments of honest human encounters, is it because the Holy Spirit has abandoned us or because we have been afraid to put ourselves into the kind of situation where the love he gives is possible?

We cannot force the Spirit of God to work. But we *can* risk taking the first step which opens up the possibility of receiving new life in our everyday lives and in our relationships with other people around us. For each one of us this first step will mean something different. What would it mean for you? Or to put it another way: Recognizing that to speak of the gift of new life means that the initiative lies with the Spirit, what could *you* do to put yourself in the position to receive that gift?[3]

The Holy Spirit and Truth

According to the New Testament, the Holy Spirit is the source of new life: a new personal relationship with God and other people. But that is not his only gift. He is also the source of truth. He is the "Spirit of truth" (John 14:17). He is himself the truth (1 John 5:7).

Pietistic Christians and the Pentecostal churches have traditionally emphasized the Spirit's gift of rebirth and new life. Orthodox Christians and the "main-line" churches have emphasized the connection between the Spirit and truth. In the previous section we tried to see what is right about the former emphasis and at the same time see that new life means far more than an emotional, individualistic religious experience. Now, in a similar way, we have to consider the orthodox emphasis on truth. First we shall criticize its limitations. Then we shall discuss what is right about it. Finally, we shall ask again how we can receive the gift of the Spirit.

1. Personal truth. What is the truth which the Holy Spirit gives us? Classical Protestantism has properly emphasized that it is the truth given in Scripture. The Holy Spirit is the "breath" of God working through the biblical writers to give us his truth. The same Spirit illumines our minds so that we can receive and understand this truth.

But what is the truth given to us in Scripture? Orthodox Protestantism has had a tendency to think of it primarily as divinely given, *intellectual* truth—correct ideas and doctrines about God, man and the world. "Orthodox" means "right thinking." The man in whom the Spirit is present is the man whose *mind is* enlightened.

This is too narrow an understanding of biblical truth. That truth is not just intellectual but personal. To accept the truth of Scripture is not just to know something new, but to enter into a new personal relationship with the God we meet there. This means that the Spirit's gift of truth is life-changing as well as mind-informing truth. One way of testing the spirits is to ask whether the man who claims to hold to the truth given by the Spirit in Scripture demonstrates that truth in the kind of new personal relationships with God and other people we have discussed above. A man may understand all mysteries and all knowledge, but if he does not have love for his fellowmen, he has missed the whole point (1 Corinthians 13:2). He may have the most orthodox intellectual convictions, but if his faith does not result in active obedience to God, his faith is dead (James 2:17). Unless our intellectual and doctrinal truth becomes personal, reconciling truth, it is not his truth, no matter how correct it may be in itself.

2. Intellectual truth. We have been arguing that the truth which comes from the Holy Spirit changes men's hearts, as well as their minds, and creates instead of destroying community among men. But when we have said that, we must go on to recognize that the Spirit does work also in the minds of men. His truth is in fact also intellectual truth.

In 1 Corinthians 14:6–33 Paul argues against those Christians who think that to have the Spirit means only to have the irrational, emotional experience of speaking in tongues which are meaningful to the speaker but not to anyone else. What good is such a religious experience, Paul asks, if it is not *intelligible* (verse 9), if one does not know the *meaning* of what is said (verse 11), if my *mind* is unfruitful (verse 14)? Even if ecstatic experiences are legitimate in private, "in the church I would rather speak five words with my mind, in order to instruct others, than ten thousand words in a tongue" (verse 19). In other words, the Christian faith is not anti-intellectual. It is not just a matter of subjective feelings and experiences. It makes sense and can be communicated.

Another way of saying this is to say that the Holy Spirit works not only to give us a feeling of God's presence, but to give us _wisdom._ How is this said in 1 Corinthians 2:6–13? The Spirit enables us to love God with our _minds_ as well as with our hearts and souls (Matthew 22:37).

This means that the Holy Spirit is as much at work when we study as when we pray, when we share our thoughts as when we share our feelings, when we work to understand Christian truth as when we are at worship. It means that Christian love for other people expresses itself not just in sentimental emotions, but in intelligent, clear-minded search for understanding of these other people. It means, as orthodox Christians have always insisted, that true Christian unity between individual Christians, between Christian denominations, and between Christians and non-Christians is a unity also of mind as well as heart.

The spirit of love and community is a test of whether the truth we think we have received from the Spirit is really his truth. But truth—the truth written down in intelligible words and interpreted by rational Christian doctrines—is a test of whether our emotional experience, love and community are really the Spirit's work.

3. The gift of truth. How can we have the Holy Spirit's gift of truth? The understanding of the truth of God is a gift we cannot give to ourselves—not even armed with the Bible. Unless the Holy Spirit illumines our minds, we cannot even recognize that the Bible contains the truth. Many intelligent people, including some who sincerely would like to believe, simply cannot honestly accept the biblical witness as true. Nor can those of us who do acknowledge the truth of this witness understand what we read there without the help of the Spirit. Have not all of us at times felt that we were reading "just words" when we read the Bible?

But as in the case of faith, love and hope, this does not mean that we can do nothing at all. Although we cannot tell ourselves or discover for ourselves the truth of God, we can put ourselves in a position where it becomes possible to receive this gift. There are at least two things we can do to make our minds receptive to the Holy Spirit's work.

a. In reading the Bible, we can ask ourselves again and again whether we really *want* to hear the truth it offers. Do we really want to find only confirmation and support for the ideas, opinions and prejudices we already have? Are we willing to let the Scriptures change and correct what we think we already know? If we only use the Bible to justify our own theological, political and social ideas, we do not really want the guidance of the Spirit, nor can we expect it. If, on the other hand, we go to the Bible and listen to it preached with a sincere willingness to learn, to change, to be corrected, then we will be open to hear what God's Spirit has to say to us.

b. We can remind ourselves that while the Holy Spirit is promised to us especially when we read the Scriptures, he is free to work when, where and how he chooses—also outside of Scripture and the church. The Spirit of God is the fountain of *all* truth, Calvin tells us, whether it is specifically biblical or Christian truth or not (*Institutes*, II, 2, 15). If we really want the Spirit's gift of truth, we will not be afraid of truth from *any* source, whether it comes from Catholics or Protestants, non-Christians or Christians. We need not be afraid of scientific truth, the results of impartial historical investigation of the biblical sources and church tradition, or the discoveries of the psychological and sociological sciences about human nature. If we are willing to listen to and learn only from people who already think exactly as we do, is it really truth we want or is it again only support for what we already think? If we want to know the *whole* truth, *God's* truth, how can we refuse to listen to and learn also from those who think differently from us? Why should we not be willing to recognize the same Spirit who speaks to us in Scripture when he comes to us unexpectedly from other places?

There is a sense in which we Christians believe that we already have the truth insofar as we have the biblical witness to God and his revelation of who he is, who we are and what is going on in the world. But it is always questionable whether we have correctly *perceived* that truth and its implications. Insofar as we are convinced that we have already arrived in understanding the truth, we neither want nor will we receive the guidance of the Spirit. But insofar as we are willing to recognize that "our knowledge is imperfect" and that "now we see in a mirror dimly" (1 Corinthians 13:9, 12); insofar as we are willing to admit that all the truth may not be on our side; insofar as we recognize that we are not the only ones seeking the truth of God and that others may have learned from him some things we do not know yet but can learn from them—to that extent, we may prepare the way for the guidance of the Spirit of truth in our individual lives and our church.

The Holy Spirit and the Christian Community

"The Holy Spirit . . . The Holy Catholic Church." The two go together when we confess our faith. And they go together in the New Testament. The Holy Spirit first came not to isolated individuals but when "they were all together" (Acts 2:1). "To each is given the manifestation of the Spirit for the common good" (1 Corinthians 12:7). "Since you are eager for manifestations of the Spirit, strive to excel in building up the church" (1 Corinthians 14:12).

In one sense it is quite logical that building up and holding together the Christian community should be an essential part of the Holy Spirit's work. The *new life* he brings reconciles men to God and their fellowmen and establishes a new relationship between them. New life results in new community. The *truth* he brings is first of all and primarily the truth about God, man and the world recorded in the Bible. But the Bible is the church's book; the church is the community of men gathered and held together by the truth contained in this book. New life, truth, community— the three naturally go together as related works of the one Spirit of God.

1. The problem of unity. But in practice, as we saw at the beginning of this chapter, it does not always work out that way. Those Christians who are especially concerned for the vitality and new life of the Spirit often feel that the church is made up of people who show no signs of real rebirth and newness of life. Perhaps there are too many immoral people in the church. Or perhaps the very church which preaches the reconciling work of Christ refuses to be reconciled with and include in its fellowship people of the "wrong" color or class. Newness of life and the existing community seem mutually exclusive. To stick with the community means to compromise the Spirit's gift of new life. But to leave the church to form a new group of "real" Christians is to break the unity of the church which is a gift of the same Spirit.

Again, those Christians who are especially concerned for the truth given by the Scriptures often feel that the church is not faithful to that truth. Its preaching, its educational literature, its faith and practice are either too liberal or too conservative. Which is it to be—truth or the unity of the church? Can we have one gift of the Spirit at the expense of another?

The solution generally has been to sacrifice community in the interest of new life or truth. The "Holy Catholic Church" is in fact split into many different churches, each of which claims to be guided by the Spirit. Even when there is not an open split, many congregations and denominations are split internally into warring camps, each of which is sure that it has on its side the Spirit's gift of real Christian truth or real Christian personal experience and life.

But the New Testament unmistakably warns that "there is one body and one Spirit . . . one hope . . . one Lord . . . one faith . . . one baptism . . . one God and Father of us all" (Ephesians 4:4–6). Where the Holy Spirit is, there Christians are *drawn together*. There is unity, community—peace (Romans 8:6). Is it really the experience of new life which comes from the Holy Spirit, if it sets Christians against each other instead of reconciling them to one another? Can it really be *his* truth if it divides Christians into the same kinds of parties and enemy camps into which non-Christians are divided? It obviously will not do to pretend that all the churches and parties within the churches are spiritually one, when in fact they are suspicious of each other, sometimes refuse to worship together, often will not even talk (much less listen) to one another, and question whether the others are really Christian at all. The blunt truth is that we are *not* spiritually united.

In short, our lack of community seriously calls into question whether we really have received *any* of the gifts of the Spirit.

With these considerations we have run into a problem too

important for us to deal with in a few words now: "Just what is the community brought together and held together by the Holy Spirit?" We shall have to give a whole chapter to this question. What we can do now is to conclude our study of the Holy Spirit and his work by asking for the third time, "How can we have the gifts of the Spirit?" It is a question which is all the more urgent now that we have encountered the painful claim of the New Testament that where the Spirit is, there is gathered and held together a *community* of Christians.

2. **The gift of unity.** First of all we must acknowledge once again that we cannot give ourselves the gifts of the Spirit. Only the Spirit, not we ourselves, can make us into a community in which love and truth exist in unity and peace. Nor can we force the Spirit to work according to our scheduling and plans. There is no guarantee that we will achieve real Christian unity, or that the Spirit will give it to us, just because we enter into ecumenical conversations, work for organizational unions, set up interdenominational conferences, or bring hostile factions within the given churches together to work things out. The Spirit of God works—or does not work—when, where and how *he* chooses.

But once again, this does not mean that we can sit back complacently with the attitude that we can go on with our external and internal divisions, telling ourselves that when he is ready, the Spirit will move among us. There are some things we can do to make ourselves receptive to the Spirit, to prove that we sincerely *want* the gift only he can give. Here are some suggestions. Do you agree with them? What other concrete steps do you think we could take?

a. If we want the power of the community-creating work of the Holy Spirit, *we can strive to build up the church* (1 Corinthians 14:12). When the Spirit works, he builds up; he does not tear down. If we want the Spirit, then, we will work not to create or maintain divisions without or within, but to overcome divisions. Sometimes, of course, it is necessary to tear down old structures in order to build new ones. But everything depends on whether we tear down *in order* to build again. If we are satisfied with the present divisions in the church, or if we are working further to fragment the church community, we show that we do not really want the Spirit. Nor can we expect him. Only he who earnestly desires to *build* community really wants and can expect him.

b. If we want the Spirit's gift of community, *we can examine ourselves* before we criticize the faith and life of other denominations or groups within our denomination. Is it really our steadfast holding to the truth and our seriousness about the new life of the Spirit which separates us from the others? Could it be that we are separated because deep down we only want to build up *ourselves*— like the Pharisee who thanked God that he was better than other men? Is it the *church* we are interested in or only our denomination or our party within the denomination? If we are already perfectly sure of ourselves, of our understanding of the truth, and of our version of the Christian life, then we do not even think we need the Holy Spirit. Nor can we expect him. Only those who recognize also their own as well as others' need for him want and can expect him.

c. If we want the Spirit's community-building power among us, we *must be open to talk and to listen* to other denominations and other groups within our denomination. What if the Spirit of God is also at work among them? If we are too afraid or too suspicious to have anything to do with them, might we not deprive ourselves of something very important the Spirit is saying to us or doing for us through them? Unless we let them speak for themselves, how can we know whether their version of the Christian faith and life is corrupt? Have we rejected fellowship with Catholics or Methodists, or conservatives or liberals within our own church, on the basis of what they really believe and how they really live—or only on the basis of the prejudiced caricature we have made of them? (Is it fair to assume that modern Catholics are just like the Catholics Luther and Calvin confronted? Do we listen to *everything* the "liberals" or "conservatives" in our own church say, or do we hear only what we "knew" beforehand they would say?) If we think we can expect the work of the Spirit only in our denomination or party, we do not really want the Spirit at all. We only want self-confirmation and self-justification. Only those who are open to the presence and work among other Christians gathered in his name really want and can expect him.

d. If we want the Spirit's gift of community, *we must recognize that unity does not mean uniformity.* Within the Christian community there are "varieties of gifts, but the same Spirit; and varieties of service, but the same Lord; and there are varieties of working, but it is the same God who inspires them all in every one" (1 Corinthians 12:4). All Christians do not have to think or live exactly alike. (How is this shown in Acts 15:1–21?) Are we sure that the different interpretations of Christian truth and practice among other denominations and parties are of community-splitting significance? Even if the others seem to be one-sided in one direction or another, might we not need fellowship with them to correct one-sidedness on our part? If we demand that everyone else be just like us before we will have fellowship with them, it is not the richness of the Holy Spirit we want, but only our own poverty. Only those who seek community in which there is room for differences really want and may expect the coming of the Holy Spirit.

e. Finally, if we want the Spirit's gift of community, *we must be willing to confess that we never "have" or "possess" him or any of his gifts, but stand constantly in need of them.* With this point we summarize this whole chapter and everything we have said about all the gifts of the Spirit we have discussed. Every new day we must be open afresh to his coming again to judge our own as well as others sinfulness (John 16:8), to give us *new* truth and *new* Christian fellowship. True, the new life, truth and community the Spirit brings are not just any new thing. His work is always the work of the Father and Son we come to know in the "old" book. But the God whom we meet in Christ in Scriptures is a living God. He did not stop working 2,000 years ago. He is still at work, continuing his creative, reconciling, renewing work in every new time and situation in ways we cannot anticipate. To know him and to want his Spirit is to be unwilling to stay where we are and to be eager to move forward into the revolutionary new and unexpected at his leading. It is to be unwilling to stay born again "babies," but to seek his power to grow and change in our understanding of Christian truth, life and community. It is to be open to *new* expressions of reconciliation with God and our fellowmen, *new* perception of biblical-theological truth, *new* forms of Christian community.

If we mean what we say when we say we believe in the Holy Ghost, we must have the courage to "forget what lies behind" and to "strain forward to what lies ahead" (Philippians 3:13). We can never dream of settling down comfortably or defensively where we are. We must pray every new day, and be willing to have our prayer answered in surprising ways, an ancient prayer of the church: *Come,* Holy Spirit.

FOR FURTHER REFLECTION AND STUDY

1. All Christians would admit that the Spirit's gifts of new life, truth and unity in the church are all important. But all of us tend to be one-sided in one way or another. In which direction are *you* one-sided? What about your denomination as a whole? What about other denominations?

2. What difference does it make to insist that the Holy Spirit is the Spirit of Christ?

3. Do you agree that the Holy Spirit is also at work in the world, outside the church, among and in people who are not Christians? Could the Spirit be at work in a night club? In a political party? On the golf course at eleven o'clock on Sunday morning? How could we tell whether or not he is at work in such unexpected places?

4. Read the description of what it means to be children of God through the Spirit in Romans 8:12–39. Are God's children promised success, happiness and prosperity in the world? What is the relationship between the present and future life for the children of God?

5. Read Paul's description of the gifts of the Holy Spirit in 1 Corinthians 12–14. What gifts are mentioned? Why are they given? Do they conflict with each other? Do all Christians receive the same gifts? What is the greatest gift? What does Paul think of "speaking in tongues"?

6. In light of the biblical understanding of the meaning of the word "spiritual," what would be a spiritual relationship between a man and his wife? Between an employer and his employees?

7. What does it mean to be "born again"?

8. If faith, hope and love are gifts which we can only receive from the Holy Spirit and not something we can achieve for ourselves, should we blame or condemn people who do not have these gifts?
9. Is a Christian "egghead" likely to be less Spirit-filled than a "simple" Christian?
10. How can we be faithful to the Christian convictions we already hold and yet open to let ourselves be corrected by the Holy Spirit?
11. Should individual Protestants or Protestant denominations cooperate with the ecumenical movement to unite divided Protestant churches? Should we be sympathetic to the new dialogue between the Protestant and Roman Catholic Churches?
12. Do you agree that it is wrong to speak of "having" the Holy Spirit?
13. Could the Holy Spirit lead us to think and do things not specifically contained in the Bible?

16

Are You a Christian?

Are you a Christian? How would you answer someone who asked point-blank? Many of us would suspect that it is a trick question meant to trap us. Any answer we give involves us in embarrassing self-contradictions.

Suppose I answer, "Yes. I belong to the First Presbyterian or Reformed Church." Then I'm a dead duck if my questioner knows anything at all. Are "Presbyterian-Reformed" and "Christian" synonymous? Since there are so many denominations, with so many versions of Christianity, how do you know yours is the really Christian one? Why is there so much un-Christian pettiness and feuding in the church? Why does the church so often simply echo the class and race prejudices of its environment and spend all its time keeping the organization going instead of serving the world? Church membership is no guarantee that I take seriously either the Christian faith or the Christian life.

Suppose I answer, "Yes, I am a Christian. I believe in Jesus Christ as my personal Lord and Savior." Then my questioner can begin asking uncomfortable questions about my *life*. If you believe in Christ, then why are you so impatient with your children? Why do you talk about other people behind their backs? Do you pay your maid or the employees in your business a fair wage? What are you doing to obey Jesus' command to minister to the poor, the oppressed, the imprisoned? It doesn't take long to expose the contradictions between my professed faith and my life. But if I begin to argue that it's not what I *do* but what I *believe* that makes me a Christian, I open myself up to the charge of being a fake and hypocrite.

Suppose, then, I am more cautious and answer, "Well, I *try* to be a Christian." That invites my questioner to take another tack. How *hard* do you try? The temptation is to begin adding up the score: I go to church, read the Bible, pray, try to be kind to other people, and so on. But the total score will not stand close examination. Is it enough? *Why* do you do all that? Is it really out of love for God and your fellowmen, or is it at least partially out of the desire to buy the approval of God and admiration of other people? So long as I allow the conversation to turn around my efforts in believing and doing, it will always be doubtful both to myself and to other people whether I am even trying very hard to be a Christian, much less how well I have succeeded.

But on the other hand, if I try to turn the conversation from myself and the state of my faith and life to talk about God and what he has done and is doing, I seem to be avoiding the original question about whether *I* am a Christian.

What *does* it mean to be a Christian? How are Christian faith and Christian life related? What is the connection between what God gives us and does for us, and what he requires *us* to do? In other words, how do we receive and make our own the Holy Spirit's gifts of faith and new life we discussed in the last chapter? These are the questions we shall deal with in this and the following chapters. The church has tried to answer them with the doctrines of justification and sanctification, and these are the doctrines which will guide our discussion. Study them not only to learn in general what a Christian is, but to discover how you would answer the question, "Are *you* a Christian?"

The Problem of Justification

Every Protestant who knows anything at all about Protestant beliefs knows that justification by faith was what got the Reformation started. Luther was a man tormented by doubts about how he stood with God. He knew that God was a righteous God who would not let sin go unpunished, and he was terrified that he was not good enough to escape God's wrathful judgment. "How can I find a *gracious* God?" was the question that plagued his life. He became a monk and gave himself full time to the attempt to earn God's acceptance by an extraordinary religious life. But the harder he tried, the more he realized that he would never be good enough to merit salvation, and the more anxious, despairing and guilt-ridden he became. Finally, he stumbled across the Good News of the New Testament that we do not have to save ourselves by "being good" to satisfy God's righteous demands. What we cannot do for ourselves, God has done for us in Christ. We are "justified"—made right with God—not by our own efforts to climb up to God but by his free grace in coming to us. Just when we give up the futile attempt to merit God's love, acknowledge that we are and always will be unworthy in ourselves, and trust his goodness instead of our own—just then we will discover that salvation is not a prize to be won by our good works, but a gift to be accepted by faith. How is this expressed in Romans 3:21–26 and Ephesians 2:8–9?

Most Protestants (and, by the way, many modern Roman Catholics)[1] agree in theory that Luther was right. But the words, "justification by faith," no longer evoke in us the same overwhelming joy and sense of glorious freedom they gave Luther and the first Protestants. Why? One reason is probably that it is hard for us to see that we are in the same desperate predicament that Luther was in when he "discovered" this doctrine. Quite apart from whether we *ought* to or not, how many of us take God and his righteousness so seriously that we live in daily terror that we might be eternally damned? Who of us could say that every day, all day, his life is soured by the fear that God does not love him? Who of us ever thought seriously of giving up everything in order to escape the wrath of God and earn salvation by striving to live a perfect life? If we are to grasp something of the joy and freedom of justification, we must first translate the desperate situation to which it speaks into more contemporary terms. When we have done that, we shall then speak of what the doctrine itself can mean to us modern men.

Most of us do not try to justify ourselves as young Luther did. But we have other ways of doing the same thing—with the same results.

Many American men try to justify themselves not so much by good works as by just plain work. Hard work and success are what make a man worth something. They give him self-respect. They prove that he is a good husband and father. They win for him the approval and admiration of other men. So a man works harder and harder. But the very work which was supposed to give his life meaning becomes a cruel slave driver which turns his life into a treadmill. It was supposed to give him self-respect, but he is constantly threatened by the fear that he has not performed well enough or climbed high enough—and constantly tormented by the thought of failure, loss of work, or retirement. The work which was supposed to have made him a good, responsible husband and father takes so much time that he neglects his family. It was supposed to win the approval of other men, but it turns them into rivals and opponents to be defeated and dominated. The very work which he thought would justify his existence to himself and before other people becomes self-destructive and alienates him from them.

If we can believe television, many American women try to justify themselves to their husbands by working constantly and frantically to stay young and beautiful. How can a woman accept herself or expect to be loved otherwise? Old age and the middle-aged spread are a terrifying threat ever before them. Every new wrinkle, every additional pound, every gray hair is a source of anxious concern. But how can a woman constantly preoccupied with herself and her lovableness love or let herself be loved? She offers not herself but youth and beauty to be loved. She is so concerned about herself that she is not free to love her mate. The very quest which was supposed to make the marriage is what breaks the marriage, inwardly if not outwardly.

Some of us try to justify ourselves by being critical of other people, thinking that if we can make them look little, we will look big. But the need to run down others is itself a sign of our own insecurity and of our desperate need to be able to accept ourselves and to be accepted by them. The more we try to build ourselves up by tearing other people down, the more insecure, unlovable and lonely we become. We are trapped and condemned by the very means by which we thought to save ourselves.

Others of us, on the other hand, try to justify ourselves by being critical of *ourselves,* thinking that the more humbly self-accusing and self-rejecting we are, the more admirable we will be. But the need to run down myself is not a sign of genuine humility; it is a sign of arrogant pride: I'm more humble than anyone—and therefore *better* than anyone. Such self-depreciation sometimes seems to lead to self-sacrifice and "selfless" service of others, but in fact it is only *self*-serving and a means of manipulating others. The very means by which we try to justify ourselves condemns us to a lonely, guilty life of self-centeredness.

Still others of us try to justify ourselves by trying to be good—not so much, like Luther, to win God's approval, as to convince ourselves of our own worth and to win the love of other people. If I can't justify myself by being rich or powerful or intellectual or attractive, perhaps I can do it by achieving moral superiority. Even if I can't be anything else, I can be good! Or can I? The quest for self-justifying virtue is also self-defeating. It leads to constant, anxious circling round and round ourselves: Have I forgotten something? Have I done enough? Am I *really* good? Even when the quest does get beyond self-criticism, it never really reaches others. I only *use* other people as objects to practice my goodness on. I am not really interested in *them,* but only in the warm glow their thankfulness and indebtedness give me. But how can I expect them really to love and respect me, when they sense that I am only using them to build up my own ego and satisfy my own needs? The very quest which should justify me in fact damns me. The very means by which I thought to buy the love of other people alienates me from them.

Depending on what is important to us and what is possible for us, all of us spend our lives trying to justify ourselves in one way or another. But whatever the means, the result is always the same. We are alternately too proud or too despairing of our own worth. Our lives are driven, anxious, guilty. No matter how hard we try, we cannot save ourselves or buy the respect, love and acceptance of others. Whoever looks to himself and tries to measure and guarantee his own worth by his own achievements destroys himself, alienates himself from his fellowmen—and misses the one way in which his existence *can* be justified: God.

But that means that the predicament of us modern men, though it is expressed in a different way, is exactly the same as the predicament of Luther! Perhaps the New Testament truth he stumbled upon is after all more relevant than we thought. Maybe it is not just an appropriate theme for Reformation Sunday once a year, but a truth that could make a difference every day of our lives.

Justification by Grace

You *cannot* justify yourself. That was our first point. The doctrine of justification is a call first of all to give up. Surrender. Stop trying to be something you are not. Put aside all the ways you so desperately and futilely try to use to convince God, yourself and other people that you are deserving of their admiration, love and respect. It won't work. You can't bring it off—not even by the negative way of trying to prove that you are deserving of admiration, love and respect because you are so humble and selfless, or because you so earnestly beat your breast and confess that you are a no-good sinner. You cannot justify yourself. Only *God* can make things right within you and in your personal relationships.

But we will never understand the first point until we understand a second one: You *can* give up all your attempts to justify yourself, because you do not *need* to give yourself to the anxious, frantic, self-defeating task of justifying yourself. Only God can, but God *does* justify us. Now we shall try to understand what this means in our relation to God himself. Later we shall see how we also become right with ourselves and with other people as we become right with God.

The meaning of justification is really very simple. It seems complicated to us only because it sounds too good to be true. Justification by grace, as a "gift" (Romans 3:24), means quite simply: You do not have to try to buy God's love and acceptance, because you are *already* loved and accepted by God—without any qualification or prerequisites.[2] God does not say, "I will love you *if* you are good, *if* you prove yourself worthy, *if* you do so and so, *if* you first love me." He does not even say, "I will love you, *if* you first have faith in me, or *if* you first humiliate yourself and grovel on the ground before me." He says simply, "I love you just as you are—*you*, not your righteousness, your humility, your faith, or your accomplishments of one kind or another."

That does not mean that God's love is blind. He sees us as we really are. Justification is a big "nevertheless." God says to us: "You may fool other people, but you cannot fool me. I see behind all the masks and defenses and pretensions by which you try to convince yourself and other people that you are somebody and not nobody. I see *you*—even more clearly than you see yourself when no one else is around and you admit to yourself who the real you is behind the front you usually hide behind. *Nevertheless* I love and accept you—*despite* your open and secret sins, *despite* your unworthiness and unlovableness, *despite* what you do to other people and yourself by your inability and unwillingness to love and let them love you."

Justification means that despite the fact that things are *not* right in our inner lives and our personal relationships, God forgives and accepts us nevertheless. *Therefore*, there is no need for our compulsive, anxious, defensive attempts to make things right ourselves or to give up in despair because we cannot do so.

How do we know this is true? Because that is what God himself has told us and proved by his actions. "While we were yet helpless, at the right time Christ died for the ungodly . . . while we were yet sinners Christ died for us" (Romans 5:6–8). God is not for those who first do what they can to help themselves, but for the helpless. He is not for those who first believe in him, but for those who have lived without him or against him. He is not for the righteous, but for the unrighteous—including those who are unrighteous just because they think they are righteous, or because of their self-righteous confession that they are unrighteous! Christ means that God's love is not a reward for what we do or confess that we have not done, but a *gift* given absolutely freely, with no strings attached.

And the result? We are justified—in Christ. That means that things are "made right" between us and God—not because we love God, but because in Christ God loves us. Our existence is "justified" not insofar as we make ourselves worthy of being loved, but simply because in loving us God gives us a worth we do not have in ourselves. It is not what we do for God, but what he has done for us; not what we *give* but what we *receive* that makes us "somebody" and not "nobody."

The Justice of Justification

We can better understand the meaning of justification by grace if we look at what it means in the light of a problem traditionally considered in connection with this doctrine. The problem arises from the fact that its terminology is borrowed from a law court. God is a righteous or just Judge. We are accused and convicted of unrighteousness. Justification means that the Judge declares us to be just or righteous in the eyes of the law. We who are guilty are forgiven and set free. This analogy raises obvious difficulties. If God is a just Judge, how can he forgive or declare righteous those who are in fact guilty? If he accepts us as righteous, and treats us "as if" we were in the right with him and his law, does he not wink at sin and pretend that a lie is the truth? Traditionally, the answer has been that when he judges us, he looks at *Christ's* righteousness and accepts us for Christ's sake, on the basis of *his* merit. But the problem still remains. Can righteousness be transferred? Are *we* not still guilty? Even if God lets us get by, are we not still trapped in our sin?

The problem is unsolvable so long as we take the legal imagery literally and think of justification in exclusively moral or ethical terms. What the legal imagery intends to say is not that God pretends we are not guilty and falsely declares us to be morally perfect and thus deserving of salvation. Justification has to do not so much with morality as with our personal relationships. It says that in Christ God has acted to make right not just the wrong things we have *done* but the wrong persons we *are*. It deals not just with our sin and guilt but with the *cause* of sin and guilt within us. It means that in Christ God was and is at work not just to enable us to escape the price we ought to pay for our sins, but to heal the twisted relationships which lie at the bottom of all our particular sins. It is not a matter of God's pretending that we are something we really are not, but his freeing us to be something we are not. Perhaps we can best understand this by an analogy. Think of a problem child in school. He is noisy, uncooperative, insolent with his teachers, a troublemaker and bully among his fellow pupils. What should be done with such a child? "Justice" might demand that he be punished. But punishment does not solve his problem; it only makes him more hostile, even if it squelches him. Or think of the child who is a problem because he withdraws into himself. He does poor work because he is paralyzed by the fear of his own inadequacy, and he is rejected by his fellow pupils because in his withdrawal he seems "stuck-up." It might seem proper to threaten the child that if he does not work harder and listen to the teacher, he will fail, and to warn him that if he does not make an effort to get along better with other people, he never will have any friends. But threats and pep-talks only make him feel more insecure and afraid, so that he withdraws and fails all the more. Any good psychologist knows that what both children need is first of all to be loved. If the troublemaker learns that he is accepted for himself, he no longer has to draw attention to himself by rebellion against authority and order. If the withdrawn child learns that someone cares about him, he is freed from the insecure self-depreciation which defeats him and isolates him from other people. Neither punishment nor threats can change either child or solve his problem. But love can.

Justification is something like that. It says, "God loves you. God accepts you. God forgives you. Without demanding that you be punished, without demanding that you torment and punish yourself, without demanding that you do anything to make up for what you have done or not done. Is that just? In a sense, no. No judge in any court could treat guilty men that way. If the just requirements of the law are not met, the guilty party must pay up and suffer the consequences in one way or another. But on the other hand, the good news of justification does not simply leave us where we are, overlooking all the ways we put ourselves in the wrong with God and our fellowmen. It means that the relationship between ourselves and God is changed. He restores fellowship where for one reason or another we have rejected or destroyed fellowship. And that new relationship with God inevitably *changes* us.

There are many ways to express how the good news of God's love *for* us results in a real change *in* us. 1 John 4:18 says it this way: "Perfect love casts out fear." When we learn that God loves us just as we are, then we are free from the fear which expresses itself in hostile or defensive attempts to buy off or manipulate God and our fellowmen in order to build up ourselves. We are freed from the fear which expresses itself in despairing, self-hating attempts to escape God and our fellowmen by running and hiding from them to nurse our insecurity in self-centered isolation. Seemingly just punishment and threats and demands only increase fear and lead to increased alienation and separation. But seemingly unjust love does away with fear and leads to reconciliation with God, our fellowmen and ourselves.

The love, forgiveness and acceptance of God in Christ, in other words, make possible within us precisely what his righteousness and justice demand of us—that we love him with our whole beings and our neighbor as ourselves. Justification is God's way of giving what he demands. It is not his closing his eyes to the truth and pretending that everything is in order in our lives. It is his way of beginning to *create* order just because he knows very well how hopelessly "fouled-up" we are.

Justification Through Faith

Suppose we begin to understand what justification by grace means. The question still remains, "How can we have this assurance of God's love which frees us *from* ourselves, frees us *for* God, for other people and for true self-fulfillment?" The church answers this question by speaking of justification through *faith*.

We have deliberately waited until the end of our discussion of justification to speak of faith because we wanted to avoid a common misunderstanding. It is often said that instead of the idea that man's good works make him acceptable to God, Protestantism teaches that all we have to do is have faith in order to win God's approval and acceptance. This is a serious distortion, because it only substitutes another requirement which men must fulfill in order to earn salvation. In the last analysis it makes us just as insecure as does justification by other means. Instead of anxiously examining my *life* to discover whether it is good enough, now I must anxiously examine my *faith* to see whether it is sure and strong enough to earn God's love. Justification by faith in this sense is only another means of self-justification and self-salvation.

According to true Protestantism, neither our good works *nor* our faith justifies us. God alone does it by his free grace in Christ. It is not confidence in the goodness of our life *or* in the strength of our faith, but confidence in *him* which gives us the assurance that we are right with him. Robert McAfee Brown puts it this way: "The gospel does not say, 'Trust God and he will love you,' the gospel says, 'God already loves you, so trust him.' Faith is not a 'work' that saves us; it is our acknowledgment that we are saved."[3]

This does not mean that faith is unimportant. While it is not the cause of God's loving us, it is the indispensable means by which we accept and live from his love. Faith does not make us right with God, but no one is made right with God without faith.

Another analogy from human relationships can help clarify the part faith plays in justification. If a man's wife does not already love him, his faith in her cannot force her to love him, no matter how complete it is. But on the other hand, no matter how much she loves him, he can neither receive nor return her love if he does not have faith in her. If he constantly doubts whether she is really faithful to him, or if he constantly questions whether he is good enough for her, the marriage will be hopelessly spoiled by his suspicion of her, or anxiety about his lovableness. The marriage can be a happy one only when he believes that her declarations and demonstrations of love are genuine.

So it is with us and God. Our faith in him does not force or enable him to love us, but it is our way of acknowledging, receiving, enjoying—and returning—the love he had for us long before we ever thought of believing in and loving him. We are not made right with God *by* our faith, but we are made right with him *through* our faith. Our faith does not change God from being against us into being for us, but it does change us from being closed into being open to receive the love he has always had for us.

What is this faith we have been talking about? In order to answer this question, we have only to underline what we have already said not only in the present discussion of justification but throughout this book. Very simply, faith is *trust*. It is not intellectual acceptance of biblical or theological doctrines *about* God—not even the doctrines of Christ or of justification. It is confidence in God himself. Faith is not believing in the Bible; it is not, in Calvin's words, "assent to the gospel history" (*Institutes* III, 2, 1). It is not believing in a book, but believing in the God we come to know in the book. Christian faith is not confidence in our own faith; it is confidence not in faith that saves ("saving faith"), but in the *God* who saves. The faith we have been talking about, in other words is a kind of personal relationship—a total commitment of ourselves to the living God who has proved himself trustworthy by his powerful and loving action for us in the life, death and resurrection of Christ. Calvin puts it this way: Faith is "a firm and certain knowledge of God's benevolence toward us, founded upon the truth of the freely given promise in Christ, both revealed to our minds and sealed upon our hearts through the Holy Spirit" (*Institutes* III, 2, 7).

But as soon as we say that, we run again into a problem we have met before. How can we have such faith? How can we be so sure of God's love that we are freed from the unnecessary, self-defeating attempt to justify ourselves? How can we trust God so completely that we do not have to trust our own goodness or faith? Here we run again into the problem we wrestled with in the previous chapter. Faith, trust, or assurance in God is a *gift*. We can no more simply decide to trust him than we can by sheer will power decide to trust another human being. The faith which trusts in the love of God is itself the work of God's love, "revealed to our minds and sealed upon our hearts by the Holy Spirit."

But the fact that we cannot give ourselves faith does not mean that we must say fatalistically that everyone either has it or he doesn't, God either gives it or he doesn't, and there is nothing we can do about it. As we said in the last chapter about all the gifts of the Spirit, there are some things we can do to put ourselves in a situation where the gift of faith is promised and received. In the present context, we mention three specific things we can do. Especially the last two raise questions which lead us to the two following chapters.

First, if we want a faith that trusts in the love of God which frees us from the necessity of trying to justify and save ourselves, *we can admit honestly that none of us has such faith*, at least not always. Even those who do not have intellectual doubts about the truth of biblical and Christian doctrines do not have such confidence in God's love that they are free from the fearful or proud compulsion to build themselves up in one way or another before God, other people and in their own self-estimation. None of us has faith in the sense of the carefree, relaxed trust Jesus speaks of in Matthew 6:25–26. Whoever wants real faith, therefore, must paradoxically admit that he does *not* have it and pray every new day that he may *receive* it afresh. "I believe. Help my unbelief!"

In the second place, faith (trust in God's love) becomes possible *when we put ourselves in the situation where we can hear about and experience his love over and over again*. That situation is above all the *church*, the community of God's people.

Just as a child or husband or wife needs to hear over and over again from parents or mate that he or she is loved, so we Christians need to hear over and over again the unbelievably good news that God loves, forgives and accepts us despite everything we have been and done. Trust in God becomes possible as we learn constantly afresh what kind of God he is. It is in the church that we may expect to hear this good news; there faith thus becomes real.

But hearing is not enough. A child could not trust a parent, or a husband or wife his or her mate, if there were not visible demonstrations that the parent's or mate's declarations of love are genuine. It is not enough simply to hear the words that God loves us. We need to *experience* his love. Once again, it is above all in the fellowship of the church that we are promised that this will happen. We experience *God's* forgiveness, acceptance and love primarily as we experience the forgiveness, acceptance and love of the people in this community. It is by definition the community of God's forgiveness for guilty men, God's acceptance of those who in themselves are unacceptable, God's love for those who know they cannot earn the right to be loved. It is the place where people can risk putting aside all their defenses and masks, knowing that they will be accepted just as they are, with all their faults, whatever they have done, however unacceptable they are by the moral and social standards of the world. How can those who know themselves to be forgiven sinners not forgive other sinners?

To summarize, we cannot give ourselves the gift of faith which is trust in God's love for us just as we are. But we can put ourselves in the situation—in the church—where we can hear about and experience his faith-creating love. To say this, of course, raises another question. Is the church really such a community of forgiveness, love and acceptance? We shall have to give a whole chapter to the "problem" of the church. But if we are faithful to biblical doctrine, we must, despite all the difficulties involved, hold to this promise: If we want to know about and experience the love of God which makes things right in our lives, we can and we must expect to find it first of all in his church. We can recognize, experience and trust it *everywhere* when we first find it *there*.

What can we do to put ourselves in the situation where faith becomes possible? We can admit that we do not have it, but need ever afresh to receive it. We can participate in the community of faith. Finally, *we can risk beginning to do what faith requires. Faith in God is only possible when we live by faith.* How will we ever learn that God is trustworthy until we give up trusting in ourselves? How can we trust him if we do not willingly and thankfully obey him? How can we believe that we unworthy, undeserving people are forgiven, loved and accepted until we begin to forgive, love and accept other unworthy, undeserving people? How can we believe that we are made free for a right relationship with God, our fellowmen and ourselves until we risk giving up our self-defensive, self-destroying attempts to ignore or use God and fellowmen to serve ourselves, and learn that we find ourselves by losing ourselves in serving them? Faith comes with obedience. Without obedience, there can be no faith. Or to put it in the classical language of the doctrine of justification, we are not made right with God *by* good works, but we are not made right with him *without* good works.

Dietrich Bonhoeffer beautifully describes the connection between faith and obedience in an imaginary conversation of a man with his pastor:

"I have lost the faith I once had." "You must listen to the Word as it is spoken to you in the sermon." "I do; but I cannot get anything out of it, it just falls on deaf ears as far as I am concerned." "The trouble is, you don't really want to listen." "On the contrary, I do." And here they generally break off, because the pastor is at a loss what to say next . . . . The pastor feels himself confronted with the ultimate riddle of predestination. God grants faith to some and withholds it from others. So the pastor throws up the sponge and leaves the poor man to his fate. And yet this ought to be the turning-point of the interview . . . . The pastor should give up arguing with him, and stop taking his difficulties seriously. That will really be in the man's own interest, for he is only trying to hide himself behind them. It is now time to take the bull by the horns and say: "Only those who obey believe . . . . You are disobedient, you are trying to keep some part of your life under your own control. That is what is preventing you from listening to Christ and believing in his grace. You cannot hear Christ because you are wilfully disobedient. Somewhere in your heart you are refusing to listen to his call. Your difficulty is your sins . . . . Tear yourself away from all other attachments and follow him."[4]

"No one should be surprised at the difficulty of faith," Bonhoeffer writes, "if there is some part of his life where he is consciously resisting or disobeying the commandment of Jesus" —some sinful passion, some animosity, some selfish hope.

If so, you must not be surprised that you have not received the Holy Spirit, that prayer is difficult, or that your request for faith remains unanswered. Go rather and be reconciled with your brother, renounce the sin which holds you fast— and then you will recover your faith! If you dismiss the word of God's command, you will not receive his word of grace. How can you hope to enter into communion with him when at some point in your life you are running away from him? The man who disobeys cannot believe, for only he who obeys can believe.[5]

Now we have come to the point where the doctrine of justification leads to the doctrine of sanctification, the subject of
our next chapter. We must begin there where we leave off now,
with the connection between Christian faith and Christian life.
Now it is important only to see this much of the connection: If
we want to receive the gift of the assurance of God's love, forgiveness and acceptance which frees us in turn to accept him,
other people and ourselves, we must be willing to enter into the
life of faith, to *do* what faith requires.

By way of conclusion, let us go back to the question with
which we began this chapter: Are you a Christian? According
to the doctrine of justification, a Christian is one who knows
that he is guilty of offending God and of hurting other people
and himself by his attempts to justify himself. He is one who
believes that *nevertheless*, despite everything, he is forgiven,
loved and accepted by God's grace in Jesus Christ. And as he
experiences freedom from the anxious or proud need to justify
himself, he also experiences a new freedom for God and other
people, and a new freedom to accept and be himself. How would
you summarize in your own words what this means? On the basis
of what you have learned in this chapter, how would you begin
to answer the question, "Are *you* a Christian"?

FOR FURTHER REFLECTION AND STUDY

1. Read Paul's doctrine of justification in Romans 3:21–26.
   Compare his statement with Jesus' parable in Luke 18:10–14.
   Does Jesus' story help you to understand what Paul was talking about?
2. At the beginning of this chapter we spoke of various ways in
   which some people try to justify themselves. Do you recognize yourself in any of these examples? In what other ways
   could we try to justify ourselves before God, other people,
   and ourselves?
3. Is self-depreciation more Christian than self-exaltation?
4. Why is it impossible to earn the love of God? Why is it
   impossible to earn the love of other people?
5. Why do you think some Christians believe an over-emphasis
   on justification by grace to be dangerous? Do you agree?

6. How would you answer the objection that it is impossible for a God who is a just and righteous Judge to forgive, accept and love sinful men?

7. Do you agree that it is wrong to speak of "saving faith"? Defend your answer.

8. If God loves us anyway, why does it matter whether we love him in return?

9. What is faith?

10. Do you agree that the main way we experience God's love, forgiveness and acceptance is through other people? In what other ways could we experience it in our daily lives?

11. Compare Bonhoeffer's description of the relation between faith and obedience with what Paul says about it in Romans 6:1–23. Do they say the same thing?

17

Are You a Christian?

THE DOCTRINE OF
SANCTIFICATION

Albert Camus, a remarkably sensitive agnostic who fought
courageously with the French underground during World War II,
was once asked to speak to a group of Christians. Taking them to
task for their compromising silence or safely ambiguous theological
jargon while millions of Jews were slaughtered, he spoke some
words relevant to all Christians in all times:

> What the world expects of Christians is that Christians should
> speak out, loud and clear, and that they should voice their
> condemnation in such a way that never a doubt, never the
> slightest doubt, could rise in the heart of the simplest man.
> That they should get away from abstraction and confront the
> blood-stained face history has taken on today. The grouping
> we need is a grouping of men resolved to speak out clearly
> and to pay up personally . . . Perhaps we cannot prevent this
> world from being a world in which children are tortured. But
> we can reduce the number of tortured children. And if you
> don't help us, who else in the world can help us do this? . . .
> It may be, I am well aware, that Christianity will answer
> negatively. Oh, not by your mouths, I am convinced. But it
> may be, and this is even more probable, that Christianity will
> insist on maintaining a compromise or else on giving its con-
> demnations the obscure form of the encyclical. Possibly it
> will insist on losing once and for all the virtue of revolt and

indignation that belonged to it long ago. In that case
Christians will live and Christianity will die. In that case the
others will in fact pay for the sacrifice. In any case such a
future is not within my province to decide, despite all the
hope and anguish it awakens in me. I can speak only of what
I know. And what I know—which sometimes creates a deep
longing in me—is that if Christians made up their mind to it,
millions of voices—millions, I say—throughout the world would
be added to the appeal of a handful of isolated individuals
who, without any sort of affiliation, today intercede almost
everywhere and ceaselessly for children and for men.[1]

What this unbeliever wants to hear is that Christians take
seriously their own doctrine of sanctification.

Let us put it another way. In order to answer the question,
"Are you a Christian?" we spoke in the last chapter of the doctrine
of justification, which describes how a man becomes a Christian:
Giving up all attempts at self-justification, he comes to trust in
God's forgiving acceptance of him despite the fact that he is not
good and deserving in himself.

But that is only a part of the answer. If I am asked whether I
am a Christian, it is not enough for me to answer, "Yes. I am a
sinner who believes that nevertheless I am accepted, loved and
forgiven by God through Jesus Christ." A Christian is not just a
man who passively trusts God to accept him as he is, solve his
problems, meet his personal and family needs, comfort and save
him. He is a man who *responds* to God's love, forgiveness and
acceptance with thankful *obedience* in every area of his life. To
be a Christian is not only to believe and receive, but to *live* and
serve as a Christian. In other words, we cannot answer outsiders'
criticisms of Christians and the church, or answer the question
whether we ourselves are Christians, until we go on from the doctrine of justification to talk about the doctrine of sanctification.

Justification tells us how a person becomes a Christian. Sanctification tells us how a person grows in the Christian life.

Justification tells us about God's gracious action toward man.
Sanctification tells us about man's response with obedient action
toward God.

Justification tells us that God is *for* us, forgiving and saving us from sin. Sanctification tells us that by his Holy Spirit the same God works *in* us, helping us to leave our sin behind and begin a new and radically different kind of life.

In justification the covenant-making God makes a promise: "I will be your God." In sanctification, the same God also gives an inescapable command: "You shall be my people."

Justification tells us that Christ is our Savior, who died for us. Sanctification tells us that the same Christ is our Lord, who commands us to live for him.

Justification tells us that God adopts us to be his children. Santification tells us that God expects us to *live* as his children— and therefore as brothers and sisters of one another.

Justification tells us that we are made free *from* the self-justification which breaks relationship with God and with our fellowmen and therefore ruins our own lives. Santification tells us what it means to *live* as free men—free *for* God, *for* fellowmen and therefore free *for* our own true self-fulfillment.

Justification and sanctification are related as gift and task, creed and deed, theology and ethics, faith and life, passively receiving and actively giving in return. No one is a Christian until he is both justified *and* sanctified.

That is what we have to try to understand in this chapter. It is all the more important that we learn what sanctification means because we live in a time in which outsiders are highly critical of the church, not so much because its faith is out of date as because it does not practice the faith it already has. And it is all the more important, because so many of us insiders like to hear about God's love and forgiveness, but are angered by or simply cannot imagine the kind of costly Christianity Camus yearned to see.

We shall think first of all about the relationship between justification and santification as we have defined them. Then we shall think in more detail about what sanctification as such means.

Christian Faith and Christian Action

The Reformed confessions deal with the problem of the relation between justification and sanctification in terms of the relation between faith and good works, or faith and the fruits of faith. We mean the same thing when we speak of Christian faith and Christian action. The point we have to make in several different ways is the same point the Reformers made: Justification-faith and sanctification-action must be distinguished from each other, but they can never be separated. They are two different aspects of the one gracious work of the same God.

✓ **1. There can be no Christian faith without Christian action.** It is easy enough for all of us to agree in theory with this general statement. We know that faith without works is dead (James 2:14–26). But in practice, we main-line Protestants have so strongly emphasized salvation by grace alone that we are often suspicious of any talk about good works. Some versions of Christian orthodoxy have so strongly and exclusively emphasized right Christian belief and pure doctrine that they simply ignore the Christian life; all that matters is to believe the right things. Some forms of pietistic Christianity have been so exclusively concerned with the salvation of souls that in practice, if not in theory, they have acted as if all that matters is leading people to make a confession of faith and join the church. Once they are saved, they can be forgotten. Their growth in the Christian life can be ignored, while we go out to win more converts.

This split between Christian faith and Christian life, justification and sanctification, lies behind many of the arguments in the church today.

Many people sincerely could not understand why a whole year of the Covenant Life Curriculum was devoted to the study of *The Christian Life.* They wanted to study the Bible *instead of* Christian ethics.

There is currently a big debate in the church whether evangelism should emphasize Christ as the Savior who saves us from our sins *or* Christ as the Lord who calls us to serve him in every sphere of everyday life. Is the mission of the church to save souls *or* to engage in Christian social action which tries to bring the good news of God's love and justice to bear on life in the world?

Many people really cannot understand why preachers do not "stick to the Bible" and talk about "spiritual things" *rather than* "meddling" by talking concretely about what it means to live as a Christian in face of the sexual, racial, social and political crises of our time.

The result of thinking that we can be saved or justified without obediently *living* as those who have been forgiven and saved is what Bonhoeffer calls "cheap grace."[2] Cheap grace is grace without obedience. It means that we are not freed from our sins, but that we can settle down with them comfortably, assured that God will forgive, whatever we do—so long as we believe in the doctrine of justification. It says that grace alone does everything, so everything in our lives can remain as it was before. It reasons that since we depend on God's grace and not our works for salvation anyway, we can model our lives on the world's standards. It means that the Christian life is reduced to middle-class respectability, which makes no costly demands, but is safe and painless. "The upshot of it all is that my only duty as a Christian is to leave the world for an hour or so on a Sunday morning and go to church to be assured that my sins are forgiven."[3]

The Christian answer to this split between justification and sanctification, and the cheap grace which follows from it, is that there is no such thing as Christian faith without Christian action. To be justified or saved is to commit our whole lives to the God who justifies and saves us.

To know God is to know him as the God who not only graciously forgives, accepts and loves us as we are, but claims our lives —*all* of them. How is this relation between God's grace and God's command expressed in Deuteronomy 6:20–25? In Exodus 20:1–18?

To be elected or chosen by God is not to be given special privilege and indulgence, or only to be guaranteed salvation when we die. It is to be chosen in order to *serve* him here and now. How is this said in Ephesians 1:4 and Colossians 1:21–22?

We cannot know Christ as Savior *for* us without acknowledging him also as Lord *over* us. To have faith in him means inevitably also to *follow* him. How is this said in Matthew 7:21?

To receive the Holy Spirit is not just to get an emotional charge, or to experience God's nearness and love. It is to be renewed *to go to work*, living a different kind of life. Galatians 5:22–25 again!

To belong to the church is not just to belong to a community

of believers who come together only to "get something out of" a
church service, to be "fed" and "blessed." It is to belong to a
community of people who come together to be renewed so that
they can go back into the world to serve God as they serve their
fellowmen. How does 1 Peter 2:9 say this?

Just when we take the Bible seriously, we discover that it
hardly ever speaks of faith without corresponding obedience, of
 theology without corresponding ethics. What relation between
justification and sanctification is implied, for instance, in the great
Christological passage, Philippians 2:1–13?

"Can we believe that we are justified without doing good
works? That is impossible. For to believe in Jesus Christ is to
receive Him as he is given to us. He promises not only to deliver
us from death and to restore us to favor with his Father, through
the merit of his innocence, but also to regenerate us by his Spirit,
that we may be enabled to live in holiness" (Calvin's Geneva
Catechism, Q. 126).

That is the first thing we have to emphasize. There is no such
thing as Christian faith without Christian life. Christian faith does
not free us *from* but *for* Christian action. God does not forgive,
accept and love us *on condition that* we become righteous, but he
does forgive, accept us *in order that* we may become righteous.

2. God's action makes possible man's action. When
we talked about justification, we said that by ourselves we cannot
achieve a right relationship with God and other people, or a meaningful life for ourselves. We are totally dependent upon God's
forgiveness, acceptance and love. Do we not contradict ourselves
now when we begin to talk about Christian action and quote
Camus' call for Christians to get to work to make the world a better
place to live? Does not the doctrine of santification shift the emphasis from trusting in God's grace to trusting in man's good works?

This would be a legitimate objection if a popular view were
correct in saying that justification means that God does his part
to forgive and help us, and sanctification means that man takes it
up from there, working on his own to do his part. But this is not
the Christian view. Sanctification is just as much the work of God's

grace as justification. Effective Christian action in our individual relationships and in the life of the world is possible, not because we are optimistic about men in general or even about Christian men, but because we are optimistic about the renewing power of God in men's lives. We can confidently give ourselves to obedient Christian action, and we can hope for progress in our own lives and in the world, not because we have faith in ourselves and our own goodness, but because we have faith that God does not stop with forgiving our sins, loving and accepting us. He promises also to work in us, accompanying us every step of the way, enabling us to do what we could never do alone, helping us to achieve results we could never hope for if we were left to ourselves. How does Paul emphasize this in Philippians 2:13?

It is not individual and social Christian action, but the apparently pious pessimism which refuses to engage in Christian action, which is faithless. Christian faith in God's grace alone is not an excuse for us to do nothing, hopelessly sitting around waiting for God to do something. It is the courage to risk challenging all the difficulties, dangers and obstacles of our own and the world's sinfulness, just because we believe in a God who is with us not only at the beginning but throughout our Christian lives. Sanctification, in other words, means that an emphasis on man's action does not exclude faith in God's action. It is just faith in God's action which gives man the ability, courage and hope to act. We cannot make the world a better place to live, but God can—working in and through us.

All this means, by the way, that the obedient Christian life is not a terrible burden and necessity we unfortunately have to accept if we are really Christians. For Christians God's law is not the threat that we had better obey or else suffer the consequences. Sanctification means that God promises to give us the ability to do what he commands us to do. He says to us not only, "You *must* do what I command," but, "By my grace you *can* do whatever is necessary to obey my command." The Christian life is not easy. It is difficult and costly. But it is not a life of grim, teeth-gritting determination. The Christian can enter upon the serious responsibilities of the Christian life with a kind of light-hearted, cheerful confidence, just because he knows that God himself gives what he demands. How is this attitude toward Christian obedience to the requirements of God expressed in Matthew 11:28–30, and 2 Corinthians 4:7–12?

In summary: Sanctification means (a) that faith in God's action does not exclude but includes Christian action in the world, and (b) that the Christian life is not only a great task but a great privilege. How are both these points underlined in John 14:12–24?

3. **Being a Christian is growing up.** Justification has to do with becoming a Christian; sanctification with living out the Christian life. In justification we passively receive God's grace by faith. In sanctification by God's grace we become active servants of God and neighbor.

Does this mean that when we are sanctified, we leave justification behind us, switching from one kind of grace to another? There is a kind of Christian perfectionism which interprets the relation between justification and sanctification in this way. Once a person is converted and receives the Holy Spirit, he no longer has to live from God's forgiveness. He can live from his own righteousness (which, of course, he acknowledges to be God-given). He no longer has seriously to confess his sin and ask for forgiveness. This way of relating justification and sanctification in a temporal sequence (first one, then the other) is unbiblical. "If we say we have no sin, we deceive ourselves, and the truth is not in us" (1 John 1:8). Jesus taught us to pray over and over again, "Forgive us our debts." We *never* leave behind us our need to receive God's forgiveness for what we do to him, other people and ourselves by our lack of love and refusal to let ourselves be loved. Sanctification —the Christian life, Christian action—does not mean that we who once were sinners can now congratulate ourselves and thank God that we are no longer sinners. Such a "sanctified" life would be the very essence of sinfulness!

But how can we understand the Christian life then? We have said on the one hand that we cannot remain only passive, helpless babies in the Christian faith. New birth to Christian faith in God's grace leads to strong, confident, responsible Christian action by

God's grace. But now we seem to say that we never get past the beginning of the Christian life. No matter how long we live, every day we have to confess all over again what we confessed the very first day we knew what it is all about: "God be merciful to me, a sinner."

There is a biblical image which helps us clarify this seemingly complicated situation. It summarizes not only everything we have been trying to say about the relation between justification and sanctification, but also everything we have tried to say about what it means to be a Christian.

The image is that of the growth of a child to maturity which we find in Ephesians 4:13–16. To be a Christian is to be "growing up." It means to be moving toward "mature manhood"—the complete or whole humanity which is the "stature of the fulness of Christ." Seen from this point of view, the question we have to ask ourselves (and be willing for people like Camus to ask us!) concerning our Christian life and action is not: "How perfect are you? What degree of righteousness have you achieved?" The question is: "Are you *growing?* Have you settled down comfortably with the growth you have behind you, or are you willing to keep up the painful, constant struggle to keep on changing? Is your Christian life an attempt simply to hold on to what you think you have already achieved in your relation to God and other people? Or are you willing to risk what you have already learned and accomplished to explore new and more complete ways of loving God and other people? Do you spend your life defending and protecting yourself as you are, or are you willing to subject yourself to the dangers of admitting that you are still immature in your beliefs and way of life and need to plow into new ways of thinking and living?"

To be a Christian is not to have arrived at some state or condition of Christian existence. It is to be constantly having growing pains. It is not to *be* something but to be *becoming* something. It is never to think that we have arrived, but to be constantly on the way (Philippians 3:12–16).

But this means that we never leave our need for the justifying grace of God. Even when we do keep growing, we never reach the stage where we no longer need God's forgiveness, his love and his acceptance of us despite our "immaturity." In fact, the more progress we make toward the whole or complete humanity of Christ (sanctification), the more sensitive we become to our own inhumanity and need for forgiveness and renewal (justification). A Christian is one who every day, all through his life, lives both from God's sanctifying *and* his justifying grace.

But what is this "mature manhood," this "stature of the fulness of Christ," this complete or whole humanity, Christians are moving toward? What is the nature of genuinely Christian life and Christian action? That is what we have to talk about next.

In But Not of the World

There are many ways we might try to describe the Christian life. But in the context of the doctrine of sanctification, the obvious way is to describe it as a holy life. The verb "to sanctify" means "to make holy." Growth in sanctification is growth in holiness. A Christian is by definition a *holy* person. And that means that he is a "saint," for that is the translation of the New Testament word for "holy one."

Most of us probably react negatively at first when we hear that Christians are supposed to be saints who lead holy lives. Our minds jump from "saint" to "super-human," from "holy" to "holier-than-thou," from "sanctified" to "sanctimonious." We think of very pious people who live by a long list of thou-shalt-nots and are rewarded for their sacrifice of a normal life in the world by the assurance that they are superior to everyone else.

If we are to understand the true meaning of holiness, we have to get rid of this negative, self-righteous, world-denying view. But at the same time we must not fall into the opposite view that the Christian life means only a kind of mild moral respectability which fits comfortably into the world and its standards. The holy life of the saints, in other words, is life *in* the world, but not *of* the world. How does Jesus say this in John 17:14–19?

In this section we shall try to understand what it means to live as Christians "in but not of" the world, and in the next section we shall look at some of the commandments Jesus gave which illustrate concretely what such a holy life is like.[4]

The basic meaning of the word *holy* is "separate" or "different." In the Old Testament, the people of God are holy, and in the New Testament the church is a community of saints, because they are set apart from other people by virtue of their belonging to God. God's people are not "conformed" to the world but are "transformed" by the renewal of their minds in order to serve God and not the world (Romans 12:1–2). Jesus said, "My kingship is not of this world" (John 18:36). Christians have their "citizenship" not on earth but in heaven (Philippians 3:20). We could cite many more passages which make it clear that Christians are not of this world. They are *holy*—different, separate, from the world. But this does not mean that the Christian life is one which flees the problems and responsibilities of life in the world. Christians are not different or separate in that they retire from the world into a spiritual realm of tranquil isolation and safety. The communion of the saints is not a purely religious community divorced from and uninterested in secular affairs. To be holy means to be *in* the world even as we are not *of* it. We can see why this is so, and what it means, in several different ways.

1. The holiness of God. In the Old Testament, God is often called the "Holy One of Israel." He is different from all the other gods in that he is completely free from any dependence upon the world and the claims of men in it. Yet his holiness does not mean that he has nothing to do with the world. It is just as the Holy One that he is the covenant-making God who binds himself to a particular people in the world. He is not holy *despite* but *because* of the fact that he involves himself in every aspect of the very worldly history of a very worldly people.

In the New Testament, Jesus, the "Holy One of God" (Mark 1:24; John 6:69), accomplished his work not only in the synagogue and Temple, but in the marketplace, on public roads, in a courtroom, and at the place where garbage and criminals were disposed of. He was holy not *despite* but *because* of the fact that he entered into the world and lived a fully human life in it.

In other words, we learn from the holiness of God or Jesus

that holiness does not mean being unrelated to the world, but being related to it in a particular way. What that way is will be the topic of the next two points.

2. The holiness which is against the world. The Kingdom of God is not only different from the kingdoms of this world; it *invades, confronts, opposes* and *contradicts* them. Christians are different in that they refuse to conform to the world; but that means their loyalty to God takes precedence over all other loyalties. Holiness means a *protest* against the ways and claims of the world. In the words of Camus, whom we quoted at the beginning of this chapter, to be a Christian in such a world as ours means inevitably "condemnation," "revolt," "indignation."

But how can an effective holy protest *against* the world be made except *in* the world? A Christianity which refuses to have anything to do with political and economic questions, or does nothing to question the generally accepted way of life around it, can make no holy protest. By its inactivity and silence it gives an unholy *consent* to the worldly status quo. Its very otherworldliness lends support to the sinful world by letting it go unchallenged. A holy protest can be made only by those who, "loud and clear," in word and action, call into question the ideals, institutions and practices which have absolute validity for other people.

We can make the same point in another way. The New Testament makes it unmistakably clear that a holy life in following the Holy One involves self-denial, cross-bearing, and sacrifice. (Calvin understood this to be the total sum of the Christian life. See his *Institutes*, III, 7.) How is this stated in Mark 8:34-36 and in Romans 12:1? Jesus often warned that those who followed him would be so at odds with the world that they would be hated and persecuted. See John 15:18-21 and Mark 13:9-13.

But this kind of costly holiness is only possible when Christians are different from the world *in* the world—when they openly do what others do not do, and do not do what others do; when they publicly refuse automatically to conform to the political systems and ideologies, business practices and even the standards of family responsibility and moral integrity which others around them consider unquestionable. A Christianity which withdraws into a purely religious church or restricts itself to purely private spirituality will obviously stir up no trouble and therefore demand no cross-bearing, cost no sacrifices. The world may shrug off such a harmless, inoffensive Christianity. It may laugh at its pious pretentiousness. But the world will not be threatened enough by such an otherworldly Christianity even to take it seriously, much less to hate or persecute Christians.

This is not to say that Christians are to go out looking for trouble, seeking to be martyrs. It is to say that as with the Holy One himself, so also with his followers, to be holy means to risk being different *within* the structures of the world—and to be prepared to "pay up personally" (Camus) when that holy protest has painful repercussions. The alternative to such holy worldliness? Camus put it bluntly: "Christians will live and Christianity will die."

3. The holiness which is for the world. The holiness of God, of Christ, and therefore of Christians means protest against the sinful world. But they are *against* the world only in order to be *for* it. The holy God judges his disobedient people because he loves them and wants them to return to him for their own good. Jesus stirred up so much trouble in the world of his time that they killed him; but he did it "not to condemn the world, but that the world might be saved through him" (John 3:17). The agnostic Camus' purpose, when he asked Christians to voice their condemnation, indignation and revolt against the "bloodstained" world we live in, was to plead with Christians to join those who "intercede everywhere and ceaselessly for children and for men."

Other gods and other men may seek their own honor, glory, purity and superiority above everything else. They may withdraw in isolated splendor, or condemn, or use people to defend and advance their own spiritual or material interests. But the holy God and his people are "different." They are holy just because they are willing to risk their own honor, power and spiritual and material self-interests for the sake of other people. To be holy means to be not only for oneself but for other men. It means to look not only to our own interests but to the interests of others (Philippians 2:4). It means not to serve oneself, but to serve God and to serve other people. That is how Christians are different, separate, not of the world.

But that means, once again, that the truly holy life can only be lived *in* the world. How can we possibly be genuinely and effectively with and for our fellowmen if we withdraw into a self-serving church or a self-serving, private religion? How can we possibly be holy as God is holy so long as we think that to be holy means to be a spiritual elite who preserves their holiness by refusing to have anything to do with people, institutions and places which are not holy? To be holy in the biblical sense is to abandon a self-protecting, world-denying concern for our own safety and purity—even for our own salvation (Mark 8:35)! It is to risk *denying* and *sacrificing* ourselves to "intercede for children and for men" wherever and however they are hurt or destroyed in the world.

The Holiness Jesus Commands

So far we have spoken of the holy life, in but not of the world, in a very general way. Now we shall become painfully and controversially concrete. We shall look at some examples of the kind of life Jesus required of those who would follow him. The sayings we shall look at are radical and difficult to interpret. Here are some guidelines to help you: (1) Remember that Jesus spoke always to particular people in particular situations. It would be wrong automatically to conclude that everyone, always, is required to do exactly the same thing he required of them, in exactly the same way. (2) On the other hand, it would also be wrong to spiritualize all the hard sayings of Jesus. We cannot escape the holy life he demanded by saying that he did not mean it literally, and that we have only to take his commandments in a "spiritual" sense. Jesus spoke specifically and concretely about how his disciples should live in the world. Although we cannot make a legalistic set of general rules out of his commands, we must try to learn what it means faithfully and obediently to echo his attitude toward these worldly realities in our everyday lives. (3) Since he spoke as the "Holy One," we may expect Jesus to criticize the attitudes and practices the world takes for granted. He demands a costly nonconformity. But on the other hand, since he spoke as the Holy One who gave himself for the world, we may expect that his hard commandments will also bring freedom—freedom *from* enslaving loyalties to the world, freedom *for* God and our fellowmen.

1. Holiness and money. Read Matthew 5:40–42; 6:24–33; Mark 10:17–22. Jesus said again and again that whoever would follow him must give up his attachment to material possessions. The lives of other men (and of some churches?) may be determined exclusively by what is good business, by practical financial considerations, by sound fiscal policies, and by what will pay off with a good financial return. But the followers of Jesus are to be holy—different from the world. They have to be willing to give up what belongs to them. Why? Not because wealth is bad and poverty is good, but because individuals (and churches!) cannot place their faith and hope in God and in financial security at the same time. Because trust in God *frees* men from the anxious, self-seeking, self-destructive trust in possessions. And surely it is no accident that Jesus mentioned *poor people* (not religious institutions!) as the beneficiaries of such a loose attitude toward money. To be holy means to risk one's own material comfort and security for *their* sakes.

Impractical? Meddling in nonreligious business affairs and economic problems? Of course! Jesus was talking about what it means to be holy *in* the world.

2. Holiness and the use of force. Read Matthew 5:38–39, 43–48; 10:28; 26:47–54; Luke 9:51–56. Other men may believe that when an individual or nation is attacked, self-defense is an automatic right. They may take for granted that the use of force against threatening enemies, or for the protection and guarantee of their own way of life, is self-evidently legitimate. But not the disciples of Jesus. They do not live by the standards and "self-evident" assumptions of the world. They are neither to fear force used against them, nor to exercise force against others, nor even passively to support those who are willing to do the dirty work for them. They are to be like the Holy One who sacrificed his own life, even when he could have had twelve legions of angels to fight for him.

Why this "pacifism" of Jesus and his disciples? Its purpose is not that they may preserve their own purity and righteousness. They are pacifists because they do not hate, slaughter and maim, but *love*, their enemies.

But that raises all kinds of very complicated political and social problems—about Communism, war and the civil rights movement, for instance. Such talk is dangerous. Subversive. Unrealistic. Of course! We are talking about *holiness*—not conforming to the general accepted ways of the world, but being transformed. We are talking about being in but not of the world.

The point is not to argue a theory of pacifism in principle or to say that there are no conditions under which the state may use force—such as the exercise of police power to preserve law and order. But it is to ask seriously whether at the very least Christians ought not to give sympathetic support to those who do follow literally the commands of Jesus himself against the use of force.

3. Holiness and family responsibilities. Read Matthew 10:34–39; Luke 9:57–62; 14:25–26. For other men, nothing may be more important than husband or wife, children or parents, brother or sister. Everything else may be sacrificed for the good of one's family; the welfare of his family cannot be called into question by anything. Me and my family, my family and me—nothing can take precedence over our happiness, comfort, security, and responsibility to and for one another.

But the disciples of Jesus are called to be holy. They do not live by the standards of the world—not even by its highest standards. They are commanded to renounce any absolute attachment to family. They may have to break with family, sacrifice the best interests of family, disturb the peace and harmony within the family. They may be called upon to *hate*, not father and mother, wife and children as such, but the enslaving hold they have.

Why this family-threatening holiness of Jesus and his followers? Not because the Christian faith is against sex, marriage and family life as such, but because God and his Kingdom call into question _all_ other attachments and loyalties. Because holiness is a protest made for the sake of _right_ worldly relationships. Because an exclusive, self-centered withdrawal into a clannish concern only for me and mine means that the needs and rights of other people (whom God loves as much as he loves us) are ignored and trampled. Because when family is made absolute, the warmth of family attachments can become smothering; the closeness of family relationships, a prison. Children are so tied to parents that they are prevented from growing up into mature, independent human beings. Husbands and wives lose their identity and become simply the echo or tool of the other. The lives of parents become empty and meaningless when the children are gone.

The family-threatening holiness Jesus demands does not destroy the family; it cuts apron strings and breaks the tyranny which family members exercise over one another when family is the be-all and end-all.

In any case, the holiness Jesus commands with his harsh saying about the family is far more than that of religious activities. It has to do with sex, the discipline and letting-be of children, the family budget and care for the aged. It is holiness _in_ the world.

4. **Holiness and piety.** Read Matthew 5:21–48; 6:1–16; Mark 2:15–3:6. Other people may think they are good when they obey the law (not killing, committing adultery, stealing, swearing, and so on); when they pray, go to church and give a little money to help others; and when they preserve their own moral and religious integrity by avoiding the company of those whose morality, patriotism and religious sincerity are questionable. But Jesus and his followers are different. They are not merely moral, religious and pure; they are _holy_—set apart.

On the one hand, their righteousness is _more than_ that of others. Strict legal faithfulness to your spouse does not make you an "innocent party" in your marriage, and your marriage itself a sound one. _Inner_ fidelity is what really matters; you can be legally innocent and yet just as guilty of adultery as someone who sleeps around. Not killing is not enough; hating another person is just as bad. Loving only those who are like you in tastes, way of life, political and theological views and race is not enough; holy people love their *enemies*.

On the other hand, the nonconforming holiness of Jesus and his followers can *break* the moral and religious conventions which seem absolute to others. Those who follow Jesus may seem irreligious because they refuse to advertise their piety. They do their praying in private (rather than at football games). They do their giving in secret (rather than publicizing their tithing). They risk seeming immoral and politically subversive because they have the wrong friends and do not let their concern for undeserving sinners be stopped by the warning that "birds of a feather flock together."

Why Jesus' harsh criticism of law-abiding, God-fearing people? Why this suspicious nonconformity to the moral and religious conventions of the "best" people? Not because Jesus and his followers are against morality and religion as such (Matthew 5:17!). Rather because, not being of the world, they are more concerned about the verdict of God who sees into the hearts of men than about the approval or condemnation of other people. Because, once again, Christian holiness is *against* the world only in order to be *for* it. Christians criticize and refuse to conform to conventional morality and religion for the sake of *true* morality and religion. They are holy—different—just because they have learned from Jesus that *the needs of human beings take precedence over conventional moral and religious rules. People are more important to Jesus and his followers than their own legal purity and reputation.* Men do not live for the sake of laws; laws are there to be obeyed—and sometimes broken!—for the sake of men (Mark 2:27).

Such holiness is dangerous and costly, of course. You can get a bad reputation with it. You may be rejected by some solid citizens and by some pious church members. You may get into trouble with the law (like Jesus and Paul). But that is just what it means to be holy—to run the risk of being in the world without being of the world, to be transformed instead of conformed to the world.

A serious investigation of the radical requirements Jesus made of those who follow him results in a sequence of thoughts which lead us to look first backward, then forward, in the course of our study.

The first result is painful self-examination: "If *that* is what it means to be a Christian, do I really want to be one? Am I willing to pay the cost of discipleship? Do I really want to be holy, if holiness means not just a little moral respectability, a little religious piety, a little orthodox theology, but such a dangerously different nonconforming life? Many people who were with Jesus at first turned away when they heard him spell out what was involved in following him. Could it be that the same thing would happen today, if we took seriously the call of Christian discipleship to 'speak out clearly and pay up personally'? Not everyone wants to be a Christian. Perhaps not even everyone whose name is on the church roll. Do I?"

The second result of listening to Jesus' descripton of the life his followers must live is thankful remembrance that sanctification never leaves justification behind. Even when we seriously want to, who of us ever obeys the radical call of Jesus so completely that we do not have to pray at the end of every day, "Forgive us our debts"? What good news to know that we do not *have* to depend on our own holiness, but that at the end of every day we *can* remember again that God forgives, accepts and loves us *despite* our failures. That does not excuse us from the life of discipleship. It does give us the courage and confidence to keep starting out all over again every new day—to keep growing.

Thirdly, the requirements of Jesus remind us that holiness is a gift. Who of us ever has the wisdom to make faithful yet responsible decisions in the Christian use of money? In knowing what to say and do about the use of force in light of the character of modern warfare? In being a good husband or wife, parent or child? Even when we do know what we should do, who of us has the courage and ability to do it? The good news of Christ is that we are not left to ourselves to make decisions and act alone. We have the promise of the guidance and help of God's Spirit to help us when we cannot help ourselves.

But that only raises again the same problem we have wrestled with before: How can we have this gift? What are the answers we tried to give in the last two chapters, when we discussed the doctrines of the Holy Spirit and justification? In the present context, when we have been discussing the meaning of holiness, one particular answer stands out. It is significant that in the New Testament no individual person is ever called "holy" or a "holy one" (saint)—with the exception of the one individual who is *the* Holy One of God. No one can be holy by himself. A Christian is never a "Lone Ranger who rides off in lonely individualism to serve God and become righteous."[5] Holy people or saints are found only in the plural, in the *"communion* of the saints." In other words, the gift of the Holy Spirit, who enables people to be holy people, is given in and with the *church.*

What that means, and whether we can believe it (Does that sound like the church *you* belong to?)—that is what we have to talk about in the next chapter.

FOR FURTHER REFLECTION AND STUDY
1. What is the relation between God's action and man's action in Philippians 2:1–13?
2. Should evangelism emphasize Christ as the Savior of men or Christ as the Lord of men?
3. Some Christians argue that Christians should have nothing to do with organizations such as the Peace Corps or the United Nations, because our hope is in salvation through Christ, not in human efforts toward world improvement. What do you think?
4. Why do you think The Heidelberg Catechism places the title "Thankfulness" over its exposition of the Ten Commandments?
5. Is it correct to think of sanctification in terms of growing, or "being on the move"? Would an outsider like Camus be satisfied with such thinking?
6. Describe in your own words what it means to be in but not of the world. How are Christians both *against* and *for* the world at the same time?

7. Do you think we ought to take Jesus' commandments in the Sermon on the Mount literally?
8. On *"holiness and money"*:
   a. What should a Christian do when his neighborhood is integrated by block-busting, and property values begin to go down?
   b. Evaluate this bumper slogan from a Christian point of view: "I fight poverty—I work."
9. On *"holiness and the use of force"*: Answer the following questions about war in light of Jesus' statements and attitudes about the use of force: Can any Christian in good conscience support the mass killing of civilians as a means to an end? Can the Christian church count itself part of any ruling establishment that condones this? Does the doctrine of "massive retaliation" fall in with Christian concepts? Is expediency ever a proper motive for a committed Christian?[6]
10. On *"holiness and family responsibilities"*:
    a. What factors should be considered in the decision to keep an aged parent in your own home or to place him in an institutional home for senior citizens?
    b. "She worships the ground he walks on." "He adores her." "They live only for their children." What should Christians think of such expressions of family love?
11. On *"holiness and piety"*:
    a. In the light of Matthew 6:5 f., what do you think of prayers over the loudspeaker before football games and public meetings?
    b. Should the church receive into its fellowship alcoholics and dope addicts? Men and women known to be sexually promiscuous? Homosexuals? People with questionable occupations—night club entertainers, liquor dealers, and such?
    c. Is civil disobedience ever allowed or required of people who take the Christian faith seriously?

18

Living or Dead?

The trouble with the church is: (Check the answers which express your opinion.)

"It's too worldly. Too many of its members (even officers) drink, violate the Sabbath and do not believe in the Bible."
 "It's too worldly. It is guilty of the same race, class, economic and social discrimination as any secular organization and club."

"The preacher's sermons are boring. They're nothing but vague, unrealistic generalities which give me no help in my day-to-day living."
 "The preacher's sermons meddle too much in practical questions that are none of his business. He ought to stick to religious values and the salvation of souls."

"All the church does is serve itself. Its members raise money mostly to spend on themselves, their building and their denomination. All they do is have meetings, programs, luncheons, dinners, committees and organizations to entertain and edify themselves. They ignore the terrible individual suffering and social problems in the world around them and spend all their time bickering about such trivial issues as what color to paint the sanctuary or whether to get new choir robes."
 "The church is getting to be too much of a social welfare

organization. Too much money and support is given for doubt-ful causes in cooperation with questionable outside agencies. Too much time is spent on nonspiritual things."

"The church is compromising the truth of the gospel with all this ecumenical dialogue and plans for uniting with other denomina-tions. Now they're even beginning to play footsie with the Catho-lics."

"The church is too narrow-minded and intolerant. Every denomination thinks it has a monopoly on the truth and is too proud and suspicious to give an inch on its old confess-ional formulas."

"It's too inclusive. So long as you make a pledge of financial sup-port, it doesn't matter what you believe or how you live."

"It's too exclusive. If you are not the right color, don't wear the right clothes, or don't have the right political ideas, you are not welcome."

We could continue the list indefinitely:
"Too old-fashioned and conservative.
Too modernistic and liberal.
Too much hellfire and damnation.
Not enough hellfire and damnation.
Too chummy.
Too cold.
Too intellectual.
Too superficial."

The point is, almost everyone is unhappy about the church for one reason or another. Some of the gripes are petty. Some of them simply reflect the general confusion and unrest of our rapidly changing world. All of them cannot be legitimate, since many of the criticisms expressed are diametrically opposed. But there is much evidence to confirm the fact that the church is in serious trouble. The evidence has been collected in a whole series of books analyzing what is wrong with the church from sociological, psy-chological and theological points of view.

Survey after survey shows that while religion is still popular in our country, the Christian church and its message do not significantly influence church members. Their attitudes and practices in sex, marriage and divorce, and race relations; their ideas about poverty, war and other social issues; their dread of old age, attitude toward death, and the way they conduct their funeral:—in all these ways church members are generally indistinguishable from non-Christians. They consider religion to be a good thing so long—and only so long—as it gives them personal comfort and confirms the generally accepted "American way of life."

The enrollment in seminaries is falling off. Even within the seminaries, a large number of ministerial students do not want to become pastors of local parishes. They want specialized ministries in hospitals, on college campuses, or in inner-city projects. "That's where the action is. In a local congregation you never get around to the real task of preaching, teaching and counseling, because all your time is taken just to keep the organization going. You are not allowed to bring the gospel to bear on the real issues of life, because all the people want is someone who will not rock the boat."

Thousands of young people are simply not interested in the church any more—not even interested enough to attack it and debate its beliefs. They just ignore it as harmless and irrelevent and look to the Peace Corps, the civil rights movement, or the poverty program to find something worthwhile and challenging. On the other hand, many other people are angrily leaving churches because they think the church is *too much* involved in secular affairs.

The church *is* in trouble. On the inside, it is torn by confusion and strife, or endured with a listless going-through-the-motions of business as usual. On the outside, it is increasingly ignored or laughed at for its irrelevant piety.

This is the situation in which we have to talk about what it means to say, "I believe in the Holy Ghost, the holy Catholic Church, the communion of the saints . . ." We cannot let the present situation determine what we believe about the church. We have to learn that from the biblical source of our faith. But neither can we ignore the present situation, and act as if all we have to do is hold firmly to past ways of thinking and doing things. A part of the Reformed faith is that in obedience to the living God we must be constantly reforming in every new time and situation.

We shall look at the classical doctrine of the church, then, and ask what it could mean for a renewal of the church in our time. We will not solve all the problems and answer all the questions we have raised. No easy, glib answers will do. Nobody knows exactly how the church should go about fulfilling its task in our time. But perhaps we can at least identify what the real problems and legitimate criticisms are. Perhaps we can discover which possibilities are closed and which are open for further exploration, if we are to learn what it means to be a faithful *and* relevant church in an increasingly secular age.

This will be our procedure: First we shall try to understand what it means to say that the church is "the people of God." Then we shall ask about the importance of the church. Finally, we shall study the nature and task of the church in terms of the classical description of it in the Nicene Creed as the "one Holy Catholic and Apostolic Church." In following this procedure we shall not try to summarize everything that could be said about the doctrine of the church. We shall rather concentrate on those points where there seems to be widespread misunderstanding and confusion today.

The People of God

The Greek word used in the New Testament for church means "called out." The church is a community of people called out of the world by God to belong to him and be his people. The purpose of their coming together is twofold. First, they receive God's judging, forgiving, renewing grace. Secondly, they come together in order to be sent out again to be God's agents of judgment, forgiveness, reconciliation and renewal in the world. We shall speak later of the gift and task involved in church membership. Now we are concerned to simply say what it means that the church is a community of people called together by God.

1. *You* are the church. The church is not a board or agency in Atlanta or Richmond or New York (not to mention

Geneva or Rome!). It is not only the ordained preachers and leaders of the church. When we talk about the church, we are not talking about "them," but about "us." *We* are the church. Whenever a group of Christians are gathered in the name of Christ, there the church is. In the New Testament, the church is first of all and primarily a local congregation—the church in Jerusalem or Antioch or Rome. It is not limited to individual local congregations, of course. Paul could also speak of the churches in a wide geographical area. Nor do the individual congregations exist independently and self-sufficiently. They exist in mutual cooperation and support, united as "members" of the one "body" of the one Lord. Nevertheless, the church always exists concretely whenever and wherever a group of Christians are together. This means that whenever we say, "Why doesn't the church do so and so?" or, "The trouble with the church is . . . ," we are asking why *we* don't do so and so and are complaining about our own faults.

2. The church is not a *building*. It is hard for us to grasp this, because we are so used to thinking of the church as centered in a building which stands in the neighborhood where the members live. But it has not always been so. For the first three centuries the church had no buildings. Christians met together in homes (1 Corinthians 16:19; Colossians 4:15), or in the places where their secular occupation brought them together ("Caesar's household," Philippians 4:22). Later, when buildings were built, they were not built in local neighborhoods, but at the crossroads of life—in market towns or places of central government. It was not until the Middle Ages that the kind of parish church we know came into being.[1]

It is important in our time to understand that the church does not depend on a church building. This raises some serious questions about our present church structures and suggests some interesting possibilities for the future. Have we given so much time, money and effort to erecting, furnishing and maintaining buildings that we have lost sight of the real nature and purpose of the church —not to serve ourselves, but to serve God and our fellowmen in the world? In removing the church from homes and from places of business and government where secular life brings Christians together, have we come to think that the Christian faith and life has only to do with what goes on in an isolated building once or twice a week?

As our society changes, our lives are less and less centered in the neighborhood where we live. Many people find their friends, do their business, take their leisure—spend most of their lives— outside the neighborhood where their homes are. Can we afford to continue thinking of the church primarily as a neighborhood institution? If the church is wherever and whenever Christians come together for worship, study and service in the name of Christ, do they not just as surely "go to church" when they meet at the factory or downtown during their lunch hour, when they gather at the lake where they keep their boats, when they join together in service projects away from the church building, when they meet for prayer and study in someone's house? The point is not to deny that our local church is still important. It is to say that as our society changes and the neighborhood becomes less and less important in our lives, the church does not have to be less and less important. We can be open to experiment with new and (to us) strange forms of the church, because the church is not a building. It is God's people, whenever, wherever, however they come together.

3. God creates the church. One final implication of the fact that the church is the people called out by God: According to the Reformed churches (in distinction, for example, from Congregationalists or Baptists), the church is not a "voluntary association" of believers who get together and decide to form a church. It is God who creates the church and calls men into it. The church, therefore, is not like a club or fraternity or group of like-minded people who enjoy each other's company, form an organization for their mutual benefit and enjoyment and set up the constitution and rules of membership to suit themselves. It is not our church but God's church.

This understanding of the church is dramatically emphasized by the practice of infant baptism. Before we chose God, he had chosen us. Before we decided to be a member of the church, he claimed us to be one of his people. Before we loved him, he had loved us and adopted us to belong to him. He wants us to respond to his call with thankful obedience and to return his love by freely participating in the community of his people. But it is he who initiates, governs, and maintains the community. Its members are bound to serve him, not their own wishes and preferences. They must seek to express *his* will, not just the personal opinions of the leaders of the church, or the popular opinions of the church members. The church belongs to *him*, not to the clergy *or* the laity, the individual church members *or* the preachers, the local congregation *or* official church assemblies *or* the various boards and agencies.

A People in Community

One of the main images used in the New Testament to talk about the church is that of the "Body of Christ." Christians are related to each other as parts of the human body, and they are related to Christ as the body is related to the head. This image will guide the rest of our thinking about what the church is.

The first thing implied by it is that it is just as impossible for anyone to be a Christian by himself as it is for an arm or a leg to live and function apart from the body and the head. To be a Christian is by definition to belong to the church. There is no such thing as a purely individualistic relationship to Christ. "There is no purely private Christianity, for to be in Christ is to be in the church and to be in the church is to be in Christ, and any attempt to separate relation to Christ in faith from membership in the church is a perversion of the New Testament understanding."[2]

Notice that we have not said that in order to be good or to be moral, you must belong to the church. The old claim that "you can be just as good without going to church" is true. We only have to look around us to see that many people who never darken the door of the church are not only morally beyond reproach, but fine, sensitive people. Remember the unbelieving Camus we spoke of in the last chapter! Many non-Christians put some Christians to shame by their personal integrity, their warm and loving family life, their willingness to "speak out and pay up" in behalf of those whom society in general ignores or rejects. Why should we not be happy and grateful—and repentant!—when we meet such people?

But to be a *Christian* means inevitably to belong to the church. To believe in and follow Christ is to join in the community he draws together around himself. To be reconciled with God in Christ is to be reconciled also with other men; it is to be led out of my sinful attempt to live in self-sufficient isolation above or apart from others, and to be drawn into the community where all barriers which separate men are broken down. If I want to receive the Holy Spirit and his gifts of faith, hope and love, then I must be a part of the community to whom the life-renewing power of the Spirit is promised. To be saved is not just to be assured that I will go to heaven when I die; it is to enter into a new relationship with God and fellowmen in the community of God's people *here and now*. How can I know that the forgiveness, love and help of God in Christ are real, if I do not experience them through the community of people who belong to him? How can I be a Christian, if I do not participate in the community gathered to share with others the forgiveness, love and help they themselves have received?

To belong to Christ is to belong to the Body of Christ, for it is in and with his body that he himself promises to make himself known in the world "between the times"—between his resurrection and coming again. Whoever tries to do without the church, tries to do without Christ. Whoever is too good for the church (with all its weaknesses and faults), is too good for Christ himself.

This inseparable connection between being a Christian and belonging to the church has led many theologians to say that there is no salvation outside the church. Both Luther and Calvin took this position (see Calvin's *Institutes*, IV, 1, 4, and his Geneva Catechism, Questions 104 and 105). The Westminster Confession says more carefully that outside the church "there is no *ordinary* possibility of salvation" (XXV, 2).

Is the church that essential? We must be very careful here. It is not the church but Christ who saves men. And while it is true that the church is bound to Christ, it is not true that Christ is trapped in the church. He came to express God's love not just for Christians and the church, but for all men, in the whole world. He

is the risen Lord who is at work not only in the church but everywhere—even among men and societies who do not recognize or
acknowledge his reconciling, healing work. He himself said, "I have
other sheep which are not of this fold" (John 10:16). God may have
provided some other way for those who are never reached by
the church. We can say that there is no salvation outside God's
work in *Christ*, but can we say that there is no salvation outside
the *church*? Calvin himself said that "God's power is not bound
to outward means" (*Institutes*, IV, 1, 4).

What we can say for sure is that although God is not bound
to the church, *we* are bound to it. That is where the God who is
at work in his loving power everywhere is specifically known,
thankfully trusted and obeyed. And if that is so, then not only
are we bound to the church ourselves, but we are bound to invite
all other men into it so that they too may accept and live by the
forgiveness, love, help and command of the God who cared for
them and was at work for their good, even before they knew it.

A Holy People

"The *holy* Catholic Church, the communion of the saints (or
holy ones)." What do we mean when we confess that the church
is holy? From what we learned in the last chapter, it must mean
that the church is set apart or "different" from other organizations
and societies. But how is the church different?

First, let us clear away a misunderstanding church members
all too often have about themselves, much to the world's amusement or disgust. The people of God are *not* holy in that they are
morally superior to other people, or because they have a better
understanding of and purer commitment to the truth of God.
There is no sin to be found in the world which cannot also be found
both among individual Christians and among whole denominations: blind prejudice and intolerance; personal immorality and
legalistic self-righteousness; cut-throat competition; misrepresen-
tation or misuse of the truth for personal gain; lust for money,
prestige, power and success at all costs; pious rationalization for
social injustice, nationalistic arrogance, bloody wars and economic
exploitation.

There is no point in denying this or trying to explain it away.

It is perfectly obvious to the rest of the world even if it is not to us. Nor do we need to deny it. The Bible is perfectly open about the sinfulness of God's people. Think of the prophets' preaching against the individual and social sinfulness which Israel tried to conceal with pious words and religious ceremonies (Isaiah 1:1–17; Jeremiah 6:13; 7:1–26; Amos 5:21–27). Think of the sins to be found among the saints to whom Paul addressed his letters (1 Corinthians 1:10–13; 5:1, 9–13; 11:20–22; Galatians 2:11–14; Philippians 1:15–17). Whatever the holiness of the church means, it does not mean that the world and people in it are sinful, whereas Christians are not. We shall never understand the holiness of the church until we get rid of the idea that it is the community of the pure, who know better and live better than everyone else.

This leads us to three ways in which we *can* say that the church is holy or different.

First, the church is distinguished from other societies precisely in that it is a community of people who *know* they are sinners, and freely *admit* that they are not good or superior. Charles C. Morrison puts it this way:

> The church is not a society of good people, it is a society of sinners. It is the only organization in human society that takes sinners into its membership just because they are sinners. It is the only organization that keeps on saying week after week, year after year, age after age: "We have left undone those things which we ought to have done, and we have done those things which we ought not to have done."[3]

Secondly, the church is holy in that it is a community of *dissatisfied* sinners. They are not satisfied with themselves, or with the way things are in the world around them. They are gathered together not to justify their present way of life or to advertise their piety, but to admit publicly that they need to be *forgiven* for what they are, and that they want to *change* and need *help*. The people of God, in other words, are holy not because of what they *have* or what they *are*, but because of what they are seeking to *receive* and to *become*.

Finally, the church is different from all other societies in that it is gathered in the name of Jesus Christ. Here we run again into the image of the body and the Head. The body is holy only because the Head is *the* "Holy One." Holiness is not found in the church and its members as such, but in him from whom they seek forgiveness, change, help and new direction. When asked about the holiness of the church, Christians cannot proudly or defensively begin arguing about the church's (i.e., their own!) goodness, strength, purity and wisdom. They can only point to *his* goodness, strength, purity and wisdom.

On the other hand, it also follows from the fact that the church lives from the holiness of its Head that it cannot be only a passively receiving people. The Head directs, controls and activates the body. The church freely admits its sinfulness, but if it is a community of *dissatisfied* sinners, it cannot settle down comfortably with its confession of sin. If it is serious about wanting to change and be helped, it can only be willing to follow its Head. How can it claim to be the holy community gathered in the name of Christ, if, instead of reflecting his reconciling work among men, it goes on reflecting the same social and personal hostilities as worldly groups? How can its members live from him, if, instead of reflecting his self-giving love for guilty and suffering men everywhere, they go on reflecting only a worldly concern for their own present and future happiness, peace of mind, personal comfort and security? How can they say they believe in the truth he brings, if in practice they think and live just like everyone else?

The dependence of the body on the Head means the confession that the people of God are sinful, and he only is holy. But it also means inevitably the demand that they at least get up and start moving, set out on the way that leaves their sinfulness behind and moves toward his holiness.

That is what the Lord's Supper is all about. On the one hand it is a way of reminding us constantly that we do not live from our own strength. We have to be fed, nourished, given new life over and over again. But on the other hand the Lord's Supper means that we *are* fed, nourished and given new life—not just so that we may flex our spiritual muscles for everyone to admire, but so that we can get to work growing up "in every way into him who is the head, into Christ" (Ephesians 4:15).

A United, Catholic People[4]

It follows from the fact that there is one Savior and Lord of the church that the community of people who are the Body of Christ are united in faith, hope, love, worship and service (1 Corinthians 10:16–17; 12:4–27; Ephesians 2:11–22; 4:1–7, 11–16; Romans 12:4–6). Closely related to the idea of the church's unity is that of its catholicity. "Catholic" means "universal" or "whole"—including Christians in all places; of all races, classes, languages, cultures, nationalities; in all kinds of political, social and economic situations. Without using the word catholic, the New Testament expresses its meaning in Galatians 3:28. One Lord, one Spirit, one God, one baptism—and therefore one Body, the "holy *catholic* church" (Ephesians 4:4–6).

That is what Presbyterian and Reformed Christians say they believe (although they are split into different denominations and factions which debate who is *really and truly* Presbyterian and Reformed!). So do the Roman Catholics, Methodists, Lutherans, Baptists—and the hundreds of other denominations in our country. The splintering of the church into many churches screams that we are *not* one, *not* catholic. And that implies that we do not have one but many lords, are not led by one but by many spirits.

What is the reason for the disunity of the church? Preachers and theologians think first of all of great doctrinal issues: predestination, the authority of Scripture, infant baptism, the Lord's Supper, and so on. There is good evidence, however, that most people belong to their particular church for quite untheological reasons. Everyone knows that the Episcopal Church is for "high society" and intellectuals; the Presbyterian for the wealthy, those "on the way up," or the "solid middle class"; the Methodist and Baptist for the "ordinary man"; the Lutheran for those with a German background; the Pentecostals for the "lower classes" and uneducated. Then, of course, there are separate denominations, or congregations within denominations, for Negroes, who "wouldn't feel at home" in white churches—or for whites who wouldn't feel at home in integrated churches. Why do *you* belong to your particular congregation and particular denomination?

There are two nice-sounding but unsatisfactory ways of arguing that the divisions among and within the churches do not contradict what the Bible tells us about the unity and catholicity of the church.

The first argument is that the true church is invisible. There is a spiritual or invisible unity and catholicity which remains in spite of the external divisions. The different denominations, or factions within them, may not talk together, worship together, or work together. They may be suspicious of each other, question the genuineness of the other's faith and worship, work in competition with each other. Yet they are "spiritually" one!

There is a sense in which the true nature of the church is in fact invisible. There is no external proof that God is really uniquely at work in this very ordinary-looking group of people—just as there is no proof that he was uniquely present and acting in the Jew named Jesus. As with Jesus, so with them: We cannot *see*, we can only *believe* that it is so. But on the other hand, as with Jesus himself, so with the church which is his Body, God works in a very earthly, this-worldly, *human* way. It simply will not do for us to try to explain away the embarrassing facts by piously talking of a disembodied, real church somewhere above or apart from the concrete church organizations we see around us. The world may not be able to see *why* it is so, but it ought to be able to see very clearly *that* in and among all the churches gathered in the name of the one Lord there are present the fruits of his Spirit which are mentioned in Galatians 5:22–25; Ephesians 4:30–32, and Philippians 2:1–3. Look at these texts again. Do they describe *your* local church? your denomination as a whole? the relation of your denomination with other denominations?

A second way of arguing that our divisions do not contradict our unity and catholicity is the "branch theory." According to it, the various denominations and groups within them are like different branches of the same tree. Is it just natural for rich and poor, educated and uneducated, white and black, liberals and conservatives, to come together with their own kind and have a version of Christianity which appeals to them. But of course all these divisions are still bound together by their common faith in Christ.

There is something right also about this argument. According to the New Testament, the unity of the body of Christ is not a rigid uniformity. There *are* legitimate differences among the various members of the body (1 Corinthians 12:14–31; Romans 12:4–8). But in the first place, the differences mentioned in the New Testament are not sociological or even theological differences, but differences of gift and task. And secondly, nowhere does the New Testament suggest that the different members of the body can live in self-sufficient isolation or in downright opposition to each other. On the contrary, Paul's point is just that they all need each other and must live together in mutual cooperation, if the whole body is to function properly. "To each is given the manifestation of the Spirit for the *common* good" (1 Corinthians 12:7).

The branch theory, which separates Christians according to natural or sociological differences, is a plain contradiction of the reconciling work of Christ, who *breaks down* and *overcomes* the natural barriers between men in the world. Donald Miller puts it this way:

> There is diversity within a large family—different aptitudes, different tastes, different personal characteristics. It would be a strange family, nonetheless, which would set up separate living arrangements to satisfy the particular peculiarities of each member. In a real family, the diversity is held within the unity of the family. The family lives in the same house, eats together, carries forward its group activities as a unity. In this way, the diversity of tastes enriches the whole family life, and each benefits from the other.[5]

Insofar as it attempts to justify denominational and factional separation, therefore, the branch theory is no more acceptable than the invisible church theory. On the contrary, it is helpful only insofar as it works in the opposite direction.

What then can we do about the glaring contradictions between the unity and catholicity of the church we say we believe in, and its brokenness in practice? We can give up all attempts to excuse or explain away the scandalous contradiction between our faith and our practice. We can acknowledge the sinfulness of our divisions. We can get to work to give concrete, visible expression to the unity and catholicity Christians do already have in the one Christ they already believe in. That is what the World Council of Churches on the international level and the National Council of Churches in our own country are attempting to do. It is also the meaning of Protestant-Catholic dialogue which is taking place around the world.

In chapter 15, in dealing with the doctrine of the Holy Spirit, we talked about some attitudes and actions which contribute to the fulfillment of the ecumenical task of the church. Go back and look at the list again (pp. 307-310). How would you change or add to the list now that we have thought about the church not only as the community of the Spirit but as the Body of Christ?

An Apostolic People

"The one Holy Catholic and Apostolic Church." "Apostolic" means "in line with the Apostles." Some churches have interpreted this to mean that the bishops of the church are connected by historical succession with the original Apostles and therefore speak and act with the same authority. Most Protestant churches interpret "Apostolic" to mean that the church must let itself be constantly judged and corrected by the original Apostles as we know them in the Bible. In this sense "Apostolic" is almost synonymous with "biblical."

But even if we consider ourselves correct in this interpretation, we must confess that just at this point we run into a very serious failure not only in the classical confessions of the Reformed churches but in Calvin himself. According to them the "marks" of the true, apostolic-biblical church are the pure preaching of the Word of God and the right administration of the sacraments according to the ordinances of Christ. Proper administration of discipline is sometimes added. What is wrong here is what is *not* said. This classical description of the true church says nothing about the church's having a *task* or *mission* to fulfill. Preaching, sacraments and internal discipline are indispensable, but they are all ways in which the people of God are *ministered to*. A too exclusive emphasis on these marks of the church has resulted in the idea that the main function of the church is to care for itself and tend to the needs of its own members. But that is only half of it. The word "Apostle" means "one who is sent." According to the New Testament, Christians enter into the company of God's people by baptism, hear the Word of God, receive new life and strength as they break bread together, and discipline themselves, *in order to be sent back into the world as servants or "ambassadors" of Christ* (2 Corinthians 5:20). After all, the Christ who is proclaimed in word and sacrament was himself an "Apostle"—one sent by God into the world not to be served but to serve and give his life for many (Mark 10:45). His followers in the New Testament heard him say not only, "Come unto me," but also, "Go!" "As the Father has sent me, even so I send you" (John 20:21). Since we have listened to what the Reformed fathers taught us about the authority of Scripture, therefore, we have to go beyond them at this point to say that an apostolic people of God not only listen to sermons and receive the sacraments when they come together among themselves, but also are a people who are called out in order to be *sent* out, receive in order to *give*, are helped in order to *serve*. In short, an "apostolic" church is by definition a church commissioned with a task to fulfill—and equipped by God himself to do it. (How is this expressly stated in Ephesians 4:11?)

We can be grateful to the new Confession of 1967 of The United Presbyterian Church in the United States of America for recovering this biblical understanding of the apostolic nature of the church which has been so sadly neglected in the confessions of the past. After it has spoken of God's reconciling work in Christ, it moves on to speak of the church's ministry of reconciliation:

> To be reconciled to God is to be sent into the world as his reconciling community. This community, the church universal, is entrusted with God's message of reconciliation and shares his labor of healing the enmities which separate men from God and from each other. Christ has called the church to this mission and given it the gift of the Holy Spirit. The church maintains continuity with the apostles and with Israel by faithful obedience to his call (II, A, 1).

Before we talk about how the people of God fulfill their mission, we must correct another serious failure closely related to the first. *Who* is sent? It is easy enough to see how incorrectly we have in practice answered this question by asking some other questions: Who is a missionary? a servant of God? a priest? a minister? Automatically we think of the clergy or other professional Christians. But this is contrary to the biblical understanding. Accordling to the Old Testament, *all* of God's people are called to be priests (i.e., those who bring God to men and men to God and thus fulfill a mediating or reconciling function). See Exodus 19:6. According to the New Testament certain functions in the church are given to only a few. (What are they? See 1 Corinthians 12:28–31, and Ephesians 4:11.) But nowhere does the New Testament suggest that only a few are called to be priests or servants of God or ministers to other people. As in the Old Testament, *all* God's people are called to this task. See 1 Peter 2:9.

Luther saw this and emphasized it with his doctrine of the "priesthood of all believers." He did not mean by this phrase simply that every man is his own priest, with his own private access to God. He meant that every Christian is called to be a priest to *every other man,* bringing to him God's forgiveness, love, help and reconciliation. But this doctrine of the priesthood of all believers was soon lost in Protestantism. A split lasting until our day was made between clergy and laity, professional and "second-class" Christians. The first were expected to be the really active, "full-time" representatives of Christ in the world. The second were expected to be mostly passive recipients of the benefits of the church, or at best only part-time helpers of the clergy.

As the Reformed churches (along with other churches, including the Roman Catholic)[6] have rediscovered in our time the biblical idea that "Apostolic" means sent with a task, so they are also discovering again the biblical and Reformation idea that the apostolic task is given not just to a few people with a special calling, but to the *whole* Christian community and to *every one* of its members. Only a few are called to stand behind the pulpit or baptismal font or communion table. But the task—and privilege—of the ministry of reconciliation is given to *all,* clergy and laity

alike. Not just preachers in a local congregation, "foreign" missionaries, "home" missionaries in especially needy areas, or professional
evangelists who travel around are "Apostles." *You* also are sent
into the world wherever you work or play or live as a priest, missionary and servant of God, with a ministry of reconciliation. That
is what it means to belong to an apostolic church.

How, then, does a truly apostolic church go about its task?
Here are some suggestions meant to apply both to the whole community of Christians (the church as such) and to every individual
Christian (you personally). Do you agree with them? How would
you change or add to them?

1. The servant church. The purpose of the church's
and the individual Christian's sending, like that of Jesus himself, is
to serve God and fellowmen. This means that our purpose is *not* to
serve ourselves in one way or another. The goal of the church in
its missionary or evangelistic work is not to build itself up so that
it can become as big, powerful and influential as possible. And the
goal of individual Christians is not to impress others (and perhaps
also convince themselves) how good or loving they are, or to earn
stars in their crowns later on. No matter how busy we are with
church work or how self-sacrificing for others we may appear, we
are only using God and other people to serve ourselves when we
are consciously or unconsciously motivated by such concerns—and
other people will very quickly recognize that they are only being
used. As the one who was *the* Servant of God gave himself out of
pure love for God and man without asking what he personally
would get out of it for himself, so will his Body and its members
give themselves—even if the result is failure and not success,
weakness and not power, a cross and not a crown. How does
Jesus say this in Matthew 20:25–28 and Mark 8:34–35?

2. The church for the world. As God sent his Son
into the sinful world because he loved it, so the church and individual Christians are *for* the sinful world into which they are sent.
We cannot look at people outside the church with suspicion or
belligerence or contempt as enemies to be conquered, forced to

surrender, tamed and placed under the control of the church and
our beliefs. Sometimes the church has given itself to evangelism or
missions in the world in order to *defeat* godless communists or the
followers of some other ideology. Sometimes Christian individuals
approach non-Christians as opponents or victims to be "sold" or
out-argued or frightened by threats into giving up and joining up.
As if a victory for our side were our main interest! But that cannot
be the way of a church and its members who follow their Head. We
go into the world not as conquerors but as agents of reconciliation,
not with hostility for sinful non-Christians but with the compassion
with which Jesus looked on those who were trapped in the inhumanity of their twisted relationships with God, other people, and
themselves. Without participating in their sin, without in any way
condoning it, not hesitating to speak against it, Jesus was their
friend and gave his life for just such people. That must be our
model also. However great their unbelief, however shocking their
immorality or their equally sinful, self-righteous morality, we will
be interested in them as human beings whom God loves, not
simply as potential converts to our way. We will listen to them as
well as talk to them—and be open to hear something worth listening
to. We will not only expect them to come to us, but we will be willing to go to them wherever they live and work and play—even if it
means going to dirty slums or sinful suburbs, union halls or execu-
tive suites, cheap taverns or elegant country clubs, jails or the
P.T.A.

   3. The church with the world. We must be careful
when we say that, like Christ himself, the church and individual
Christians have a servant's task to fulfill for the sake of the sinful
world. We are not Christ, and we cannot do what he does. We
Christians are in no position to judge sinners; we ourselves are
sinners who *are* judged. We cannot forgive the sins of others; we
need to be forgiven for our own sins. We are not the saviors of
mankind or even "soul-savers" of a few individuals; we too are
dependent on God for our own salvation. We cannot reconcile men
to God and each other; we ourselves are disobedient, unloving
people who constantly need to *be* reconciled. Sometimes the

church and individual Christians have thought they could approach unbelievers in a sinful world as the wise to the foolish, the strong to the weak, the righteous to the unrighteous, the superior to the inferior. In a condescending, patronizing, or pitying way, we have acted as if we "have it made," and as if our task is to help others think and live like us. No wonder people outside the church have been angry—or only laughed—at such arrogance.

We will properly fulfill our servant task in and for the world only when we never forget that we are *not* Christ and cannot do what he does. We are only his Body and its members, and we are just as dependent on him as anyone else is. We never stand *above* the sinful, guilty, needy world. We can only stand *with* it, knowing that we *share* its sin, guilt and need for forgiveness and renewed humanity. The only difference between us Christians and other people is that we know where help is to be found. We go to them not as healthy rich men to sick beggars, but as beggars to other beggars with the good news of where food and health are to be found. We are not sent with the mission to point to ourselves and our spiritual or moral achievements, but to *him* and the new humanity *he* brings.

    4. Body and soul. There is an old argument about whether the church should be more concerned about the souls and the spiritual needs of men, or about their bodies and physical needs. The biblical answer is that we should be concerned about neither bodies nor souls, but about *human beings—people.* There are no such things as bodiless souls or soulless bodies. What kind of ambassadors for Christ would we be if we said in effect, "God loves you—but of course he only cares about saving your soul. He is not interested in whether you are hungry, poor, sick, homeless, overworked and under-paid. All that is unimportant." On the other hand, what kind of ambassadors would we be if we said in effect, "God loves you. He wants you to have all the good things of this life. But he is not interested in the fears, hostilities, prejudices, alienation and idolatrous worship of false gods which enslave you, ruin your life, sour your relationship with the true God and with your husband or wife, family and the other people around you.

That's your problem to work out as best you can, however you see fit." In both cases, the response would be quite correctly, "These Christians and their God may be interested in my soul or in my body, but they are not interested in *me*." Like Christ himself, who healed bodies *and* broken relationships with God and other people, the church and we Christians are sent to minister to *whole* men, body and soul, and to be concerned for the *wholeness* of their lives, not just fragments of it.

5. **Words and action.** Another old argument, which we have run into before, is whether the church's and the individual Christian's responsibility is primarily to talk or to act, to proclaim the gospel in words or in deeds. This is another false alternative. Sometimes we have said with our mouths, "God accepts you, forgives you, loves you, wants to help you. So turn to him and trust your life to him." Then by our actions (or simply by our failure to do anything), we have said, "But we Christians don't accept you. We can't forgive you, we don't love you and we don't want to have anything to do with you. So don't expect any help from us—except pious advice." How can we expect people to believe the message of the ambassadors of Christ when their actions deny the truth of their own message? On the other hand, if we are only ambassadors and not the Lord and Savior of men ourselves, must we not explain very carefully that whatever new humanity we have received ourselves and can make possible for others is at best only a pale reflection of that which God makes possible in Christ? Jesus, who was himself *the* Word of God, both *spoke* of the saving love of God and *demonstrated* it by living as the man with and for other men. He sends us out not only to talk about but to *live* the new relationship with God and with other people which we have experienced in him. And he sends us out not only to live it, but to tell the secret of it, so that other men may experience it too.

6. **Individuals and society.** Still another big debate concerning the mission of the church turns around whether we are sent as representatives of Christ only to individuals or to the society in which they live. Is social action a part of the church's task, or

only the evangelization of individuals? We have already learned that this is still another false alternative. If a man cannot work to support his family because he does not have the skills to work in an automated economic system; or if he is exploited and discriminated against, and his children are deprived of the opportunities other children have; or if his home is bombed and his family killed or mutilated because he happens to live in the wrong place at the wrong time—how can we expect him to belive us when we proclaim the goods news that Christ loved and died for him and is now the risen Lord over the whole world for his good? How can we refuse as servants of this Lord to do what we can to make the justice, love and freedom of his Kingdom visible in the economic, social and political spheres which have such a big influence on the lives of individuals? If we do not take our own gospel about the lordship of Christ seriously, how can we expect anyone else to take it seriously?

On the other hand, how can we expect individuals to believe that God loves *them,* if we are in fact more interested in this or that social or political cause than in their personal problems and needs? What good does it do to say, "God loves you. Give your life to him," if in practice we sacrifice the individual human beings to whom we say this to the cause of capitalism, or integration, or abstract social justice, or the Democratic or Republican ideology, or Americanism—or some other cause which may be very noble in itself? The Christ who sends us into the world as his ambassadors knows and cares for every single individual, and at the same time he is the Lord over all the nations and societies which shape the lives of individuals. Our assignment is not to make one or the other but *both* facts known. How else can we proclaim convincingly that "God was in Christ reconciling the *world* to himself . . . So we beseech *you,* be reconciled to God" (2 Corinthians 5:19 f.)?

7. Can we do it? Everything we have said about our sending into the world means that as a church and as individual Christians we have been given a difficult task. It would be an impossibly difficult one if our mission were, as it is sometimes put, to "take" Christ to the world. Or if our task were to "win the world for Christ"—as if we were *his* sponsors, defenders and protectors.

But our understanding of our task changes completely when we are modest enough to acknowledge that we Christians and our church are neither required nor allowed to think that we have to be the saviors of men or the rulers of the world. Just when we remember our own gospel about what God has done on Good Friday and Easter and is still doing in Christ "between the times"; just when we are willing to let *him* be Savior and Lord—then our task becomes an unbelievably confident, even carefree, enterprise. Jesus Christ *is* the world's Lord and Savior! The world *already* belongs to him!

That means that there is no place we can go where he is not already at work before us—no nation (not even those which are our enemies), no home (not even those where there are marital difficulties, or no partner at all), no hospital, no voting booth, no place of business or entertainment. We do not have to go into the hostile or indifferent world anxiously or defensively. We may go thankfully, confidently and joyfully, because we go not to *take* him but to *meet* him. Long before we ever thought of going into the world, he entered into it and identified himself with it. Long before we became concerned about men suffering from their own and others' inhumanity, he cared for them and gave his life for them. Long before we ever dreamed of going to do battle with the forces of darkness and evil and death in the world, he triumphed over them. Long before it ever occurred to us to go as ministers of reconciliation to live among and minister to unbelievers near at hand or far away, he was living among them, ministering to them, and he still is. Wherever we look, wherever we go, he is already there—he to whom a torn and broken world already belongs. That is the comfort and certainty, joy and freedom, of our apostolic mission. We do not have to shoulder the impossibly heavy burden of doing his work for him. We are simply invited to participate with him in the work he himself has done, is doing, and will do.

We can summarize everything we have been trying to say about the apostolic church by quoting Matthew's version of Jesus' last words to his disciples. He left us a *command:* "Go and make disciples of all nations." But *before* he gave us this task, he said,

"All authority in heaven and on earth has been given to *me*." And *after* he gave it, he promised, "*I* am with you always, to the close of the age" (Matthew 28:18–20).

We began this chapter talking about what is wrong with the church today and the trouble it is in. Then we discussed what the church is according to the Bible and the tradition all Christian churches have in common. All the way along we have tried to do two things: to be realistic and honest about what the church as we know it is really like, and to be faithful to Scripture and the teaching of our church fathers. Now that we have finished, several questions remain which you must answer for yourself. Have we been *realistic and honest?* (Think of your local congregation, your denomination, the church in general.) Have we been *faithful?* (Think of the biblical and creedal doctrines of the church.) Have we dealt with all the problems and objections we raised at the beginning? What problems and objections are left over in your mind? The following suggestions for further reflection and study are meant to help you answer these questions.

FOR FURTHER REFLECTION AND STUDY
On "The People of God"
1. When you hear the word "church," what comes first of all to your mind?
2. What does your local church do other than what takes place within the church building? What could it do?
3. What percentage of your local church's budget is spent on maintaining the building and activities that take place in the building?
4. How does the Presbyterian-Reformed form of church government differ from that of a congregationalist church? How does it differ from the form of government of the United States?
On "A People in Community"
1. In this whole chapter, we depended especially on the image of the head and the body to talk about the relationship between Christ and the church. Look up the other images used in the following New Testament passages: (a) John 10:1–18; Luke 15:1–7. (b) 1 Peter 2:6–7; 1 Corinthians 3:9; Ephesians

2:20–21; Hebrews 10:21. (c) 2 Corinthians 11:2; Ephesians 5:21–33; Revelation 21:2, 9. (d) Hebrews 10:11, 16 f.; 12:22; 13:14. What aspects of the relation between Christ and the church are suggested by these images which are not suggested by the body-head image?

2. Evaluate the following statements:

> a. You can be just as good without belonging to the church.
>
> b. You can be a Christian without belonging to the church.
>
> c. Everyone who does not belong to a Christian church is going to hell.

3. Can the members of *your* local congregation learn something about the acceptance, forgiveness, love and help of God from your attitudes toward each other? Does your church's attitude toward the surrounding community bear witness to the acceptance, forgiveness, love and help of God in Christ?

On "A Holy People"

1. Evaluate this observation from a late medieval manuscript: "The church is something like Noah's ark. If it weren't for the storm outside, you couldn't stand the stink inside."

2. Is it too cynical to say that church members are just as sinful as other people? (Remember what we learned in chapter 11 about the meaning of sin.)

3. Are we exaggerating when we say in the prayer of confession, "There is no health in us. . . . have mercy on us, miserable offenders"?

4. A familiar accusation is that "the church is full of hypocrites." Is it true?

5. Do you think that we were realistic and honest when we said that the church is a community of *dissatisfied* sinners who want to *change*? Is it true of *you*? Does this affect your social and political views? Your theological views?

On "A United, Catholic People"

1. Do you agree that denominational divisions are a sinful denial of the unity and catholicity of the church?

2. Do you agree that in practice the disunity of the church in

our country is caused more by sociological than by theological differences? Are sociological differences a legitimate reason for our divisions?

3. Do you think it is honest to say that the different denominations are spiritually one?
4. What could the denominations do, without losing their integrity, toward making the unity we have in Christ visible?

On "An Apostolic People"

1. To what extent would it be accurate to say that your church is apostolic? In what ways do you personally go beyond a purely passive relationship with the church to live as one who is sent out with a ministry of reconciliation?
2. Evaluate this statement: "A lay religion which is theologically uninformed and secularized, or narrowly cramped and traditionalized, may be as disastrous to the church as clericalism."[7]
3. "The world does not exist for the sake of the church, but the church for the sake of the world." Do you agree?
4. Discuss the following statements in the light of Matthew 28:18–20:

    a. It is wrong to speak of the "soul-saving" work of the church or of individual Christians.

    b. It is wrong to speak of "taking" Christ to the world.

    c. It is wrong to speak of "winning the world for Christ."

5. Having studied the apostolic task of the church, how would you define the task of evangelism and of missions?
6. How could Christ be at work among men who never heard of him, or, having heard, do not accept him as Lord and Savior?

19

What's Going to Happen to Us?

THE DOCTRINE OF
THE CHRISTIAN HOPE
FOR THE FUTURE

You are going to die. So is everyone you love—your husband or wife, your children, your parents, your friends. It may happen tomorrow, or day after tomorrow, or not for several years. It may come quickly and easily or slowly and painfully. But you are all going to die. One day you will be put in a hole in the ground and covered up with dirt. Or—who knows?—like millions of other people in our time, you too may be blown into irretrievable bits and never buried at all. But in one way or another, sooner or later, we are all going to die—you, I, everyone of us.

We may try to fool ourselves and other people. Women may dress like adolescents, learn the latest teen-age dance steps, spend a fortune on age-defying cosmetics and other beauty aids. Men may sit glued to the TV, dreaming that they are still college athletes; they may literally, or only in fantasy, chase women to convince themselves that they are still virile young lovers; they may keep frantically busy to convince themselves that to work always is to live always. But whatever our way of trying to fool ourselves, we can't bring it off. We are all getting older every day; every day we are one day nearer to death, the grave, the end.

Is there any more hope for the world in general than for us individuals? Fifty years ago we fought the war that was supposed once and for all to "make the world safe for democracy." Are we better off now than we were then? Is there any less hatred, greed, brutality or equally cruel indifference among men now than there was a *thousand* years ago? Is it realistic to hope that even in the *next* thousand years we will reach the point where there will be no more wars or rumors of wars, injustice, poverty, crime, persecution of minorities, the physical and psychological crippling of children as a result of the inhumanity of their elders? The forms of our inhumanity change, of course. Nuclear bombs instead of rocks. Economic exploitation instead of slave trade and land-grabbing. But can we really expect that *man himself* will change? Even if America could have its way all over the world? Even if Christians and the church could control everything?

It is considered bad taste to talk about dying in our time. Death has replaced sex as the subject too obscene for polite society. (Now we say "passed on" instead of "died," and "memorial park" instead of "graveyard"—just as we once said "limbs" instead of "legs.") And it is downright un-American to suggest that we cannot eventually solve all our own and the world's problems if we work at it long and hard enough, if we can only get the rest of the world to follow the American way of life. But that's the way it is: You are going to die, and your body will rot either under or above the ground. The suspicion will not go away that the American dream for ourselves and the rest of the world, along with all other utopian dreams, is *only* a dream.

In this last chapter we are going to discuss what Christians have to say about these brutal facts of life. This is how we shall go about it: First we shall eliminate the answers Christians *cannot* accept. Then we shall try to fix some guidelines to help us approach the Christian answer properly. Third, we shall discuss the Christian hope for the *world*. Finally, we shall discuss the Christian hope for *individuals*.

Some Non-Christian Answers

The Christian answer to the tragic facts of life about the world we live in is that Jesus Christ is coming again "to judge the quick and the dead" and to establish forever his Kingdom of justice and love. And the Christian answer to the tragic certainties about our individual destiny is the "resurrection of the body and the life everlasting." Later we shall discuss what this means in detail. But simply to say this much enables us to rule out from the very beginning some answers a genuinely biblical faith must reject. Some of them are clearly un-Christian; some of them are less clearly so and are sometimes mistakenly confused with the Christian position.

1. **Non-Christian attitudes about the world's future.** Here there are two basic answers Christians cannot accept. We can summarize them quickly, because we have already run into them before. Look again at our discussion of the implications of the doctrine of creation on pages 159-168 and of the Kingdom of God on pages 270-282.

a. The first view is based on a *false optimism*. The Christian hope for the world is that God, and God only, can and will overcome the inhumanity of men and the resulting inhumanity of their social, political and economic structures. The Kingdom of perfect justice and love will never come *in* history. It will only come at the *end* of history. Even then it will come because of what *he* will do, and not because of what men will have achieved.

This means for Christians the end of all idealistic, utopian schemes in history. Neither the communistic *nor* the democratic ideology can save the world. It will not be saved by the nonviolent, pacifistic philosophy of the "doves," *or* by the aggressive, "realistic" philosophy of the "hawks." Neither revolution which hopes to change everything overnight, *nor* evolution which says we have to go slowly, can achieve "one world" or "a world safe for democracy"—or even a "Christian nation under God." Neither non-Christian *nor* Christian programs, plans, causes or crusades will ever achieve a new world and a new humanity. The Christian hope for the God who will come in Christ to straighten things out only at the end of history means the end of *all* "liberal" hopes for the perfection of the world, or even part of it.

b. The second position is based on a *false pessimism*. The Christian hope for the world is that the God who *will* come to judge and save is the same God who *is* the powerful and loving Creator and Ruler of this world. He is at work here and now so that we can live genuinely human lives, loving him and neighbor as self. The Christ who *will* come is the same Christ who loved the world even when it became inhuman, living against God, against neighbor, and therefore in self-contradiction. He entered into this world, and as a result of his death and resurrection he already *has been* and *is* at work to overcome its inhumanity and to restore its God-willed humanity.

This means that an openly unbelieving or an apparently pious despair or indifference about what can be accomplished in this world is just as impossible for Christians as secular or religious utopianism. Christians cannot hope for utopia. But neither can we live in faithless pessimism and irresponsibility. Not because we believe in the perfectibility of men, but because we trust in the sovereign power and love of the Creator, we can and we must do what we can to achieve at least a little more justice and humanity among men. Not because we believe in them as such, but because we believe in a living Lord who rules over them (whether they themselves know it or not), we can and we must join forces with those worldly programs, causes and organizations which seek to alleviate human suffering and set limits to the destructive power of hatred, greed, war and oppression.

In short, Christians do not hope for the coming of the Creator, Lord and Savior at the end of the world *instead of* trying to make the world a more human place now. On the contrary, *just because* they know about him and expect his coming victory at the end, they have the courage to get to work, confidently expecting here and now at least real preliminary signs of the totally new heaven and earth he will bring then.

2. Non-Christian attitudes about the destiny of individuals.

Once again we shall discuss a too pessimistic and too optimistic answer Christians cannot accept.

a. *False pessimism* takes death too seriously.

As he came from his mother's womb he shall go again, naked as he came, and shall take nothing for his toil, which he may carry away in his hand ... just as he came, so shall he go; and what gain has he that he toiled for the wind, and spent all his

days in darkness and grief, in much vexation and sickness and
resentment?

Everything before them is [emptiness] since one fate
comes to all, to the righteous and the wicked, to the good and
the evil, to the clean and the unclean, to him who sacrifices
and him who does not sacrifice . . . the dead know nothing,
and they have no more reward; but the memory of them is
lost . . . Enjoy life with the wife whom you love, all the days
of your vain life which he has given you under the sun,
because that is your portion in life and in your toil at which
you toil under the sun . . . for there is no work or thought or
knowledge or wisdom in [the kingdom of the dead] to which
you are going.

These words were not written by an atheist. They were written
by a "preacher" who could also say, "Fear God and keep his
commandments; for this is the whole duty of man." They are
included in the book which Christians believe to be the Word of
God. Stop now and read through the whole book of Ecclesiastes—
or at least plan to read it before you leave this section.

What shall we make of such strange words coming from the
Bible itself? Here are some conclusions we may draw from Ecclesiastes. Some of them are questionable, so you had better examine
them carefully.

First, if death has the last word and there is no hope for the
future, then my life *here and now* will be meaningless. All I can
do is live like "the preacher," swinging back and forth between a
weary, depressed cynicism and a frantic, joyless attempt to wring
what little pleasure I can from this fleeting life. *An empty future
means an empty present.*

Second, it is not necessarily true that only those who believe
in a life after death can believe in God and live honorable, responsible lives in relation to other people. Important as they may be,
it is not so (as some Christians have argued) that only the promise
of heaven and the threat of hell can prevent wild, lawless, godless
living. Who can fail to admire "the preacher" and others like him,
who, knowing neither heaven nor hell, yet are courageous, mod-

erate and even deeply religious in the face of what they believe to be the emptiness of life?

Third, compassion and not condemnation is called for when we meet people like "the preacher." How can we fail to sympathize with those who, having no future, have no alternative but to swing back and forth between paralyzing despair and the desperate attempt to escape the emptiness of life in simple earthly pleasures, or perhaps in plain hard work? People who are trapped need to be loved, not damned; they are *already* tragically damned.

Finally, no one can talk convincingly about life after death who does not face as honestly as "the preacher" the stark reality of death and the cloud it casts over all of life. No cheap talk will do about a happy ending to come. If we are honest with ourselves, who of us does not sometimes suspect that what he tells us is the truth?

But having said all this, we Christians can still say that because we know about the resurrection of Christ we believe in the resurrection from the dead for all men. Death is real and certain, but it does not have the last word. For us there can be no ultimate pessimism about the future—and therefore no cynicism about the value of life in the present (the value of *other* men's lives as well as of our own!). We move not only toward the *end* but toward the *fulfillment* of life—the genuinely human life which God the Creator v illed for us from the beginning, and which God the Savior is already at work here and now to restore and renew in us. There may be some question of how seriously we take our own gospel. (Do Christians in fact find more joy and meaning in life *now* because of their hope for the future?) But the Christian gospel itself declares that all gloomy philosophies of life like that of "the preacher" in Ecclesiastes have been superceded by the promise of another "preacher" in 1 Cor. 15:54–57: "Death is swallowed up in victory . . . . thanks be to God, who gives us the victory through our Lord Jesus Christ."

b. We have been talking about a point of view which takes death *too* seriously. Now we have to talk about *false optimism*, which does not take death seriously enough. It is the belief in the immortality of the soul. This doctrine was not taught by the bibli-

cal writers themselves, but it was common in the Greek and
Oriental religions of the ancient world in which the Christian
church was born. Some of the earliest Christian theologians were
influenced by it, read the Bible in the light of it and introduced it
into the thinking of the church. It has been with us ever since,
influencing even the Reformed confessions (see the Westminster
Confession, XXXII; the Belgic Confession, Art. XXXVII).

According to this doctrine only my body can die, but I myself
do not really die. My body is only the shell of my true self. It is not
me; it is only the earthly-physical prison in which the real "I" is
trapped. My true self is my soul, which, because it is spiritual and
not physical, is like God and therefore shares God's immortality
(inability to die). What happens at death, then, is that my immortal soul escapes from my mortal body. My body dies, but I
myself live on and return to the spiritual realm from which I came
and to which I really belong.

If we hold to the genuinely biblical hope for the future, we
must firmly reject this doctrine of the soul's immortality for several
reasons:

First the Christian faith does not pretend that death is not so
bad after all since we ourselves do not actually die at all, but only
"pass on" to a new form of existence when our souls escape from
our bodies. For the biblical writers death is real, total and terrible.
Jesus himself did not face death with the calmness of one only
"passing over to the other side." He faced it "with loud cries and
tears" (Hebrews 5:7) and blood-sweating dread (Luke 22:44;
Mark 14:32–42). For Paul death was not a friend to be welcomed
because it meant only "entering into a wider room"; it was the "last
enemy" to be fought and destroyed (1 Corinthians 15:26). Unlike
the doctrine of the soul's immortality, there is no pious denial of
the horror of death in genuine Christian teaching. Christians face
the facts with unflinching honesty: Death *is* hideous, because, so
far as we are concerned, it means the end of *us,* not just the death
of our bodies.

Secondly, Christians reject the doctrine of the soul's immortality because the Christian hope is not in the indestructibility of man,
but in the creative power of God, who by the power of his word

can call life into being out of nothing and make dead men live. The Bible is clear about this. God alone has immortality (1 Timothy 6:16). If there is life beyond death for men, it is not because they possess in themselves some immortal quality death cannot destroy, but because God *gives* them eternal life or immortality (Romans 2:7). It is not because *they* are strong enough to conquer death, but because *Christ* is, and because *he* has triumphed over death *for* them (2 Timothy 1:10). As in general, so at this point, Christians are not optimistic about man and the potentialities he has in himself, but about God and what he can and will do. Is that not a far greater and far more certain hope?

Finally, Christians reject the doctrine of the immortality of the soul because of the unbiblical split it makes between body and soul, physical-earthly and spiritual-heavenly life. If the concept of the soul's innate immortality is too optimistic from the Christian point of view, its contempt for the body and its earthly life is un-biblically pessimistic. The Bible does not teach that the body is only a worthless or evil prison which degrades our true selves. It teaches rather that we were created and *are* body ("male and female"!) as well as soul, and that bodily as well as spiritual life is willed and blessed by God himself. And the biblical hope is not for the soul's escape from the bodily-physical into some purely spiritual realm. Our hope is for the renewal of our *total* human existence. This means that also from the point of view of God's future plans for us, he places his stamp of approval upon our bodily as well as our spiritual interests and pleasures here and now.

Here we run into the Christian alternative to the doctrine of the immortality of the soul: the resurrection of the body. We shall ask later what that means. The point right now is that whether we look at it in terms of our future hope or in terms of the meaning of our present lives, the hope for the immortality of the soul is less than Christian. On the one hand, Christians are far more honest about the total threat and reality of death than that. On the other hand, the Christian hope is far greater than that, just because their hope is not in their own deathless spirituality but in the God who creates and re-creates whole men, not just disembodied souls. "I believe," we say in the creed, "in the resurrection of the *body*."

Asking the Right Questions

Having eliminated some hopes for the future (and therefore also some concepts of the present) which Christians *cannot* accept, we are now ready to focus on the Christian hope as such. Our purpose in this section is to set some limits to the questions we may legitimately ask and to answers we may expect to discover. This can save us from all the wild speculations and fantasies which are especially a danger at this point in Christian theology. Not everyone would agree with all the following points. Do you?

1. **We must not want to know too much.** "It is unwise for Christians to claim any knowledge of either the furniture of heaven or the temperature of hell; or to be too certain about any details of the Kingdom of God in which history is consummated."[1] Why? First of all because no one knows the answers to all the questions our curiosity leads us to ask about the future. Not even the biblical writers claim such knowledge: "It does not yet appear what we shall be" (1 John 3:2). Not even Jesus himself knew (Mark 13:32). Moreover, as a rule the biblical writers are not even interested in the details of "what it will be like." They understand their own lives and the history of the world by looking forward to the future of what they believe God has already begun in Christ. But just for that reason, they have no time to sit around with folded hands waiting for the future to arrive. They are too busy *living* the new life to spend too much time speculating about what the new life will be like.

We will do well to follow their example. Where the Bible is silent, we ought not to ask too many questions or claim that we know too many answers. And where the Bible places its emphasis, we ought to place ours: living in the present in light of our future hope rather than abandoning the present in order to spend our time dreaming of the future.

2. **Biblical language about the future is symbolical.** (See the articles on heaven, hell, death, and so on in the various theological word books.) When the biblical writers or Jesus himself

talk about the end of the world or what happens after death, they use the concepts of human experience to talk about something that is beyond all human experience. They try to express in the categories of time and space truth which lies beyond all temporal and spatial categories. Not only that, they do this in terms of human experiences and understanding of space and time which belong to an ancient culture quite different from ours. Therefore, we cannot take the images and pictures they use literally. Rather, we must try to understand the truth they are trying to convey with the images and pictures. Let us illustrate with some examples.

When Jesus said to the thief on the cross, "Today you will be with me in *paradise*" (Luke 23:43), he used a word which was originally a Persian word for a nobleman's park or garden. If we want to understand what heaven is like, we will not investigate what a rich man's property in the ancient Near East was like; we will try to understand what it might mean to be *with Jesus*.

When Jesus spoke about his coming again, he said he would be "coming on the clouds of heaven" (Matthew 26:64). We have only to ask the question which naturally follows to see how absurd it would be to take such a statement literally: *Where* will he appear on the clouds? Palestine? New York? Alabama? South Africa? The point is obviously not *how* and *where* he will come, but *that* God in Christ will be the Judge and Savior of men at the end of history.

Paul pictures Christ coming "with the sound of the trumpet of God" (1 Thessalonians 4:16). His point is surely not that God will blow a trumpet, but that a great victory is coming.

In the New Testament hell is sometimes described in terms of "fire" (Matthew 18:8-9; 25:41), but sometimes as "darkness" (Matthew 8:12; 22:13; 25:30). How can it be both fire and darkness at the same time? The problem is solved as soon as we stop thinking of these as literal descriptions of hell and consider them as images which say the same thing in different ways. For the Jews "fire" was the symbol for the destruction of everything displeasing to the holy God. "Darkness" was the opposite of light, the symbol of salvation. The images are not intended to describe the physical characteristics of hell, but a kind of relation to God. But, while we must recognize that the Bible speaks in symbols, we must also think of the symbols as standing for something significant. Symbols by definition symbolize something!

As with the particular pictures we have used as examples, so in general we may apply two rules for the proper interpretation of all biblical language describing the future: (a) It is not to be taken as a literal description of *how* things will be, but as a symbolic description of the fact *that* at the end of our individual lives, and at the end of history in general, God will be there in Christ as the Judge and Savior of men. (b) The Bible uses the earthly, human categories of time and space not primarily to describe literally *where* we will be and *how* we will exist "after time," but to describe symbolically *who* we will be. It is not primarily interested in the "furniture of heaven" or the "temperature of hell," but in *people,* and whether they will be together with or separated from God.

3. There is no one consistent biblical picture of the future, but a development in its thought. In the Old Testament in general there is no hope at all beyond this world. There is no heaven and no hell, nor any real life after death. Everyone who dies goes to the same place, Sheol, "the land of gloom and deep darkness" (Job 10:21), a region where all the dead have a kind of shadowy, unreal existence completely cut off from God and even forgotten by him (Psalm 88:4–6, 10–12). Toward the end of the Old Testament, the hope began to rise that God would finally triumph at the end of history over all his own and his people's enemies. At that time the dead would be raised to "everlasting life" or to "shame and everlasting contempt" (Daniel 12:2). With Jesus' coming, and especially with his death and resurrection, hope for a final world judgment and resurrection of the dead became a part of the Christian faith. But even then there was no agreement about just when and how these things would happen. Jesus himself seems to have thought that the end of the world and the resurrection of the dead would come very soon (Mark 13:30). In his earlier writings, Paul still expects the end very soon (1 Thessalonians 4:13–18). But in his later writings (Romans, for instance), he seems to postpone the end to an indefinite future.

We are not concerned here to trace the details of this develop-

ment, but only to make his one point about its significance: We
cannot expect to find one neat biblical timetable for the future. Nor
can we expect to combine all the relevant texts into one neat
scheme describing the way everything will happen. The details of
the biblical hope change from time to time and from situation to
situation. What we do learn (from the New Testament, at least) is
that, however conflicting and difficult to harmonize are the pictures
we are given in different writings, at different points in the development of biblical thinking, they all agree on the two basic points we
have already emphasized: (a) God in Christ stands at the end of
history in general. (b) God in Christ stands at the end of the life
of every individual person. In the last analysis that is all we know.
Just when and just how these two things will happen, we cannot
know and do not need to know.

    **4. The best insight we have into what God *will* do
is found by looking at what he *has* done.** What may we expect to
happen at the end of our lives and at the end of the world? We may
expect the victory and confirmation of what God intended from the
very beginning when he created the world. Or, to say the same
thing in other words, we may expect the victory and confirmation
of what he was at work to accomplish in Christ 2,000 years ago. The
most certain clue to what will happen to us in the *future* is what
God has been doing with us and for us all along in the *past*. Two
consequences, one negative and one positive, follow from this.

    The negative conclusion is this: The clearest biblical sources
for helping us to understand our hope for the future are *not* those
apocalyptic books, Daniel and Revelation, which speak most exclusively and explicitly about the future. We do not say that there
is nothing to be learned from them, or that they are not true. We
only say that they are not the *clearest* sources for understanding
our Christian hope. They are highly symbolical, filled with all
kinds of weird beasts, angels, demons, visions, mystical numbers
and cosmic conflicts, which are utterly strange to us. Some people
spend years making charts, timetables and diagrams trying to
figure all this out. Whole sects have been formed on the basis of
interpretations of this one part of Scripture. But we will do well

to follow the example of Calvin and the Reformed confessions in not getting bogged down in the apocalyptic writings. Christians do not place their hope in all kinds of fantastic predictions and speculations about a future they cannot really know anything about. They place their hope in the God they *know*, confident that the God we *will* meet is none other than the God who *has* made himself and his will known to us. This means that just when we think about the future, we cannot forget about all the rest of the Bible or read it in terms of the apocalyptic writings. On the contrary, we must read these difficult writings in the light of what we already know from the rest of the Bible.

The positive conclusion to be drawn from the relation we have suggested between past and future is this: What we look forward to is not the destruction but the *fulfillment* of the created world and our creaturely lives in it. To look forward to a final judgment of the world is not to look forward to the annihilation of the world and a purely spiritual Kingdom of God, but to look forward to a "new heaven and a new earth" (Revelation 21:1)—the completion and perfection of *this* world, which in itself always has been and still is the good creation of God. To look forward to "life after death" is not to look forward to being angels or ghosts or little gods, but to being a "new creation" (2 Corinthians 5:17), "new men" (Ephesians 2:15). It is to expect not escape from our humanity, or the annihilation of our humanity, but the completion and perfection of our humanity—the human existence which God willed for us from the beginning and which he was and is already at work to restore to us through his Son, the *man* Jesus Christ. This means that whatever we say about the future of the world or about our future as individuals must take the form of good news we can thankfully and gladly hear, not bad news we unfortunately have to accept. For the future hope of Christians is not a world-denying hope which is disinterested in or contemptuous of genuinely human, earthly life. The "end" we Christians look forward to is not only the conclusion (*finis*) but the fulfilled goal and purpose (*telos*) of our earthly, worldly, human life here and now. To say what this good news means in detail is our task for the rest of this chapter.

The Christian Hope for the World

Is it always going to be this way? World War I, depression, World War II, cold war, Korea, Viet Nam. Then China? Africa? Husbands and wives, parents and children, rich and poor, red and yellow, black and white hurting each other and being hurt by each other? No! It will not always be that way. For "he is coming to judge the quick and the dead" and to create "a new heaven and a new earth." That is the promise and hope we have to try to understand in this section.

1. **The Last Judgment.** When we hear this phrase, even those of us who have not seen Michelangelo's picture of it in the Sistine Chapel in Rome or other medieval pictures of the "last day" probably think of a day of gloom and doom on which Christ, with clinched fist and a sword, sternly separates those on the right, who are floating upward into rosy clouds, from those on the left, who are being dragged down by hideous demons into all kinds of excruciating torture. (Why is it that those at the bottom of such pictures are so much more interesting than those at the top? Is it because the "blessed" are so piously and boringly passive, while something is at least going on among the "damned"?) If we are to think about the future of the world in a biblical way, we have to get rid of such half-pagan mythology. By way of contrast, we shall emphasize two particular aspects of the Christian hope.

a. "In the Biblical world of thought the judge is not primarily the one who rewards some and punishes the others; he is the man who creates order and restores what has been destroyed."[2] The first thought that comes to Christians when they think about the end of history ought not to be the self-centered or vindictive thought about who will be "in" and who will be "out." It ought to be the thankful and joyful thought that we may confidently look forward to the time when the way of the world's Creator, Reconciler and Savior will prevail once and for all—when justice will finally triumph over injustice, love over hatred and greed, peace over hostility, humanity over inhumanity, the Kingdom of God over the kingdom of evil. The last judgment will come not against but for the good of the world. Therefore, we may eagerly, not reluctantly, look forward to the future.

b. The new creation and restoration of world order does, of course, imply also the judgment of individual men. In the ominous words of the Westminster Confession, all men must "appear before the tribunal of Christ to give an account of their thoughts, words and deeds; and to receive according to what they have done in the body, whether good or evil" (XXXIII, 1). If that were the whole story, the medieval pictures of the last judgment would be justified. In fact they would be too optimistic, since *no one* could survive if salvation depended on the absolute purity demanded by God. *All* of us would have to look forward to the end with stark terror. Who of us, no matter how moral or pious, would not have to be counted among the wicked for our failure to love God with our whole being and our neighbor as ourselves?

But the whole picture changes as soon as we remember who the Judge will be. Not blind justice, not a vengeful or even unbiased judge, but Christ himself! The one who will judge sinful men is the very one who loved and gave his life for sinners! The triumphant Judge who stands at the end is none other than the dying man on a cross who has already taken the judgment of God on himself for the sake of the whole world. "We should not then fear the last judgment and have a horror of it?" Calvin asks in his Geneva Catechism. He answers, "No, since we are not to come before any other Judge than he who is our Advocate and who has taken our cause in hand" (Q. 87). "What comfort does the return of Christ to judge the quick and the dead give you?" asks the Heidelberg Catechism. "That in all affliction and persecution I may await with head held high the very Judge from heaven who has already submitted himself to the judgment of God for me and has removed all curse from me . . ." (Q. 52). Because he is *this* Judge, we look forward to the final judgment not with fear and horror but, like Calvin and his followers, "with head held high."

But what of those who do not know this Judge, or, knowing, still prefer to stand on the record of their own moral and religious innocence in thought, word and deed? We have already dealt at length with this question (see pp. 114-120 above), and we shall return to it again presently. In the present context, we make only this observation: If we listen to the gospel they themselves taught us, we cannot follow the Reformed fathers in the almost sadistic pleasure with which some of them seem to look forward to the time when God "will cast all his and our enemies into everlasting condemnation" (The Heidelberg Catechism, Q. 52), or when we shall "see the terrible vengeance which God shall execute on the wicked" (Belgic Confession, Art. XXXVII). The Good News of Christ is that God does not hate and will the destruction of sinful men who are his enemies, but loves them and acts for their reconciliation and salvation. He also commands *us* to love his and our enemies, not gleefully to look forward to the time when we can enjoy seeing them "get what they have coming to them," and can say, "I told you so." Moreover, if we know that, while we ourselves were "helpless," "ungodly" sinners and enemies of God, Christ died for us (Romans 5:6–11), how can we not do what we can by our words and actions to let those other sinners and enemies know that the same good news is for them too? If we believe that it applies to us, how can we not believe that it applies for them too? If we do not believe it for them, how can we believe it for ourselves? If we know that the only hope any of us has is that all of us will one day stand before the Judge who is the "friend of sinners" (Luke 7:34), must we not hope *for* rather than *against* the wicked who are his and our enemies?

　　　　　2. **The new world.** We have emphasized that we must not speculate about what the future will be like in detail. So if we come now to talk about the "new heaven and new earth" which the last judgment will bring, we must be careful not to begin thinking about gold streets, fluffy clouds, white robes, halos, harps and the like. Nevertheless, without giving us any literal pictures, Scripture does permit us to say something about the future Kingdom of God which, once again, is important not only because of what it tells us about the future, but also because of what it tells us about our lives here and now.

　　　　　a. No more church! "And I saw no temple in the city, for its temple is the Lord God Almighty and the Lamb" (Revelation 21:22). What a relief to know that it will not be like being in church all the time! What could be more boring than to spend eternity sitting around singing hymns, listening to sermons, praying and listening to prayers (some of which already seem to last forever)! There won't even be any church as we usually think of it when the Kingdom of God comes in its fullness. Why? Because there will be no more need for it. At the end and goal of history there will no longer be only a limited group of people who know about the Kingdom of God and the new humanity brought by Christ. *Everyone* will know. There will no longer be only a relatively small community of people in the world who submit to the judging, forgiving and renewing Lordship of the one in whom true humanity and deity are together. The *whole world* will openly belong to him. There will be no more need for missions and evangelism to invite hostile, alienated, self-contradicting men to find their own true selves as they are reconciled to God and fellowman. "All things, whether on earth or in heaven" will be reconciled (Colossians 1:20) or united (Ephesians 1:10) in him. The church's function will have been accomplished. We may eagerly and joyfully look forward to the day when the church will be out of business once and for all!

This good news about the future extinction of the church underlines something we have already learned about the nature and task of the church "between the times." The world does not exist for the sake of the church, but the church for the sake of the world. The church's task is not to serve itself, but to serve men in the world. We are called not to make clear that God accepts, loves and wants to help only Christians and their church, but that he accepts, loves and wants to help all men, everywhere. For it is not the world but the church which will disappear when the Kingdom of God comes in power and glory!

b. We will all live in the city![3] We continue the same line of thought if we note that when the New Testament talks about what it will be like when "the old has passed away and the new has come" (2 Corinthians 5:17), it does not use a churchly but a *political* image. The new earth and new heaven we hope for will be like a *city* (Revelation 21:1–27), and we will be like "citizens" of a city (Philippians 3:20). It would be wrong to push this analogy too far, but the following reflections about its significance are hopefully consistent with what we know about God's plan for the world in general.

We do not have to look forward to an eternal life of isolated loneliness—as pictured in the typical cartoon of a man sitting all by himself on his little private cloud in a vast empty sky. Nor can we think of a lazy pastoral scene in which there is nothing to do but lie around in bored idleness. The Bible chooses rather the picture of city life. A city is a place where there is work to be done, where there is excitement and action, where new building and new ways of doing things are always in progress. It is a complex, cosmopolitan place where all kinds of people, of different races, classes, nationalities and religions have to learn to live together, work together, depend on each other, cooperate with each other, be responsible to and for each other. On the other hand, a city is a place where there is room for real individuality, freedom from the smothering conformity and rigid conventions often imposed on people who live in small towns.

That is what the City of God will be like. Not a static, frozen— dead—perfection in which there is nothing more to do, think, achieve. Rather a creative, dynamic "moving from perfection to perfection"[4] in which there will always be new things to learn, new things to do, new tasks to perform—under the God whose own perfection is not static and lifeless, but the perfection of the God who always will be a living, active Creator. In the "New Jerusalem" there will be community without uniformity, individuality without irresponsibility. The problem of individual rights vs. community welfare will be solved in such a way that community serves individual, and individual serves the community, in "a commonwealth of free responsible beings united in love."[5] Does not this image of a perfect city draw together everything we are told that God the Creator willed from the beginning when he created men to find their individual fulfillment as they live not alone, but together, helping each other to subdue and have dominion over the earth (Genesis 1:27–31; 2:18)? Does it not summarize the new humanity of Christ which frees us to be ourselves as we are reconciled with God and with people who used to be strangers or enemies?

If we are right in this train of thought, then a new light is thrown on the rapid urbanization of our lives in the twentieth century. Protestants have a tendency to be suspicious of this development. We are threatened by the way it breaks down old patterns of life in church and society. We are frightened by the difficult social, economic, political, racial and religious problems which arise when all kinds of people are forced to live together in a complex system of interrelatedness and interdependence. We have a tendency to resist the change and to dream of the good old days when everything was simpler and clearer and easier. This reaction is understandable. Our cities are hardly reflections of the City of God right now. They only magnify and multiply the God-denying, brother-hating, self-destroying hostilities, the self-centeredness, alienation, loneliness and indifference to the need and suffering of others which were characteristic of sinful men also in the good old days, but which were easier to ignore and hide from then. Nevertheless, if we Christians look forward to a new heaven and new earth which will be like a *city,* how can we not welcome the challenge and opportunities of urbanization? The structure of urban life has been hallowed by God himself. That is what the kingdom of God will be like—the Kingdom which we believe can and does break into the world here and now. Why should we not welcome urbanization, with all its difficulties and problems, as a gift and sign of the possibilities of that Kingdom?

The Christian Hope for Individuals

Having discussed the Christian hope for the world, now we move on to discuss the hope of Christian individuals for themselves. What is going to happen to *me* and those whom I love? Christians answer: "I believe in the resurrection of the body and the life everlasting."

1. **The resurrection of the body.** In this section we shall discuss three questions: (a) What is the source of this Christian alternative to belief in the immortality of the soul? (b) What is its meaning? (c) When does it happen?

a. Where do we get the idea of the resurrection of the body? The idea was current in the Judaism of the New Testament period, but the certainty of its meaning and reality came with the resurrection of Jesus himself. Unlike the hope that the soul is immortal, Christian faith in the resurrection of the body did not arise from wishful thinking or theoretical speculation, but from the conviction of the early Christians that it had actually happened: A man rose bodily from the dead. He was not just *a* man, so that the event could be considered a freak accident. He was *Man,* the representative of *all* men. The secret of the meaning of *every* man's humanity is found in his humanity. What happened to him is the clue to what is going to happen to *every* man. Because he rose bodily from the dead, we may hope that we too will so rise. How is this connection between what happened to Jesus and what will happen to all men made in 1 Corinthians 15:12–22 and Romans 8:11? Once again we see that the Christian hope for the *future* is based on what has already happened in the *past.*

b. What does "resurrection of the body" mean? We began to answer this question in our discussion of the resurrection of Jesus. Go back and read pages 268-270 again. We take up here where we left off there. The key to understanding this doctrine is the fact that for the biblical writers "body" or "flesh" is simply a synonym for "man." Resurrection of the body means resurrection of *man.* To believe in it is to believe that my human self or person, the human being that "I" am, will live again. I will not be someone or something different from who and what I am now. I will be *myself.* The same holds good, of course, also for other people.

Now for the biblical writers (as for realistic modern men) it is impossible to think of a man without a body. It is a person's body which makes him a distinct, identifiable human being. How could we love, praise and serve God, and how could we recognize, communicate with and relate personally to other people without eyes, ears, mouths, noses, hands, feet—and the male or female sexual characteristics which make us the men or women we are? For the biblical writers, then, the resurrection of man meant necessarily also the resurrection of his body.

This does not mean simply the rehabilitation of our present physical bodies. The biblical writers knew as well as we do that these bodies may be sick or deformed, and that in any case after

death they decompose and "return to dust." Straining to express
the inexpressible, Paul said that we will have perfect "spiritual"
bodies (1 Corinthians 15:42–44). We cannot and need not try to
conceive of what that might mean. All we need to know is that we
will not (as the classical idea of immortality held) lose our personal identity and be melted or dissolved into some kind of universal spirit or realm of spirituality, like a drop of water returning
to the ocean. At our resurrection we shall possess whatever in the
new heaven and new earth corresponds to our bodies in the present
world—that which makes us who we are, individual, distinct *human*
beings with the ability to have genuinely personal relationships
with God and other human beings.

   c. *When* will this resurrection take place? Immediately at the
death of every individual, or only at the fulfillment of all history?
Here we run into two problems which ought to warn us not to
expect or want to know too much at this point: the problem of the
development and apparent inconsistency of biblical thinking
about the future, and the symbolical character of what it says. On
the one hand we are told that immediately at death we may expect
to be with Christ (Luke 23:43; Philippians 1:23). On the other
hand, it is suggested that there is something like a waiting "sleep"
of all the dead until they are all raised at once on the last day (1
Thessalonians 4:13–18).

   The classical Reformed confessions solve this problem neatly
by combining the doctrines of the immortality of the soul and the
resurrection of the dead. At death, the soul of every man is judged
and goes to its eternal destiny, while his body remains in the grave.
On the last day the body is raised again and reunited with the
soul for a final judgment (Westminster Confession, XXXIV; Belgic
Confession, Art. XXXVII). This theory can be criticized for several
reasons: (1) Its separation of body and soul is unbiblical. (2)
While it does combine various elements of the biblical hope, the
Bible itself does not give us this neat system. The confessions de-
vise an artificial solution to a problem the Bible itself is content to
leave unanswered. (3) The final judgment seems completely
superfluous if the souls of the righteous and wicked are assigned
their permanent places immediately after death. (4) This theory

hopelessly confuses the categories of time and eternity. After death a person is beyond our creaturely categories of space and time. Present and future and the time between them (as well as the spatial categories of up and down) are no longer applicable. The Bible recognizes this when it says that "with the Lord one day is as a thousand years" (2 Peter 3:8), and that "Jesus Christ is the same yesterday and today and for ever" (Hebrews 13:8). Events which from our point of view seem widely separated in time may from the standpoint of "God's eternal Now" occur simultaneously.

The contemporary Reformed theologian, Emil Brunner, puts it this way:

> The New Testament bears witness both to "departing and being with Christ" and to the appearing of the glory of Christ and his world of the resurrection as one and the same hope. He who believes in Jesus as the Christ knows that both things are true: I go to him and he comes to the world.[6]

Without even trying to spell out the details, is it not better to leave it at that—as the New Testament itself does?

2. The life everlasting. The New Testament teaches that there are two possible kinds of life waiting for men at the end of this life: life in heaven and life in hell. That is what we are going to talk about in this last section. At this point too we must follow the rules we have learned for thinking about the future from a Christian point of view. (a) We must not take literally, but seek the *meaning* of the symbolical language of Jesus and the New Testament writers. (b) The best way to do this is to remember that the clearest clue we have to the *future* lies in what God has already been up to in the *past,* and is therefore already true of the *present.* According to the Gospel of John, Jesus himself invited us to do this: "He who hears my word, and believes him who sent me, *has* eternal life; he does not come into judgment, but *has* passed from death to life" (John 5:24). And on the other hand: "He who does not believe is condemned *already,* because he has not believed in the name of the only Son of God" (John 3:18).

What, then, is *heaven?* Everything we have learned not only in this chapter but throughout this whole book leads us to this answer: *Heaven is an eternal life of genuine, complete, free realization of our humanity.* That is, it is the life originally willed for us by God the Creator, lived for us by his Son (the Man!) Jesus, and worked in us by his Spirit. It is an eternal life of the self-fulfillment which comes in loving, praising and serving God; and in loving and letting ourselves be loved by, helping and being helped by, other human beings. Life in heaven can be described as "entering into rest" (Hebrews 4:1 ff.), but that does not mean lying down and doing nothing forever. It means rest from all the frustrations, tensions, conflicts and self-contradictions of our present struggle with the God-denying and brother-denying inhumanity in and around us. It means coming to rest or peace with our true selves, so that we are free to live a creative, active human life in the image of the living, active Creator God. (See the word "rest" in the various theological word books.)

And what is *hell? Hell is an eternal life of unfulfilled and self-contradictory humanity.* It is living in hostility toward God and toward other people, and therefore denying one's own true self, forever. It is living forever without loving or the willingness to be loved, helping or letting oneself be helped. It is *never* coming to rest, but living *forever* in the frantic, self-destroying attempt to be what one is not and never can be. It is eternally attempting to be a human being without or against God and fellowmen. Hell, in other words, is not a kind of eternal life at all; it is a kind of eternal living *death.*

Who is going where? We shall not repeat what we have already learned about the problem of salvation and damnation in general (see pp. 139-141 above). Instead we shall try to correct a common misunderstanding of the meaning of heaven and hell in particular. The misunderstanding is that heaven is the reward for being good, and hell the punishment for being bad—like an eternal lollipop or an eternal spanking promised to good or bad children.

According to Jesus and the New Testament, the real situation is just the opposite. *Heaven is for sinners and hell is for "good" people!* To whom did Jesus address his gracious words of invitation

THE CHRISTIAN HOPE FOR THE FUTURE

and promise? To people who were obviously guilty—dishonest tax collectors, prostitutes, political and social outcasts rejected by respectable people. And to whom did he address his sternest warning of hell-fire and eternal misery? He almost never mentioned hell except when he spoke to the scribes and Pharisees—the very moral, very religious, complacent, church-going people of his day (see Matthew 25:31–45). In Matthew 21:31 he said it with shocking bluntness: "Truly, I say to you, the tax collectors and the harlots go into the kingdom of God before you." Again and again he predicted a surprising reversal between "righteous" and "wicked," "first" and "last" (Matthew 19:23–30; 20:1–16).

Why this complete contradiction of our popular moralistic understanding of the way God ought to dispense rewards and punishments? The point is not, of course, that God approves of immorality and condemns morality. The point is that only people who are sinful and know it can be aware of their need for the acceptance, forgiveness, love and help of God and their fellowmen. Only they can love the God who loves *sinners*. Only they are moved to care for other undeserving, sinful people. Only they who know that they do not *have* it can be open to *seek* and *find* the new humanity which comes with the Kingdom of God. On the other hand, those who are convinced that they are good and can take care of themselves—they do not know God as the Father who freely loves and forgives. They know him only as a great heavenly Paymaster who is there to pay off for services rendered; therefore they do not know the true God at all. They know their sinful fellowmen not as brothers whom they need, but only as inferiors to be rejected, or ignored, or perhaps patronizingly *used* as objects to practice their superior virtue and wisdom on. So long as they persist in their proud inhumanity, they can never enter into the Kingdom of God. Nor will they want to on the terms in which it is offered.

So heaven is for sinners and hell is for "good" people. To say this is only to state the inevitable consequences of the Protestant insistence that salvation comes by God's free grace alone and not by our good works (not even by our *faith* considered as a good work). And when we see this, then the doctrine of heaven and hell ceases to be a pagan matter of anxiously or arrogantly adding up

the score to decide who is "in" and who is "out," who will be rewarded and who punished. It becomes the essence of the Good
News of Jesus Christ. This Good News does have two sides to it,
warning and promise. But it is warning to "good" people and
promise to sinners.

This is the warning: Do you want to live independently and
self-sufficiently, without God or (basically the same thing) thinking of God only as a Scorekeeper for the credit you have chalked
up, safely cutting yourself off from the disturbing and sometimes
painful *love* of God? Do you want to be free from depending upon
and having responsibility to and for other people, especially those
unworthy of your concern? Very well, you may have what you
want. You may live in opposition to God and to other people now
and forever. You have *chosen* the living death of hell.

And this is the promise: Are you willing to admit that, no
matter how religious (or irreligious) or moral (or immoral) you
are, you are constantly getting "lost" in life, losing sight of who you
are and what you are here for? Are you willing to admit that it is
your own fault—that you keep losing your own identity, because
in one way or another you have cut yourself off from the God and
the fellowmen who alone can enable you to find yourself? Are you
willing to risk the pain of giving up your proud or fearful inhumanity to be *reconciled* with God and your fellowmen (*all* of
them)? Do you want to be born again to be a truly free, truly human man or woman—free to be yourself because you are free for
the disturbing, demanding love of God and other people? Then you
may enter into the Kingdom of God, no matter how sinful you may
have been in your irreligion or religion, your immorality or morality. You may have eternal life not only in the future but already
now. All you have to do is choose the God who has already chosen
just such lost sinners as you. That is, all you have to do is find yourself in surrender to the one man who was totally for God and
totally for other men, and therefore totally human.

That is the Good News addressed both to obviously sinful
"outsiders" and to us sinful insiders. For God so loved the world—
the *sinful* world, including inhuman sinners such as *all* of us are
—that he gave his only Son, that whoever believes in him should

not perish but have eternal life. For God sent his Son into the world, not to *condemn* the world, but that the world might be *saved* through him (John 3:16–17).

FOR FURTHER REFLECTION AND STUDY
On "Some Non-Christian Answers"
1. Do you say "died" or "passed on"? Why?
2. Is Christianity a utopian religion?
3. Read Ecclesiastes now if you did not do it before. Should this book be in the Bible? What can Christians learn from it?
4. Is it true that if there is no hope for the future, the present will be meaningless?
5. Some Christians have argued that we ought not to be overly concerned about all the suffering and deaths caused by war, since this life is not really important anyway. Do you agree?
6. Do you think that most Christians in fact live more freely and joyfully than people who do not hope for a future life?
7. Summarize the reasons for arguing that the doctrine of the immortality of the soul is less than Christian. Do you think they are valid?

On "Asking the Right Questions"
1. Does the discussion of the symbolical character of the New Testament's language about the future undermine for you the authority of Scripture? What about the discussion of the development and inconsistency of the biblical hope?
2. Do you agree that the writers of the Reformed confessions were wise in not trying to give detailed descriptions of the end of the world based on Daniel and Revelation?
3. Why is the past the clearest indication of what the future will be like?

On "The Christian Hope for the World"
1. Why is it important to emphasize that *Christ* will judge the world?
2. Do you agree that it is wrong for Christians to look forward to the time when God "will cast all his and our enemies into

everlasting condemnation"? What about people like Hitler? The communists? Those who have persecuted Negroes in our country?

3. Were you glad or sorry to read that in the life to come we will not be idle, but will have work to do?

4. What do you think of the argument that life in God's new world will be city life?

On "The Christian Hope for Individuals"

1. Read 1 Corinthians 15:35–50. What does Paul think our resurrected bodies will be like? How does verse 49 help solve the problem? Compare this verse with 1 John 3:2.

2. How would you answer the common question of whether or not we will recognize our loved ones in heaven?

3. Will there be sex in heaven? What is the meaning of Jesus' words in Mark 12:18–25?

4. Do you think we were right in our criticism of (and our alternative to) the position of the Reformed confessions on the question of what happens between the death of an individual and the final judgment of the world?

5 Jean-Paul Sartre wrote a play about hell called *No Exit*. He has one of the characters say: "There's no need for red-hot pokers. Hell is—other people!"[7] What do you think he meant? Does this statement agree with our interpretation of hell? What do you think of it?

6. Look again at G. B. Shaw's idea of hell quoted on page 220 above. Does it agree with our interpretation in this chapter? Do *you* agree?

7. Would it be more biblical or Christian to think about eternal life in heaven as an angelic or divine life rather than as a fulfilled *human* life?

8. How would you try to comfort someone who is dying? Someone who has recently lost a loved one?

Where Do We Go from Here?

What do you do now? You have finished this study of the major doctrines of the Christian faith. But if you have learned anything at all, you will feel that you are just beginning to be a theologian. There are too many questions still unanswered, too many problems still unsolved. In fact, if you have really made progress, you will have *more* questions and problems now than when you began. The more you learn about the majesty and mystery of God, the more you realize that he will always be beyond the farthest reaches of our understanding and imagination. As we finish this study, then, we have not come to the end of the road; we are only a little further along it. So what do you do now? Keep moving! Continue growing! We end this study with some suggestions for *further* study. We shall arrange them in three parts corresponding to the three questions any traveler must ask himself if he is to move on true course toward his destination: (1) Where have we come from? (2) Where are we? (3) What lies ahead?

Where Have We Come From?

In some ways, our whole study has been backward looking. The source and norm of our work has been an ancient Bible. Our outline has been shaped by the Apostles' Creed, the earliest version of which was probably formulated in the second century. We have been especially guided by the confessions of Reformed forefathers written three or four hundred years ago. "Back to . . ." is not a good slogan for Christians. Like Abraham, we believe in a living God who calls us to leave the safe past behind, serve him here and now and follow him confidently into an unknown future. But we Christians also believe that we discover what this living God is saying and doing in our time as we learn what he has said and done in the past. We learn where we are and where we are going as we look back to see where he *has* been leading us. There·

fore even the most contemporary Christian theology can never be finished with Christian tradition.

This means that your continuing study of theology must include further study of those Christians who before us have sought to understand what it means to think about God, man and the world in the light of Jesus Christ as we know him in Scripture. We shall limit our suggestions here and throughout this postscript primarily to relatively short books, available in paperback, written in language understandable to nonprofessional theologians.

A good study of the Apostles' Creed is Karl Barth, *Dogmatics in Outline* (New York: Harper & Row, Publishers Incorporated, 1961).

John Leith, *Creeds of the Churches* (New York: Doubleday and Company, Inc., 1963), is a collection of the major creeds of all the churches—protestant, Roman Catholic, and Eastern Orthodox. It also includes a brief discussion of the history and main characteristics of each.

Some works interpreting specifically Reformed confessions are: Allen O. Miller and M. Eugene Osterhaven, *The Heidelberg Catechism with Commentary* (Philadelphia: United Church Press, 1963); Karl Barth, *The Faith of the Church: A Commentary on the Apostles' Creed According to Calvin's Catechism* (New York: Meridian Books, 1958); Karl Barth, *The Heidelberg Catechism for Today* (Richmond: John Knox Press, 1964); George S. Hendry, *The Westminster Confession for Today* (Richmond: John Knox Press, 1960).

An excellent history of the development of Protestant thought is John Dillenberger and Claude Welch, *Protestant Christianity* (New York: Charles Scribner's Sons, 1954). This work covers the history of Protestantism in Europe and America. It includes a comparative study of the different denominational traditions and of the different types of theology (i.e., orthodox, liberal, pietistic, fundamentalistic, neoorthodox, and so on).

Robert McAfee Brown, *The Spirit of Protestantism* (New York: Oxford University Press, 1965), treats classical Protestantism more topically than historically. After comparing the different "varieties" of Protestantism, Brown discusses some of the main doctrinal affirmations of Protestants. Then he deals with some contemporary theological problems in a section entitled "Ongoing Protestant Concerns." This is a book which achieves the rare combination of theological depth and simple clarity.

Where Are We?

In 1918 a pastor of the Swiss Reformed Church named Karl Barth wrote a book which began a brand new period in the history of Christian thought. Not too surprisingly, it was a commentary on Paul's Letter to the Romans, the same biblical book which four hundred years ago led Martin Luther to "new" insights which radically reformed the church. The result was what has been tagged "neoorthodoxy," an understanding of the Christian faith which dominated the theological scene until the early 1960's. Even those who opposed this new movement from the left or from the right were controlled by it to the extent that they had to define their own position in relation to it. Not only Protestants but also Roman Catholics have been influenced by it. In the last third of the twentieth century, theologians are speaking of neoorthodoxy as a movement which has had its day, but it has been so influential that no one can ignore it. The way into the future lies *through* the new insights of the neoorthodox theologians.

Neoorthodoxy is so called because it was a protest against the liberal theology which dominated the nineteenth century. Liberalism was optimistic about the goodness of man, his ability to know and obey God and his ability to overcome evil in the institutions of the world. It thus emphasized the immanence of God in man's heart and mind, and the God-likeness of man. Fresh study of the Bible and the brutal facts of life in the twentieth century (two world wars and a worldwide depression) convinced many theologians that liberal theology was neither biblical nor realistic. These theologians called for a return to the theology of the Reformation with its emphasis on the *distance* between God and man. They spoke of the sovereignty and transcendence of God, and of the creatureliness and sinfulness of man. Their theme was man's *inability* to help himself and transform the world, his total dependence on the grace of God in Christ. On the other hand, the new orthodoxy was not simply a return to the "old" orthodoxy of the sixteenth and seventeenth centuries. Rejection of a literalistic interpretation of Scripture and free use of moden biblical scholarship, emphasis on the relevance of the Christian message to man's social and political life, and a concern to relate Christian truth to modern scientific thought—these were some characteristics of liberalism gladly retained by the neoorthodox theologians.

In order to understand neoorthodoxy, in other words, you need to understand how it is like and how it is different from both classical orthodoxy and classical liberalism. As we have already mentioned, these similarities and differences are discussed in *Protestant Christianity* by Dillenberger and Welch. Another book which compares and contrasts these types of theology is William Hordern, *A Layman's Guide to Protestant Theology* (New York: The Macmillan Company, 1955). Hordern deals with orthodoxy, fundamentalism, liberalism and the different versions of neoorthodoxy in terms of representative theologians.

It would be a mistake to think that the neoorthodox theologians are all exactly alike. Within the general framework we have described, they differ widely in their theological approach and in the degree to which they accept or reject the presuppositions of orthodoxy and liberalism. Once you have the general characteristics of neoorthodoxy in mind, you will want to move on to study the thought of the different representatives of this movement for themselves.

Karl Barth's theology may be called "the theology of the Word of God." Barth wants always to begin with the self-revelation of God in Christ as we know him through Scripture in the church. Then he wants to relate the grace and judgment of this God to man's life in the world. It is no accident that we have often referred to Barth throughout our study. Along with Emil Brunner, he is a Reformed theologian who has tried to write a theology for the twentieth century in line with the Reformed tradition. Barth's great theological achievement is a monumental work in thirteen volumes, *Church Dogmatics*. A good introduction to his thought (which in good Reformed tradition has kept developing and changing over the years) would be to compare an earlier collection of essays, *The Word of God and the Word of Man* (New York: Harper & Row, Publishers, Inc., 1957), with a later collection, *The Humanity of God* (Richmond: John Knox Press, 1960).

Paul Tillich, who died in 1966, identified his theology as "the theology of correlation." He was concerned to correlate the questions asked by philosophers, artists and psychologists about the meaning of life with the answers which are given in Jesus the Christ. Unlike Barth's thought, which moves from the gospel to the world, Tillich's thought moves from the world to the gospel. Tillich also differs from Barth in that his language is not that of the Bible or of traditional theology but of metaphysical philosophy (philosophy which deals with the problem of "being"). Tillich's great work is his three-volume *Systematic Theology*. A good introduction to his thought would be three smaller works: *The Courage to Be* (New Haven: Yale University Press, 1952); *Dynamics of Faith* (New York: Harper & Row, 1957); and a collection of sermons, *The New Being* (New York: Charles Scribner's Sons, 1955). A good book about Tillich's life and thought written for laymen is John Heywood Thomas, *Paul Tillich* (Richmond: John Knox Press, 1966).

Rudolph Bultmann is a New Testament scholar rather than a systematic theologian, but he has been another very influential voice in the theology of our time. Bultmann is like Tillich in that his thought moves from an analysis of the situation of man in the world to the message of the gospel. But Bultmann believes that it is the philosophy of existentialism (particularly that of Martin Heidegger) which furnishes us with the beginning point and framework of a theology relevant to modern men. Two good introductions to what existentialism is all about are William Barrett, *Irrational Man* (New York: Doubleday and Co., 1958); and David E. Roberts, *Existentialism and Religious Belief* (New York: Oxford University Press, 1959). Bultmann is especially interested in existentialism because he believes that it helps us to translate what he calls "the mythological form" in which Christian truth is expressed in the New Testament into a form which is understandable to scientifically oriented twentieth-century men. He wants to "demythologize" the New Testament not in order to change or water down Christian truth, but in order to relate it to the "self-understanding" of modern men in the same way that the biblical writers related it to the self-understanding of men in the first century. Two small works which furnish a good introduction to Bultmann's thought are "The New Testament and Mythology," in H. W. Bartsch (ed.), *Kerygma and Myth* (New York: Harper & Row, Publishers, Inc., 1961); and Bultmann's *Jesus Christ and Mythology* (New York: Charles Scribner's Sons, 1958).

Reinhold Niebuhr, perhaps the greatest theologian America has ever produced, has called his theology "Christian Realism." He also begins with an analysis of man's situation in the world. But in typically American style, he begins not with philosophical problems, but with the practical problems of man's political, social and economic life. He first came to share neoorthodox theological convictions because of his disillusionment with liberalism's idealistic confidence in man's ability to solve his personal and social problems by himself. Niebuhr's whole theology is based on the conviction that *political* realism demands a *biblical* realism about the sinfulness of man and all his institutions and ideologies, and about man's constant need, both individually and socially, for the judgment and grace of God in Christ. Niebuhr's most important work is *The Nature and Destiny of Man* (New York: Charles Scribner's Sons, 1949). Another work, very important because it marked the turn from liberalism to neoorthodoxy in the main stream of American theology, is *Moral Man and Immoral Society* (New York: Charles Scribner's Sons, 1932).

What Lies Ahead?

During the 1960's theology began to take a new turn. The great creative work of men like Barth, Tillich, Bultmann and Niebuhr has not been forgotten. But a new situation demands that younger theologians, all of whom have been the students of these masters, take up where their teachers left off and ask all over again the same question their theological fathers asked: What is God saying and doing *now*, and how can we faithfully and intelligently speak about him in *our* time and place? When we look at what is going on around us in the present, it is difficult to distinguish between what are merely passing theological fads and what will be of lasting value. And it is always dangerous to predict what is going to happen in the future. But everything seems to indicate at least three areas in which major changes are already taking place and in which we may expect further theological development in the coming years: (1) the relation between Protestants and Roman Catholics, (2) the relation between the Christian faith and other religions, (3) the Christian witness in an increasingly secularized world.

A good general preparation for a study of what is going on in the present period of change is Daniel Day Williams, *What Present-Day Theologians Are Thinking* (New York: Harper & Row, Publishers, Inc., 1959). See especially Chapter III, "God and the World."

1. Protestant-Catholic relations. An event which will probably be as important in the history of Christianity as the Reformation was four hundred years ago is the meeting of the Second Vatican Council during the years 1962–1964. It marked such a radical renewal in the Roman Catholic Church that some observers believe the Roman Church in our time is more ready to reform itself according to the Word of God than are the Protestant churches. In any case, the council opened up a brand-new period in Protestant-Catholic relations. Instead of simply ignoring each other, or fighting against each other, now Protestants and Catholics are talking and cooperating with each other as never before. We may even hope that we are living through the beginning stages of the healing of a split which has divided the Body of Christ for four hundred years. You can best understand (and participate in) what is happening in this area by reading the documents of the council itself. They are collected in Walter M. Abbott, S. J. (ed.), *The Documents of Vatican II* (New York: Association Press, 1966). Included with this collection is a series of essays by noted Protestant theologians commenting on each of the council's decisions.

2. The Chrisitan faith and non-Christian religions. The problem of the relation between the Christian faith and other faiths was a burning one at the end of the nineteenth century. But the history of the first part of the twentieth century made it necessary for the neoorthodox theologians to push it aside. The collapse of liberal theology and a whole series of political and cultural crises within Western civilization made it imperative for them to rediscover the *Christian* faith and its relevance for the modern *Western* world. But now, when all the old barriers between people of different religions and cultures are breaking down, many theologians are saying that we can no longer work in such isolation. Do we Christians mean something totally different from the followers of other religions when we say the word "God"? When we enter into a conversation with them, how can we on the one hand avoid the arrogant attitude that we have everything to give and nothing to receive, and, on the other hand, avoid compromising the Christian faith? How can we distinguish between what is essential to the Christian faith and what is really only the cultural form it has taken in Western civilization? This is a problem which will probably occupy Christian thinkers more in the future. Some books which will introduce you to this whole area are: George W. Carpenter, *Encounter of the Faiths* (New York: Friendship Press, 1967); David M. Stowe, *When Faith Meets Faith* (New York: Friendship Press, 1967); Paul Tillich, *Christianity and the Encounter of the World Religions* (New York: Columbia University Press, 1963); Hendrik Kraemer, *Why Christianity of All Religions?* (Philadelphia: The Westminster Press, 1962).

3. **The Christian faith in a secularized world.** The achievement of neoorthodoxy was its rediscovery of the biblical emphasis on the distance between a transcendent God and creaturely-sinful men, and on the gracious revelation by which God speaks and acts in Jesus Christ to reconcile men to himself. Without necessarily denying the *truth* of this emphasis, many theologians now are perplexed about its *meaning*. Just *how* does God "speak" and "act" in the world? Does he interfere with the operation of scientific laws and the natural working of events? Is he present and at work *only* where Jesus Christ is known? Is he a great problem solver who steps in to do for us what we cannot do for ourselves?

Behind such questions is the recognition of the fact that modern man has become thoroughly secularized. We no longer really expect God to "do" anything in the world. Most of the time we do not even think we need him. We turn not to God but to the physician, the psychiatrist, the engineer, the scientist, the political and social leader—sometimes even to a computer!—to solve our problems. Even when we do need God, he does not seem to be present. What has he done to help the suffering caused by modern warfare, poverty, racial injustice and the comfortable emptiness of our affluent society? Where and how does God really make a difference in the world? Many theologians now are concerned to discover how we can still speak of God in a time when God seems at best absent and silent and at worst irrelevant—the very word "God" meaningless to many people. We mention only a few of the attempts to deal with the so-called "God problem" (whether the problem is with God or with us is a debatable point!).

The best introduction to the problem itself is Dietrich Bonhoeffer's *Letters and Papers from Prison* (New York: The Macmillan Company, 1962). The letters and papers collected here were written during the years 1943–1945, when this brilliant young theologian was a prisoner of the Nazis. They have had a very great influence on the younger generation of preachers and theologians. The belief that the world has "come of age" so that it no longer needs "religion" to answer its questions and solve its problems; criticism of traditional ways of speaking of God; and search for a new theology which is genuinely Christ-centered, yet expresses a "religionless Christianity" and a "holy worldliness"—these are ideas of Bonhoeffer which describe the starting point of much "postneoorthodox theology." A good book on the life and thought of Bonhoeffer is E. H. Robertson, *Dietrich Bonhoeffer* (Richmond: John Knox Press, 1966).

One thinker who has wrestled with the problem Bonhoeffer described is the English bishop, John A .T. Robinson. Christians around the world have read and discussed his *Honest to God* (Philadelphia: The Westminster Press, 1963) and the more recent *The New Reformation?* (Philadelphia: The Westminster Press, 1965). See also David L. Edwards (ed.), *The Honest to God Debate* (Philadelphia: The Westminster Press, 1963).

Another widely read book is that by the American theologian Harvey Cox, *The Secular City* (New York: The Macmillan Company, 1965). Cox analyzes secularized urban American society and tries to speak of God and his action in political and social rather than in traditional metaphysical categories. See also Daniel Callahan (ed.), *The Secular City Debate* (New York: The Macmillan Company, 1966).

The controversial "death of God" theologians have dealt with the "God problem" in a different way. They want to hold on to the importance of Jesus, but instead of trying to understand God in a new way, they try to work out a "theology" without God. See Thomas J. J. Altizer and William Hamilton, *Radical Theology and the Death of God* (New York: Bobbs-Merrill Co., 1966), and Thomas W. Ogletree (ed.), *The Death of God Controversy* (New York: The Abingdon Press, 1966).

A quite different attempt to speak meaningfully of God in our time is that of the process theologians. Like the philosophers Alfred N. Whitehead and Charles Hartshorne, they think that we can make theology consistent with the modern world view if we give up the idea of God as a personal Being who literally speaks and acts. Instead, we must learn to think of God as the fundamental creative process which gives life and meaning to all reality, both natural and human. One version of this approach which has aroused much interest and excitement is that of the French Catholic theologian, Teilhard de Chardin, who tries to understand the scientific evolutionary process in a way which expresses a mystical religious view of the world. Bernard Towers, *Teilhard de Chardin* (Richmond: John Knox Press, 1967), discusses the life and thought of Teilhard. The best place to begin studying his own writings is *The Phenomenon of Man* (New York: Harper & Row, Publishers, Inc., 1961).

A representative sampling of the problems which are occupying the attention of theologians, and of the various approaches to these problems, is given by a series of paperbacks which collect from various theological journals some recent articles by a number of thinkers. Edited by Martin E. Marty and Dean G. Peerman, and published by The Macmillan Company, this series includes *New*

Theology No. 1 (1964), *New Theology No. 2* (1965), and *New Theology No. 3* (1966).

Everything we have said suggests that in the church as well as in the world around us we are living in a period of change, uncertainty and confusion. While no one knows exactly what lies ahead for Christian theology, indications are that we must be prepared for a while to expect only partial answers and fragments of the truth, not the defense of neat comprehensive systems or the building of new ones. We must hope not so much for sure conclusions as for faithful and intelligent searching. We must be satisfied if instead of arriving at right answers, we can discover the right questions. There will be experiments with new terminology and concepts as men struggle to think both as Christians and as modern men. Some of these experiments will lead to blind alleys. All of them will be temporary, inadequate and in need of correction.

But we need not be frightened or threatened by this situation. We can welcome it. It only underlines what we ourselves have always said: The church must be always reforming, because no man or group of men, in *any* period, can master the truth of God. In this sense our time is no different from any other time for genuinely Reformed Christians. It is not an unfortunate necessity but an essential part of our faith in the living God that we are both allowed and required to let our thoughts and language about him be constantly reformed. Our Reformed heritage, in other words, gives us the courage to risk the questionable experimental ways of studying theology that our time requires. We may do it thankfully and joyfully, because we serve the God who said, "Behold, I make all things *new*" (Revelation 21:5).

Acknowledgments

PART I
1. The first question of several Christian catechisms.

CHAPTER 1
1. Karl Barth, *Church Dogmatics,* I/2 (Edinburgh: T. & T. Clark, 1956), pp. 607 ff.

CHAPTER 2
1. From *The German Phoenix,* by Franklin Hamlin Littell. Copyright © 1960 by Franklin Hamlin Littell. Reprinted by permission of Doubleday & Company, Inc. Pp. 180 ff
2. *Ibid.*
3. John H. Leith, *Creeds of the Churches* (New York: Doubleday & Company, Inc., 1963), p. 5.
4. The Confession of Basel (Switzerland, 1531) says: "We submit this our confession to the judgment of the divine Scripture, and hold ourselves ready always thankfully to obey God and his Word if we should be corrected out of holy Scriptures."
   The Belgic Confession (Art. VII) says: ". . . neither may we compare any writings of men, though ever so holy, with those of divine scriptures; nor ought we to compare custom, or the great multitude, or antiquity, or succession of times and persons, or councils, decrees, or statutes, with the truth of God, for the truth is above all; for all men are of themselves liars, and more vain than vanity itself."

PART II
1. I am indebted in this section to Paul Tillich's definition of faith as "ultimate concern," and to his understanding of any man's god as that about which he is ultimately concerned. See his *Dynamics of Faith* (New York: Harper & Row, Publishers, Incorporated, 1957), and *Systematic Theology,* Vol. I (Chicago: University of Chicago Press, 1951), pp. 12–14.
2. *Calvin: Institutes of the Christian Religion,* ed. John T. McNeill, tr. Ford Lewis Battles (Philadelphia: The Westminster Press, 1960), I, 1, 1.

CHAPTER 3
1. Karl Barth, *Theological Existence To-Day!* (London: Hodder and Stoughton, 1933), p. 52.
2. The fact of such a "natural" knowledge of God does not necessarily mean (as some opponents of general revelation have insisted) a false confidence in man's ability to "climb up to God." It means rather that God

does not make himself known only in Jesus, the Bible and the Christian church. The same God we know in this "special" way can and does make at least something of himself known in other ways to other people. The doctrine of general revelation and the natural knowledge of God can be interpreted to point not to the goodness and greatness of man but to the goodness and greatness of God.

3. George S. Hendry, *The Westminster Confession for Today* (Richmond: John Knox Press, 1960), p. 23.
4. See Karl Barth, *Church Dogmatics*, II/1 (Edinburgh: T. & T. Clark, 1957), chapter 5; and *Dogmatics in Outline* (New York: Harper & Row, Publishers, Incorporated, 1959), chapter 3.
5. See Paul Tillich, *Biblical Religion and the Search for Ultimate Reality* (Chicago: University of Chicago Press, 1955); *Dynamics of Faith;* and *Systematic Theology,* Vol. I, Part I.
6. J. Dillenberger and Claude Welch, *Protestant Christianity* (New York: Charles Scribner's Sons, 1954), p. 238.
7. Charles C. West, *Outside the Camp* (New York: Doubleday & Company, Inc., 1959), p. 56.

Chapter 4

1. The confessional statements of the Reformed Churches recognize that God's Word, or God's revelation of himself, comes in a threefold way. They usually emphasize the written Word, the Bible, but they also recognize the other two forms:
(1) *The eventful-personal Word.* The first chapter of the Westminster Confession deals with Scripture as the Word of God. But it says that *before* God spoke in Scripture "it pleased the Lord, at sundry times, and in divers manners, to reveal [1]himself and to declare that his will unto his church; and afterwards . . . to commit the same wholly unto writing" (I, 1). Jesus himself is not specifically acknowledged as the Word of God here, but the Confession indirectly points to the fact that God's self-revelation of himself reached its climax in Jesus by referring to Hebrews 1:1: "In many and various ways God spoke to our fathers by the prophets; but in the last days he has spoken to us by a Son . . ."
(2) *The written Word.* Here we may quote the Belgic Confession as typical of all the Reformed confessional writings: "We confess that this Word of God was not sent nor delivered by the will of man, but that holy men of God spake as they were moved by the Holy Ghost, as the Apostle Peter saith. And that afterwards God, from a special care which he has for us and our salvation, commanded his servants, the Prophets and Apostles, to commit his revealed Word to writing; and he himself wrote with his own fingure the two tables of the law. Therefore we call such writings holy and divine Scriptures" (Art. III).
(3) *The proclaimed Word.* "Preaching" is not often mentioned as a form or revelation, but the Second Helvetic Confession says, having first referred to the Scriptures, "Wherefore when this Word of God is now preached in the church by preachers lawfully called, we believe that the very Word of God is preached . . . and that neither any other Word of God is to be feigned, nor to be expected from heaven" (Chapter I). And Luther once said, "Now I and any other man who speaks Christ's words may freely boast that his mouth is Christ's mouth. I am certain that my word is not

mine but Christ's word, therefore my mouth must be his whose Word it preaches" (Karl Barth, *Church Dogmatics*, I/1, 107). In our time we would want to supplement this preacher-centered and *spoken*-word-centered statement by saying that when *any* Christian bears witness to this word in speaking *and* in acting "the very Word of God is preached." In any case, it is suggested here that God not only spoke in the past; he still speaks in the present.

According to the Bible and the confessions of the church, then, there is a unity in the different ways in which God reveals himself. There are, as we shall see presently, important differences between his revelation of himself in Israel's history and in Jesus, in the Bible, and in the community of his witnessing people. But all three of these ways of revelation are the word of the one true God.

2. Paul Tillich discusses the issues we have considered in this section on the freedom of God in terms of the "Spiritual Presence" which manifests itself in individuals and communities outside the Christian sphere. God's presence can make a "spiritual community" even of people who are not Christians. See his *Systematic Theology*, Vol. III (Chicago: University of Chicago Press, 1963), pp. 152–155.

Chapter 5

1. Karl Barth, *Church Dogmatics* (London: T. & T. Clark, 1936), I/1, 422.
2. From *The Christian Doctrine of God*, by Emil Brunner, translated by Olive Wyon. The Westminster Press. Copyright 1950 by W. L. Jenkins. Used by permission. Pp. 211 f.
3. Karl Barth, *Church Dogmatics*, I/1, 403.
4. Rachel Henderlite, *A Call to Faith* (Richmond: John Knox Press, 1955), p. 106.
5. *The Heidelberg Catechism*, 400th Anniversary Edition. United Church Press, 1962.
6. George S. Hendry, *The Westminster Confession for Today*, p. 43.
7. Karl Barth, *Church Dogmatics*, I/1, 415.
8. *Ibid.*, p. 418.
9. R. P. C. Hanson, *God: Creator, Saviour, Spirit* (London: SCM Press, 1960), p. 86.
10. Paul Tillich, *Systematic Theology*, Vol. III (Chicago: University of Chicago Press, 1963), p. 283.
11. George S. Hendry, *The Westminster Confession for Today*, pp. 45 f.

Chapter 6

1. See George S. Hendry, *The Westminster Confession for Today*, pp. 46–48.

Chapter 7

1. C. P. Snow, *The Light and the Dark* (Harmondsworth, England: Penguin Books, 1962), pp. 73, 203. Used by permission of Macmillan & Co., Ltd.
2. Karl Barth, *Church Dogmatics*, II/2 (Edinburgh: T. &. T. Clark, 1957), p. 326. Barth is the first Reformed theologian ever to have interpreted predestination exclusively "in Christ." We are indebted to him for many of the insights in this chapter.
3. Dietrich Bonhoeffer, *The Cost of Discipleship* (New York: The Macmillan Company, 1963), p. 99.

PART III

CHAPTER 8
1. In this and the following discussions I am indebted to Langdon Gilkey's *Maker of Heaven and Earth* (New York: Doubleday & Company, Inc., 1959).
2. Emil Brunner, *The Christian Doctrine of Creation and Redemption* (Philadelphia: The Westminster Press, 1952), p. 34.
3. See Calvin's whole discussion here on how we are to enjoy the good things of this life.
4. See Reinhold Niebuhr, *Faith and History* (New York: Charles Scribner's Sons, 1949). Niebuhr's works are especially helpful for an understanding of the Christian view of history.

CHAPTER 9
1. From *Maker of Heaven and Earth*, by Langdon Gilkey. Copyright © 1959 by Langdon Gilkey. Reprinted by permission of Doubleday & Company, Inc.
2. *Ibid.*, p. 227.
3. See Reinhold Niebuhr, *The Nature and Destiny of Man* (New York: Charles Scribner's Sons, 1949) I, 93 ff.

CHAPTER 10
1. For this expression and in the following discussion we follow Karl Barth, *Church Dogmatics*, III/2 (Edinburgh: T. & T. Clark, 1960), pp. 222 ff.

CHAPTER 11
1. See Calvin's *Institutes*, II, 1, 11, for a discussion of this paradox. When the New Testament speaks of natural man as sinful, or when the Reformed confessions speak of man as being a sinner by nature, they are referring to man who is helplessly trapped in his denial of his truly natural self.
2. See Reinhold Neibuhr, *The Nature and Destiny of Man*, I, 228–240.
3. Franklin Hamlin Littell, *From State Church to Pluralism* (New York: Doubleday & Company, Inc., 1962), p. 134.
4. George Bernard Shaw, *Man and Superman* (Baltimore: Penguin Books, Inc., 1952), p. 130.

PART IV

CHAPTER 12
1. In the following discussion I have been helped by Karl Barth's discussion of "The Miracle of Christmas," *Church Dogmatics*, I/2, 172 ff.
2. See Oscar Cullmann, *The Christology of the New Testament* (Philadelphia: The Westminster Press, 1959), pp. 270 ff.
3. See Karl Barth, *The Humanity of God* (Richmond: John Knox Press, 1960), pp. 37 ff.

CHAPTER 13
1. See Rachel Henderlite, *A Call to Faith*, pp. 84 ff. for a helpful discussion of the doctrine of the atonement.

2. See George S. Hendry, *The Westminster Confession for Today*, pp. 110 ff.
3. See Donald M. Baillie, *God Was in Christ* (New York: Charles Scribner's Sons, 1948), pp. 157 ff.

CHAPTER 14
1. See Oscar Cullmann and A. J. B. Higgins, *The Early Church* (Philadelphia· The Westminster Press, 1956), pp. 106 ff.; Oscar Cullmann, *The Christology of the New Testament*, pp. 195 ff.; and Karl Barth, *Dogmatics in Outline*, pp. 121 ff.
2. See Rachel Henderlite, *A Call to Faith*, pp. 124 ff.
3. Karl Barth, *Dogmatics in Outline* (New York: Harper & Row, Publishers, Inc., 1959), p. 123.

PART V

CHAPTER 15
1. George S. Hendry, *The Holy Spirit in Christian Theology* (Philadelphia: The Westminster Press, 1965), pp. 118, points this out and carefully develops the work of the Holy Spirit from these three points of view.
2. John Macquarrie, *Principles of Christian Theology* (New York: Charles Scribner's Sons, 1966), p. 295.
3. See Dietrich Bonhoeffer, *The Cost of Discipleship*, pp. 61 ff.

CHAPTER 16
1. See, for instance, Hans Küng, *Justification: The Doctrine of Karl Barth and a Catholic Reflection* (New York: Nelson, Thomas & Sons, 1964).
2. No one has said this more movingly than Paul Tillich in his great sermon, "You Are Accepted," *The Shaking of the Foundations* (New York: Charles Scribner's Sons, 1948), pp. 153 ff.
3. Robert McAfee Brown, *The Spirit of Protestantism* (New York: Oxford University Press, 1961), p. 63.
4. Reprinted with permission of The Macmillan Company from *The Cost of Discipleship* by Dietrich Bonhoeffer. Second edition © SCM Press, Ltd. 1959, pp. 75–76.
5. *Ibid.*, pp. 72–73.

CHAPTER 17
1. Albert Camus, *Resistance, Rebellion and Death* (New York: Alfred A. Knopf, Inc., 1961), pp. 71–74. Used by permission.
2. See Dietrich Bonhoeffer, *The Cost of Discipleship*, chapter 1.
3. *Ibid.*, p. 34.
4. The rest of this chapter roughly follows Karl Barth, *Church Dogmatics*, IV/2 (London: T. & T. Clark, 1958), pp. 543–553.
5. William Hordern, *New Directions in Theology Today*, Vol. I (Philadelphia: The Westminster Press, 1966), p. 112.
6. Pierre Berton, *The Comfortable Pew* (New York: J. P. Lippincott, 1965), p. 23.

CHAPTER 18
1. See Colin W. Williams, *Where in the World?* (New York: National

Council of Churches Office of Publication, 1963), pp. 4 ff.

2. Claude Welch, *The Reality of the Church* (New York: Charles Scribner's Sons, 1958), p. 165.
3. Robert McAfee Brown, *The Spirit of Protestantism*, p. 99.
4. In the following discussion I have been especially helped by Donald G. Miller, *The Nature and Mission of the Church* (Richmond: John Knox Press, 1957), pp. 119 ff.
5. Donald G. Miller, *The Nature and Mission of the Church,* (Richmond: John Knox Press, 1957), p. 126.
6. See "Decree of the Apostolate of the Laity," *The Documents of Vatican II,* ed. Walter M. Abbott, S. J. (New York: American Press, 1966).
7. Donald G. Miller, *The Nature and Mission of the Church,* p. 90.

CHAPTER 19

1. Reinhold Niebuhr, *The Nature and Destiny of Man,* Vol. II (New York: Charles Scribner's Sons, 1949), p. 294.
2. Karl Barth, *Dogmatics in Outline,* p. 135. See also our discussion of the meaning of God's justice on pages 116–120 above.
3. See Harvey Cox, *The Secular City* (New York: The Macmillan Company, 1965).
4. John Macquarrie, *Principles of Christian Theology,* p. 320.
5. *Ibid.,* p. 321.
6. Emil Brunner, *The Christian Doctrine of the Church, Faith and Consummation* (Philadelphia: The Westminster Press, 1962), p. 393.
7. Jean-Paul Sartre, *No Exit* (New York: Vintage Books, 1958), p. 47.

The devices are geometric designs based on historic Christian symbolism. A description of every element in each symbol might deny the reader the opportunity to see them fresh, to make discoveries and connotations of his own. Is there a parallel between the method and task of geometry which, using ruler and compass, explores the nature of the universe and organizes and applies the knowledge learned, and the method and task of theology? Is there significance in the stars and compass for man's seeking to know the beyond, or for his being led to God?

Some information about the symbols may add to the reader's understanding. The basic star is eight-pointed, the star of regeneration symbolizing the "eighth day of creation" when Christ renews all things. (Is the baptismal font in your church eight-sided?) The six-pointed star is the Creator's star, and the four-pointed star is used for the Son. In the Hebrew tradition and in the early church the numbers were significant: *one*, God; *three*, Trinity; *four*, the whole world (four corners of the earth, four points of the compass); *seven*, perfection (the gifts of the Holy Spirit); *ten*, human completeness (from ten fingers, ten toes); *twelve*, the Hebrew tribes, the Apostles, hence the church. Multiples of ten also had special meaning and were often symbolic rather than literal: forty days, seventy disciples sent out by Jesus.

Other symbols to be found in the devices include: the all-seeing eye of God the Father, the cross and fish symbols for the Son; the dove and flames or fire for the Holy Spirit; equilateral triangle and triquetra for the Trinity.